Media and Media Policy in West Germany

GERMAN STUDIES SERIES
General Editor: Eva Kolinsky

Volker R. Berghahn and Detlev Karsten, *Industrial Relations in West Germany* (cloth and paper editions available)
Eva Kolinsky (ed.), *The Greens in West Germany: Organisation and Policy Making*
Eva Kolinsky, *Women in West Germany: Life, Work and Politics*

In preparation

Eckhard Jesse, *Elections: The Federal Republic of Germany in Comparison*
Josef Esser, *The Politics of Industrial Policy in West Germany: Case Studies of Steel and Telecommunication*
Richard Stoess, *Right-wing Extremism in West Germany: Its Roots, Development and Organisation*
Alan Kramer, *West German Economy, 1945–1955*
Douglas Webber, *Health Policy in West Germany*
Michael Fichter, *Labour Unions in West Germany*
J.K.A. Thomaneck, *Workers and Trade Unions in the GDR*
Thomas Hummel, *International Marketing in West Germany*
Detlev Bald, *The Bundeswehr: Its Origins, Structure and Role in West German Society*

GERMAN STUDIES SERIES

Media and Media Policy in West Germany

The Press and Broadcasting since 1945

Peter J. Humphreys

BERG
New York / Oxford / Munich
Distributed exclusively in the US and Canada by
St. Martin's Press, New York

First published in 1990 by
Berg Publishers Limited
Editorial Offices:
165 Taber Avenue, Providence R.I. 02906, USA
150 Cowley Road, Oxford OX4 1JJ, UK
Westermühlstraße 26, 8000 München 5, FRG

© Berg Publishers Limited 1990

All rights reserved.
No part of this publication may be reproduced
in any form or by any means without
the permission of Berg Publishers Limited.

Library of Congress Cataloging-in-Publication Data

Humphreys, Peter.
Media and media policy in West Germany: the press and
broadcasting since 1945 / Peter Humphreys.
p. cm.
Bibliography: p.
ISBN 0-85496-187-9: $42.50 (est.)
1. Mass Media policy—Germany (West)—History. 2. Mass media–
Germany (West)—Planning—History. I. Title.
P95.82.G3h88 1989   89-35876
302.23'0943—dc20   CIP

British Library Cataloguing in Publication Data

Humphreys, Peter J.
Media and media policy in West Germany: the press and
broadcasting since 1945. — (German studies series)
1. West Germany. Mass media, history
I. Title II. Series
302.2'34'0943
ISBN 0-85496-187-9

Printed and bound in Great Britain by
Short Run Press Ltd
Exeter, Devon

Contents

List of Tables, Figures and Appendices — viii
Preface — xi
Introduction — 1
  'Stunde Null' 3
  The Policy Approach 5
  Specialist Terminology: 'Policy Community' and 'Policy Network' 9
  'Closed' or 'Open' Policy Communities? 10

1 The Historical Origins and Early Post-War Development of the West German Press System — 13
  The Emergence of the Mass-Circulation Press 13
  The Weimar Republic 15
  The Third Reich 21
  The Allied Occupation 24
  The Organisations of the Press and the Birth of the BDZV 43
  The Journalists' Associations in the Early Post-War Period 48
  The Legal Basis of the Press 52
  The Press Council – A 'Self-Control' Organ 59
  The West German News Agencies 60
  The Significance of 'Stunde Null' 65

2 Controversies Over the West German Press System — 68
  The Conflict Between the Broadcasters and the Press 69
  The Controversy Over State Security and the Press 71
  Press-Concentration 74
  An Overview of the Main Newspaper and Magazine Publishing Groups 83
  The Political Balance of the West German Press 89
  The 'Springer Press' 92

Contents

State Policy on Press-Concentration 99
The Debate About 'Internal Press Freedom' 104
The Conflict Over the Introduction of New
Technologies 111
The 'Alternative' Press 117

3 The Historical Origins and Early Development of the West German Broadcasting System 124
The Weimar Republic 124
The Third Reich 126
The Allied Occupation 128
The Broadcasting 'Constitution' 132
The Legal Basis of Broadcasting as Laid Down by
Legislation of the Länder 136
The ARD 148
The Significance of 'Stunde Null' 152

4 Controversies Over the Public-Service Broadcasting System 155
The Attempts to Centralise Broadcasting 155
ZDF 164
The 'Third Channel' 168
The Financial Basis of West German Broadcasting 170
Party-Political Pressures on Broadcasting 176
The Statute Movement 187
Commercial Television 190

5 The Controversy Over the Introduction of the New Media 193
The KtK: Kommission für den Ausbau des technischen
Kommunikationssystems 194
The Group Politics of the Broadcasting
Revolution 195
The Cable Pilot-Projects 212
The 'Expert Commissions' 229
Satellite Broadcasting 231
The FRAG Judgement 235

6 The 'Dual Broadcasting System' and Multimedia Diversification 239
The 'Machtwende' (Change of Power) in Bonn 240
CDU/CSU Land Legislation 241
SPD Land Legislation 247

Satellite Broadcasting and the Need for a New
'Staatsvertrag' 256
Dramatic Action by the Bundespost to Rescue National
Media Policy: New Measures to Promote Commercial
Broadcasting 263
A Dual Broadcasting System 270
The 'Staatsvertrag for the Reform of the Broadcasting
System of the Federal Republic' 275
Patterns of Multimedia Diversification and
Cross-ownership of the Press and Broadcasting in the
Dual Broadcasting System 280

Conclusion 293
The Historical Legacy 293
Post-War West German Media Policy 294
The Performance of Key Media Functions 301
Whither the Media? The Deregulation Debate 304

Afterword 310

Appendices 313

Glossary 325

Chronology 331

Bibliography 337

Index 345

List of Tables, Figures and Appendices

Tables

1.1	Press structure in 1947: circulation statistics	38
1.2	The explosion of newspaper foundings after the end of licensing	41
1.3	The explosion of newspaper foundings after the end of licensing: the situation in the US zone of occupation	41
1.4	The structure of the West German press when the Germans received back their full sovereignty from the Allies in 1955: the 'multiple editions' phenomenon	67
2.1	Data on the development of the daily press in the Federal Republic of Germany, 1954–87	75
4.1	Development of licence-fees: cost per month	171
6.1	Shareholders in SAT 1	285

Figures

3.1	Radio and television in the Federal Republic of Germany	140
3.2	Structure of a broadcasting corporation	143

Both figures by kind permission of Zahlenbilder, Eric Schmidt Verlag.

Appendices

1(a) Economic concentration in the daily press ('Tagespresse'): market-shares of the ten largest

List of Tables, Figures and Appendices

	publishers of daily newspapers in 1987	313
1(b)	Market-shares of the five largest newspaper publishing groups (at given moments in time)	315
1(c)	Economic concentration in the market for popular illustrated magazines ('Publikumszeitschriften'): market-shares of the four main publishers of illustrated magazines in 1986	316
1(d)	Economic concentration in the market for popular illustrated magazines ('Publikumszeitschriften'): development of the market-shares of the four main publishers since the early 1970s (figure for the fourth quarter of each year)	317
1(e)	Market-shares of the leading papers sold on the street ('Boulevardzeitungen') in the third quarter of 1987	318
2	The key broadcasting judgements of the Federal Constitutional Court: a résumé of the main points with selected extracts	319
(a)	The 'First TV Judgement' of 28 February 1961	319
(b)	The 'Second TV Judgement' or the 'Value Added Tax Ruling' of 27 July 1971	319
(c)	The 'Third TV Judgement' or 'FRAG Judgement' of 16 June 1981	320
(d)	The 'Fourth TV Judgement' of 4 November 1986: the ruling on the Lower Saxony Broadcasting Law	320
3	New regulations for broadcasting adopted by the Länder	323

Preface

The publication of this book is well timed for two main reasons. In the first place, in 1989 the Federal Republic of Germany is officially forty years old. Its media system is hardly older. Forty years seems to be a reasonable enough period of time to justify an in-depth stocktaking exercise. This book is primarily a study of one of the most important areas of the Federal Republic's social life. The health of the Republic's media system must be considered to be one of the major criteria of judgement of the success of its economic, social and political system. Written from a political science perspective, the book aims to explore the legacy of West Germany's authoritarian and totalitarian past, and against this background, to give a full and fair account of the construction of a media system which, despite its flaws, can stand positive comparison with any other media system in the Western liberal democratic world.

In the second place, the fortieth anniversary of the Federal Republic of Germany marks a distinct watershed in the development of the country's media system: the unmistakable contours of a new media order are already emerging as the Republic comes of age. Under the impact of technological change, mainly in the sphere of broadcasting, the policy-makers have had to produce a regulatory framework which responds to new commercial pressures while at the same time safeguarding the very considerable public-service achievements of the past forty years. While this book can describe this process, and make some major critical points about it, the verdict must necessarily come at a much later date: perhaps, another forty years hence. In this respect, this book will at least serve to illuminate the policy process whereby the new order came into being.

The people who have helped me gather the information for this book are too numerous for me to mention personally here. Therefore I acknowledge my deep gratitude to all those individuals whom I have interviewed in West Germany over the last

Preface

few years and to all those who responded so fulsomely to my written requests for information. I am particularly indebted to the following for the support, inspiration and friendship which they have given me: Professor Wolfgang Hoffmann-Riem, Director of the Hans-Bredow-Institut at the University of Hamburg; Professor Hans J. Kleinsteuber, in the Political Science Department of Hamburg University; and Professor Kenneth Dyson, in the School of European Studies at Bradford University, with whom I have collaborated particularly closely in researching the field of the 'new media'. In addition, I would like to thank all the members of the Hans-Bredow-Institut, and especially its librarian, Dipl.-Bibl. Jutta Simon. Similarly, I extend my warm gratitude to all the members of the European Institute of the Media at the University of Manchester and its Director, Professor George Wedell. I would particularly like to thank its librarian, Brigitte Meyer, who never once complained whenever I made urgent calls upon her patience in searching for source material or other kinds of elusive information. Thanks must also go to Dr Eva Kolinsky, Senior Lecturer in German at Aston University, for her useful comments on the first draft; and to Dr John Sandford, Reader in German at Reading University, for the generosity with which he has shared his acclaimed expertise in this particular subject area. I should also note my thanks to Justin Dyer, of Berg Publishers, for the close attention to detail and the praiseworthy efficiency which he has displayed in helping to produce the final draft.

I am also indebted to the Economic and Social Research Council (ESRC) for funding much of the research upon which this book is based. This grant allowed me to make several extended trips to West Germany over the period from 1984 to 1986. Another grant under the ESRC – DFG academic exchange scheme made it possible for me to return for shorter periods in 1988 and 1989.

Finally, I would like to thank my wife, Sarah, and my two-year-old daughter, Kate, for allowing me to disappear into the attic at all kinds of strange hours in order to produce this piece of work.

Peter J. Humphreys (Govt Dept, University of Manchester)
June 1989

Introduction

From its historical origins onwards the broadcasting system has been the object of power-political attempts to influence and control it. Media policy has always been about power politics.[1]

Press freedom is the freedom of two hundred rich men to disseminate their opinions . . . the Constitution gives [the citizen] the right to express his opinion, economic realities take it away.[2]

The first comment was made by a leading West German academic expert in an important recent study of the 'battle for power over radio and television' in the Federal Republic of Germany. The second cynical comment was made by none other than one of West Germany's leading conservative journalists, Paul Sethe, shortly before his death in 1965. It caused a general public stir, not least because he had long worked on a newspaper, *Die Welt*, owned by one of the most powerful press barons in the history of the world's press, Axel Springer. He had also worked on another leading conservative daily, the *Frankfurter Allgemeine Zeitung*. These two comments introduce the main aim of this book, to explore the social, economic and political power-relations behind the media system of the Federal Republic of Germany.

For the sake of manageability, the study is limited to the press and broadcasting sectors, a conscious decision having been taken to exclude other phenomena of the media, such as cinema, records and advertising. The press and broadcasting are

---

1. H. Kleinsteuber, *Rundfunkpolitik in der Bundesrepublik*, Opladen: Leske Verlag & Budrich GmbH, 1982, p. 95.
2. Paul Sethe in *Der Spiegel* 19/1965, p. 118, quoted by E. Spoo, 'Pressekonzentration, Springer-Dominanz und journalistische Arbeit', in B. Jannsen and A. Klönne (eds.), *Imperium Springer: Macht und Manipulation*, Cologne: Pahl-Rugenstein Verlag, 1968, p. 206.

Introduction

the main instruments of the mass media and the principal means by which mass communication occurs in advanced industrial societies. No other media have a greater impact, or are 'consumed' to a greater degree. The press and broadcasting are the most important sources or mediators of contemporary political information and current affairs and they are one of the key agents of socialisation and integration in complex modern society. More than most other fields of public policy-making, the press and broadcasting have a pervasive effect on all areas of social and political life in advanced industrial society.

Furthermore, mass communication does not exist in a vacuum. Inevitably, a study of the mass media will shed light on the social and political system of any given society. In this respect, West Germany is a particularly interesting case-study of the mass media in a liberal democracy. The origins and development of the mass media system of the Federal Republic illustrate and underline the dramatic break with an unacceptable and undemocratic past. The book is premised on the belief that the mass media system is a very useful mirror in which to examine the level of democratic progress and health achieved by the new democracy. As Arthur Williams has put it in the introduction to his path-breaking work on the West German broadcasting system, an examination of the West German mass media is no less than 'indirectly an exploration of the state of society in the Federal Republic'.[3]

Indeed, hardly a people in history has found itself in such a dramatically transformed situation as the result of a break in historical continuity as the German people at the end of the Second World War. The country was geographically truncated, politically divided and, for a significant period, under the complete direction of the Allied occupation powers. The choice of socio-economic system was largely imposed from outside and the traditional political culture was profoundly attenuated and delegitimised. Most significantly, the media system too was largely imposed from outside. There can be no better reason than this for taking 'Stunde Null' ('Zero Hour') or 'Das Jahr Null' ('Year Zero') as the main starting-point.

3. A. Williams, *Broadcasting and Democracy in West Germany*, London: Bradford University Press/Crosby Lockwood Staples, 1976, pp. 1–2.

Introduction

'Stunde Null'

The break with the past is powerfully and neatly symbolised by the concept of 'Stunde Null', 1945. It has been widely held that the shock and dislocation of losing the Second World War fractured traditional patterns of institutional sclerosis in Germany and that this was the prerequisite of West Germany's spectacular subsequent success as a liberal democracy. The conventional wisdom holds that the combined impact of the Nazi interlude, the World War and, most importantly, the Allied occupation removed once and for ever the negative features of German tradition and society and paved the way for a fundamental democratic modernisation of the country.[4] Yet, the 'Stunde Null' concept, with its stress on renewal, has been strongly contested, generally by marxists who have argued that, in the case of West Germany (if not East Germany), a 'restoration' has taken place. For example, in a detailed study of the post-war press, Rüdiger Liedtke has suggested that Allied policy during the occupation period 'sought to realise a formal democratic ideal, while at the same time suppressing all discussion about alternative economic models' (i.e. to the 'capitalist' one).[5] The essence of this argument is that as a result of a combination of developments within the Federal Republic and the agency of external forces (the policies of the Western Allies) there has occurred a resurgence of similar conditions to those of pre-Hitlerian Germany. As will be seen, in the brief historical sections of the text, during the Weimar Republic the media system came to be characterised by such non-democratic features as the overweening control of broadcasting by the state and the massive concentration of ownership of the press in the

---

4. See R. Dahrendorf, *Society and Democracy in Germany*, London: Weidenfeld and Nicolson, 1968; M. Olson, *The Rise and Decline of Nations: Economic Growth and Social Rigidity*, New Haven: Yale U.P., 1982; G. Smith, *Democracy in Western Germany*, London: Heinemann, 1979.

5. Rüdiger Liedtke, *Die verschenkte Presse – Die Geschichte der Lizenzierung von Zeitungen nach 1945*, Berlin: Verlag für Ausbildung und Studium in der Elefanten Presse, 1982. For more general representative examples of this kind of marxist analysis see R. Badstübner and S. Thomas, *Entstehung und Entwicklung der Bundesrepublik Deutschland – Restauration und Spaltung 1945–55*, Cologne: Pahl Rugenstein, 1979; E. Schmidt, *Die verhinderte Neuordnung 1945–52*, Frankfurt/Main: Athenäum, 1981 (8th edn).

Introduction

hands of the right-wing Hugenberg press empire. These developments were part of an anti-democratic syndrome which severely weakened the fragile democracy of Weimar and prepared the way for the National Socialist takeover.

However, there is a powerful counterargument. The very memory of the capture and abuse of the press and broadcasting by the National Socialist propaganda machine during the Third Reich exerted a profound and far-reaching formative influence on the early development of the West German media system. Thus the Western Allies, and the Germans whom they chose to make responsible for the resurrection of the post-war media system, took special pains to ensure the installation of a strong press and broadcasting system designed to withstand every attempt at state subordination and domination by unhealthy concentrations of media power. In very different ways in each sub-sector, policy-makers – both Allied and native German – conscientiously sought to ensure pluralism in the press and broadcasting system. Similarly, wholly new constitutional and legal principles operative for both the press and broadcasting placed a special duty of pluralism on the new communicators, whether it was to be the result of a 'natural' competition of interests and diversity of viewpoints ('Tendenzen'), as in the case of the press, or an 'artificial' product of direct regulatory intervention, as in the case of public-service broadcasting. The early post-war policy-makers, at first under the leadership of the Western Allies, started from the first principle that the mass media were an important instrument for the (re)formation of public opinion and, over an extended period of time, the (re)shaping of the country's political culture.

Bearing in mind the gravity of the marxist critique, the following examination of the mass media will focus on such central questions as the real state of independence, degree of concentration and amount of pluralism in the media system of the still young republic. In this respect, it is a central assumption of the book that the task of evaluating German democracy can be approached by means of the singularly illuminating prism of its mass media system.

Introduction

The Policy Approach

It needs to be stated at the outset that this work reflects the interests of a political scientist, working in the field of public policy analysis, not those of a media sociologist. In examining the origins, development and current state of the mass media in West Germany, the empirical material will be presented, organised and analysed from the perspective of the mass media as an area of 'public policy'. If a major criterion for designating a sphere of activity as 'public policy' is the breadth of the social consequence of actions taken in the public domain, then there can surely be few areas of human activity that have a broader effect than the mass media. Another distinguishing feature of 'public policy' in liberal democracies is the characteristic involvement of both public and private actors in the policy process. In this respect, the organisation of the mass media system in a liberal democracy involves, more than most areas, addressing the crucial and quintessentially 'political' question of the proper balance of public and private involvement in policy-making.

The term 'media policy' or 'communications policy' is relatively new. In the Federal Republic it was only during the 1970s that the political parties and government began to employ the explicit term 'media policy' ('Medienpolitik') to denote the area of mass media as an important sphere of political debate in its own right. Nevertheless, although not yet referred to as 'media policy', the juridicial basis and organisational structures of the mass media were shaped decisively during the formative years of the Federal Republic by that characteristic combination of public and private initiative that can best be referred to as 'public policy'. This book seeks to examine the totality of measures taken by the state, including external state forces in the period of Allied occupation, and by the political parties and other social organisations which have shaped the mass media system of the Federal Republic since 1945.

The book deliberately adopts a 'structural' approach, concentrating on addressing such questions as: the nature of the policy-making system and processes; the institutions, social groups and interests involved in the policy process; the distribution of power and influence within the policy-making system; and the role of government and the state in the policy process. It

5

Introduction

is important to note straightaway that the state is not the exclusive actor in the field of media policy. Indeed, in the Federal Republic the 1949 Constitution (called the 'Basic Law') explicitly precluded such a state of affairs. Any study of media policy has to take into account all the various interests which seek to influence the development of the media. This means all kinds of actors, encompassing:

(1) governments, both central government (the 'Bund') and regional ('Land') authorities in West Germany's federal system;
(2) the political parties, both at 'official' and 'grass-roots' level;
(3) other powerful organisational interests, such as the interest groups or 'associations' ('Verbände'), the economic interests such as the publishers of the press, and the officially recognised 'socially significant groups' ('sozial relevante Gruppen'), which play such an important role in West Germany's public-service broadcasting system;
(4) the 'citizens', for example, through grass-roots organisation in 'citizens' initiative groups' ('Bürgerinitiativen') and the 'new social movements' such as the 'Greens' ('die Grünen');
(5) and in a country where law ('Recht') plays a very special role, the independent judiciary (the 'Rechtsstaat') will be seen to have had a very crucial role in determining the parameters and overall direction of media policy.

Beyond identifying the actors, it is also an aim of this work to ask some important related questions. What motivates their activity? What are their aims? To what extent are they pursuing an economic logic? To what effect? To what extent are their goals political? Are they pursuing the latter in an 'ideological' or a 'pragmatic' manner? Are they 'interested' or 'disinterested'? (For example, it might be assumed that the independent judiciary acts in a 'disinterested' way.) What are the constellations or 'coalitions' of interest? What is the balance of power between these actors and 'coalitions' of actors? Moreover, the range of actors, the extent, depth and effectiveness of their involvement, and their various motivations and behaviour will all depend on

Introduction

the nature of the issues raised by media policy.

Obviously, in the immediate aftermath of twelve years of National Socialist totalitarianism, the most urgent issue was how to reorganise the media on a democratic and pluralist basis. This involved making important decisions about the degree of regulation to which the media should be subject or the amount of self-regulation which they would be allowed. In addition, the matter of regulation raised the important questions of: by whom, by what methods, to what effect? In particular, to what extent should the state be involved in the media? Another early problem was the question of what should be the desired public/ private mix of media operators? What degree of commercialism and private capitalistic enterprise should be permitted? What kinds of alternative economic models – such as cooperatives ('Genossenschaften'), public-service institutions ('öffentlich-rechtlichen Anstalten') or public foundations ('gemeinnützige Stiftungen') – were explored, encouraged or (as the 'restoration theorists' argued) discouraged? The important issue of how the media should be financed had to be addressed. Other important early issues related to the structure of a democratic and pluralist media system. What should be the desired degree of regional and local provision? Should control be decentralised or should the central state have an important role? By what means might cultural and political diversity and 'fairness' be provided and safeguarded? What should be the appropriate mixture of entertainment, comment and information? To what extent did the mode of organisation, regulation and finance of the media affect the latter question?

Another set of issues which appeared on the policy agenda at a very early stage related to the relationship between press and broadcasting, the interaction of the media and the degree to which the press and broadcasting sectors should be kept distinct from each other, particularly in matters of ownership and control. As will be seen, this particular issue has been an enduring theme of media policy throughout the history of the Federal Republic. Indeed, in the recent period it has been probably the single hottest political potato in the field of the media. Another very controversial and related political issue is the degree to which media concentration has developed. This raises the questions: To what extent has pluralism been reduced or replaced by

7

Introduction

oligopolies/monopolies? Why has media-concentration, especially press-concentration, developed? What are its effects? How might it be controlled or restrained? Most importantly, should press-concentration be allowed to extend into the field of broadcasting?

Since it has been suggested that 'media policy is about power-politics', it is also important to examine the extent to which 'politics' has impinged on the 'freedom' of the media. This too has been a recurring theme of, at times very heated, media policy debate in the Federal Republic. The book provides a thorough exploration of the degree to which, for example, the notionally 'independent' public-service broadcasting system has been subject to the threat of politicisation by the political parties and leading figures of political authority (e.g. Chancellor Konrad Adenauer). Since political parties and powerful politicians are by no means the only politically 'interested' actors, attention will also be given to the 'political' motivations and orientations of leading publishing houses of the press. Political influence may stem from parties, it may equally derive from the editorial policies of powerful proprietors of influential newspapers and magazines. Therefore, the quintessentially important question of the regulation of editorial policy, both in the press and broadcasting, commands a very considerable measure of attention. In addition, various attempts by the journalists, broadcasters and even 'lay-journalists' and other social groups to affect mass communication are examined in detail. This in turn raises important questions. How 'open' or 'closed' are the media, both in terms of access and representation? What are the entrance thresholds? Are they high or low? Are they determined by financial consideration or by regulation? Are they determined by political resources?

Another major set of questions relates to the impact of new technologies on the media. What policy issues have emerged from the introduction of new technologies in the print sector or in the broadcasting system? How have governments responded to them? How have they affected established interests, such as the production staff or the printworkers? Have they had an impact on traditional regulatory policies? For instance, have they, as has been suggested, led to a 'paradigm change' from a model of public-service broadcasting to a market model of com-

Introduction

munication? What has been the impact of 'technocratic' impulses on policy-making? What have been the respective impacts of international market change, political tradition, ideology and institutional structures on policy development?[6]

Specialist Terminology: 'Policy Community' and 'Policy Network'

At this stage, it is important briefly to introduce two key, and essentially quite straightforward, analytical specialist terms from the field of political science (and policy studies in particular), which will recur at intervals throughout the text. The concept of 'policy community' will henceforth be employed to denote the complex web of interactions and resource dependencies between the various groups and actors closely involved in the policy process. The term implies a fairly structured and formal pattern of relationships between all those actors with a common interest in media policy. In particular, these actors will share a common understanding about the 'rules of the game' according to which policy is made in their sector. In fact, the 'community' may be very clearly defined by law, even constitutional law, as in the case of West German broadcasting regulation. A useful refinement of the notion of policy community has recently been offered by Maurice Wright and Stephen Wilks, who distinguish between the 'policy community' at the sectoral level (i.e. the 'press' sector or the 'broadcasting' sector) and the possibility of a more exclusive 'policy network' relating to specific issues.[7]

This work will apply the concept of 'policy network' in the following way. Firstly, it is a very useful way of viewing the kind of relationship between groups and actors which may often be less 'official', less formalised and perhaps less durable than

---

6. On this theme see K. Dyson and P. Humphreys, *Broadcasting and New Media Policies in Western Europe: A Comparative Study of Technological Change and Public Policy*, London: Routledge and Kegan Paul, 1988.

7. See S. Wilks and M. Wright, 'Conclusion: Comparing Government–Industry Relations: States, Sectors and Networks', in S. Wilks and M. Wright (eds.), *Comparative Government–Industry Relations: Western Europe, United States and Japan*, Oxford: Clarendon Press, 1987, pp. 275–313.

9

would merit the description of 'policy community'. Secondly, a policy 'network' may occur, for example, as the result of a destabilisation of an established 'policy community' by a new issue (e.g. the attempt to introduce commercial broadcasting, or the introduction of new technologies). In this connection, a 'network' may arise as the result of new entrants to the sector (e.g. publishers of the press seeking to embark on broadcasting operations). For example, new entrants to a sector might seek to establish a new relationship with the official policy-makers which circumvents the 'established' policy community regulating that sector. Similarly, political actors might see advantage in such a relationship (as in the case of the CDU with the publishers over the issue of commercial broadcasting). Therefore, the notion of 'network' may well imply a certain degree of 'conspiracy of interest'. Thirdly, in a similar way, the term 'policy network' might refer to the processing of an issue by an 'inner circle' within the more formal and broader 'policy community' to the exclusion of certain members of the latter.

'Closed' or 'Open' Policy Communities?

In the past, both the press and broadcasting in Germany had always been confined to a tightly circumscribed body of elites, a quintessentially 'closed' policy community. From the following account of the mass media system in the Federal Republic, the reader may conclude that the system remains essentially 'closed'. Such a view might be justified in view of, for example: the extensive permeation of the media system by the political parties; the concentration of media power in the hands of a few giant concerns which exert irresistible pressure on the state; or the existence of a restrictive corporatist policy-making 'elite cartel' and the resultant exclusive nature of policy communities, which denies access to 'marginal' groups and even to those working in the production process of the media. On the other hand, the reader may feel that an acceptable and meritworthy degree of political and social pluralism has replaced traditional German elitism. This view might stress the historic struggle against censorship and state control, the hard-won establishment of the central principle of competing opinions, the exist-

Introduction

ence of countervailing influences and pressures on the media system and commitment to a concept of 'media freedom' that rules out monopolies and undue concentrations of media power. This ideal-type pluralist view is the 'official' view, or the 'conventional wisdom', of the Federal Republic's media system. It is the way the country projects itself, as indeed all the Western democracies do, in comparison with Eastern Europe or Third World dictatorships. Of course, the truth may be not so easy to paint in black or white terms: it may lie somewhere in between these polar viewpoints.

Whatever conclusion the reader may arrive at, the importance of the subject-matter can hardly be in doubt. As Hans-Matthias Kepplinger, another leading media expert in the Federal Republic, has suggested: media 'policy' is as old as the media themselves. It began with the struggle between the feudal state and the liberal modernising bourgeoisie ('liberales Bürgertum'). In Germany, this struggle was only very imperfectly resolved until the period following 'Stunde Null', 1945. Yet, above all in Germany, historical experience – particularly, the period of National Socialist totalitarianism – provoked an awareness of the central significance of the media to liberal democracy.[8] As will be explained, during the post-war period, controversies over press-concentration in the 1960s and 1970s, 'press freedom' and 'broadcasting freedom' in the 1970s, and the 'new media' and the introduction of commercial television in the 1970s and 1980s (merely to mention the most important instances), have all contributed to broaden still further the public awareness that the field of the mass media entails making very serious public-policy choices ('ordnungspolitische Entscheidungen').

---

8. Hans-Matthias Kepplinger, *Massenkommunikation: Rechtsgrundlagen, Medienstrukturen, Kommunikationspolitik*, Stuttgart: Teubner Studienskripte, 1982, p. 9.

1
The Historical Origins and Early Post-War Development of the West German Press System

The Emergence of the Mass-Circulation Press

The history of the press in Germany goes back as far as the seventeenth century and that of the printed word even further to the invention of the movable letter-press by Johannes Gutenberg in the mid-fifteenth century. In fact, it would be no exaggeration to suggest that Germany was the birthplace of European intellectual journalism. However, the rise of the press as a truly mass medium was for a long time frustrated by the fragmented state of 'Germany' during the seventeenth, eighteenth and much of the nineteenth centuries. As a consequence, events lagged somewhat behind comparable developments in the Anglo-Saxon world. Moreover, for most of this period the infant press system remained severely constrained by the pervasive practice of censorship and political control that was the rule in most of the vast patchwork of German states during this long period of stultifying authoritarianism and relative economic stagnation. Authoritarian government remained the norm in most parts of Germany even after the French Revolution and the Napoleonic Wars introduced the spirit of liberalism to the Continent at the end of the eighteenth century and the beginning of the nineteenth century.

Any significant development of the mass press in Germany was delayed until the latter decades of the nineteenth century. At this historical juncture, a sudden massive expansion of the print media accompanied Germany's belated but very rapid industrial 'take off' process following national unification in 1870/1. This development resulted from a combination of factors: the growth of literacy, the dramatic expansion of other forms of communication and the concomitant undermining of

13

parochialism, and technological advances in printing. The latter factor was particularly important: it would hardly be an exaggeration to suggest that the modern press was brought into being by technological progress. After centuries of virtual stagnation the invention of the typesetting machine ('Setzmaschine') and the application, from 1873 onwards, of rotary printing ('Rotationsdruck') revolutionised the German press. Also most important was the rise of large new social classes as the result of industrialisation. The industrial and commercial 'bourgeoisie' and the burgeoning working class in the mushrooming urban conglomerations were both hungry for information and social comment.

Moreover, in 1874, following national unification, Bismarck's first government enacted the 'Reichspressegesetz' ('Imperial press law') which brought a measure of long overdue rationalisation to the highly fragmented system and created the basis for a national press. Most notably, the law replaced the existing profusion of regional press laws with a national legal framework. The law also abolished the practice of pre-publication censorship ('Vorzensur') and the state licensing of most publications. Post-publication censorship ('Nachzensur') was certainly not dispensed with and the law provided for the continued suppression of certain publications, but at least a first major step towards a more commercial climate of publishing had been taken. As the result, the 'Generalanzeigerpresse' – a healthy provincial and profit-oriented mass-circulation press – sprang into life. Nevertheless, the political climate under Bismarck was hardly liberal, as demonstrated by his immediate launching of a ruthless campaign against the country's large Catholic minority (the 'Kulturkampf'), followed swiftly by another against socialism. The enactment of the 'Anti-Socialist Law' ('Sozialistengesetz') of 1878 outlawed the publication of socialist opinions. Above all, the limited 'liberalisation' of press law reflected the rising power and influence of the industrial and commercial middle classes.[1]

In this climate, the 'Generalanzeigerpresse' remained generally apolitical and objectively conservative. However, an em-

---

1. H. Kleinsteuber, *Rundfunkpolitik in der Bundesrepublik*, Opladen: Leske Verlag & Budrich GmbH, 1982, p. 43.

bryonic political press had grown up during the course of the nineteenth century. The period leading up to and following the abortive 1848 revolution had seen the rise of the liberal and radical press, witness the famous *Neue Rheinische Zeitung* which Karl Marx helped to establish in 1848. The rise of social democracy in Germany during the 1860s and 1870s saw the founding of the socialist press, most notably the establishment in 1876 of *Vorwärts*, the organ of the newly formed Social Democratic Party of Germany (Sozialdemokratische Partei Deutschlands – SPD). Ironically, both the SPD and *Vorwärts* thrived as the result of the repression, which was, in any event, generally lifted with Bismarck's retirement in 1890.

During this period, the mass press started to develop its modern industrial and commercial character as advertisers were now attracted by the newspapers' growing mass circulations. The German press had traditionally relied upon subscription ('Abonnement') for its income and this form of finance continued to remain important. In the early years of the twentieth century a third important kind of newspaper began to thrive in the shape of the so-called 'boulevard' press ('Boulevardzeitung') sold directly on the street. Significantly, these processes were accompanied by a tendency towards press-concentration. By the beginning of the twentieth century a large part of the commercial German press market was the preserve of three press magnates, namely Rudolf Mosse, Leopold Ullstein and August Scherl.[2]

The Weimar Republic

Despite the political cultural legacy of the authoritarian Imperial state ('Obrigkeitsstaat'), the German press exhibited some quite diverse features during the Weimar Republic (1918–33). In the highly politicised and more liberal climate of the 1920s, most newspapers developed political allegiances. A very large body

---

2. J. Sandford, *The Mass Media of the German-Speaking Countries*, London: Oswald Wolff, 1976, p. 10. On the mass-circulation press in Germany during the Imperial period, including detailed information on the Ullstein, Mosse and Scherl concerns, see Chapter 1 of H.-D. Müller, *Der Springer Konzern. Eine kritische Studie*, Munich: R. Piper & Co Verlag, 1968, pp. 13–36.

of newspapers – almost six hundred – were Catholic in orientation and therefore supported the Catholic Centre Party (Zentrum). The socialist and communist press also thrived, with the Social Democrats (SPD) running almost two hundred papers, including *Vorwärts*, and the Communists (KPD) no less than fifty. The SPD papers, in particular, developed into an impressive mass-circulation press after making a supremely successful effort to modernise and broaden their appeal, incorporating sports, news, photos, entertainment, women's pages and even business sections into their format. By contrast, the communist papers remained heavily doctrinaire. In addition, the mainstream press embraced many quality papers with a liberal orientation, perhaps best exemplified by Theodor Wolff's famous *Berliner Tageblatt* established in 1871. However, a very large number of the mainstream newspapers remained extremely conservative and about eighty reflected very right-wing 'German national' views. By the year 1932, around 30% of the German newspapers were still 'party papers'. The Catholic Centre Party and the Bavarian People's Party (Bayerische Volkspartei – also Catholic) had no less than 434. The Social Democrats had 149. By this stage the Nazi Party too had a 'mere' 120. The vast majority, however, was still accounted for by the commercial mass-circulation 'Generalanzeiger' press and the provincial 'Heimatzeitungen'.[3]

However, concentration proceeded apace, at least in the commercial mass press market. In 1913 the press concerns of August Scherl had been taken over, in the utmost secrecy, by a consortium of conservative businessmen and politicians led by the leading industrialist Alfred Hugenberg. During the Weimar Republic Hugenberg went on to build up Europe's first and mightiest 'multimedia' empire. By the end of the period, the mass commercial press market was dominated by this single giant concern, a state of affairs partially disguised by the superficial veneer of pluralism provided by the political press. In reality, both financially and in terms of its mass 'reach', the Hugenberg press empire eclipsed by far the still limited re-

---

3. M. Haler, *Basic Law Guarantees Freedom of Opinion – Mass Media in the FRG*, Bonn: Inter Nationes, 1982, p. 15. Also: Rüdiger Liedtke, *Die verschenkte Presse – die Geschichte der Lizenzierung von Zeitungen nach 1945*, Berlin: Verlag für Ausbildung und Studium in der Elefanten Presse, 1982, pp. 17–18.

sources and appeal of much of the political press, and it increasingly dwarfed the liberal quality press. According to one leading authority on the German press, Hugenberg operated his media empire according to three main principles: he sought to 'industrialise' the press following American practice; he endeavoured to apply capitalistic and technical methods to promote press-concentration and to pitch his appeal to the masses; and lastly, he aimed to achieve a much deeper, wider and enduring political impact than the 'conservative' press had hitherto accomplished.[4]

Hugenberg himself was an extreme conservative. Until the end of the First World War he had been chairman of the directorate ('Vorsitzender des Direktoriums') of the Krupp steel and armaments concern. He had also been closely involved with the Prussian government service, and had had a hand in the colonial administration of Prussia's Polish territories. From 1920 onwards he was a leading member of parliament for the anti-democratic and extreme right-wing nationalist German National People's Party (Deutschnationale Volkspartei – DNVP). Hugenberg and his party were fiercely nationalistic and anti-socialist. Moreover, they were the one of the more extreme voices of anti-Weimar revisionism. Immediately, Hugenberg's press empire became the main mouthpiece of the barons of heavy industry and the DNVP. Inexorably, Hugenberg expanded his influence on the fragile republic's mass communications system. With the backing of the industrial barons of the Ruhr, he had founded an advertising agency in 1914 called 'Ala' (standing for the Allgemeine Anzeigengesellschaft or the General Advertising Company) which came to control a significant section of the commercial market and helped its owner to achieve a nationwide measure of influence on the Weimar press system. After the Great War Hugenberg immediately acquired the Telegraphen-Union news agency, which extended his effective editorial control to hundreds of newspapers beyond the very many that he now actually owned outright. In 1922 he went on to establish 'Wipro' (standing for Wirtschaftsstelle der Provinz-

---

4. Chapter on the 'Hugenberg Konzern' in H.-D. Müller, *Der Springer Konzern*, p. 25. Also see D. Guratzch, *Macht durch Organisation. Die Grundlegung des Hugenbergschen Presseimperiums*, Wiesbaden: Westdeutscher Verlag, 1974.

presse which roughly translates as 'economic office of the provincial press'), a syndicate which existed specifically to supply news and information to the country's vast provincial press (the so-called 'Heimatzeitungen'). But his interests were not limited to written information. Quite early on in the Weimar period, he established the German Cinematic Society (Deutsche Lichtbildgesellschaft) in order to exert a propagandistic influence on the infant German film industry as well. Later, in 1927, he extended his communications empire even further by taking over the heavily indebted Universum-Filmaktiengesellschaft ('Ufa'), which produced about three-quarters of German-made cinema films and provided the weekly 'Wochenschau' news service for the cinema. Later, he established his own separate cinema news company called the Wochenschau-Produktion Deuligfilm company. A system of banks, serving as holding companies and concealing the true extent of his backing by Germany's giant industrial capitalists, gave the Hugenberg concern a firm financial foundation. The tone of the Hugenberg concern's message has been eloquently described as being 'an unbridled falsification of the circumstances and causes of Germany's defeat in the Great War, the substitution of national self-pity in place of its self-respect, a renewed incitement of "Angst" and hatred against a world of enemies, and an unchristian interlacing of religion and politics, which called upon God to ratify this creed of richly emotive nationalism'.[5]

As the Weimar Republic lurched to the right in 1925, symbolised by the election of Field Marshal von Hindenburg to the presidency in that year, the influence of Hugenberg's media empire became increasingly pernicious. In fact, right from the inauguration of the Weimar Republic in 1918 onwards, Hugenberg conducted a media campaign against Germany's first experiment with liberal democracy. From 1925 until 1928 the DNVP participated in a series of broadly-based but inherently unstable coalition governments. In October 1928 Hugenberg became the chairman of the DNVP and, at the notorious Bad Harzburg conference, he subsequently committed his party to a 'national front' (the Harzburger Front) with the National Social-

5. See Müller, *Der Springer Konzern*, pp. 27–30. Also see Sandford, *The Mass Media*, p. 12.

Historical Origins of the West German Press System

ists, in order to defeat the Weimar system presumed to have been 'poisoned' by marxist 'cultural bolshevism' ('marxistisch-Kulturbolshewismus'). The editorial might of his vast media empire was now turned with devastating effect against the best efforts of the SPD-led 'Grand Coalition' of 1928–30 to stabilise the political system. After 1930, as the Republic entered into its crisis years, the DNVP declined as the National Socialists gained mass support. Ironically, this transfer of support was facilitated by the 'common front' tactics pursued by Hugenberg and his party. In 1932, the support of Hugenberg and the DNVP was crucial for Hitler to be able to command a parliamentary majority and for his subsequent fateful election to the post of chancellor on 30 January 1933. Hugenberg entered Hitler's first government of 'national renewal' as the Imperial Minister for the Economy and Food Supply (Reichsminister für Wirtschaft und Ernährung). Five months later, he left the cabinet with his tail between his legs following a minor dispute with Hitler. Hugenberg felt that Hitler had betrayed him by virtually ignoring him. Throughout the short history of the Weimar Republic Hugenberg's media empire served the cause of anti-democratic forces, at each stage contributing greatly to the atmosphere of decline, panic, anti-semitism and anti-democratic revanchism. Ironically, Hugenberg's only reward was to have his press empire subsequently demolished by the Nazis.

In comparison with the proliferation of Catholic, socialist and communist newspapers during the Weimar Republic, the Nazi press, at least during the Weimar period, was relatively unimpressive. As Oron Hale has pointed out, 'the circulation successes of the Nazi press came after and not before the [Nazi] accession to power'. During the Weimar Republic, 'millions of copies were printed for which there were no subscribers or street sales, but which were distributed for purposes of political propaganda'. Thus by the early 1930s, the Nazi press was encountering very severe financial difficulties, such that 'if Hitler had not come to power in 1933, the party press would have withered and disappeared quite as rapidly as it had blossomed'.[6]

6. O. Hale, *The Captive Press in the Third Reich*, Princeton, NJ: Princeton University Press, 1964, pp. 59–60. (Also in German: O. Hale, *Presse in der Zwangsjacke 1933–45*, trans. by Wilhelm and Modeste Pferdekamp, Düsseldorf: Droste Verlag, 1965).

The Nazi press first appeared in significant measure as a rash of weekly newspapers from the mid-1920s onwards. Not until 1930 did they generally convert to daily publication. Before this point, the number and circulation of Nazi daily newspapers had remained very low. According to Hale, in 1927 there were only 3 Nazi dailies with a meagre total circulation of 17,800. By 1929 there were still only 10, with a relatively insignificant total circulation of 72,590. By 1930 their number and circulation had grown but they still did not constitute an important part of the Weimar press: there were now 19 Nazi daily newspapers with a total circulation of 253,925. By 1932, their number had grown to 59 with a circulation of 782,121. However, it was only after the Nazi seizure of power ('Machtergreifung') in 1933 that these figures were transformed. In 1934, there were no fewer than 97 Nazi daily newspapers with a total circulation of 3,375,757 and the following year the hundred mark was achieved with a total circulation of 3,900,080. By 1939, these latter figures had doubled. Yet, to call most of them 'newspapers' is to some extent a misnomer. As Hale notes, they were

> primarily propaganda organs . . . with few regular subscribers, no capital, little or no advertising, no news service, no local correspondents, few trained journalists . . . [and] the editorial and management staff were volunteers. Most were from the ranks of the fanatics, the salvation seekers, the rootless and the unemployed. They [the papers] were violent and crude, [they] could have been the work of juvenile delinquents.[7]

The main organ of the National Socialist German Workers Party (Nationalsozialistische Deutsche Arbeiterpartei – NSDAP) was the *Völkischer Beobachter*, which was founded in Munich as early as 1920. This newspaper was an outgrowth of a tradition of small but vituperously anti-semitic, 'folkish' ('völkisch') and extreme nationalist newspapers that had grown up in the nineteenth century. Following the abortive 1923 Munich Putsch, the newspaper was banned, but this ban was subsequently lifted following the Republic's lurch to the right in 1925. The *Völkischer Beobachter* provided the gullible, the bigoted and, after 1929, the

---

7. Ibid., p. 50. The figures are from ibid., p. 59.

Historical Origins of the West German Press System

dispossessed, the unemployed and the hopeless with a simple but effective message: salvation would follow a National Socialist victory over the un-German forces of Judaism and Bolshevism. The National Socialist press included a number of similar 'agitprop' papers ('Kampfblätter') such as Julius Streicher's luridly anti-semitic *Der Stürmer* and Josef Goebbels' *Der Angriff*. It is difficult to gauge the effectiveness of such papers, since they seem to have had such a limited audience. However, their low circulation (until 1933) is a dubious indicator of their effectiveness. It is certainly the case, however, that a very similar underlying message was conveyed to a truly mass readership by the organs of the Hugenberg press empire.

In the end, the Weimar press system, like the political system, proved itself to be deeply flawed. Apart from the Hugenberg concern and a few exceptionally successful papers, the press rested on weak economic foundations. Moreover, it was deeply penetrated by special social and political interests. Thus, the polarisation of politics and society was reflected in the highly partisan nature of much reporting and the inability of the press, like the political parties, to act 'responsibly' and contribute to the consensus-building which the Republic direly needed for its very survival. The freedom of the press, too, was not adequately enshrined in the Republic's Constitution. In particular, the 'Law for the Defence of the Republic' of 1922 gave the political authorities the potential power to curb the press. This opened the way for the penultimate blow to press freedom which was actually dealt by the emergency decrees of the Brüning and von Papen governments in the crisis years of 1931–2 (the 'Pressenotverordnungen' of March, July and August 1931 and July 1932). Thus press freedom became a casualty even before the Nazi 'seizure of power' ('Machtergreifung') of 1933. In sum, the Weimar press fell victim to a fatal combination of its own weaknesses, the prevailing uncertainty, fear and finally panic of the population, and the irreconcilable opposition of the social and political interests and ideologies of the time.

The Third Reich

When Hitler came to power, the situation of the Nazi 'party

papers' was transformed virtually overnight. Hale notes that

> bank credit suddenly became available, there was a rush by opportunists to subscribe and advertise in them, and the 'Gau' press [i.e. local Nazi press] received the windfall of property confiscated from the socialists and communists. Soon the Nazi papers were nested into the former premises of the so-called marxist press and for the first time began to publish their papers from well-equipped printing plants and business offices.[8]

Nor were the 'bourgeois' papers spared from the tidal wave of confiscations that occurred after the Nazi seizure of power. After the socialist and communist press, especially blacklisted were those liberal middle-class papers, of which there were a respectable number, which had dared to remain critical of the Nazis until the last minute.

Shortly after their accession to power in 1933, the National Socialists enacted the 'Emergency Decree for the Protection of State and Nation', followed by the infamous 'Editors Law' ('Schriftleitergesetz' – 'Schriftleiter' actually meaning 'anyone who wrote'). This latter law laid the foundations for the Nazi Party's control of press freedom. It was primarily directed at controlling the work of editors and journalists rather than the newspaper proprietors directly. It placed explicit controls on the qualification for admission to the profession. The most notorious of these was the stipulation that all members of the profession be of pure 'Aryan' racial stock: it simply banned Jews from the press. The law also laid down a number of strict duties and rules of conduct. Effectively, editors and journalists were reduced to being state servants. Editors now became the direct link between the Nazi state and the press, as a result of which the actual newspaper proprietors were reduced to being merely the 'paymasters'.[9]

Although the widespread expropriations had led to a farreaching extension of the Nazi press, and its own publishing house, the Eher Verlag, at first the National Socialists did not appear to aim for an entirely state-owned press. They were more clever than this. They allowed many of the old and

8. Ibid., p. 61.
9. Ibid., p. 83.

Historical Origins of the West German Press System

established newspapers to continue under previous ownership. Yet these 'independent' papers were pressured into forms of 'cooperation' with Nazi competitors. Many were given over into the hands of 'reliable' people. Many others were passed into the control of camouflaged holding companies connected to the Eher Verlag. At the same time, the process of 'Gleichschaltung' (coordination within the Nazi order) involved a very strict control of the press. All areas of intellectual and cultural life fell under the control of Josef Goebbels' Imperial Ministry for Popular Enlightenment and Propaganda (Reichsministerium für Volksaufklärung und Propaganda). This ministry contained a range of special departments supervising radio, cinema, theatre, literature, advertising and the press. In addition, all editors had to become members of a National Socialist Press Chamber (Reichspressekammer), from which all non-Aryans and anti-Nazis were automatically banned.

Under such conditions, a form of self-censorship naturally developed. Moreover, a subtle but near absolute effective control of news and information was brought about by the merging of the two German new agencies of the Weimar period into a single National Socialist-controlled German News Agency (the Deutsches Nachrichtenbüro) in 1933. Thus, during much of the Third Reich there remained a superficial appearance of 'pluralism' even under conditions of *de facto* Nazi Party monopoly and absolute control of information. However, after the outbreak of the war there was an even more rigorous clamp-down on the press, and many more newspapers were now actually closed or taken over directly by the Nazis. By 1943 nearly one thousand publishers had been shut down. Many were bought up or simply confiscated by the Nazis, so that it has been calculated that no less than 82.5% of the total circulation capacity was in Nazi ownership by 1945. The Eher Verlag had become the largest newspaper concern in the world.[10]

10. Apart from ibid. see: J. Wulf (ed.), *Presse und Funk im Dritten Reich. Eine Dokumentation*, Gütersloh: S. Mohn Verlag, 1964; K.-D. Abel, *Presselenkung im NS-Staat. Eine Studie zur Geschichte der Publizistik in der nationalsozialistischen Zeit*, Berlin: Colloquium Verlag/Wissenschaftsverlag Volker Spiess, 1968 (2nd edn, 1987); and W. Hagemann, *Publizistik im Dritten Reich. Ein Beitrag zur Methodik der Massenführung*, Hamburg: Hansischer Gildenverlag – Joachim Heitmann & Co., 1948.

The Allied Occupation

Such a brutal rupture was the Third Reich in the historical development of the German press that the press in West Germany today is almost solely the product of the post-war years. In the first place, very many newspapers had been closed down or completely taken over by the Nazis. Secondly, the remaining so-called 'Altverleger' ('old established publishers') were thoroughly compromised. According to Hermann Meyn, 'after twelve years of central political direction and control the psychological starting conditions ['Ausgangslage'] for the rebuilding of the German press in 1945 were very poor indeed despite the general hunger for news. The spoken and printed word was hopelessly compromised.'[11] Thirdly, the effects of heavy Allied bombing meant that much of the production capacity of the German press lay in literal as well as moral ruins. Finally, this dire situation was exacerbated by shortages of paper and newsprint. After the collapse of the Third Reich, the Allied occupation authorities saw to it that those old and established newspaper owners classified under the loose term 'Altverleger' were disbarred from press activity during the occupation.

Moreover, it was the Western Allies who now played by far the most decisive role in giving the future shape to the West German press. On 24 November 1944, the Allies had drafted a very detailed plan of action for their control of the press following Germany's inevitable defeat. Immediately following the German surrender, this plan was largely put into action by the enactment of 'Law No. 191' on 12 May 1945 of the Allied Control Council, the joint Allied body responsible for the administration of the occupied territories. According to this law the defeated Germans were denied the use of any form of public communication whatsoever. In effect, the entire German press was proscribed regardless of its political or philosophical orientation. Along with this general law, the Western Allies enacted 'Directive for the control of news, no. 1' ('Nachrichten Kontrollvorschrift Nr 1'), which specified more narrowly the conditions under which certain exceptions might be allowed in their zones

---

11. H. Meyn, *Massenmedien in der Bundesrepublik Deutschland*, Berlin: Colloquium Verlag, 1979, p. 37.

of occupation. As a result, every magazine published and every single broadcast, film or theatrical performance in both Western- and Soviet-controlled occupation zones required signed permission from the military governments. In short, the press was to be reintroduced under licence.

The Licensed Press

In the early summer of 1945 the military governments issued the first licences. In the meantime the population's communication and information needs were met by the so-called 'army-group newspapers' ('Heeresgruppenzeitungen') which were published weekly or bi-weekly by press-officers of the military authorities. In addition, the occupation authorities each distributed their own newspaper in their respective zones: the *Neue Zeitung* (American zone), *Die Welt* (British zone), the *Nouvelles de France* (French zone) and the *Tägliche Rundschau* (Soviet zone). The Soviets were the first to issue licences in June 1945. They were followed by the Americans at the end of July 1945, the French in August 1945 and lastly by the British in January 1946.[12]

Above all, both the Western Allies and the Soviets were determined to 'reeducate' and thoroughly 'democratise' the Germans. The immediate aims were to conduct a complete denazification of editorially influential personnel and to 'reeducate' the Germans in an 'Anti-Fascist' direction. There were also a number of immediate concerns: most notably to persuade the Germans of their war guilt, in particular their collective guilt for war crimes such as the concentration camps. Significantly, there was to be no discussion of the future of the German nation unless the Allies made an exception to this rule.[13] However, to achieve the main goal of 'reeducating' the Germans towards 'democracy', the methods adopted by the Western Allies and by the Soviets differed according to their very different respective

12. H. Hurwitz, 'Die Pressepolitik der Allierten', in H. Pross (ed.), *Deutsche Presse seit 1945*, Berne/Munich/Vienna: Scherz Verlag, 1965, pp. 27–55; also H. Hurwitz, *Die Stunde Null der deutschen Presse*, Cologne: Verlag Wissenschaft und Politik, Berend von Nottbeck, 1972.
13. K. Giebel, *Medienschungel. Eine kritische Bestandsaufnahme*, Stuttgart: Bleicher Verlag, 1983, pp. 185–6.

interpretations of the causes of fascism and of the concept 'democracy' itself.

The Soviets quickly embarked on a course of action which, by the temporary expedient of their encouragement of an 'Anti-Fascist bloc', paved the way for the future establishment of full-blown Communist hegemony in the eastern occupation zone. The marxist analysis of the causes of fascism stressed capitalism as the major culprit, therefore the Soviets' ultimate concern was to socialise all major areas of social and economic activity, including the media. Although at first all of the 'Anti-Fascist' parties, licensed by the Soviet military occupation forces as early as June 1945, were allowed to develop their own press, very quickly it transpired that the Communists (the KPD) benefited from Soviet patronage. The Social Democratic and 'bourgeois' papers were customarily denied adequate paper and newsprint, while the communist press received generous financial and material support from the Soviets. After the 'shot-gun marriage' of the KPD and the SPD to form the marxist-leninist Socialist Unity Party of Germany (Sozialistische Einheitspartei Deutschlands – SED) in April 1946, the Soviets made every effort to disadvantage and suppress the 'bourgeois' press. In the end, the non-communist parties were simply absorbed into the SED-dominated National Front and their press was constrained to toe the SED line. The main official organ of the East German press soon became the party paper modelled on the Soviet *Pravda*, namely *Neues Deutschland*. Throughout this transition period towards an overtly marxist-leninist press system, the support given to the East German communist press by the Soviets was, in the words of one authority, 'particularly crass' ('besonders krass'). The situation had quite simply been a case of 'a one-sidedly manipulated press censorship' ('eine einseitig gehandhabte Pressezensur').[14]

By contrast, the Western Allies opted in favour of the gradual and controlled reestablishment of a privately-owned, commer-

---

14. H.-D. Fischer, *Parteien und Presse in Deutschland seit 1945*, Bremen: Schünemann Universitätsverlag, 1971, pp. 74–85, in particular pp. 76–7. Also see: E. Hermann, *Zur Theorie und Praxis der Presse in der Sowjetischen Besatzungszone Deutschlands*, Berlin: Colloquium Verlag, 1963; and K. Koszyk, *Pressepolitik für Deutsche 1945–49*, Part IV of *Geschichte der deutschen Presse*, ed. B. Sösemann, Berlin: Colloquium Verlag, 1986, pp. 325–54.

Historical Origins of the West German Press System

cial organisation of the press. For this reason they sought to return the ownership of the new German press into the hands of individual or groups of individual licensees, about whose commitment to democracy they were confident (see p. 29 below). During the period of licensing, the Allies even ruled against the operation of a free capitalistic share ownership of the press. Moreover, the Western Allies clearly aimed to install a press system which was to be free from central state control. Partly to this end, they supported the decentralist idea that the press, like the political parties, had to be rebuilt from the local and regional level upwards. In this manner, the Germans were to be reeducated gradually into the habits of a decentralised pluralist democracy, which was to be characterised by the widest possible dispersion of political and socio-economic power. This too contrasted with the centralising instincts of socialist democracy. By adopting this decentralised approach, the Western Allies also aimed to prevent the development of the kind of press-concentration that had characterised the Weimar press. At least, there can be little doubt that this was the intention. Another important policy was to ensure the strict separation of news and commentary. This typically Anglo-Saxon notion was quite new to the German press tradition. It was set to endure as a central principle of the new democratic press system that this distinction should be made clear. The role of the American *Neue Zeitung* deserves a special mention in this connection. Revealingly, the *Neue Zeitung* was sub-titled an 'American newspaper for the German population'. Its first edition appeared on 18 October 1945 and contained an article by General Dwight Eisenhower, in which he announced that 'the *Neue Zeitung* would serve to give the German press an example by its objective reporting [strict separation of news and comment], its respect for the truth, and its high journalistic standard'.[15]

Ironically, or perhaps symbolically, the *Neue Zeitung* was printed on the Munich press of the notorious *Völkischer Beobachter*. Unlike the licensed press, it contained very little local or regional reporting, since its primary aim was to have a national audience. Indeed, the *Neue Zeitung* immediately achieved a

15. E. Matz, *Die Zeitungen der US-Armee für die deutsche Bevölkerung (1944–46)*, Münster: Verlag C. J. Fahle, Studien zur Publizistik, Bremer Reihe, Band 12, 1969, pp. 16–17. Also see Liedtke, *Die verschenkte Presse*, pp. 54–64.

wide readership of about 1.5 million, although mainly in the American occupation zone. It received very generous amounts of financial and material support from its American backers. Its format contained some important innovations. Apart from containing the usual amounts of entertainment, sport and the traditional German 'feuilleton', it introduced a politics section, a foreign affairs section and most importantly a readers' letters section called 'Das Freie Wort'. It immediately became a forum for debate about the reconstitution of German democracy. Among others, such leading 'Anti-Fascist' writers as Carl Zuckmeyer, Thomas Mann and John Steinbeck wrote for the paper. Under the distinguished editorial guidance of Hans Habe and later of Hans Wallenberg, the *Neue Zeitung* generally achieved its main purpose of furnishing the new German press with a worthy model of Anglo-Saxon style democratic reporting. In addition, the paper undoubtedly served to bring home to many Germans the then official line of their 'collective responsibility' for the Third Reich, but at the same time it was by no means uncritical of the occupation authorities. Indeed, this openness to self-criticism was entirely new in the German experience of the press. In sum, until it finally closed down in 1955 when the Germans received back their full sovereignty from the occupation powers, the *Neue Zeitung* played an important role in the rebirth of German democracy and the establishment of a new kind of press.

To return to the question of the licensed press, the issue of every licence was accompanied by regulations ('Vorschriften') specifying the kind of company that would produce the newspaper and guidelines for its fundamental orientation. These regulations also explicitly forbade the expression of any nationalistic, pan-German, militaristic, fascist or otherwise anti-democratic views. They specifically banned all terminology or expressions that had a 'Nazi' ring. They stipulated that the source of all news and information had to be made very clear. Allied press officers acted as watchdogs to ensure compliance. The rationing of paper was a useful additional means of exerting pressure, and many papers were in any case directly dependent upon the Allies for financial support. The ultimate sanction was, of course, the removal of the licence itself. However, Harold Hurwitz notes that 'in general, the supervision . . . was practised in a restrained manner. Praise and advise was to be much more frequently heard than reproach. Sanctions were only enacted on the most seldom occasions.'[16]

In practice, there was a very considerable variation of approach adopted by the different occupation authorities. The Americans favoured 'independent' or 'above-party' newspapers. A party press was totally incongruent with the American conception of a free press and was a wholly unfamiliar notion. They therefore distributed licences to individuals or boards of editors with different group affiliations in their southern German occupation zone. The Americans either insisted upon licensees taking a non-party line or else they sought to manufacture a pluralist balance of opinion and political orientation by appointing licences to groups of individuals of different group identification. Consensus was to be reached prior to publication, and accordingly a contrived balance of opinion presented to the readers. At least, this was the theory. However, this policy quickly ran into some practical difficulties. Rüdiger Liedtke has pointed out that because most of the untainted or 'active Anti-Nazis' were socialistically inclined – of one shade or another – the licensees had often to be found among these circles. Thus, in the case of the *Frankfurter Rundschau*, one of the earliest and the best-known newspapers to reappear in the American zone, the original group licence-holders consisted of three Social Democrats, two members of the KPD, a KPD sympathiser and a left-wing Catholic of the old 'Zentrum' party. Similarly, Liedtke points to the case of the *Rhein-Neckar Zeitung* which was given over into the joint responsibility of one Social Democrat, one Communist and a leading Liberal (Theodor Heuss). In Liedtke's words, 'the selection of Anti-Nazis . . . inevitably led to a contradiction between what the US aimed for and what their denazification programme supported'.[17]

However, with the advent of the Cold War and the increasing anti-communism of the British and Americans, the period of the 'Anti-Fascist' press proved to be short-lived. The number of

16. Hurwitz, *Die Stunde Null*, p. 145.
17. Liedtke, *Die verschenkte Presse*, p. 73. For a far more positive evaluation of press policy in the American occupation zone see: Hurwitz, *Die Stunde Null der deutschen Presse*; and K. Koszyk, *Pressepolitik für Deutsche 1945–49*, pp. 39–122.

licensees on the boards of newspapers in the US zone quickly diminished as it proved increasingly difficult to reach the hoped-for editorial consensus. Moreover, licences were also progressively withdrawn from Communists, and in some notable cases from Social Democrats as well. Liedtke states that 'in August 1948, after the onset of the first Berlin crisis, the last Communist licensee of a daily newspaper in the US zone had his licence withdrawn'.[18] The Americans also sought to balance the left orientation of the *Frankfurter Rundschau* (which remained in the control of a Social Democrat licensee) by deliberately founding the *Frankfurter Neue Presse* and giving the licence to two Catholic sympathisers of the Christian Democratic Union (Christlich-Demokratische Union – CDU).[19]

Unlike the Americans, the British had no qualms about issuing licences in their northern German occupation zone to newspapers with a distinct political orientation (the so-called 'Parteirichtungszeitungen'). From the outset, individuals or groups issued with a licence were allowed to retain and reflect a particular ideological bias. In this case overall balance was supposedly assured by the resultant competition of different viewpoints in the political/readership marketplace. At the same time, however, the British were careful to ensure that these papers did not fall directly under party ownership or control. In order to prevent the newspapers becoming literally party organs, the licences were only awarded to ordinary members or sympathisers of a party. Only in thinly populated areas of the British zone which could only be expected to support a single paper was the 'American model' adopted and care taken to establish 'above party' newspapers.[20] Significantly, the British authorities also granted licences to a certain Axel Springer to publish a radio magazine, called *Hör zu*, and a local newspaper called the *Hamburger Abendblatt*, thus setting him on his path towards erecting a huge press empire. The French distributed licences according to both the British and American models. At first they seemed to favour the American model, but after 1947 they also adopted the British one.[21]

18. See Liedtke, *Die verschenkte Presse*, p. 162.
19. Ibid., pp. 144–5.
20. See Meyn, *Massenmedien*, p. 38.
21. On press policy in the British occupation zone see Koszyk, *Pressepolitik für*

Historical Origins of the West German Press System

Generally, therefore, the Allied military authorities were very careful to issue licences to people who were able to offer unequivocal proof of their 'Anti-Fascist' credentials. Both the licensee publishers and the journalists themselves were not only required not to have been members of the Nazi Party, they also had to be free of any suspicion of support, connivance or collaboration with the Nazis. Licences were not issued to any formerly active Nazis by any of the occupation authorities. However, as already mentioned, this ban extended even to many publishers who had lost their papers to the Nazis. Therefore most of the so-called 'old publishers' ('Altverleger') were similarly banned from reappearing. Furthermore the licensees were to be the 'trustees' of the Allied occupation powers and, in this sense, the immediate representatives of Allied policies to the German people. This limitation meant that much new blood was injected, of necessity, into the press sector. New people were attracted to it who had little or no previous experience of publishing or journalism. According to Herbert Meyn, 'of the 113 licence-holders in the American zone a substantial quarter came from other branches of activity'.[22]

This also had the effect that most of the newspapers established during the occupation period in the Western zones, as in the East, were effectively produced on expropriated presses, if only on a temporary basis. In the American zone especially, many 'Altverleger' had to lease their printing works to licence-holders (although it was the latter who most often had to bear the costs of repairing war-damage). After 1948, this compulsory leasing procedure was gradually replaced by the signing of actual leasehold contracts. From the beginning, the British were mainly content to see simple printing contracts signed, while the French often issued licences without any such conditions attached.[23]

Deutsche 1945–49, pp. 123–259. Also see H. Fischer, *Reeducations- und Pressepolitik unter britischem Besatzungsstatus. Die Zonenzeitung 'Die Welt' 1946–50*, Düsseldorf: Droste Verlag, 1978. On policy in the French zone see K. Koszyk, *Pressepolitik für Deutsche 1945–49*, pp. 260–318. Also see S. Schölzel, *Die Pressepolitik in der französischen Besatzungszone 1945–49*, Mainz: Hase und Koehler Verlag, 1986 (Veröffentlichung der Kommission des Landtags für die Geschichte des Landes Rheinland-Pfalz).
22. See Meyn, *Massenmedien*, p. 37.
23. V. Schulze, *Der Bundesverband Deutscher Zeitungsverleger*, Düsseldorf: Droste Verlag, 1985, p. 33.

The degree of editorial control by the Allies also varied both between spheres of influence and over time. In the Soviet occupation zone, state control of the press by the National Socialists was replaced very quickly by a similar degree of effective state control first by the Soviets and then progressively by their East German Communist allies. In the Western zone, too, the occupation forces kept all journalistic reporting on a tight rein. However, in the latter case, it was a fundamental tenet that the press should henceforth be free of state control. Moreover, the main purpose of licensing was that the Germans themselves should be guided back into taking responsibility for the rebirth of a privately owned and pluralistic, rather than monopolistic, press system. In this way, the Germans themselves were to play an important role in the reconstruction of liberal democracy in West Germany. At the same time, however, the Allied licensing and control system placed very considerable constraints on press freedom.

As early as September 1945 the Americans gave up pre-publication censorship ('Vorzensur') of the press in their zone and shortly afterwards the British and the French followed suit. Nevertheless, a strict control in the form of a post-publication censorship ('Nachzensur') continued. For a considerable period of time afterwards, Allied 'press control officers' could demand subsequent alteration, amending or even withdrawal of information. According to one informed source, corrections actually increased rather than decreased after the change from 'Vorzensur' to 'Nachzensur'.[24] By this and other regulatory means, the military authorities of the Western Allies ensured that the nascent German press respected the rules that they had prescribed, especially those stipulating a strict separation of news and commentary and a ban of any criticism of the Allied occupation powers. Both the early 'Vorzensur' and the continuance of the practice of 'Nachzensur' prevented the establishment and distribution of newspapers, whose general orientation ('Tendenz') was not in harmony with the interests of the respective occupation power.

24. G. Steinhausen, *Gründung und Entwicklung der westdeutschen Nachrichtenagenturen nach dem 2. Weltkrieg*, Dissertation, Heidelberg 1959, p. 39, quoted in H.-W. Gross, *Die Deutsche Presse-Agentur*, Frankfurt/Main: Haag & Herchen Verlag 1982, p. 53.

Historical Origins of the West German Press System

Moreover, the nascent German press remained exclusively dependent upon information furnished by the Allies' own news agencies. Each of the Allied occupation powers used their own zonal news agencies as a more subtle and less obtrusive form of control of information than direct and overt control of the individual licensed newspapers (see p. 62 below). In the words of one US government official: it was 'more important to invest American capital in a German news agency than in German industry'.[25] All the Allies subjected the licensed press in their respective zones to regulations which strictly delimited their access to information sources and effectively gave the zonal agencies an information monopoly for internal news and the Allied Press Service (APS) a monopoly of all external 'world' news.[26] Even though these regulations were subsequently lifted, the respective authorities retained considerable control.

Hurwitz describes how German journalists were not allowed to enjoy the same freedom of movement and status (therefore 'access' to information) as their Allied counterparts until 1949. They remained totally dependent upon 'official' news sources: apart from the news agencies that meant the public relations departments and press releases of the military governments. Until late 1946, they were not even allowed to buy foreign publications. The French were the strictest in enforcing the maintenance of their news agency's monopoly. Hurwitz also describes how absolute was this dependency of the licensed press upon the information supply of the agencies and points out how this bred distrust and resentment, which was fortified by the sometimes insensitively pedagogic behaviour of the occupiers towards the Germans.[27] In sum, during the occupation the German population could only be informed as the Allies themselves wished them to be.[28]

---

25. F. Sänger, *Verborgene Faden*, Bonn, 1978, p. 142 quoted by Gross, *Die Deutsche Presse-Agentur*, p. 52.
26. R. Greuner, *Lizenzpresse – Auftrag und Ende. Der Einfluß der anglo-amerikanischen Besatzungspolitik auf die Wiedererrichtung eines imperialistischen Pressewesens in Westdeutschland*, Berlin (East): Rütten und Loening, 1962, p. 270.
27. See Hurwitz, *Die Stunde Null*, pp. 198–9.
28. B. Mettler, *Demokratisierung und Kalter Krieg. Zur amerikanischen Informations- und Rundfunkpolitik in Westdeutschland 1945–49*, Berlin: Wissenschaftsverlag Volker Spiess, 1975; G. Kieslich, 'Zum Aufbau des Zeitungswesens in der Bundesrepublik Deutschland nach 1945', *Publizistik*, no. 8, 1968, pp. 274–81;

Media and Media Policy in West Germany

The Licensed Press and Capitalist Competition

From a financial point of view, the first three years after the end of the war were halcyon days for the licensed press. The demand for information far exceeded the scarce supply, so the producers dominated. Moreover, the licensed press benefited from protection from competition. The Allies regulated everything from sales areas, numbers of copies published (i.e. the circulation), through to sales price and advertising rates. Under these circumstances not a few licensees were able to amass small fortunes (Axel Springer was set on his trajectory towards becoming a press magnate in this way).

However, there was a dark shadow on the horizon. In most cases, the licensees did not own the means of production of their publications. In the Western occupation zones at least, the Allied occupiers had not gone so far as to dispossess the 'Altverleger'. As seen, the licensees had been compelled to conclude rental and leasehold agreements with the 'Altverleger' for the use of whatever remained of their property. Accordingly, the latter were well-placed to endure and outlive the occupation and the ban on their publishing activities. They could afford to be fairly optimistic and patiently confident about their prospects of soon returning to business. By contrast, the licensees had a driving incentive to accumulate capital as rapidly as possible during the brief period of the occupation and compulsory licensing (the period of so-called 'Lizenzpflicht') in order to be able to break free of this disguised dependency.

In this respect, the currency reform of June 1948 which set the stage for West Germany's astounding economic reconstruction during the 1950s, marked a very important moment. In the British and American zones of occupation, by now merged into the so-called 'bizone' (and shortly to be joined by the French zone), a German Economic Council had already been created, giving 'West Germany' its first central administrative authority. Preparations for the Marshall Plan and the European Recovery

---

K. Koszyk, *Pressepolitik für Deutsche 1945–49*; J. Leithauser, *Journalisten zwischen zwei Welten. Die Nachkriegsjahre der Berliner Presse*, Berlin: Colloquium Verlag, 1960; K. Otzen, *Lizenzpresse, Altverleger und Politik, Kontroverse um die 'Kieler Nachrichten' in den Jahren 1945–52* (Duisburger Studien) St. Augustin: Hans Richarz Publikation Service, 1980.

Programme were well advanced. A reform of the vastly inflated 'Reich' currency was required in order to free the market and lock the West German economy into the Western capitalist system. The resultant currency reform was accompanied by the unilateral abolition of wage and price controls by Ludwig Erhard, who was at that time the chief German economist in the Frankfurt Economic Council. Together, these measures restored the primacy of supply and demand and put West Germany firmly on the tracks of a free-market capitalistic development.[29]

In fact, the currency reform was more than a landmark in the economic development of West Germany. By this point in time, the Cold-War division of the Western and Eastern zones of occupation was looming fast. In March 1948 the Soviets had walked out of the Allied Control Council. On 16 June 1948 the Soviets similarly terminated the four-power Allied Kommandatura in Berlin. Two days later the political division of Germany was effectively sealed by the enactment of the currency reform for the three Western occupation zones and the Western sectors of Berlin. This unilateral measure laid the basis for a separate socio-economic system in what was shortly to become the Federal Republic and broke the link agreed at Potsdam between the Western- and the Soviet-occupied parts of Germany. The Soviet response was the Berlin blockade.

There were few areas of social and economic life that were unaffected by the currency reform. As far as the embryonic press system of the Federal Republic was concerned, it had a profound impact. For those licensees that had not yet been able to acquire a press, the devaluation of their money holdings amounted to a serious set-back. At the same time, the currency reform unleashed a very considerable wave of increased competition among them. As seen, most of the economic regulations were lifted around about this time and the free market was restored. As a consequence, suddenly the competition for market-shares, readers and advertising revenue began in earnest.

A fierce sales war ensued as licensees reacted by driving down their prices and increasing their reliance on advertising.

29. J. Leaman, *The Political Economy of West Germany*, Houndmills and London: Macmillan Press, 1988, pp. 29, 33, and 56.

The logic was simple. By taking this risk, they gambled on increasing their circulation and thereby attracting more advertisers. A common strategy for trying to break into each others' sales areas was the adoption of the so-called 'Nebenausgabe' or strategy of 'multiple editions'. By producing slightly different local editions of what was effectively the same newspaper, the publishers thus sought to expand their circulations. Alongside their main editions ('Hauptausgaben'), competitive and expansionist publishers began to produce a multitude of local supplements ('Nebenausgaben' or 'Bezirksausgaben'). Often these latter differed from the former in little more than title alone, yet they appealed to traditional German localism and acted as a spearhead for the assault on rivals' territories. According to Hurwitz, by August 1949 there were 183 'Nebenausgaben' in the US zone, 169 in the French zone and no less than 379 in the British zone.[30] This is the origin of the most striking characteristic of the West German press landscape to this day, namely the superficial pluralism and the multiplicity of titles for a much smaller number of genuine papers. At the same time as competition increased dramatically in this way, the profitability of the licensed press fell (mainly as paper prices rose after the abolition of price controls). In the struggle to maintain their market-share and to survive, the papers were compelled to increase their advertising business. Many became indebted to banks and other sources of finance. Gross notes that, as a result, 'even before the final abolition of compulsory licensing ['Lizenzpflicht'] in September 1949 and the restoration of complete business freedom, all the essential features of a capitalist press had developed'.[31]

Between 31 July 1945, when the *Frankfurter Rundschau* was licensed, until the foundation of the Federal Republic of Germany in September 1949, no less than 169 papers were licensed: the British licensed 71, the Americans 58, the French 20, and 20 were licensed in jointly-occupied West Berlin.[32] The basic character of the West German newspaper scene was thus clearly established by the Allies. New 'model' newspapers, heavily influenced by the Anglo-Saxon style, were set on their feet in

30. See Hurwitz, *Die Stunde Null*, p. 213.
31. See Gross, *Die Deutsche Presse-Agentur*, p. 61.
32. See Giebel, *Mediendschungel*, p. 186.

Historical Origins of the West German Press System

the key urban centres during the occupation period. The more traditional German 'Heimatzeitung' (local newspaper) or the 'Generalanzeiger' (popular local newspaper with no particular affiliation) of the 'Altverleger' were denied an early entrance on the scene and later they were to find it difficult to compete with those newspapers that were already established.[33] The pattern of press structure that emerged from the period of compulsory licensing differed from zone to zone. The press in the largely rural and less densely-populated US zone was characterised by a high proportion of small and medium-sized newspapers. By contrast, the conurbations of the British zone quickly produced a greater number of large and powerful newspapers with much higher circulations. Gross calculates that, by the end of the period of licensing, there were no less than 24 newspapers with a circulation of over 100,000 in the British zone, as opposed to 15 in the US zone; while there were 23 papers in the US zone with a circulation of between 50,000 and 99,999 and only 16 in the British zone; finally, there were only 4 papers in the British zone with a circulation of less than 50,000, while there were 8 in the US zone (see Table 1.1 below).

Like 'denazification', at the time licensing was generally accepted by the Germans as a necessary evil. However, it was not without its critics. Since the 1960s, the 'new left' has tended to blame Allied policy for giving the West German press structure its private commercial structure, and for helping certain licence-holders (e.g. Axel Springer) to accumulate massive private resources. Two major and detailed academic studies, namely those of Reinhard Greuner (1962), an East German view, and Rüdiger Liedtke (1982), have seen the licensed press as being an instrument to reintroduce and safeguard capitalistic structures in Germany. For instance, Liedtke points out that 'the numerous demands for a really democratic press with other organisational structures [i.e. other than private ownership], such as those of the cooperative ['Genossenschaft'], the public service body ['öffentlich-rechtliches Institut'] or the public foundation

---

33. In the literature there is contradictory information on the number of licensed newspapers or 'Lizenzzeitungen': Harold Hurwitz speaks of 169 in Hurwitz, 'Die Pressepolitik der Alliierten', in H. Pross, *Deutsche Presse seit 1945*, p. 255. The *Handbuch der Weltpresse* produced by the Institut für Publizistik der Universität Münster, Cologne-Opladen, 1970, Bd. 1, p. 119 counts 161.

Table 1.1 Press structure in 1947: circulation statistics

Circulation	British zone	American zone	French zone
Below 50,000	4	8	4
50,000 to 99,999	16	23	9
Above 100,000	24	15	11

Source: H.-W. Gross, *Die Deutsche Presse-Agentur*, Frankfurt/Main: Haag & Herchen Verlag, 1982, p. 62

['gemeinnützige Stiftung'] . . . were made taboo subjects or often resisted as attempts to socialise the press'. Generally, such works attempt to prove that the worst features of the West German press system had their origin in the licensing policies of the Western Allies.[34]

In actual fact, official Allied policy had clearly aimed at establishing a decentralised press system that would be both democratic (in the liberal sense) and free from the state and from the kind of press-concentration that had scarred the Weimar press. Paradoxically, it was after the ending of compulsory licensing that press-concentration really started to reemerge.

The Development of the Press after the End of Compulsory Licensing

As during the spring of 1949 the future state entity of the Federal Republic of Germany began to become increasingly clearly defined, the occupation powers began to dismantle step-by-step the regulatory system that had accompanied licensing. On 23 May 1949, the Federal Republic's constitution or 'Basic Law' ('Grundgesetz') was promulgated and it came into effect the following day. The first federal election, in August 1949, was won by the new conservative 'alliance', Konrad Adenauer's Christian Democratic Union and its Bavarian sister party, the Christian Social Union of Franz Josef Strauss (CDU/CSU). The Basic Law contained an important guarantee of press freedom

---

34. See Liedtke, *Die verschenkte Presse*, quote from p. 8; and Greuner, *Lizenzpresse*. Liedtke's book is an interesting study which examines the practice of licensing by the Americans using as examples the *Süddeutsche Zeitung*, the *Frankfurter Rundschau* and the *Rhein-Neckar Zeitung*, all very famous West German papers. It also has informative sections on the British and French practice.

(Article 5). Even before this important development, laws about the freedom of the press had been passed in three Länder in the American zone, namely Bremen, Württemberg-Baden and Hessen. Moreover, on 4 May 1949 the Americans had announced that shortly the licensing system would be abolished in their zone by the enactment of a general licence ('Generallizenz'). Twenty-seven days later, on 31 May, compulsory licensing ended in Württemberg-Baden. Only four months later the other Länder in the Western zones followed this example. Finally, on 21 September 1949 the Allied High Commission promulgated 'Law No. 5 Concerning the Press, Broadcasting, and Other Organs of Reporting and Entertainment' ('Gesetz Nr. 5 über die Presse, Rundfunk, die Berichterstattung und die Unterhaltungsstätten').

This law allowed the right to every German living in the Federal Republic, with the exception of those identified by the words 'Hauptschuldige' (specially guilty) or 'als Belastete eingestufte ehemalige Nationalsozialisten' (former Nazis classified as 'guilty'), to produce a magazine, newspaper or article without prior permission from the Allied authorities. Significantly, the lifting of compulsory licensing also now allowed the 'Altverleger' to begin publishing again. There immediately occurred a wave of new newspapers, mainly founded by the 'Altverleger' rushing to reenter the business, which reached a high-water mark in April 1950 and ebbed away again until 1952/3. According to Meyn, within half a year the number of newspapers had risen by around 400 (i.e. roughly trebled) to attain the grand figure of 568.[35] Within a year, no less than 750 new titles had appeared, although Gross notes that few of these gained a circulation of over 20,000.[36] The sudden increase in the number of newspapers was particularly spectacular in the American zone. This did not so much reflect any deliberate American policy as the fact that, as seen, the American zone contained a much greater number of small and dispersed rural communities, each of which aspired to have its own newspaper (see Tables 1.2 and 1.3). By contrast, the British zone was more urbanised and was therefore more fertile territory for a greater degree of press-

---

35. See Meyn, *Massenmedien*, p. 39.
36. See Gross, *Die Deutsche Presse-Agentur*, p. 90.

concentration. Around 1949/50, fierce competition grew up between the old and the new publishers. The old publishers were disadvantaged to the extent that they now had to reconquer their former areas of circulation under very difficult conditions, most notably severe paper shortages and competition from already established licensed papers. They were often only able to withstand this competition by means of mergers and amalgamations. This was a great stimulus towards the pattern of press-concentration that had already begun to appear among the licensed press.[37]

With the end of licensing, the control of the presses themselves, which as seen the Allies had merely confiscated from the old publishers and temporarily leased to the licence-holders, ended too. After the foundation of the Federal Republic, more and more presses began to pass back into the hands of their former owners as these leasehold agreements made during the period of occupation expired. Despite this, the prospects of survival for many of the new papers were not at all promising. From several hundred reemergent 'Altverleger', only 29 managed to attain a circulation of 20,000, which Gross suggests was the critical threshold for a newspaper to be able to stand by itself and support its own production facilities. In fact, the return of the so-called 'Heimatpresse' soon transpired to be much less of a competitive threat than previously anticipated by the licensed press.[38]

Among the 'Altverleger', the main beneficiaries of the return of market forces and the abolition of compulsory licensing were the owners of the very large printing and publishing concerns in the larger provincial cities. Within a very short period of time many of the latter had driven the licensed papers, which their presses had hitherto printed, completely out of business and had taken over their subscribers. However, the majority of 'Altverleger' were smaller publishers of local papers ('Heimatzeitungen'). Many of the latter folded or were compelled by the competition to relinquish their independence. As a result, these smaller publishers were often taken over by more efficient and

---

37. See Meyn, *Massenmedien*, pp. 39–40; also see Sandford, *The Mass Media*, pp. 28–9.
38. See Gross, *Die Deutsche Presse-Agentur*, p. 90.

Historical Origins of the West German Press System

Table 1.2 The explosion of newspaper foundings after the end of licensing

	Newspapers	Editions
Mid-1947	113	500
March 1949	140	—*
Sept. 1949	187	—*
End of licensing 21 Sept. 1949		
End 1949	527	—*
Feb/March 1950	755	1 041

Note: *Unfortunately the data are incomplete due to the lack of accurate records.
Source: Günther Kieslich, 'Zum Aufbau des Zeitungswesens in der Bundesrepublik Deutschland nach 1945', *Publizistik*, no. 8, 1963, pp. 274–81, pp. 276–7

Table 1.3 The explosion of newspaper foundings after the end of licensing: the situation in the US zone of occupation

	Licensed papers 1 June 1949		After the ending of licensing 31 October 1949	
	Number of papers	Circulation	Number of papers	Circulation
Württemberg-Baden	16	992 000	122	1 000 000
Hessen	14	994 000	82	1 187 872
Bavaria	27	1 900 000	500	2 150 102
Bremen	2	209 000	2	262 563
Total	59	4 095 000	706	4 600 537

Note: These figures illustrate graphically the tremendous increase in competition following the end of licensing. The number of newspapers increases by nearly twelvefold. By comparison, the total circulation registers a very modest increase. Much of the increase can be accounted for by 'multiple editions' and this would account for the obvious discrepancy with the first table above. Nevertheless, the increased competition for a limited pool of readers is still striking.
Source: H. Hurwitz, *Die Stunde Null der Deutschen Presse. Die amerikanische Pressepolitik in Deutschland 1945–49*, Cologne: Verlag Wissenschaft und Politik, 1972, p. 237

powerful larger publishers. Many also amalgamated or inaugurated new kinds of cooperation with other small papers in the same predicament. This development was a very significant stimulus to press-concentration.

41

It soon became apparent that the 'licensed press' had already established itself enough to be able generally to withstand this storm. Gross notes that only 21 from a total of 131 licensed newspapers fell victim to this fierce wave of new competition in the years 1949 and 1950. In sum, the 'Altverleger' managed to achieve a circulation of around 1.5 million by the end of 1952. The share of total circulation achieved by the 'Altverleger' then remained constant at a modest 22% during the first few years following the abolition of compulsory licensing. By comparison, the share of the 'licensed press' was no less than 72%, with the occupation powers' publications and party political papers accounting for the remainder. Yet, the halcyon days of the 'licensed press' were now well and truly over: looked at another way the figures produced by Gross showed that, by the end of 1950, the licensed press had lost almost 30% of its circulation.[39] Indeed, after the abolition of compulsory licensing, many licensed newspapers could only continue to produce by virtue of credits granted by the Allies to enable them to buy printing facilities and premises. Some licensed publishers were already struggling, with the end of their leasehold contracts now increasingly in view. The sudden newspaper boom, allied with the attempt of the 'old publishers' to regain their former distribution areas, sharpened still further the edge of already fierce competition and contributed to the process of press concentration.

The overall outcome of this intense mêlée of competition during the latter years of the Allied occupation was that a very large number of very small papers was soon confronted by a much smaller number of very large ones. Approximately half of all papers in the year 1952 had a circulation of less than 5,000. Against this, those with a circulation of over 100,000 constituted around 5% of the total number of newspapers. The latter, around 28 large dailies ('Tageszeitungen'), however, accounted for no less than 41% of total circulation. They were nearly all former 'licensed papers'.[40] On the other hand, not a few less successful 'licensed papers', particularly those that had been unable or

39. Ibid., pp. 90–1.
40. C. Ossario-Capella, *Der Zeitungsmarkt in der Bundesrepublik Deutschland*, Frankfurt/Main: Athenäum, 1972, p. 73.

otherwise not disposed to acquire their own presses, had fallen either entirely or at least partially into the hands of powerful reemergent 'Altverleger' while others had merged with these older publishers. Thus, the battle-lines between the 'licensed press' and the 'Altverleger' soon became very confused and even meaningless. The initially sharply-defined conflict between 'licensed press' and 'Altverleger' had led, after a short period, to a complex web of cooperation, integration and even fusion. According to Manfred Knoche, a community of interest developed between the licensed press and the owners of printing works, leading to many mergers and other forms of combination between old and new publishers. Many licensees also sold up to the old publishers entirely. Many owners of print facilities pressured them out of business by raising the rental on their facilities. Thus, the early polarisation between licensed press and 'Altverleger' progressively diminished as time passed.[41]

As a result, the two 'sub-sectors' of the press, which had arisen during this period, had merged by the mid 1950s. This process was symbolised most clearly by the rapprochement of the two publishers' organisations which had meanwhile arisen to defend the interests of the infant West German press, namely the Gesamtverband Deutscher Zeitungsverleger (GDZV, for the 'licensed publishers') and the Verein Deutscher Zeitungsverleger (VDZV, for the 'Altverleger'). In 1954, they merged into the Bundesverband Deutscher Zeitungsverleger (BDZV).

The Organisations of the Press and the Birth of the BDZV

Although the Allied occupation powers were the main actors in the policy process which gave the future West German press system its underlying shape and character, it would be a mistake to overlook the role played by indigenous forces in establishing its most important feature, namely the centrality of the principle of self-regulation. The concern of the Western Allies

---

41. M. Knoche, *Einführung in die Pressekonzentrationsforschung. Theoretische und empirische Grundlagen – Kommunikationspolitische Voraussetzungen*, Berlin: Wissenschaftsverlag Volker Spiess, 1978, p. 34.

that the future press system should be private and commercial in nature and free of all but minimal state regulation was powerfully reinforced by the rapid reconstitution of the West German publishers' own power and influence. In this latter respect, the early collective lobbying power of the publishers' associations was a decisive factor in preempting other forces seeking to subject the press to greater regulatory pressures. Even before the foundation of the new state, the publishers had begun to consolidate their position.

The Early Organisation of the Licensed Press

During the period of compulsory licensing, the Allied occupation powers retained a strict fiduciary control of the assets of the licensed press. The latter also had to pay a licence fee to the respective military governments. On occasions, licensees were even compelled to surrender their newspapers to the respective occupation authorities. Under such restrictive conditions, the new German publishers had an immediate and powerful incentive to organise themselves to gain collective strength and lobbying power. Therefore, wherever opportunity presented itself, the licensees sought to make contact with each other and soon established loose organisations out of which slowly and gradually characteristic regional (Land-based) professional associations grew. The first such organisations appeared as early on as the end of 1945 in the American and British occupation zones and from October 1946 onwards in the French zone. In Berlin a single association gave collective representation to the Berlin publishers. The Western Allies generally viewed these associations positively and authorised their activities, perceiving them to be embryonic organisations of self-regulation and necessary elements of a developing democratic culture. Moreover, they also saw them as useful organisations which could help to simplify and expedite cooperation between the newspaper publishers and the occupation authorities.

According to their founding statutes, the main purpose and task of these publishers' associations was to 'represent and promote the professional and economic interests' of their members. In actual fact, this abstract formula covered a whole catalogue of immediately pressing tasks: such as the thorny question of the equitable supply and distribution of scarce raw materials like paper and print dyes; the reconstruction of news agencies and other services important to the industry; and not least, the collective representation of the publishers *vis-à-vis* the occupation authorities. In particular, the associations lobbied for the removal of compulsory leasing and also for the abolition of measures that had placed strict constraints on shareholding in the new enterprises.[42]

The Early Organisation of the 'Altverleger'

Although debarred from publishing during the immediate post-war period, the 'Altverleger' were no less anxious to reestablish contact with each other. In their case, the main incentive for collective organisation was to lobby for the removal of compulsory licensing and for a speedy return of control over their printing facilities. In a very similar way to the licensed publishers, the 'Altverleger' rapidly established a network of regional associations which were soon formally linked by the foundation of a national association called the Arbeitsgemeinschaft für Pressefragen e. V. At its birth, the latter gave collective representation to around 150 publishing houses.

When the Parliamentary Council commenced its deliberations upon the Basic Law at the beginning of September 1948, this Arbeitsgemeinschaft judged that the time had arrived to face up to the Allies and demand the reintroduction of 'press freedom'. Accordingly, it elaborated a manifesto entitled 'Press Freedom and Democracy' ('Pressefreiheit und Demokratie') calling for an end of restrictions on the activities of the 'Altverleger'. This document was lent considerable force by the fact that it carried the signatures of leading democratic politicians such as Konrad Adenauer, shortly to be elected as first CDU Chancellor of the Federal Republic, and Professor Carlo Schmid, an influential and highly distinguished member of the SPD. The manifesto was widely distributed in West Germany and also presented to

42. See Schulze, *Der Bundesverband Deutscher Zeitungsverleger*, pp. 34–5. Also on the BDZV see R. Richter *Kommunikationsfreiheit = Verlegerfreiheit. Zur kommunikationspolitik der Zeitungsverleger in der Bundesrepublik Deutschland 1945–69* (Dortmunder Beiträge zur Zeitungsforschung), Pullach/Munich: Verlag Dokumentation, 1973.

members of the British House of Commons. Without a doubt this tremendous act of lobbying mobilised popular opinion in West Germany and encouraged the occupation powers to act to terminate compulsory licensing at a fairly early stage.[43]

On 1 September 1949, three weeks before the abolition of compulsory licensing, the Arbeitsgemeinschaft für Pressefragen e. V., by now representing no less than 220 publishers, symbolically changed its name back to the Verein Deutscher Zeitungsverleger (VDZV), the title used by the interest group of the Weimar press. The founding statute of the new body made even more explicit its ambition to reestablish itself as quickly as possible as the representative national organisation of all newspaper publishers in West Germany. Significantly, its membership was entirely comprised of individual publishers ('Altverleger').[44]

Der Gesamtverband der Deutschen Zeitungsverleger e. V. (1949–54)

However, the ambitions of the 'Altverleger' were thwarted by the existence of similar designs by the licensed publishers. Both groups anticipated the escalation of competition that was to follow the imminent removal of Allied restrictions on their operations. Both groups wanted to meet the challenge by establishing powerful national organisations. Thus, on the very same day as the 'Altverleger' refounded the Verein Deutscher Zeitungsverleger, the representatives of the various associations of licence-holders of the Western zones and West Berlin dissolved their previous Arbeitsgemeinschaft and replaced it with a new national organisation called the Gesamtverband der Deutschen Zeitungsverleger e. V. (GDZV). Unlike the very highly centralised VDZV, the GDZV adopted the federal principle of organisation. Accordingly, the general assembly, the most important decision-making organ, was to be a committee of representatives from the Land sub-associations.[45]

---

43. See Schulze, *Der Bundesverband Deutscher Zeitungsverleger*, pp. 35–6.
44. Ibid., pp. 38–9.
45. Ibid., pp. 39–40.

Historical Origins of the West German Press System

The Foundation of the Bundesverband Deutscher Zeitungsverleger

In this manner, the temporary polarisation of interests between 'old publishers' and 'new publishers' was reflected at first in a dualism of national organisations. However, the publishers very quickly realised the potential damage that this situation could do to their mutual cause. Disunity could seriously impede the process of consolidation of their autonomy of policy-making. Already, there were political voices being raised, principally from the side of the SPD and the trade unions, demanding the enactment of federal legislation to regulate the press in ways that conflicted with their interests.

A major obstacle to a rapprochement of the two camps, however, was the question of control of the presses of the 'Altverleger' which had been the object of compulsory leasing to the licensed press. However, as already seen, this particular problem was rapidly being resolved in a manner that was diminishing greatly the opposition of immediate interests of the two camps. In many cases, the erstwhile licence-holders and the 'Altverleger' were combining their operations. During the autumn of 1950, the two camps moved closer together and conducted a series of negotiations about a possible fusion of organisations. It increasingly appeared that the remaining major obstacle to fusion was more of an organisational-political nature rather than the result of any serious divergence of interest. At the same time, the need for fusion was becoming ever more urgent. A number of serious policy issues were developing which would best be answered by the publishers speaking with a strong and unified voice. As the new state took shape the policy agenda was beginning to become crowded by such difficult questions as collective bargaining with the unions, management participation ('Mitbestimmung') by the journalists, the limits of state regulation, negotiations with politicians about the possible enactment of press legislation and questions about advertising regulation, not least concerning the question of advertising by the newly established public-service broadcasters (see Chapter 3).

In the face of this objective reality, during 1951 the two camps moved significantly closer towards resolving their differences. The GDZV relinquished its claim to greater representation in the new organisation based on the much higher circulation figures achieved by the licensed press. In return, the VDZV dropped its claim to the greater representation based on its higher membership. The VDZV also agreed to drop the controversial principle of direct membership by individual publishers (which gave it its larger membership). Membership of the new national organisation would be composed of delegates from the Land sub-associations. During 1952–4, many regional sub-associations of the two sides merged to form single Land associations. This process was completed by the eventual merger of the national organisations, which took place on 15 July 1954, when a special delegate conference at Bad Godesberg founded the Bundesverband Deutscher Zeitungsverleger (BDZV). The BDZV was to be governed by a 'delegate conference' ('Delegiertenversammlung'), composed of delegates from the sub-associations of the Länder, which elected an executive in the form of a 'Präsidium'. However, the distribution of votes at the BDZV 'Delegiertenkonferenz' reflected not the number of publishers in any Land association, but rather the primary criterion of the circulation that they represented.[46] Thus, at the end of the day, it was to be the publishing groups with the strongest circulation which were to be overrepresented in the BDZV's ruling organs and, as the result, in the policy making of the BDZV their interests naturally tended to prevail. Combined with the trend towards press-concentration already noted, this contributed significantly to the emerging dominance of the large concerns in the policy community of the West German press system (see Chapter 2).

The Journalists' Associations in the Early Post-War Period

Within months of the Nazi capitulation, journalists' associations too had appeared at Land level ('Länderverbände'). Among the founders of these associations were leading Social Democrats, such as Erich Klabunde, Josef Ackermann and Fritz Sänger (later the chief editor of the German Press Agency), and liberals such as Otto Groth and Helmut Cron. After the foundation of the Federal Republic of Germany, on 10 December 1949, the various

---

46. Ibid., p. 83.

regional associations came together to form the Deutscher Journalisten-Verband (DJV). Significantly, membership of the DJV was open to publishers as well as journalists and several of the prominent leaders of the journalists were simultaneously involved in producing newspapers and periodicals.[47]

While the Allied occupation powers gradually relinquished responsibility for policy to the publishers and the latter organised themselves into a powerful collective lobbying force, the journalists' organisations remained somewhat marginalised. The conditions were adverse. The ranks of experienced journalists were depleted since many journalists were initially disbarred from reentering the profession because of their complicity during the Nazi period. The general material hardship of the post-war years meant that resources were scarce and often newspapers were struggling for survival. For a long period, many new proprietors simply refused to consider the question of journalists' rights. The journalists themselves were generally so eager to find work that many foreswore any serious union activism. After the 'completion' of denazification, there was a sudden influx of journalists looking for work and this led to an excess of supply over demand, which the publishers were further able to exploit to their advantage *vis-à-vis* the journalists. Moreover, the energies of the newly formed journalists' organisations were often diverted into recruitment drives. Unsurprisingly, under these circumstances, the DJV generally limited its activities to 'defensive' measures on behalf of its members. During the early post-war period, the main preoccupation of the journalists' organisations was to reestablish rights won during the Weimar Republic relating to such matters as collective bargaining, uniform and comprehensive contracts (the 'Mantelvertrag'), old age pensions, working conditions, sickness leave, minimum remuneration for freelance journalists and so on. The journalists' organisations were generally unwilling or unable to push more radical demands such as the demand for co-determination ('Mitbestimmung') and the principle that chief

---

47. K.-D. Funke, *Innere Pressefreiheit*, Pullach/Munich: Verlag Dokumentation, 1972, pp. 34–56; on the DJV also see H. Cron, 'Schatten des Anfangs – Der DJV nach dem Krieg', in U. Pätzold and H. Schmidt (eds.), *Solidarität gegen Abhängigkeit, Mediengewerkschaft*. Darmstadt und Neuwied: Hermann Luchterhand Verlag, 1973, pp. 116–25.

editors should be free of any binding influence from the side of the newspaper proprietors.[48]

Moreover, the journalists were not even united. The vast majority of journalists joined the German Journalists' Association (Deutscher Journalisten-Verband – DJV), which had the character more of a professional ('ständisch') association of practising journalists and editors than a trade union. However, in April 1951 a significant minority organised themselves into the Berufsgruppe der Journalisten und Schriftsteller in der IG Druck und Papier (BJS–IG D&P). As the name suggests, this was a trade union group within the huge Industrial Union of Print and Paper Workers (IG Druck und Papier) and the forerunner of the later German Journalists' Union (Deutsche Journalisten Union – DJU) within the IG Druck und Papier.[49] Founded in 1866, the IG Druck und Papier was the oldest union in German history and affiliated to the German Trade Union Federation (Deutscher Gewerkschaftsbund – DGB), which after 1949 organised West Germany's sixteen major unions. This new journalists' union (and its trade union status is what distinguished it from the DJV) reproached the DJV for being ineffective in defending the immediate interests of its members (salaries, etc.) and also, more seriously, for allowing membership to a number of editors who were simultaneously involved in publishing activities. This latter fact, it was held, disqualified the DJV from representing the journalists in collective bargaining with the employers.[50]

However, the foundation of a journalists' union did not lead to a sudden desertion of the DJV's membership, far from it. Many journalists feared reprisals from their employers. Moreover, the experience of National Socialism had engendered a certain passivity among employees, which became very evident in the early post-war period. The DJV continued (and continues) to represent around nine-tenths of the journalists and editors in the Federal Republic. Neither the IG Druck und Papier nor the DGB were willing to relinquish the DJU to the DJV. On the other

48. Ibid., pp. 60–1.
49. W. Fabian, 'Journalisten in der Gewerkschaft – die deutsche Journalisten Union in der IG Druck und Papier', in Pätzold and H. Schmidt (eds.), *Solidarität gegen Abhängigkeit*, pp. 126–34.
50. See Funke, *Innere Pressefreiheit*, pp. 62–3, and p. 66.

hand, the DJV, although much stronger in membership than the DJU, was weakened by its decentralised nature and by its non-affiliation to the powerful DGB. Both sides were weakened by their disunity and competition during this early period (compared with the quick development of organisational cohesion by the publishers).[51]

Nevertheless, albeit from a position of much greater weakness than the publishers, the journalists' organisations did raise a number of important issues in the late 1940s and early 1950s. Most notably, the DJV attempted to place on the policy agenda the question of alternative forms of press organisation such as newspapers run by trusts, foundations ('Stiftungen') and cooperatives. The journalists' organisations also lobbied hard for federal legislation to subject the press to strict public control and to gain greater representation in the policy-making process. However, these recommendations were bitterly resisted by the old and new publishers alike. That such ideas never really succeeded in being incorporated into policy simply reflected the highly unfavourable balance of forces at the time.[52]

During the early 1950s, there was one serious outbreak of industrial action, initiated by the wider trade union movement, against the federal 'Works Constitution Law' ('Betriebsverfassungsgesetz') of 1952. This law limited employees' management participation rights ('Mitbestimmung' rights) for employees in so-called 'Tendenz' firms, defined as firms with a certain moral, political or philosophical vocation, which included the press. The 'Works Constitution Law' of 1952 established the principle of the so-called 'Tendenzschutz', namely the privileged right of proprietors to determine the line of their publications, in addition to the principle of management's sole responsibility for the economic affairs of the firm. In other words, important proprietorial and managerial privileges were reserved to the press sector which was to be allowed to operate in a manner unhampered even by the limited codetermination rights for employees' representatives that were established by statute in all other

51. Cron, 'Schatten des Anfangs – Der DJV nach dem Krieg', in Pätzold and Schmidt (eds.), *Solidarität gegen Abhängigkeit*, p. 120.
52. On the history, organisation, aims and policies of the DJV see U. Koch, 'Deutscher Journalisten-Verband – Zwischen den Fronten', *Journalist*, no. 6, 1981, pp. 42–55.

industrial sectors. As a result, the IG Druck und Papier called for industrial action and between May and December 1952 a number of limited strikes broke out in the press sector. This led, in turn, to a number of successful local actions in the courts by employers demanding compensation against 'political strikes'.[53]

The abject failure of this early industrial action to combat the so-called 'Tendenzschutz' confirmed the overwhelmingly 'defensive' orientation of the journalists' organisations, which thenceforth generally confined their activities to issues of collective bargaining for the rest of the 1950s and most of the 1960s. The general strategic weakness of the journalists' organisations during this early period was symbolised by their failure even to obtain representation on the governing organ ('Aufsichtsrat') of the German Press Agency (Deutsche Presse-Agentur), which had meanwhile been established as a 'cooperative' organisation of the German press (see pp. 63–4). Moreover, according to one major expert on this subject, during the 'economic miracle' the journalists even fell behind in the national pay stakes as a result of their inferior collective muscle.[54] However, as the following chapter will describe, during the 1960s, and especially after 1968, the journalists' organisations began to mobilise much more aggressively for a sweeping reform of the internal organisation of the press sector.

The Legal Basis of the Press

The Allies and the publishers themselves were undoubtedly the major active participants (i.e. the 'policy community') in the policy processes affecting the press during the early post-war period. However, the parliamentary institutions of the Federal Republic also played a significant role in the years that followed the foundation of the new state. Moreover, the German tradition elevated the centrality of 'law in politics', and the sphere of the mass media was no exception to this rule. As John Sandford has pointed out, the Anglo-Saxon tradition confines the press largely to the sphere of general laws of the land. However, the

53. See Funke, *Innere Pressefreiheit*, pp. 74–6.
54. Ibid., p. 102.

German tradition, 'while acknowledging this principle, also provided for the enactment of specific press laws'.[55] Historically, such laws had been passed by the various principalities and provinces that constituted pre-unification 'Germany'. After unification in 1871, one major law of this kind had, as seen, also been enacted by the central government, namely the famous 'Reichspressegesetz' of 1874. In the period after 1949 the requirement to enact new legislation concerning the future character of the mass media was given a special poignancy by the recent experience of the collapse of the rule of law ('Rechtsstaat') during the last years of the Weimar Republic.

The Basic Law

Memories of the capture and abuse of the media by the National Socialists had a profound influence on the 'fathers of the Basic Law'. Hence, Article 5 of this law could hardly have been more explicit about its guarantees of freedom of the press, freedom of reporting through broadcasting and film, and its forbidding of all forms of censorship. It stated: 'Everyone shall have the right freely to express and disseminate his opinion by speech, writing and pictures and freely to inform himself from generally accessible sources. Freedom of the press and freedom of reporting by means of broadcasts and films are guaranteed. There shall be no censorship'.[56]

However, beyond this firm commitment to liberal-democratic principles of media regulation, the Basic Law had very little to say about the media. The provisions for a federal system included the principle of the cultural jurisdiction of the states ('Kulturhoheit der Länder'). This principle suggested that responsibility for regulation of the mass media fell within the sphere of state ('Land'), not federal ('Bund'), competence. As will be seen, between 1949 and 1966 the ten states and West Berlin duly enacted their own press laws. Nevertheless, accord-

55. See Sandford, *The Mass Media*, p. 53.
56. See: *The Democratic Tradition: Four German Constitutions*, ed. and with an Introduction by Elmar M. Hucko, Leamington Spa: Berg Publishers, 1987 (repr. Oxford: Berg Publishers, 1989), p. 195; and *Politics and Government in the Federal Republic of Germany, Basic Documents*, ed. C.C. Schweitzer et al., Leamington Spa: Berg Publishers, 1984, p. 117.

ing to Article 75, section 2, of the 'Basic Law', the federation ('Bund') is empowered to enact general 'framework' laws ('Rahmengesetze') for areas of Land competence. These laws provide the overall framework for further more detailed legislation and form the overall basis of policy implementation by the Länder.

The Question of a Federal Press Law

In March 1952, a federal bill for just such a framework law was introduced by the first CDU/CSU-led federal government in an attempt to ensure central harmonisation and standardisation of the decentralised arrangements for the press. However, this bill encountered immediate and fierce opposition from the interest organisations of the publishers, which as seen had powerfully reconstituted themselves during the occupation period and which were well on their way to forming a single powerful voice in the shape of the BDZV.

Above all, the publishers desired to achieve a high degree of autonomy in policy-making for their field of activity. They aimed to establish the principle and practice of self-regulation of the press and feared that the proposed bill both presaged and prepared the way for extensive government intervention in their affairs. In particular, the publishers reacted negatively to the bill's provision for a more 'pluralist' structure of policy community for dealing with affairs of the press. More specifically, the bill foresaw the establishment at both federal and Land level of so-called 'press committees' to be composed of two judges, four representatives of the publishers' and four representatives of the journalists' organisations. Worse still, from the point of view of the press, these committee members were to be nominated by both the Land and federal governments. This, the publishers feared, would amount to the thin end of the wedge; governmental intervention by stealth would thus be facilitated. The publishers also objected to provisions of the bill that sought to regulate relationships between, and the demarcation of competences of, the publishers on the one side and editors and journalists on the other. This latter question was destined to reappear hotly on the political agenda in the 1960s and '70s (see following chapter). At this stage, however, the bill was dropped because of this opposition of the publishers whose prompt organisation had allowed them to occupy a virtual 'power-vacuum' in the early post-war period.[57]

The Land Press Laws

Legislation governing the press had meanwhile been the preoccupation of the policy-makers at Land level. With the benefit of hindsight it was very clear to the post-war German elites that the traditional German 'Rechtsstaat' had been faulted. It had been characterised by form and not filled out by substantive or normative content. Therefore, there was a general determination among the West German legislators to develop a more solid legal structure and to formulate far more explicit and detailed commitments to the principles of press freedom. Under the supervision of the Allies, a number of fairly elementary and provisional press laws had been passed in the period 1948–9 in all of the Länder except Lower Saxony, Rhineland-Palatinate and the Saarland. These varied considerably in scope and contained divergent regulations (which had been the rationale for the abortive attempt to enact federal framework legislation). Therefore, in order to achieve a necessary minimum of harmonisation, the states themselves quickly established special joint commissions to elaborate a model draft Land Press Law. In 1960 such a draft was produced, upon which most states based their legislation. All in all, the following Land Press Laws were enacted:

Baden-Württemberg	Law on the Press, 14 January 1964
Bavaria	Law on the Press, 3 October 1949
Berlin	Berlin Press Law, 15 June 1965
Bremen	Law on the Press, 16 March 1965
Hamburg	Hamburg Press Law, 29 January 1965
Hessen	Hessian Law on Freedom and Right of the Press, 23 June 1949, proclamation of 20 November 1958
Lower Saxony	Lower Saxony Press Law, 22 March 1965

57. W. Mahle and R. Richter, *Communication Policy in the Federal Republic of Germany*, Paris: Unesco Press, 1974, p. 21.

North-Rhine Westphalia	Press Law for NRW, 24 May 1966
Rhineland-Palatinate	Law on the Press, 14 June 1965
Saarland	Saarland Press Law, 12 May 1965
Schleswig-Holstein	Law on the Press, 19 June 1964

In fact, although they vary in detail, these Land laws were all very similar, sometimes indistinguishable in their substantive and normative content.[58] Broadly, the state Press Laws laid down only very general guidelines. There was a common commitment to a democratic press. Accordingly, the laws enumerated a number of key principles such as freedom of the press and freedom from dependency on registration or licensing. The laws also specified a number of key functions of the press such as the dissemination of information, acting as a watchdog against malpractices in public life, and participation in the key process of opinion-forming ('Meinungsbildung'). The right of access to information was a very important innovation, and considered to be an important ingredient of the constitutionally enshrined freedom of information. It was considered indispensable to the key opinion-forming ('Meinungsbildung') function of the press that comprehensive information flowed freely to the press. Accordingly, a duty was placed on the public authorities to inform the members of the press, except in cases of secrecy and a few other exceptional circumstances denoting a 'superior' public or private interest, such as *sub judice*.

In order to fulfil the 'duty to inform' ('Auskunftspflicht'), special official press departments were established by the public authorities at federal, state and even local level. The information provided by these public bodies was designed to contribute to transparent government and administration thereby enhancing the democratic process. Press services were provided by govern-

---

58. Press Laws in 'Documents on politics and society in the Federal Republic of Germany', Bonn: Inter Nationes, 1980, pp. 12–13; M. Löffler, *Presserecht*, Vol. 1: *Die Landespressegesetze der Bundesrepublik Deutschland mit Textanhang*, Munich: Beck'sche C. H. Verlag, 1983 (new edn); also see W. Lehr and K. Berg, *Rundfunk und Presse in Deutschland: Rechtsgrundlagen der Massenmedien – Texte*, Mainz: von Hase und Koehler Verlag, 1971.

mental departments, by the parliamentary parties (Bundestagsfraktionen), by individual MPs, by the federal parliament (Bundestag) itself, by a host of public and semi-public organisations and, importantly, by the press and information office of the federal government (Bundesregierung), which continues to stage a press conference every other day. In addition, press services were supplied by the 'socially significant groups' ('sozial relevante Gruppen') making up the pluralistic fabric of West German society: among them, the political parties, trade unions, employers' organisations, churches, and many social and political minority and 'fringe' groups.

In exceptional circumstances, the state was empowered to act to restrict the information flow to the press when there was an evident danger to third parties. A prominent instance of this kind of 'censorship' was later to occur when Employers' Federation President Hanns-Martin Schleyer was kidnapped by Red Army Fraction terrorists in September 1977. The state reacted by imposing an immediate blackout of all official information concerning the negotiations with the terrorists and the investigation. However, this only applied to official news. Even on this occasion there was no restriction of journalistic investigation or reporting, although most journalists reacted with restraint until the death of the kidnap victim was ascertained.[59]

Most laws contained an obligation of accuracy and thoroughness, requiring the newspapers and magazines to check the content, origin and accuracy of all news prior to publication. In addition, newspapers and periodicals were given extensive safeguards against confiscation or seizure, which could only occur by legal authority in the public interest, and for which there was provision for compensation in the event of wrongful confiscation. It is significant that a later federal law conceded to the press the right to refuse testimony in the pursuit of its political functions. The 'Law on the Right to Refuse Testimony' (1975) granted 'persons professionally active in press and broadcasting the unrestricted right to refuse testimony, confined to the editorial component of periodical printed matter and broadcast programmes'. Running parallel to the law governing refusal of testimony was a regulation forbidding the confiscation of docu-

---

59. See Meyn, *Massenmedien*, p. 22.

ments and printed material 'in the possession of persons entitled to refuse testimony, the editorial department, the publishing house or the printing works'. This provision was intended to prevent facts which might be concealed under the terms of the right of refusal of testimony from being disclosed by the devious means of confiscation. However, the ban on confiscation does not apply when the individual entitled to refuse testimony was himself suspect of being party to a punishable act.[60]

One notable requirement was that all printed matter appearing within the area of jurisdiction of Press Laws had to carry the name of the party or firm and address of the printer and of the publisher – this was the so-called 'Impressum'. Furthermore, it should also be clear from the 'Impressum' who was editorially responsible for the publication and who were the journalists, stipulating the part of the publication or field for which they were responsible. In this way, legal accountability was ensured. Another notable requirement of the Press Laws was the right of reply ('Gegendarstellung'). Accordingly, the responsible journalist or editor and the publisher of a newspaper or periodical was obliged to publish an accredited reply by any individual or organisation who had been misrepresented over a matter of fact. Significantly, the Laws stipulated that this right to reply could not be satisfied by mere publication of a 'reader's letter', but must take the form of publication without delay of a counter item in the same type of print and in the same section of the paper as the original offending article. In practice, this provision has very often been ignored.

Apart from the general principles just outlined, the Land Press Laws placed very few material restrictions upon the press. As will be seen this was in clear contrast to the highly regulated broadcasting system.[61] Finally, it is most significant that, again in contradistinction to the public-service broadcasters' duty of

60. See Haler, *Basic Law Guarantees Freedom of Opinion*, p. 23.
61. Further useful references on West German press law are: R. Gross, *Presserecht. Einführung in Grundzüge und Schwerpunkte des deutschen Presserechts*, Wiesbaden: Deutscher-Fachschriften Verlag, 1987 (new edn); M. Löffler, *Presserecht*, Vol. 2: *Geschichte und Theorie des Presserechts*, Munich: Beck'sche C. H. Verlag, 1983 (new edn); and W. Ring, *Deutsches Presse- und Rundfunkrecht. Textsammlung mit Anmerkungen, Verweisungen und Sachregister*, Munich: F. Rehm Verlag, 1986.

impartiality in all matters, the private legal structure of the West German press ensured the right of the proprietors of newspapers and magazines to prescribe the general political, economic and cultural line of the newspaper (the so-called 'Tendenzschutz'). In addition, journalists could be legally bound to observe this line in their contracts of employment. As will be seen, the 'Tendenzschutz' later became the object of considerable political controversy, largely as the result of a trade union campaign against it (see following chapter).

The Press Council – A 'Self-Control' Organ

Despite the organised resistance of the publishers to regulation, reflected in the failure to enact federal legislation providing for extensive control organs and also in the general regulatory weakness of the Land Press Laws, there is one notable formal organ of self-control of the press in the Federal Republic which gives a voice to both sides of the industry, namely the German Press Council (Deutscher Presserat). This was founded in the autumn of 1956 by the journalists' and publishers' organisations as a sort of 'self-control' organ of the press and as an instrument to monitor and guarantee its independence. It was modelled on the British Press Council and was originally composed of five newspaper publishers and five newspaper journalists. In 1957 its membership was extended to include five representatives from each side of the magazine sector.

However, the parity principle of representation of the Press Council did not reflect a balance of forces between the publishers and the journalists during the formative years of the press system. As seen, the publishers were much more strongly placed. On the one hand, it reflected a mixture of respect for the German tradition of 'Proporz' (proportional representation) and the characteristic primacy of consensus-building in the West German policy process. On the other hand, it bore witness to the publishers' continuing fear of state regulation and might be regarded as a classic ploy to preempt further state attempts to subject the press to strict central control. It might also be seen as a significant attempt to 'incorporate' the journalists, whose organisations had been vocal advocates of legislation to establish a much more extensive and interventionist network of 'press committees' as organs of self-regulation. In actual fact, the initiative for the founding of the Press Council came from the Hamburg Journalists' Association of the DJV, but it was more an attempt to salvage something from the general failure of the journalists' more ambitious plans than a real victory. As suggested, the publishers had the most to gain from its establishment. It has been generally successful in deflecting state measures against the press, but rather less effective as a means of self-regulation.[62]

The West German News Agencies

Before proceeding in the next chapter to examine the development and controversies of the press sector after its formative period, it is first necessary to examine the origins and development of the West German news agencies. The story of the news agencies reflects clearly the balance of power that emerged between the various forces which, as just described, shaped the development of the press system in the early post-war period. In particular, it highlights the power and influence of the publishers of the press and the part played by the Allied occupation powers in bequeathing them this privileged position.

Newspapers and periodicals in the Federal Republic of Germany obtain the major part of their day to day information from five major news agencies. Three are foreign, namely the American Associated Press (AP), the French Agence France Presse (AFP) and the British company Reuter. In addition, there are two indigenous West German news agencies. The main one, the Hamburg-based giant Deutsche Presse-Agentur (DPA), was formed in 1949 from the merging of the three news agencies of the Western occupation powers. Its major significance is that it is largely owned by the West German publishers themselves (see p. 64 below). By far the smaller one, the Bonn-based Deutscher Depeschendienst (DDP), was set up by West German journalists on the staff of the American company United Press International (UPI) when the latter closed down its German-

---

62. See Mahle and Richter, *Communication Policy in the FRG*, p. 34.

language service in 1971.[63]

In addition to the five major agencies, the West German press draws its news and information, as seen, from numerous organisational press services, such as the press office of the government, the parliament, and the political parties and interest groups. The churches run their own news agencies, namely the Evangelischer Pressedienst (EPD) and the Katholische Nachrichten-Agentur (KNA). Moreover, several medium and small newspapers have founded joint news-gathering companies. Most significantly, the vast Springer group also operates its own domestic and overseas news service – the Springer Auslandsdienst (SAD).

The Pre-War Origins of the German Press Agencies

The pre-war origins of the West German press agencies, like those of their famous British (Reuter), French (Havas) and American counterparts (AP and UPI), date back to the mid-nineteenth century. The development of news and information services was both technology- and market-driven: in the first place linked to the increased demand for information that had accompanied industrialism and the expansion of world trade; in the second place promoted by the development of telegraphy. Unlike in the US, the early European telegraphic news agencies were beneficiaries of very considerable state support and state sanctioned quasi-monopoly status. This was nowhere more so than in Germany, where the state played a key role in the belated industrialisation and modernisation of the economy.

In Germany, the Wolffsches Telegraphen-Büro (WTB) took its name from its nineteenth-century founder Bernhard Wolff. During both the Imperial period of 'Obrigkeitsstaat' and the liberal-democratic Weimar Republic, the WTB was subject to strict state control. In the latter period, it became the voice of official Weimar circles and business. However, the WTB's monopoly was seriously challenged during this period by the rise of a second news agency, the Telegraphen-Union (TU). As seen, the TU was part of the mighty Hugenberg press empire

---

63. On the DDP see U. Schenck, *Nachrichtenagenturen*, Berlin: Vistas Verlag, 1985.

and a mouthpiece for the more extreme conservative industrial capitalists with an anti-Weimar viewpoint. In 1934 both agencies were merged by the National Socialists into a single organisation, the Deutsches Nachrichten-Büro (DNB) and placed under the control of the NS-Propaganda Ministry.[64]

The News Agencies Under the Allied Occupation

During the Allied occupation, separate agencies were quickly established in each of the occupation zones. The Americans established the Deutsche Allgemeine Nachrichten-Agentur (DANA) subsequently renamed Deutsche Nachrichten-Agentur (DENA), the British set up the Deutscher Presse Dienst (DPD), and the French founded the Südwestdeutsche Nachrichten-Agentur known simply as 'Südena'. Initially, these separate zonal news agencies functioned merely as instruments of the respective occupation authorities, feeding the 'Heeresgruppenzeitungen' and later the licensed press with information. The Allied staff of these zonal agencies were progressively replaced by German staff, but until they were licensed and passed into German ownership, Allied 'press control officers' remained in the leading positions within them.[65]

Both the British and US occupation authorities regarded their zonal news agencies as the foundation upon which a new 'democratic' German news agency might be built. To this end, they both shared the concern to return their respective agencies to German responsibility as quickly as possible. Significantly, they also concurred that the most appropriate organisational form was that of an association wholly owned by the German publishers. By contrast, the French sought to keep their zonal agency much more under the influence of the semi-public Agence France Presse (AFP).[66] Soon, however, it became clear that the British zonal agency, the DPD, was by far the best-placed candidate to form the basis for a unified future West German news agency. The zonal agencies' income depended mainly on the total size of their client newspapers' circulation.

64. See Gross, *Die Deutsche Presse-Agentur*, pp. 13–29.
65. Ibid., p. 37.
66. Ibid., pp. 47–8.

Historical Origins of the West German Press System

This was largest by far in the more populous British zone and very small in the French zone. However, for a period, the American military government fought a determined rear-guard action against any dilution of its influence. The Americans were particularly concerned that the British Labour government might exert a 'socialistic' influence on the future German news and information service.[67]

The Foundation of the Deutsche Presse-Agentur

The greatly increased competition between newspapers that followed the currency reform of June 1948 (the unleashing of market forces) compelled the publishers all over Germany to prioritise cost-minimisation. As a result, the weaker South German publishers suddenly had an urgent and overriding interest in seeking the rationalisation of the three existing agencies into one single agency able to benefit from economies of scale and thus supply them with cheaper services. Besides, during 1948 the separate influence of the occupation authorities in their own zones diminished necessarily with the onrush towards a single West German state. By mid-1949 most of the newspapers in the French zone were already subscribing to the DPD and in August 1949 the DPD effectively absorbed 'Südena'. Thereupon, the DENA and the DPD merged at last and formed the Deutsche Presse-Agentur (DPA).

Because of the peculiar circumstances surrounding its creation and early development, the position of the DPA seemed at first to be somewhat tenuous. Firstly, the new ruling elites in West Germany suspected that it would continue to function as a channel for foreign influence. Moreover, the CDU/CSU very soon became the dominant force in Bonn and Chancellor Adenauer, in particular, often railed against the presumed SPD bias within the DPA, which had allegedly been supported by the British Labour government (through the DPD). Moreover, the chief editor ('Chefredakteur') of the DPA, Fritz Sänger, was a well-known Social Democrat. As a result, Adenauer encouraged the waging of a long guerrilla campaign within the DPA to have Sänger removed, which was finally successful in 1959. The

67. Ibid., p. 76.

'Sänger Affair' neatly symbolised both the desire of the predominantly conservative-oriented publishers to be 'Herr-im-Hause' (master in their own house) and the entrenchment of the 'CDU state' during the first two decades of the Federal Republic. In the words of Gross, who has provided the only in-depth academic study of the DPA, 'it was no overstatement, when the SPD press service suggested that Sänger's removal from the DPA was the high point of a strategy of the wholesale "Gleichschaltung" of the largest German news agency into an agent of governmental policy'.[68]

The DPA and the Question of Pluralism

During and immediately following the period of compulsory licensing of the press, the pattern of cooperative ownership of the press agencies, including the DPA, reflected a very large number of mutually competitive publishers. However, the trend towards press concentration which followed deregulation and the resurrection of a free capitalistic press system militated against the maintenance of such a highly pluralistic structure. Within two years of the foundation of the DPA, powerful pressures had built up for a reshaping of the organisation's power structure. As the result, the purely cooperative organisational structure was soon dissolved and replaced by that of a commercial joint-stock company ('Kapitalgesellschaft'), although it still continued to function as a cooperative. In order to ensure pluralism, the maximum share taken by any single publisher was limited to 1% (a figure subsequently raised in 1975 to 1.5%) and the share of the public-service broadcasters limited to 15% of the total. However, as will be seen (in the following chapter), a remarkable degree of press-concentration soon came to characterise the West German press system. In particular, the ownership pattern of the press evolved a highly complex web of capital interpenetration ('Kapitalverflechtung') and 'cooperative' relations between firms. A limited number of giant firms came to dominate a host of dependent smaller firms. This pattern was reflected, Gross suggests, in the power-relations within the DPA (as indeed within the BDZV).

68. Ibid., pp. 110–11.

Gross points to the fact that many of the individual shareholders within the DPA were subsidiaries ('Tochtergesellschaften') of larger firms, many others were in a position of other forms of dependence through a web of 'cooperative' relations with larger firms. Moreover, the 'owners' of the DPA were also its 'customers' and as far as the latter were concerned the larger firms were by far the most important. As a result, Gross suggests, the power-relations within the DPA soon came to reflect the predominance of a limited number of giant concerns. Therefore, pluralism within the DPA was, by its very nature, a 'limited pluralism': monopoly trends within the overall press sector were faithfully reflected within the DPA and its controlling board ('Aufsichtsrat'). Moreover, as mentioned, the trade unions and journalists' organisations were denied any codetermination rights within the DPA, in accordance with the 'Tendenzschutz' paragraphs of the 'Works Constitution Law' of 1952.[69]

The Significance of 'Stunde Null'

Quite clearly, 'Stunde Null' marked an exceptional disjuncture in the history of the German press. Indeed, it can be seen as the culmination of an extended period of disjuncture, which actually commenced with the National Socialist 'Machtergreifung' of 1933. In this respect, 'Stunde Null' can easily be evaluated as a wiping of the slate clean. The Allied occupation laid the basis for a resurrection of a strong press, freed from the threat of political oppression and abuse. The twin spectres of the traditional authoritarian state ('Obrigkeitsstaat') and the modern totalitarian state were both banished, at least in Western Germany. The way was clear for the constitution of a genuinely free press, which under the Allies' tutelage was actively encouraged to play an important role in the construction of liberal democracy.

There were some other important changes. During the Weimar Republic a pluralistic political system and press had proven incapable of long-term survival. Indeed, the excessively partisan press had had a hand in the demise of Weimar democracy. The

69. Ibid., pp. 112–70.

Hugenberg press empire supplied a handy negative image to the occupation authorities, warning too against the dangers of unrestrained press-concentration. Therefore, the press had been reintroduced under licence and initially subjected to highly restrictive policies designed to limit the operation of market forces and to ensure a pluralistic ownership structure. A host of new publishers soon established themselves as the main providers of the major post-war newspapers: few of the great newspapers of the Weimar period survived this period. For a crucial initial period, major constraints were placed on the 'pure' capitalistic nature of the press, in the form of provisions against shareholding (and of course licencing itself), in order to prevent the reemergence of the great press empires of the past. This undoubtedly contributed to the reemergence of one of the earliest traditions of the German press, namely its highly decentralised nature. As the result, to this day, most West Germans read a regional or local newspaper, not a national ('überregionale') paper.

However, the ending of Allied restrictions and licencing very quickly led to the return of a quintessentially capitalistic press system. Once released from the early Allied controls, the press system very rapidly fell under the influence of powerful economic forces, which saw the return of tendencies towards a certain concentration of ownership. At first sight the infant West German press system may have appeared to be characterised by a quite exceptional degree of regionalised pluralism. Upon closer inspection, it became evident that the phenomenon of 'multiple editions' disguised the true state of affairs.

The reappearance of concentration tendencies led to accusations from some quarters that a 'restoration' had taken place. At the same time, it has to be said that these voices could not point to evidence of a new Hugenberg: Allied policies had ensured that West Germany's future press barons would be unreservedly liberal democrats. Nor should the degree of press-concentration that had occurred under the period of Allied occupation be exaggerated. Yet, radical alternatives to the free capitalistic press system had certainly been marginalised. The Allies had had little sympathy for experiments, especially those coming from the Germans. Moreover, the Cold War soon exercised its own logic: enthusiastic allegiance to liberal capitalism

Historical Origins of the West German Press System

Table 1.4 The structure of the West German press when the Germans received back their full sovereignty from the Allies in 1955: the 'multiple editions' phenomenon

	Papers	Editions
Baden-Württemberg	33	247
Bavaria	45	316
Berlin	10	23
Bremen	3	16
Hamburg	10	23
Hessen	30	144
Lower Saxony	27	155
North-Rhine Westphalia	41	411
Rhineland-Palatinate	13	89
Schleswig-Holstein	13	76
Total	225	1 500

Source: W. Schütz, 'Deutsche Tagespresse in Tatsachen und Zahlen', *Publizistik*, 1. Jahrgang, 1956, p. 33

became the West German talisman against anything smacking of 'socialism'. After the confirmation of Adenauer and the Christian Democrats in power, the domestic power structure itself was unfavourable to any flirtation with radicalism. During this early period, the proprietorial right of publishers to more or less exclusively establish the social, political and philosophical orientation of their publications was enshrined in the controversial 'Tendenzschutz', against the generally weak opposition of the journalists' organisations and the trade unions. Undoubtedly these developments stored up trouble for the future.

2
Controversies Over the West German Press System

The preceding chapter has described how the main organisational features and regulatory principles of the West German press system were established in the early post-war years. As seen, the system that emerged was characterised by a high degree of regulatory freedom for the publishers. The Western Allies had established the fundamental principle of a free and pluralist press. In particular, the press was to remain almost exclusively organised by private enterprise. Private proprietorship was held to be the best safeguard against state influence and the pluralistic competition of many different publications was considered to be an indispensable condition for the development of pluralist democracy. It had been an underlying assumption that the profit motive would act as a 'hidden hand' to ensure that the whole spectrum of public opinion would be amply catered for by the press. The publishers were allowed to determine the main orientation of their publications, but 'pluralism', it was held, would be guaranteed both by the multiplicity of publications on offer and by the constant need of the publishers to appeal to every section of the social and political spectrum. However, as will now be described, the West German press system has encountered a series of controversies which have raised the question of the degree of true pluralism of the press.

In addition, the press system has itself had to define its relations with the other main branch of the mass media, namely broadcasting. In West Germany, these two 'sub-sectors' of the media have always existed in a state of considerable tension. As will be seen (in Chapter 3), the pluralist approach to the media adopted in West Germany has stressed the central importance of combining a free and largely unregulated press system with the countervailing power of an exclusively 'public-service' and independent broadcasting system, which is highly regulated but supposedly free from undue state interference. However, the publishers of the press have never been happy with this strict separation of the two branches and they have always sought to gain a foothold in broadcasting (ultimately they have been highly successful in this respect, as Chapters 5 and 6 describe). The tension between the press and broadcasting first became manifest over the question of advertising.

The Conflict Between the Broadcasters and the Press

The conflict between the publishers of the press and the broadcasting corporations commenced in the mid-1950s. It arose because the publishers disputed the right of the public-service broadcasting corporations to run broadcast advertising on their services. The publishers regarded advertising as rightfully their reserved domain. Firstly, they argued that the economic health of the entire press system depended upon their ability to finance themselves adequately by means of advertisements as well as by subscription and street sales. Secondly, they argued that the very survival of many papers depended upon this source of finance. By implication, no less was at stake than the continued diversity of the press, which underpinned the 'pluralist' system. Thirdly, the publishers argued that the exclusively 'public-service' organisation of the broadcasters should preclude the latter from commercial operations.

The first skirmish occurred in 1956 when the BDZV instituted legal proceedings against the Bayerischer Rundfunk (the Bavarian public-service broadcasting corporation – BR) in an attempt to prevent it from introducing advertising into its television service (it was the first broadcasting station to do so). However, this action was subsequently thrown out by the Bavarian Higher Regional Court in Munich in 1957. In its ruling, the Munich court established the right of the public-service broadcasters to broadcast advertising so long as its contents did not endanger the diversity of the press.[1]

Again, in the early 1960s, the BDZV mounted a determined

---

1. W. Mahle and R. Richter, *Communication Policy in the Federal Republic of Germany*, Paris: Unesco Press, 1974, p. 18.

campaign against broadcast advertising. By this time, the publishers were alarmed by the widespread introduction of television advertising. As a result of intensive lobbying by the publishers, in April 1964 (during the CDU/FDP coalition) the Bundestag decided to establish a parliamentary 'Commission to Examine the Fairness of Competition Between the Press, Broadcasting and Film' ('Kommission zur Untersuchung der Wettbewerbgleichheit von Presse, Funk/Fernsehen und Film'). Known by the name of its chairman, Elmar Michel, the commission was overwhelmingly composed of independent experts. It submitted its report, the 'Michel Report' ('Michel-Bericht') to the federal government, by now the CDU/SPD 'Grand Coalition', in September 1967. The 'Michel Report' presented the first comprehensive account of the organisation, structure and economic development of the West German media. In particular, it explored the state of competition in the media and how the media related to competition law, constitutional law and administrative law. It concluded by making a number of suggestions for reform of the relationship between press and broadcasting.

Once more the publishers were disappointed. The 'Michel Report' rejected the publishers' claims that there was a serious distortion of competition between newspapers and broadcasting. In the commission's view the crucial factor behind the economic problems of the newspaper publishers was not adverse competition from television, but competition among the different publishers themselves. The commission justified its conclusion by pointing out that the press and television largely drew their respective advertising revenues from different advertising customers. Consequently, it was argued, the economic problems of the press were unrelated to the extent to which broadcasting was organised on public-service or commercial lines. The commission also rejected the publishers' demands to be allowed to become involved in broadcasting themselves. This, the commission concluded, would entail the undesirable development of 'multimedia' monopolies.[2]

In the meantime, a 'conservative–liberal' (CDU/CSU/FDP) bill to ban advertising on public-service broadcasting services had been dropped in the face of stiff opposition from both the SPD

---

2. Michel, Bericht, Bundestags-Drucksache V/2120, pp. 173–86.

and the Länder collectively.[3] Irrespective of the colour of their governments, the latter were above all concerned to safeguard the position of the broadcasting corporations, which had been placed entirely under their responsibility. From this point onwards, the publishers abandoned the goal of banning advertising by the broadcasters. However, they did not so easily relinquish the ambition to become involved in broadcasting. They maintained a commitment, marked by several major controversial attempts, to diversify into the other major sector of the mass media (see Chapter 4).

The Controversy Over State Security and the Press

Another important controversy affecting the West German press system arose, during the 1960s, over the question of state security. This controversy went to the heart of the question of the freedom of the press from state interference. To this extent, it raised the fundamental question about the limits of the claim of the press to enjoy self-regulation and also the degree of 'pluralism' that was permissible in a 'vigilant democracy' ('wehrhafte Demokratie' – the term used to describe the extreme defensiveness and fear of subversion which characterised the political climate during the 1950s and 1960s). The issue was given special poignancy by the Federal Republic's unique 'front-line' situation in the East–West conflict.

The Debate About the 'Emergency Laws' ('Notstandgesetze')

In West Germany, the question of special powers for the government in the event of a state emergency has always been a subject of extreme sensitivity. The reasons for this are largely historical in nature. The constitution of the Weimar Republic had endowed the government with the right to invoke 'Emergency Powers' in cases of national crisis. As seen, these powers had been abused first by the conservative nationalists and later by the National Socialists after 1930.

Nevertheless, in 1960 the CDU/CSU/FDP federal government

---

3. See Mahle and Richter, *Communication Policy*, p. 24.

attempted to give the state reserve powers for the contingency of a national emergency which included the power to restrict the press. On this occasion the draft law was defeated by the resistance of both the SPD and the Bundesrat (the second chamber of the West German parliament which gave representation to the Länder and had very considerable legislative powers, including the ability to block government and Bundestag legislation). A further attempt to introduce powers to curtail press freedom in emergencies was made in 1962 but this also failed in the face of vehement opposition from the press lobby. After years of continued debate over the issue, the 'Grand Coalition' government (CDU/CSU/SPD) then introduced a series of laws and constitutional amendments under the rubric 'Emergency Laws' ('Notstandgesetze') in 1968. This measure provoked a wave of very vigorous opposition from the trade unions, the students and intellectuals. The SPD, in particular, was fiercely criticised for having had a change of heart. However, very significantly, these latter laws did not now contain provision for curtailing the guarantee of media freedom enshrined in Article 5 of the Basic Law. It appeared that the press had achieved a significant success in consolidating and defending its prerogatives.[4]

The 'Spiegel Affair'

During this period, the specific issue of the press and state security had meanwhile erupted onto the political agenda in a very concrete and spectacular manner. The *'Spiegel* Affair' of 1962 was a serious test of the principle of press freedom from state interference.

The affair arose as the result of the publication by the *Spiegel* news magazine, on 10 October 1962, of a highly controversial article about West German defence policy. The article, by a *Spiegel* investigative reporter called Conrad Ahlers, had publicised important details of that autumn's NATO manoeuvres called 'Fallex 62'. In particular, it had suggested that the defence capabilities of the Federal Republic were highly inadequate. The government appeared, however, to so deeply resent this criti-

---

4. Ibid., pp. 23–4.

cism that it overreacted. On 23 October 1962 Ahlers was suddenly arrested by West German agents whilst on holiday in Spain. Rudolf Augstein, the liberal publisher of the *Spiegel*, was also arrested in Hamburg. Then, on the night of 26/7 October, the security forces moved against the *Spiegel* offices in Hamburg. For four weeks the premises were thoroughly searched and material was confiscated. It soon emerged that Franz Josef Strauss, then Defence Minister, had been the main instigator of the action, which the government attempted to legitimate by accusing Ahlers and Augstein of high treason.

There was an immediate public furore. Strauss's attempt to deny that it was an effort to muzzle a highly critical publication met with a wave of public scepticism and opprobium. After over three months on remand, Augstein and Ahlers were eventually released. However, the recriminations and legal disputes dragged on for several years. Finally in May 1965, the Federal Constitutional Court ruled that there had been no serious case against Augstein and Ahlers. In the meantime, the scandal had compelled Franz Josef Strauss to resign his post (though subsequent events quickly demonstrated how easily he was rehabilitated – in 1980 he became Chancellor-candidate for the CDU/CSU).

In large part as a result of the '*Spiegel* Affair', the West German Criminal Code was amended in August 1968 (by the eighth 'Strafrechtänderungsgesetz'). For a long time, the press had demanded that the Criminal Code be amended in order to strengthen the safeguards for the press against state interference under the pretext of state security. The '*Spiegel* Affair' had very dramatically highlighted the threat to 'press freedom' from this source. Accordingly, much stronger measures of protection of the press were now built into the law. Notably, the grounds for state prosecution of treasonable offences by the press were made significantly stricter. Henceforth, the press could only be punished for revealing secrets which clearly and unambiguously threatened the state's external security. The outcome of the '*Spiegel* Affair', therefore, was yet another major victory for the principle of 'press freedom'.[5]

5. D. Schoenbaum, *The Spiegel Affair*, Garden City, New York: Doubleday, 1968; J. Schöps, *Die Spiegel Affäre des Franz Josef Strauss* (Spiegel-Buch no. 40), Reinbek: Rowohlt Taschenbuch Verlag, 1983.

Press-Concentration

The lessons of German history were not confined to the perils of capture and abuse of the media by the state. The dangers of press-concentration for the political system had also been demonstrated by the dominance of the newspaper market by the Hugenberg group during the Weimar Republic. Yet, the press system that had grown up since the war appeared to present a very different picture. A healthy pluralism seemed to flourish.

At first sight, the West German daily press ('Tagespresse') appears to be characterised by a weak national press and a very strong and diverse local and regional press. Apart from the Springer tabloid, the *Bild-Zeitung*, only a handful of papers sell the greater part of their circulation without any particular connection to any area of distribution. They can therefore be referred to as 'supra-regional newspapers' ('überregionale Zeitungen'). They are the *Frankfurter Allgemeine Zeitung (FAZ)*, *Die Welt*, the *Süddeutsche Zeitung*, and the *Frankfurter Rundschau*. Two further 'specialist' papers might be added to this list: the economics and business paper, the *Handelsblatt*, and the 'alternative' paper, the *taz*. Among these, *Die Welt* has an edition for Hamburg, the *taz* has editions for Berlin and Hamburg and the *FAZ* has a special Rhein-Main edition for Frankfurt. The total circulation of these titles amounts to only 4.35 million of the total daily circulation of 14.3 million 'subscription newspapers'.

Understanding the Statistics

According to Walter Schütz, a leading West German expert on press-concentration, in 1987 a total of around 375 newspaper 'publishers' ('Verlage als Herausgeber') produced no less than 1,260 different editions ('redaktionelle Ausgaben') of daily newspapers with a sales circulation of 20.7 million.[6] However, it is immediately obvious from these statistics that in 1987 there were three times as many newspapers as there were publishers. Moreover, the figures produced by Schütz also show that these originated from as few as 121 independent editorial units ('pub-

6. W. Schütz, 'Deutsche Tagespresse', *Media Perspektiven*, 9/1987, pp. 574–97, p. 574.

Table 2.1 Data on the development of the daily press in the Federal Republic of Germany, 1954–87

\multicolumn{3}{c	}{Independent editorial units ('publizistische Einheiten')}	\multicolumn{3}{c	}{Printer/publishers' ('Verlage als Herausgeber')}	\multicolumn{3}{c	}{Editorial editions ('redaktionelle Ausgaben')}	\multicolumn{3}{c}{Sold circulation in millions}
Year	Total	Index 1954=100	Year	Total	Index 1954=100	Year	Total	Index 1954=100	Year	Total	Index 1954=100
1954	225	100	1954	624	100	1954	1 500	100	1954	13.4	100
1964	183	81	1964	573	92	1964	1 495	100	1964	17.3	129
1967	158	70	1967	535	86	1967	1 416	94	1967	18.0	134
1976	121	54	1976	403	65	1976	1 229	82	1976	19.5	146
1979	122	54	1979	400	64	1979	1 240	83	1979	20.5	153
1981	124	55	1981	392	63	1981	1 258	84	1981	20.4	152
1983	125	56	1983	385	62	1983	1 255	84	1983	21.2	158
1985	126	56	1985	382	61	1985	1 273	85	1985	20.9	156
1987	121	54	1987	375	60	1987	1 260	84	1987	20.7	155

Source: Walter J. Schütz, 'The West German Daily Press', *Media Perspektiven* 9/1987, p. 574.

lizistische Einheiten'). Therefore, real editorial diversity can only safely be considered to be offered by a much smaller total of around 121 'independent editorial units' (see Table 2.1 above).

Quite simply, this means that no less than two-thirds of the 'Verlage als Herausgeber' were limited to producing the local section of the paper and the section containing the adverts. They obtained the rest, the so-called 'Mantel' ('jacket' or 'umbrella') section, including the first few pages which provide the political news and commentary, from elsewhere, normally a cooperative editorial unit ('Gemeinschaftsredaktion') or from larger newspapers. In fact, in West Germany around four-fifths of all editions ('redaktionelle Ausgaben') are local editions covering a small district ('Kreiszeitungen'). Furthermore, a number of the smaller papers do not appear on every day of the week, although they are often counted among the dailies to inflate the overall figures.[7] A leading British authority on the West German media, John Sandford, has observed that, because of this peculiar structure of the West German press, 'German press statistics are . . . notoriously misleading. . . . many West German "dailies" are independent, individual newspapers in title only. In all important respects, they are editorially identical . . . not only with the mother paper, but also with many other small papers in the same area'.[8]

Research by Schütz and others has demonstrated that this present situation has been reached by a process of considerable growth but also of marked concentration.[9] After the initial explosion of new papers that followed the abolition of licensing by the Allies (see previous chapter), the number of publishers of daily newspapers began to decrease relentlessly. In 1954, there were as many as 624 publishers and no less than 225 independent editorial units. Between 1954 and 1987, only the total circulation of newspapers had climbed: from 13.4 million to its present level of 20.7 million (see Table 2.1).

7. W. Schütz, 'Zeitungen in der Bundesrepublik Deutschland', in *Die Presse in der deutschen Medienlandschaft*, Bundeszentrale für politische Bildung, Themenheft 6, Bonn, 1985, pp. 13–24, p. 14.
8. J. Sandford, *The Mass Media of the German-Speaking Countries*, London: Oswald Wolff, 1976, p. 29.
9. For example, also see H. H. Diederichs, *Konzentration in den Massenmedien. Systemischer Überblick zur Situation in der BRD*, Munich, Carl Hanser Verlag, 1973;

Papers with a small circulation were generally the main casualties of this development. A special government report of 1978 discovered that the reduction of 'publizistische Einheiten' from 225 in 1954 to 121 in 1976 was above all a result of the disappearance of smaller newspapers with a circulation of no more than 40,000. The number of 'publizistische Einheiten' in this category had fallen from 121 to 30, and its proportion of the total number of 'publizistische Einheiten' had fallen from 53.7% to 24.7% while its share of the total circulation had fallen from 15.4% to 3.8%. At the same time, the number of 'publizistische Einheiten' with a circulation of more than 150,000 had actually climbed from 18 to 42. The latter category's proportion of the total number of all 'publizistische Einheiten' had grown from 8.0% to 34.7% and its share of the total circulation had also risen from 37.2% to 75.5%.[10] Such trends were overwhelmingly to be explained by press-concentration processes.

The impact of press concentration on the local press has been particularly disturbing for the simple reason that, in contrast to Britain, it is normal German practice to buy a local, rather than a national, newspaper. Local newspapers are, therefore, one of the principal means by which West Germans inform themselves about national and international, as well as local, events (television being the other). Until the mid-1950s local newspaper monopolies were the exception not the rule. According to Schütz, on average three newspapers competed in each rural district ('Landkreis') or small town. However, since then the average has nearly halved. The proportion of districts with only one local newspaper has grown from 15% to 47%. In 1954 only 8% of the population lived in 'single newspaper districts', now it is around one-third of the population. Since the mid-1950s, more and more mainly smaller newspapers have fallen victim to the twin processes of press-concentration – takeovers and com-

---

IG Druck und Papier, Landesbezirk NRW (ed.), *Pressekonzentration in Nordrhein-Westfalen*, Düsseldorf, 1977; M. Knoche, 'Ansätze und Methoden der Konzentrationsforschung im Pressebereich', *Media Perspektiven*, 5/1979, pp. 288–300; and M. Knoche, 'Der Konzentrationsprozeß der Tages-Presse 1954–1978. Typenorientierte Einzelfallanalysen zum Wegfall Publizistischer Einheiten', *Media Perspektiven* 10/1978, pp. 731–47.
10. 'Medienbericht 1978', p. 12, quoted in Hans-Matthias Kepplinger, *Massenkommunikation*, Stuttgart: Teubner Studienskripten, 1982, pp. 58–9.

petition. By 1983 around 35% of all publishers of 'subscription newspapers' ('Abonnementszeitungen') enjoyed a monopoly position in their areas of distribution. Over half (52%) had a dominant position. Arguably, this process of concentration has now moved into a second phase of 'latent press-concentration'. Accordingly, most 'competing' newspapers have fallen under the influence of the same leading local/regional publisher or a web of 'friendly' (allied) publishers.[11]

The same publisher (usually based in a city) often holds a monopoly position in a number of neighbouring districts, creating sub-regional or regional monopolies. While at the national level there would appear to be a meritworthy degree of pluralism – the five largest publishers of subscription newspapers accounting for only 26.1% of a total circulation of 14.3 million – the local level reflects a very different picture indeed. In the Saarland for example, the *Saarbrücker Zeitung* (10 'different' editions) commands the entire local newspaper circulation of 192,700 as well as controlling two editions of the neighbouring *Pfalzischer Merkur*. In the Rhineland-Palatinate the total circulation of that Land is dominated by only three publishing groups which are virtually local monopolies: *Die Rheinpfalz* of Ludwigshafen (31.6%), the *Rhein-Zeitung* of Koblenz (29.2%) and the *Allgemeine Zeitung* of Mainz (21.5%).[12] By 1985 significant competition only remained between newspapers from competing publishing houses in Berlin, Munich, Münster, Bielefeld, Giessen and in the Frankfurt area as well as on the edges of overlapping distribution areas such as Dortmund, Recklinghausen, Pforzheim and Baden-Baden.[13]

Types of Concentration

Hans-Matthias Kepplinger has identified several different manifestations of concentration: concentration of publishers ('Verlagskonzentration'), concentration of circulation ('Auflagenkonzentration'), and editorial ('journalistic') concentration

11. See Schütz, 'Zeitungen in der Bundesrepublik Deutschland', p. 20.
12. A. Williams, 'Pluralism in the West German Media', *West European Politics*, vol. 8, no. 2, April 1985, p. 91, based on figures from W. Schütz, 'Die deutsche Tagespresse 1981', *Media Perspektiven*, 9/1981, p. 665.
13. See Schütz, 'Zeitungen in der Bundesrepublik Deutschland', pp. 21–2.

('publizistische Konzentration'). Concentration of publishers refers to the relentless reduction in the number of actual publishing houses as a result of mergers and close-downs. Concentration of circulation refers to the increasing domination of the market for a particular type of publication by one or several publishers. Good examples of concentration of circulation are given by the Axel Springer group's dominance of the markets for both papers sold in the street ('Straßenverkaufszeitungen') or 'Boulevardzeitungen') and Sunday papers. Editorial concentration simply means the reduction of the number of editorial units ('publizistische Einheiten') again through mergers and close-downs.[14]

Reasons for Press-Concentration

There are several main reasons for the phenomenon of press-concentration. In the first place, press-concentration has reflected the existence of a more or less free and unrestrained state of economic competition between the publishers in the Federal Republic. In a free market, characterised by cut-throat competition, publishers soon became concerned to become the principal supplier in their respective areas of distribution. The publishers deliberately sought, and struggled to achieve, a local or regional monopoly position. Radical critics of the free-market system emphasised that the rapid concentration process was a direct consequence of the 'restoration' of capitalistic production relations during the Allied occupation (see previous chapter).

Merger or amalgamation offered the opportunity to rationalise production, share the tax burden, minimise risks and spread costs. During the 1950s it quickly became apparent that it was impossible to cover the costs of production of newspapers through sales alone. In order to cover costs, newspapers were compelled to turn increasingly to the advertising market for more and more of their revenues. Very quickly advertising became the main source of revenue of daily newspapers and popular illustrated magazines alike. Newspapers that started off with a large circulation were already the most attractive to advertisers and *de facto* the best-placed in the fierce competition

14. See Kepplinger, *Massenkommunikation*, p. 64.

that, as seen, broke out in the early 1950s. Very quickly such newspapers consolidated their position and progressively increased their lead. Publishers rapidly discovered that they could establish the most favourable terms of business with their advertising customers by gaining the largest possible circulation and by gaining a monopoly, or dominant, position in the market. The share of advertising revenue in the total income of newspaper concerns rose rapidly in the period 1953–65. By the beginning of the 1960s it stood as high as around 60%. During the phase of prosperity this gave the publishers a rapid increase in profits. However, the economic recession of 1966/7 brought a stagnation and even a fall of advertising revenues. This reduced many smaller newspapers to the edge of ruin and there followed a wave of closures and mergers. The dependence of the press on advertising contracts from industry made the sector particularly vulnerable to cyclical movements of the economy. Inevitably, therefore, recessions brought an added stimulus to the concentration process. Accordingly, two giant leaps in the concentration process ('Konzentrationsschübe') can be detected following the recessions of 1966/7 and 1973/4 against a background of a more continuous broader trend towards concentration.[15]

Moreover, around the years 1967–9 the West German newspaper market reached saturation point. This meant that the ambitions of the strongest to expand further, increase their circulation, and thereby attract more advertising revenue, could no longer be satisfied by the market. The only way forward was to concentrate upon taking over smaller concerns, allowing them to appear as a local edition with a subtitle. Over the course of time, the subtitles of the larger 'mother' papers ('Hauptausgaben' or 'Kopfblätter') began to assume ever larger dimensions, so that eventually the once independent local newspapers had become little more than editions of the larger newspapers. In this way, stonger newspaper concerns continued to

15. H.-W. Gross, *Die Deutsche Presse-Agentur*, Frankfurt/Main: Haag + Herchen Verlag, 1982, p. 117. However, there is one important study which disputes the view that the press is particularly dependent on the economic conjuncture, see K.P. Kisker, M. Knoche and A. Zerdick, *Wirtschaftskonjunktur und Pressekonzentration in der Bundesrepublik Deutschland* (Dortmunder Beiträge zur Zeitungsforschung) Munich: K.G. Saur Verlag, 1979.

strengthen their own position in the market, gain higher advertising revenues, increase their turnover and win ever-wider sales areas.[16]

Advertising has remained the major source of income for the press. According to one source, some DM 5.3 billion of the total turnover of daily papers, which in 1980 amounted to around DM 7.8 billion, represented advertising. The figures for periodicals were DM 2.8 billion and DM 9.6 billion respectively.[17] Competition between the newspaper and magazine publishers for this valued source of income actually intensified during the 1970s and 1980s. During this period, the commercial press had to face increased competition from the broadcast media and from advertising-based free papers ('Anzeigenblätter').[18] During the 1970s and 1980s, the appearance and proliferation of so-called 'free-sheets', delivered free of charge to private homes, had a considerable impact in the FRG as elsewhere. The latter were totally reliant on advertising, usually small localised advertising, and contained almost exclusively local news and information content. About half of these free-sheets had some connection with the larger publishing concerns. In addition to free-sheets there also occurred a marked rise in the popularity and success of a small number of weekly illustrated papers, or supplements, which were primarily designed by the larger publishing houses in order to capture new advertising markets. The first multi-page illustrated supplement appeared in 1961. During the 1970s more and more papers carried these supplements or magazines. By 1980 no less than 11 supplements were produced, with a circulation of almost 9 million. By the 1980s, these supplements were being supplied with around half of all local and regional newspapers.[19]

In addition, press-concentration has resulted from the unequal distribution of resources and capital accumulation ca-

---

16. IG Druck und Papier, *Tendenzschutz und Pressekonzentration*, IG Druck und Papier: Stuttgart, 1971, p. 21.
17. M. Haler, *Basic Law Guarantees Freedom of Opinion – Mass Media in the FRG*, Bonn: Inter Nationes, 1982, p. 21. Note that American usage is employed throughout for 'billion' – i.e. 1 billion = 1,000 million.
18. V. Schulze, *Der Bundesverband Deutscher Zeitungsverleger*, Düsseldorf: Droste Verlag, 1985, p. 54.
19. See Haler, *Basic Law Guarantees Freedom of Opinion*, p. 17.

pacity of the publishers. The costs of typesetting and printing amount to almost half of the total expenditure of the smaller newspapers. However, as circulation increases, so this proportion diminishes and the percentage of turnover that counts as profit increases exponentially. Therefore, newspapers with larger circulations have enjoyed a much greater capital accumulation capacity than those with small circulations. Moreover, the former have much greater resources for investment in new technical installations and for increasing the concern's operations. Small newspaper concerns cannot even begin to match the enormous sums which the larger concerns can reinvest. Thus, newspapers with large circulations have a built-in competitive advantage.[20]

Concentration has also reflected the disproportionately high rise in costs in the field of the press. In this respect, personnel costs make up more than 50% of the total. During the early post-war period, as seen, the employees of the publishing houses found themselves in a generally weak bargaining situation. However, this situation soon changed as West Germany experienced the 'economic miracle' ('Wirtschaftswunder') of the 1950s and 1960s and unemployment plummeted. Concomitantly, the position of the journalists and organised labour steadily increased over time and unit costs rose accordingly. This placed the smaller and weaker newspaper concerns under increasing financial pressure and contributed to the rate of closures and takeovers. Moreover, steadily rising costs of manufacture and distribution have combined since the early 1970s with the financial constraints of investing in new automated and computerised technologies to compel smaller publishers to merge with larger ones, or at least to enter into amalgamations or associations with other smaller ones. In either case, the result has been a drift towards concentration. Faced with rapidly spiralling costs, many have simply fallen prey to takeovers by capital-rich giant predators. Often the creation of, or absorption into, a large concern has been the only course of action for the survival of financially weak newspapers.

---

20. For detailed discussion of this theme see: J. Aufermann, B.-P. Lange and A. Zerdick, 'Pressekonzentration in der BRD: Untersuchungsprobleme, Ursachen und Erscheinungsformen', in J. Aufermann, H. Bohrmann and R. Sülzer

Finally, economic causes aside, there can be little doubt that political motivations have also played a role. Certain publishers have deliberately sought to increase their political and editorial influence over public opinion by using their financial muscle to exert power over weaker publishers. In sum, as the result of all these processes, the West German press system very quickly bore witness to a progressive and disproportionate growth of the large concerns. Moreover, this process was accompanied by the rapid growth of the characteristic web of cooperation and integration ('Verflechtung') between publishing concerns that distinguishes all areas of activity in the West German press system today, including editorial matters, the procurement of adverts, typesetting, printing and distribution. In very many cases these cooperative relations are sealed with capital integration ('Kapitalverflechtung').

An Overview of the Main Newspaper and Magazine Publishing Groups

Newspapers

By 1980, the West German market for daily newspapers was dominated overwhelmingly by the Axel Springer group (the *Bild-Zeitung, Die Welt*, the *Hamburger Abendblatt, Berliner Morgenpost*, etc.) with 28.27% of the market-share. A number of other groups were also well-established in the market: notably, the Zeitungsgesellschaft E. Brost & J. Funke (the 'WAZ group') (the *Westdeutsche Allgemeine Zeitung*, the *Westfälische Rundschau*, the *Neue-Ruhr-Zeitung*, the *Westfalenpost*, etc.) with 6.00%; the 'Stuttgarter Zeitung/Rheinpfalz/*Württemberg publishers' group' (the *Stuttgarter Zeitung*, the *Stuttgarter Nachrichten*, the *Rheinpfalz*, the *Südwestpresse*, etc.) with 5.20%; the Verlag DuMont Schauberg (the *Kölner Stadtanzeiger*, the *Express*, the *Abendzeitung*) with

---

(eds.), *Gesellschaftliche Kommunikation und Information. Forschungsrichtungen und Problemstellungen. Ein Arbeitsbuch zur Massenkommunikation*, vol. 1, Frankfurt/Main: Athenäum, 1973, pp. 242–302, in particular pp. 257–9. Also see K. Farin and H.-J. Zwingmann, *Pressekonzentration. Daten. Fakten. Trends*, Ettlingen: Doku-Verlag, 1981, p. 7. They state that 'large press concerns and papers with large circulations are more rational ['rationeller']', by which they mean in a purely economic perspective.

3.73%; and the Süddeutscher Verlag group (the *Süddeutsche Zeitung*, the *Abendzeitung*, the *Donau-Kurier*) with 2.37%.[21] Research by Horst Röper, has shown that by 1987 these groups were still well-placed in the 'top ten'. In particular, the Springer group now enjoyed a market share of 28.58% (see Appendix 1(a) and 1(b)).[22]

Periodicals

There are upwards of 5,000 publications that have been described by the Federal Press Statistics as 'periodicals' in the FRG, with an annual sales circulation averaging a total of 130 million copies. However, the vast majority of these journals are simply trade journals and organisational publications. In fact, there is only a handful of truly 'popular' illustrated periodicals in the Federal Republic. The most popular, with circulations of around one million copies each, are *Stern, Bunte Illustrierte, Neue Revue* and *Quick, Tina, Das Neue Blatt, Brigitte, Bravo, Frau im Spiegel, Für Sie* and *Neue Post*. The Springer group's *Hör Zu* is the most popular radio and television magazine, closely followed by the same group's *Funk Uhr*, Bauer's *TV Hören und Sehen* and *Fernsehwoche* and Burda's *Bild und Funk*. In contrast with Britain, broadcasting corporations in the FRG do not produce their own programme journals. They are all produced by private publishers (by virtue of which, these publishers were later able to give their private commercial satellite channel an impressively well-publicised launch – see Chapter 6).

In 1980, the market for popular illustrated magazines ('Publikumszeitschriften') was dominated overwhelmingly by the Heinrich Bauer Verlag with 32.10%; the Axel Springer Verlag with 12.99%; the Burda group, with 11.01%; and the Bertelsmann/Gruner und Jahr group with 6.06%. Altogether, these four groups had a market share of 62.2% of the total.[23] By 1986, the total circulation of 'Publikumszeitschriften' surpassed the 100 million mark for the first time. The concentration – measured as the share taken by the four largest groups – had increased still

21. See Kepplinger, *Massenkommunikation*, p. 61.
22. H. Röper, 'Daten zur Konzentration der Tagespresse in der BRD im I. Quartel 1987', *Media Perspektiven*, 9/1987, pp. 563–73.
23. See Kepplinger, *Massenkommunikation*, p. 63.

further. Between them the four largest group took a market share of 66.7% of the total, broken down as follows: the Heinrich Bauer Verlag 31.52%, the Axel Springer Verlag 17.57% (up 4.58% on 1980), the Burda group 9.98% and the Bertelsmann/Gruner und Jahr group 7.00%. Moreover, the market-share of the ten largest West German publishers of 'Publikumszeitschriften' amounted to 81.05% (see Appendix 1(c) and 1(d)).[24]

The Axel Springer Group

Very clearly, with around 28% of the market-share for dailies, the right-wing Axel Springer Verlag has long occupied a dominant and unchallenged position among the West German newspaper publishers. It enjoys near complete regional monopolies in Hamburg and West Berlin (86.4% and 71.4% respectively),[25] and produces West Germany's most successful tabloid, the *Bild-Zeitung*, which has a circulation of nearly five million. Moreover, the *Bild-Zeitung* alone dominates the West German market for 'Boulevardzeitungen' (see Appendix 1(e)). The Axel Springer Verlag also produces both of West Germany's national Sunday newspapers, the *Bild am Sonntag* and the *Welt am Sonntag*. In addition, the Axel Springer Verlag produces one of the country's best-known and most widely distributed 'national' ('überregionale') quality dailies, *Die Welt*, and its largest evening newspaper, the *Hamburger Abendblatt*. Other well-known Springer papers are the Berlin *BZ* and *Berliner Morgenpost*. With holdings in many other papers and publishing houses, Axel Springer established one of the largest press empires in Western Europe, employing over 12,000 people and with an annual turnover in 1987 of around DM 2.7 billion. As will be seen (in Chapters 5 and 6) the Springer group has also recently embraced important interests in broadcasting. Therefore, it can justifiably be compared to the multi-media giants of the Anglo-Saxon world, Robert Maxwell and Rupert Murdoch.

---

24. H. Diederichs, 'Daten zur Konzentration der Publikumszeitschriften in der Bundesrepublik Deutschland im IV. Quartel 1986', *Media Perspektiven*, 8/1987, pp. 496–506.
25. According to figures supplied by Walter Schütz, 'Deutsche Tagespresse 1981', *Media Perspektiven*, 9/1981, p. 665.

Bertelsmann AG

The Springer group's major rival, Bertelsmann of Gütersloh, is one of the largest (according to some estimates, the second largest) 'multi-media' concerns in the world. Comprising over 100 firms in the FRG and abroad, Bertelsmann AG with Gruner & Jahr is a publishing giant with a world-wide annual turnover of around DM 9.2 billion in 1987. The Bertelsmann AG is a large supplier of general and specialist, including academic and scientific, literature and also a major producer of records, films and video-cassettes. Bertelsmann's 75%-owned major subsidiary, Gruner & Jahr, markets a number of highly popular illustrated periodicals, the best-known of which is the left-of-centre *Stern* magazine. Gruner & Jahr also has a holding in the 'independent' but usually centre-left oriented *Spiegel* magazine.

Bauer, Burda and Holtzbrinck

Three large conservative oriented family-owned publishing groups also deserve a special mention. The Hamburg-based Heinrich Bauer Verlag publishes, among other products, *Neue Revue, Die Neue Post, Tina, Bravo, Das Neue Blatt, Neue Mode, Riesen-Rätsel-Revue, Auto-Zeitung* and the radio and TV magazines *TV Hören und Sehen* and *Fernsehwoche*; the Burda Verlag of Offenburg produces *Bunte, Freundin, Das Haus, Freizeit-Revue* and also produces the large regional *Saarbrücker Zeitung*; while the Stuttgart-based Verlagsgruppe Georg von Holtzbrinck has shares in West Germany's two most influential economic publications, namely *Wirtschaftswoche* and the daily *Handelsblatt*.

Westdeutsche Allgemeine Zeitung Group

The 'social-liberal' or centre-left *Westdeutsche Allgemeine Zeitung* (*WAZ*) group has established a regional monopoly in North-Rhine Westphalia. The *WAZ* owns no less that 17 of the region's other newspapers, and has a majority interest in the *Westfälische Rundschau*, the *Neue Ruhr Zeitung* and the *Westfalenpost*. North-Rhine Westphalia is the most densely-populated area in the Federal Republic, taking in the major industrial conurbations of the north Rhineland and the Ruhr. This state of affairs actually puts the WAZ next to the *Bild-Zeitung* in circulation, although it is 'only' a regional newspaper.

Public Apprehension about Press-Concentration

According to at least one important longitudinal survey, there has been a general loss of public confidence in the media, particularly the daily press.[26] The public have noted the process of concentration with great disquiet. Anxiety about the loss of journalistic 'diversity' ('publizistische Vielfalt'), so essential for the functioning of liberal democracy, has engendered furious debates and led to the establishment of numerous 'media commissions' in interest groups ('Interessenverbände'), political parties, and in the federal and Land parliaments. These media commissions have striven to elaborate suggestions for the reduction of the concentration process (see p. 99).

The Publishers' Own Attempts to 'Control' Press-Concentration

The publishers themselves have been concerned to put their house in order. In the first place, they have been anxious that public disquiet and scepticism about the true degree of pluralism in the press might delegitimise the basis of their relative freedom from regulation. The official initiatives to examine the problem spurred them to give the issue serious attention. They had to be seen to be taking the duty of self-regulation seriously. Secondly, all newspaper publishers were represented within the BDZV. As a result, the stronger larger publishers were constrained to recognise the fears of the weaker smaller publishers, who as seen were the most vulnerable to the process of concentration.

Consequently, the BDZV developed the principle of 'assistance for self-help' ('Hilfe zur Selbsthilfe') and sought to ameliorate the situation by encouraging economic 'cooperation' among the publishers themselves. The latter developed many kinds of initiatives of their own. For example, in the editorial field they set up cooperative or associational editorial units

---

26. M.-L. Kiefer, 'Massenkommunikation 1964 bis 1980. Trendanalyse zur Mediennutzung und Medienbewertung', *Media Perspektiven*, 4/1981, pp. 261–86.

('Gemeinschaftsredaktionen') and correspondent agencies ('Korrespondentenbüros'). In the advertising field, they established cartels for the agreement of common advertising rates ('Tarifgemeinschaften') or 'advertising circles' ('Anzeigenringe') to facilitate the mutual procurement and pooling of advertising sections. Through 'advertising cooperatives' ('Anzeigengemeinschaften'), mainly small newspapers combined to sell advertisers a much larger 'reach' (i.e. their combined circulations). The publishers also cooperated in the field of distribution and delivery. In the technical field, they formed print-cooperatives ('Druckgemeinschaften'). Finally, the smaller publishers came together for the joint use of modern electronic ('elektronische Datenverarbeitung' – or 'electronic data processing' – EDV) facilities.[27]

Examples of this kind of development are provided by the so-called 'newspaper circles' ('Zeitungsringe') created where several newspapers joined together in a group. By the beginning of the 1970s, the Arbeitgemeinschaft Norddeutsche Allgemeine Verlags GmbH & Co. K.G. embraced no less than 26 newspapers in Schleswig-Holstein. Similarly, the Niedersächsischer Zeitungsverlag comprised 11 papers in Lower Saxony. The Westfälischer Nachrichten incorporated 8 different editions ('Ausgaben'), all of which were once independent local papers. In 1970 the Redaktionsgemeinschaft Deutscher Heimatzeitungen GmbH, in Frankfurt, could count no fewer than 54 local newspapers among its members. The complete list of such groups would be very long indeed.[28] However, cynics might argue that these attempts by the publishers themselves to ameliorate the situation have actually, objectively speaking, exacerbated the situation, leading to even greater concentration. There has been no absence of critics on the political left and particularly in the trade unions who have argued that the problems of the press system cannot properly be addressed while the 'self-regulated' press remains largely responsible for its own affairs.

---

27. See Schulze, *Der Bundesverband Deutscher Zeitungsverleger*, pp. 54–5.
28. See IG Druck und Papier, *Tendenzschutz und Pressekonzentration*, p. 18.

The Political Balance of the West German Press

The political spectrum of the West German mass press extends from centre-left to staunch conservative right. Apart from the so-called 'alternative' press with its limited readership and the residue of the political press (see p. 91 below), there are no major newspapers of a distinctly left-wing nature. In 1980 the last great unequivocally Social Democrat-oriented newspaper, the *Hamburger Morgenpost*, was sold off to a Swiss publisher. The vast majority of newspapers qualify themselves as 'above-party' ('überparteilich') or 'independent' ('unabhängig'). However, there are a large number of newspapers which are, in practice, highly sympathetic to the CDU. To some extent, the moderate conservative orientation of the majority of West German newspapers doubtless reflects the dominant political culture of the West German state itself.[29]

As elsewhere in the Western world, however, this state of affairs also reflects the capitalistic ownership and organisation of the press. As suggested, the 'Tendenzschutz' gives the West German newspaper and magazine proprietors a privileged right to determine the overall ideological orientation of their publications. Corporate organisations and wealthy individuals have thus been able to use their financial muscle to influence public opinion in a direction supportive of their own interests. The increasing corporate concentration of ownership and control of the press, which, as seen, has characterised the West German press system, has increased this discretionary power of wealthy individuals and powerful organisations. Unquestionably, the political agenda and political culture has therefore itself been shaped by this privileged position of the publishing business.

A substantial degree of political pluralism does, however, survive in West Germany. The *Süddeutsche Zeitung*, a regional quality newspaper with a national readership of around one-third of a million, is broadly centre-left in political orientation and was generally highly supportive of the 'social-liberal' (SPD/

---

29. G. Kloss, 'Die Massenmedien', in C. Edwards and H.-W. Lohneis, *Die Bundesrepublik Deutschland*, Bath: Bath University Press, 1982, pp. 126–7; also see W. La Roche and L. Maassen, *Massenmedien – Fakten – Formen – Funktionen in der Bundesrepublik Deutschland*, Heidelberg: C. F. Müller Juristischer Verlag, 1983, pp. 44–8.

FDP) coalition. Similarly, the *Frankfurter Rundschau*, effectively also a 'national' ('überregional') newspaper, with a circulation of around 185,000, is centre-left in political orientation and describes itself as 'links-liberal' (left-liberal). The *WAZ* group of newspapers, which, as seen, has a virtual monopoly in the Ruhr area and extends into much of the rest of North-Rhine Westphalia, is certainly not unfriendly to the SPD. Moreover, West Germany's most prestigious weekly quality newspaper, *Die Zeit*, leans towards the centre-left, especially in its political and cultural reporting. West Germany also has the good fortune to have a distinguished weekly news magazine (in the style of the *Economist* or *Time*) which has always had a distinctively independent but anti-conservative orientation, namely *Der Spiegel*, with a circulation of nearly one million. West Germany's largest multimedia concern, the giant Bertelsmann organisation, is distinctly 'liberal' in political orientation. Its subsidiary, Gruner & Jahr, produces another weekly news magazine (in a more 'popular' format than *Der Spiegel*) called *Stern* with a circulation of over one-and-a-half million. *Stern* has often given the impression of being SPD-oriented.

Against this, the Springer group of newspapers, which, as has been seen, has a dominant position in the West German market for dailies ('Tagespresse'), has a very right-wing political orientation. The Springer group's *Bild-Zeitung* deserves a special mention in this respect. A highly sensational tabloid, the *Bild-Zeitung's* daily sold circulation of nearly 5 million is probably a grave underestimate of its actual readership which may possibly be as high as 10 million. Its underlying philosophy ('Weltanschauung') is militantly anti-socialist and illiberal in the extreme. As seen, the Springer group also publishes the highly conservative quality newspaper *Die Welt*, originally the British occupation-zone newspaper, modelled on *The Times*, which has a readership of around 200,000.

As has been suggested, however, the majority of West German newspapers reflect a fairly moderate conservative line. Among these undoubtedly predominates the *Frankfurter Allgemeine Zeitung* (*FAZ*), with a circulation of around one-third of a million readers all over West Germany. The *FAZ* is a quality paper with a distinctively conservative orientation (although in some social questions it is 'liberal'). (More detailed circulation figures are supplied by the Informationsgemeinschaft zur Feststellung der Verbreitung von Werbeträgern e.V., in Bonn.)

The Demise of the Overtly Political Press?

The established political press, with its explicit connection to the major parties, has all but disappeared: only the weekly Social Democratic newspaper *Vorwärts*, the CDU's *Wochenzeitung* and the CSU's *Bayern-Kurier* remain of this once proud German tradition. As seen, the Weimar press had reflected the hyperpoliticised character of the period. However, the secular Federal Republic, with its unideological political parties, was not fertile soil for the continuance of the political press. A general turning away from ideology was reflected in the move towards the 'people's party' or 'Volkspartei' model of political organisation. The 'agitprop' newspaper ('Kampfblatt') was very much redolent of an outmoded image of party and it did not suit this new broadly-based and unideological model. According to one informed source, only around 50,000 of the SPD's approximately 900,000 members subscribe to *Vorwärts*.[30]

However, recently there does appear to have occurred something of a revival of the 'extreme right' press. According to one study, there are now more than 130 regularly appearing newspapers and magazines which express some kind of 'extreme right' or 'new right' ('Neue Recht') political message, with titles such as *Neue Zeit, Nation Europa, MUT, Der Republikaner* and *Deutsche National-Zeitung*. These range from the more 'respectable' *Deutschland Magazine*, the militantly anti-communist organ of the right-wing faction of the CDU/CSU, the 'Stahlhelmfraktion', to explicitly neo-nazi propaganda sheets such as the *FAP Nachrichten*, associated with Michael Kühnen's explicitly 'neonazi' Hitler-cult, the Action Front of National Socialists (Aktionsfront Nationaler Sozialisten – ANS). Generally, however, the 'new right' has avoided associating itself with the symbols of traditional Nazism and most of these publications preach what is in fact more of an extreme conservative message, though often this is similarly laced with xenophobia and racism. Most of

30. K. Giebel, *Mediendschungel. Eine kritische Bestandsaufnahme*, Stuttgart: Bleicher Verlag, 1983, p. 209.

these publications have a very tiny readership, but the *Deutsche National-Zeitung* is estimated to have achieved a weekly circulation as high as 130,000. Also, worth a special mention is *Der Republikaner*, the organ of the far-right Republican Party (Die Republikaner). This party burst into the national consciousness in January 1989 by winning nearly 10% of the vote in the West Berlin Land elections. *Der Republikaner* is extremely nationalist, populist and extremely conservative; it is estimated to have a monthly circulation of 50,000. The recent signs of a revival of the 'extreme right', especially in West Berlin, may have much to do with a general populist conservative reaction which has built up against the 'alternative' counter-culture which has appeared to thrive in West Germany, and again especially in West Berlin, since the late 1960s. This latter phenomenon, which relates to the issue of so-called 'new politics', will be explored later in this chapter.[31]

The 'Springer Press'

When talking about the 'mainstream' conservative orientation of much of the West German press, however, it is far more important to examine in greater detail the workings of the 'Springer press'. Although the party political link is not overt, it is still very real. Moreover, as seen, the Springer group enjoys a very special position of dominance in the West German press system. John Sandford has summarised the significance of the 'Springer press' succinctly: 'No discussion of the problem of press concentration in West Germany could overlook the publishing empire of Axel Cäsar Springer. Indeed, for many Springer is synonymous with all that has gone wrong with the post-war German press.'[32]

Axel Springer had launched upon his career young in pre-war Hamburg (where he had been born in 1912) working on a very modest publication called the *Altoner Nachrichten*, established by his father, whose main business was printing. During the Third

---

31. S. Jäger (ed.), *Rechtsdruck. Die Presse der Neuen Rechten*, Berlin and Bonn: Verlag J.H.W. Dietz Nachf. GmbH., 1988. The statistics are from p. 37 and p. 223.
32. See Sandford *The Mass Media*, p. 31.

Reich, the *Altoner Nachrichten* had been closed down and his father's printing works bought out by the Nazis. Subsequently, it suffered fatal war-damage. After the Nazi collapse, still in Hamburg, Springer found himself in the British zone of occupation. The difficulties experienced by his father's business meant that he was untainted by complicity in the Nazi crimes. Axel Springer therefore immediately opened negotiations with the British authorities to obtain a publishing licence. He relatively quickly acquired no less than three licences, no mean achievement considering the shortage of paper. First of all, Axel Springer founded the *Nordwestdeutsche Hefte*, a monthly critical journal which was modelled on the *Listener*, and *Hör Zu*, a listings magazine modelled on the *Radio Times*. Next Springer embarked on his long journey of conquest of the wider press market by relaunching the *Nordwestdeutsche Hefte* as a bi-monthly popular magazine called *Kristall*, with a very brash format aiming at a mass appeal, and by launching his first daily newspaper, the *Hamburger Abendblatt*, for which he also received a licence from the City of Hamburg with the blessing of the British. With its emphasis on the simple and the sensational, this latter paper anticipated the arrival in 1952 of the *Bild-Zeitung*. As mentioned, in 1953 the British sold *Die Welt* to Springer who thereby also obtained a leading quality paper for his fast-growing empire. Having thus established himself as a press magnate in his native Hamburg base, Springer soon set his sights on the former capital city of Berlin, where he bought the Ullstein publishing concern together with its well-known newspapers, the *Berliner Zeitung* and the *Berliner Morgenpost*. In 1959 he established a new headquarters for his press empire there, which later overlooked the Berlin Wall. This building provocatively flashed a neon sign message – 'Berlin bleibt frei' ('Berlin remains free') – across into East Berlin in a grand gesture of defiance of the division of Germany.

The 'New Journalism' of the Springer Press

Axel Springer brought a new kind of journalism to the German press. A central tenet was to practise a more personal, 'human' style of journalism, which was far more accessible to the masses than the traditional German press had been. It aimed to go far further in the brash commercial and 'penny-press' direction than the pre-war 'Generalanzeiger'. The 'new journalism' served the twin goals of selling more copy, and thereby serving to build the 'Springer empire', and at the same time fulfilling a self-given social and political mission. It cultivated a calculated sentimentality, promoting the (for the Germans) convenient and comforting message that the simple man is basically a good-hearted creature, but easily misled. In this spirit, Springer responded to the widespread aversion of the Germans during the 1950s and 1960s to any serious reflection.[33] Aided and abetted by the master of the 'Trivialroman' (literally 'trivial novel') Eduard Rhein, who wrote for *Nordwestdeutsche Hefte* and edited *Hör Zu* and *Kristall* during their formative years, Springer developed a formula based on an anodyne mixture of entertainment, serialised novels, puzzles, horoscopes, local sections, the heavy use of clichés and generally 'big-city romanticism'. All events seemed to be reduced to anecdote, the 'human interest' story now reigned supreme. Much of the content now focused on human catastrophes and sensationalism.

The new approach was best exemplified by the most spectacularly successful of the Springer papers, namely the *Bild-Zeitung*. With its limited vocabulary, lurid headlines and preoccupation with scandal, the *Bild-Zeitung* soon became the object of scorn by the intelligentsia. It seemed to amount to no less than a rude denial of the heavily intellectual 'German tradition' with its associated penchant for reasoning lead-articles, heavily descriptive reporting, its often high moralistic tone and its cultural, literary and philosophical 'feuilletons'. Apart from disarming the press of its objective critical function, the 'new journalism' undoubtedly contributed to the demobilisation of the political press, breaking like a tidal wave into the traditionally wide Social Democratic readership and enticing the workers into a

---

33. An anti-Springer student pamphlet distributed in West Berlin a few hours after the assassination attempt against Rudi Dutschke in 1968 carried the following slogan: 'Quote Axel Springer 1959: "Since the end of the war I have been convinced that the German reader wanted to avoid doing one thing above all, namely to reflect. I built my newspaper [i.e. the *'Bild-Zeitung'*] on this principle."' Cited in F. Brüseke and H.-M. Grosse-Ötringhaus, *Blätter von unten; Alternativzeitungen in der Bundesrepublik Deutschland*, Offenbach: Verlag 2000 GmbH., 1981, p. 11.

nominally 'classless' society. Fate and fortune were the new obsession, a sentimental 'lower middle-class' complacency, narrow-mindedness and smug contentment was the dominant ethos. It pointed the way to the 'affluent' society, confirmed the workings of the 'economic miracle' ('Wirtschaftswunder'), with its primacy to consumer/conformist values, and sought to construct a new agenda allowing little respect or tolerance to those standing beyond its cosy consensus.[34]

The Political 'Weltanschauung' of the Springer Press

Very quickly, the Springer press gained a right-wing image. Although Springer was never a member of any political party, both *Bild-Zeitung* and its more respectable stable-mate *Die Welt* bore witness to what Heinz-Dieter Müller has called Springer's 'political passion' and especially to his deep conviction that he had a special mandate to speak for the 'Volk'.[35] Indeed, the central concept of Springer's political credo was his belief in the 'Volk'. Springer's spiritual mentor was the conservative Weimar publicist and one-time chief editor of General Schleicher's christian-social *Täglische Rundschau*, Hans Zehrer, who had also cherished a special belief in the 'Volk' and had pleaded for stronger conservative political authority. After the war, Zehrer became Springer's right-hand man as chief editor of *Die Welt*. Adopting this leitmotif, Springer embarked on what might justifiably be termed a crusade to manufacture a consensus around a 'new nationalism'. According to Müller, this 'new nationalism' was a 'ragbag collection of mystical dreams of the Middle Ages, dynamic ideas of the late capitalist era, liberal ideas of the pre-industrial period and modern prescriptions for mass political leadership'.[36]

Unsurprisingly, therefore, Springer quickly became a fervent

---

34. On this 'new journalism' see, in particular: H.-D. Müller, *Der Springer-Konzern: Eine kritische Studie*, Munich: Piper, 1968 (also published in English, translated by J. Cole, as *Press Power: A Study of Axel Springer*, London: MacDonald, 1969), 'Die Schule des Neuen Journalismus: Das Hamburger Abendblatt', pp. 63–71. On the *Bild-Zeitung* see 'Ein deutsches Massenblatt: Bild', pp. 73–126 in the same.
35. See 'Der Verleger als Politiker', in Müller, *Der Springer Konzern*, pp. 185–210, p. 185.
36. Ibid., p. 191.

admirer of Chancellor Konrad Adenauer's paternalistic, highly conservative and semi-authoritarian style of 'Chancellor Democracy' ('Kanzlerdemokratie') and a healthy private correspondence ensued between them, in the course of which Springer is reputed to have constantly proffered the nation's political leader with political 'advice'. His only major disagreement with Adenauer occurred when the latter made West Germany's first tentative and exceedingly limited 'opening' towards Eastern Europe. Springer was a fierce opponent of any reconciliation whatsoever with the East. In many ways, the Springer press was quintessentially a child of the Cold War period of the 1950s, seeking to reconstruct German national sensibilities from the ignominy of the country's recent past and present division. During the later debate about Willy Brandt's 'normalisation' of West Germany's relations with the East and his recognition of the German Democratic Republic ('Ostpolitik') the Springer press adopted a militantly nationalist and anti-communist position. Springer's agitation over the 'Eastern' question sometimes verged on the irresponsibly belligerent and hysterically nationalist. For instance, during the 1961 Berlin crisis the Springer press attempted to whip up domestic German nationalist sentiment in order to pressurise President John Kennedy to take an aggressive hard-line against the Soviets. He is reported to have stated that 'if an uprising threatens in the "Zone" [i.e. the GDR], this time the West Berliners will not stand passively by to watch their fellow countrymen being shot by Soviet tanks' and also 'if there is no reunification, there will be war'. On another occasion, Springer called the GDR authorities 'the red descendants of the brownshirts'.[37]

Apart from the German Democratic Republic (always referred to as the 'so-called GDR' or in quotation-marks, although this feature is apparently about to be dropped at last), the main political target of the Springer press was the West German left. The Springer press was inclined to see subversion or decadence in every nook or cranny. During the *'Spiegel* Affair', the *Bild-Zeitung* reacted to (the Liberal) Augstein's arrest by announcing that 'treachery is a dangerous crime'.[38] The paper also accused

37. Ibid., p. 195.
38. Ibid., p. 206.

the moderate Social Democrat and world-famous West German author Günter Grass of being a 'red hooligan'.[39] Similarly, the reaction of the Springer press to the 1960s student movement was typical: they were variously accused of being 'rowdies', 'academic drop-outs' ('Gammler'), 'neurotics', 'communists', 'intellectual yobbos' ('geistige Halbstarke'), and a 'gang of hooligans' ('eine Handvoll Rabauken'). Even the more refined *Die Welt* railed against the 'intellectual unwashed' ('geistige Ungewaschenheit') and the 'red guard imitators of the ugly Peking original' ('Rote Garde, Abziehbild des häßlichen Pekinger Originals'). With not unusual licence, the Springer press reported a small and unsuccessful demonstration against the US vice-president Hubert Humphrey by a group of 'Happening-Anarchists' as an assassination attempt.[40]

Unsurprisingly, the Springer press in turn became a prime target for left-wing agitation. Following the assassination attempt on the left-wing student leader Rudi Dutschke in 1968, there was a furore. The Springer newspapers had constantly depicted Dutschke as a dangerous quasi-terrorist. In actual fact, Dutschke had been a restraining influence on the ultra hard-core within the German student movement and a proponent of peaceful demonstrations. The author of the assassination attempt duly declared himself in court to be an avid reader of *Bild-Zeitung* and he alleged that his image of Dutschke had been entirely conditioned by the Springer press. He even gave details about the newspaper commentaries that had inspired his actions. The left felt that here was a clear-cut case of incitement to violence. For a while, the student movement turned its full violence against buildings of the Springer press empire in Berlin and Hamburg.

The Springer press later contributed greatly to the hysterical reaction to terrorism in the 1970s and helped to create the 'witch-hunt' atmosphere that, for a brief period, disfigured West Germany's otherwise liberal image. This particular episode is brilliantly encaptured by Heinrich Böll's 1974 novel, *Die verlorene Ehre der Katharina Blum* (*The Lost Honour of Katharina Blum*). The

---

39. A. Klönne, 'Ein Super-Hugenberg', in B. Jansen and A. Klönne (eds.), *Imperium Springer: Macht und Manipulation*, Cologne: Pahl-Rugenstein Verlag, 1968, pp. 9–21, p. 10.
40. See Müller, *Der Springer Konzern*, p. 207.

methods of the Springer press were subsequently further exposed by a famous West German investigative journalist, Günter Wallraff, who infiltrated the *Bild-Zeitung* for a period and then wrote two highly critical books about his experiences as a 'Springer journalist'. In particular, Wallraff describes how the *Bild-Zeitung* relies on the precarious employment conditions it offers to many of its journalists as a powerful factor for 'editorial discipline'. Moreover, he exposes the way the editorial filter works often to completely distort the journalists' original reports. Beyond this, Wallraff alleges that the *Bild-Zeitung* is not averse to practising complete fabrication, without regard to the often tragic human consequences of its actions. Behind the trivial sensationalism, Wallraff detects a distinctly conservative 'Weltanschauung' at work. It must be said that Wallraff himself hardly gives the impression of political neutrality. Yet, the 'political methods' of the 'Springer press' have been confirmed by a number of critical academic works.[41]

Springer's political sensibilities (and limitations) have been succinctly summarised by Heinz-Dieter Müller as follows:

> he had no head for the art of political compromise or for the institutionalisation of political conflict. The pluralistic and liberal-democratic concern for form and procedure as well as content and goal was a foreign concept to him . . . communication, opinion construction ['Willensbildung'] and structuration in the political sense found no place in his 'Marktvolk' of consumers . . . he had all the anti-intellectualism and scepticism of liberal thinking of the archetypal self-made man.[42]

Springer's Campaign to Enter Broadcasting

During the 1970s and early 1980s the Springer press waged a

---

41. See G. Wallraff: *Der Aufmacher. Der Mann, der bei Bild Hans Esser war*, Cologne: Verlag Kiepenheuer und Witsch, 1977; *Zeugen der Anklage: Die 'Bild'-Beschreibung wird fortgesetzt*, Cologne: Verlag Kiepenheuer und Witsch, 1979; and, more recently, *Bild-Störung. Ein Handbuch*, Cologne: Verlag Kiepenheuer und Witsch, 1985. Also see: K. Arens, *Manipulation: Kommunikationspsychologische Untersuchung mit Beispielen aus Zeitungen des Springer-Konzerns*, Berlin: Wissenschaftsverlag Volker Spiess. Also see: P. Brokmeier (ed.), *Kapitalismus und Pressefreiheit. Am Beispiel Springer*, Frankfurt/Main: Europäische Verlagsanstalt, 1969.
42. See Müller, *Der Springer Konzern*, p. 191 and p. 193.

relentless media campaign to demand access for the publishers to the broadcasting system ('Verlegerfernsehen'). Not content with the degree of concentration of the media, to which he had greatly contributed, Springer was eager to branch into 'multi-media' operations. As will be seen, this fuelled the controversy which came to surround this issue during the recent period (see Chapters 5 and 6). In the end, the Springer group was to achieve this prized goal.

State Policy on Press-Concentration

The need for state action to combat press-concentration thus became increasingly apparent and calls for a redress of the situation by political action climaxed in the strident demands of the student movement of the late 1960s. Against the background of mounting public concern about the dominant position of the Springer group in the press system, the state was finally compelled to act.

The 'Günther-Bericht'

On 11 May 1967, during the CDU/SPD 'Grand Coalition', the Bundestag voted to establish an official commission of inquiry to examine the question of press concentration. The commission had the unwieldy title of 'Commission to Examine the Threat to the Economic Existence of the Press and the Consequences of Press-Concentration for the Freedom of Opinion in the FRG' ('Kommission zur Untersuchung der Gefährdung der wirtschaftlichen Existenz von Presseunternehmen und der Folgen der Konzentration für die Meinungsfreiheit in der BRD'). In the classic West German 'policy style', the commission was pluralistically composed of representatives of the relevant interest groups, among them the press, public-sector broadcasting and the general public. This included diverse publishers, journalists, and the directors-general ('Intendanten') of radio and TV corporations.

Mercifully, the title of the subsequent report of the commission was popularly abbreviated to simply the 'Günther Report' ('Günther-Bericht') after the name of the commission's chairman, Dr Eberhard Günther. It was duly submitted to the federal government on 14 June 1968 (still during the 'Grand Coalition'). However, this document noted that concentration had not yet adversely affected press freedom, but that it threatened to do so. It defined the threat of impairment of the freedom of the press as beginning when one single press concern obtained 20% of the total market share (actually achieved by the Springer press in the field of the 'Tagespresse'). However, it went on to suggest that infringement of the 'freedom of the press' would only 'directly' follow from a state of affairs in which a single press concern had accumulated a 40% marketshare of all dailies and Sunday papers.

Nevertheless, the commission now recommended a catalogue of measures against press concentration. In particular, it produced the following suggestions of ways to 'eliminate the consequences of concentration for the freedom of opinion'. Firstly, it suggested that there should be a regulatory limitation on the market-shares gained by individual press concerns. Secondly, the report recommended the drawing up of annual reports on the situation of the press for the Bundestag. Thirdly, it suggested the periodic official publication of figures making clear the pattern of ownership of the press. Finally, it suggested the creation of economic 'counterbalances to the market'. In particular, it adopted the demands of the BDZV for tax relief and cheap credit facilities for the press sector.[43]

However, most of the commission's recommendations met with an ambivalent response from the BDZV. On the question of structural policies for the press the BDZV was divided internally. Many smaller and financially weaker publishers agreed with the report's recommendations, while the larger and financially stronger publishers were naturally content with the existing press structure. In the event, the federal government only took up the commission's recommendations for the instigation of periodic structural reports on the media and for legally requiring property and stock reports by the publishers. The government had guaranteed credit and tax relief for small pub-

43. *Günther-Bericht. Schlußbericht der Kommission zur Untersuchung der Gefährdung der wirtschaftlichen Existenz von Presseunternehmen und der Folgen der Konzentration für die Meinungsfreiheiten in der Bundesrepublik – Pressekommission*, Bonn: Bundestags-Drucksache, V/3122 von 3. Juli 1968.

lishers in 1967 and small and medium-sized publishing houses already benefited from funds made available from the European Recovery Programme. However, the report's most radical suggestion, namely its recommendation of limitations on marketshares in the press sector, was dropped in face of the immediate strong opposition of the most influential publishers who argued that it would infringe the constitutional principle of 'freedom of information' ('Informationsfreiheit').

The main official action was a decision to produce a series of 'Media Reports' ('Medienberichte') in order to provide a full official account concerning the state of media news information, the state of the publishing markets, and interestingly also (in 1978) an account of emerging developments in the fields of the new media and international communications policy. The resultant official 'Medienberichte' of 1974 and 1978 were produced by the Interior Ministry (Bundesministerium des Innern) and by the Economics Ministry (Bundesministerium für Wirtschaft) in collaboration with the Press and Information Office of the Federal Government (Presse- und Informationsamt der Bundesregierung). By this means, policy-makers were at least to be kept informed.[44]

The Measures Taken by the 'Social-Liberal' (SPD/FDP) Government (1969–82) Against Press-Concentration

The SPD-led 'social-liberal' government that came to power in 1969 was confronted by a combination of continuing public concern about press-concentration and powerful political pressure from the party's 'grass-roots', urging action against the Springer press in particular. The 1968 'extra-parliamentary' opposition had radicalised the party's influential youth organisation, the so-called 'Young Socialists' ('Jungsozialisten' or simply 'Jusos') and this intra-party formation became a strong national faction pressurising the party leadership for radical reforms. Moreover, the party leadership itself, under Willy Brandt (who

---

44. See Kepplinger, *Massenkommunikation*, p. 73. See *Bericht der Bundesregierung über die Lage von Presse und Rundfunk in der Bundesrepublik Deutschland (1974)*, Bonn: Bundestags-Drucksache 7/2104, 1974; and *Bericht der Bundesregierung über die Lage von Presse und Rundfunk in der Bundesrepublik Deutschland. 'Medienbericht' (1978)*, Bonn: Bundestags-Drucksache VIII/2264, 1978.

was also Chancellor between 1969-74), was committed to 'daring more democracy'. The moment seemed appropriate to reintroduce the prospect of stricter regulation of the press onto the policy-making agenda.

Accordingly, the SPD-led 'social-liberal' government drew up plans to introduce framework legislation (a 'Presserechtsrahmengesetz') for the press sector. As will be seen, this radical orientation of the SPD did not last long. Under the Chancellorship of Helmut Schmidt (after 1974) the SPD adopted an increasingly right-wing stance. As a result, these plans for press reform were destined to come to nothing. The only notable concrete actions to combat press concentration actually taken during the period of 'social-liberal' government were: firstly, the granting of further credits from the publicly controlled 'reconstruction bank' (Kreditanstalt für Wiederaufbau) and the widening of tax allowances to favour the smaller publishers; and secondly, the amendment of the 'Law Against Restrictions on Competition' ('Gesetz gegen Wettbewerbsbeschränkungen') in 1976 to include specific reference to the press (§§ 22-4). As a result of the latter measure, the definition of market dominance ('Marktbeherrschung') and therefore of the point at which mergers became notifiable for merger control ('Fusionskontrolle') became much more strictly defined for the press than for all other sectors of the economy. Until this point, the Federal Republic's general cartel law ('Kartell-Recht') had only embraced mergers and amalgamations of companies with a gross turnover of at least DM 500 million. However, the companies involved in amalgamations and mergers of the press did not usually achieve anything like this volume of turnover. The SPD-led 'social-liberal' government therefore lowered the critical threshold to DM 25 million for the case of the press. Mergers between press concerns with a total turnover of at least DM 25 million were thus made notifiable to the Federal Cartel Office (Bundeskartellamt).

The Federal Cartel Office (Bundeskartellamt)

However, it should not be presumed that the Federal Cartel Office has been very interventionist, nor that the problem of press concentration has been solved by the mere threat of its

Controversies Over the West German Press System

intervention. In practice, the Federal Cartel Office has been generally disinclined to prevent mergers when to do so would result in the collapse of a paper. Nor can it be assumed that mergers have always been viewed unfavourably by the SPD. In December 1975 the *Westdeutsche Allgemeine Zeitung* (700,000 circulation) was allowed to merge with two smaller papers to create its virtual 'social-liberal' newspaper monopoly from Hesse across the Ruhr and as far as the Dutch border.

The best known instance of intervention by the Federal Cartel Office to prevent a merger occurred in November 1981, when the Burda publishing group was refused a 25% participation in the Springer concern. On this occasion, the Federal Cartel Office ruled that the proposed merger of press empires would have created an unacceptable degree of concentration in the publishing sector. Another significant intervention of the Federal Cartel Office did prevent the Springer group from acquiring a majority stake in the Münchner Zeitungsverlag (publisher of the *Münchner Merkur* and a major regional influence in Bavaria).[45] Generally, however, the process of concentration has continued despite the Federal Cartel Office, and the dominant position of the Springer press has remained intact.

The 'Press Statistics Law' ('Gesetz über eine Pressestatistik')

One further limited measure should be mentioned, although it hardly constituted a radical step to effectively combat concentration. Again under the initiative of the 'social-liberal' government, the Bundestag passed on 1 April 1975 a legal basis for the annual publication of press statistics, to be carried out by the Federal Statistics Office (Statistisches Bundesamt) in Wiesbaden. This law placed an obligation on press concerns to provide the federal authorities with relevant information about the legal form of the company, type and number of the workforce, turnover according to type, various different kinds of costs (salaries, wages, royalties, production, distribution, etc.), name, manner of publication of the newspapers and magazines, as well as their sales circulation, prices and advertising rates. However, arguably even this rather limited measure missed the

---
45. See La Roche and Maasen, *Massenmedien*, p. 96.

mark: the basis of the newspaper statistics was not to be 'editorial units' ('publizistische Einheiten') but rather the combined main and sub-editions ('Haupt- und Nebenausgaben'). The results of the 'Pressestatistik' are therefore only partly comparable with the long-standing surveys conducted by Walter J. Schütz and give a rather misleading insight into the true extent of press concentration.[46]

Legal Obstacles to Press Reform

Notwithstanding this marked deficit of policy-making by the federal authorities, radical demands continued for more effective economic control mechanisms for the press sector, including calls for stricter preventative merger control ('Fusionkontrolle'), limitation of the market-share of publishers, limitations on the levels of circulation of certain newspapers, and even the breaking-up of certain concerns and the nationalisation of the press. However, leading legal experts have been quick to point out that each of these suggested measures (of which only 'preventative merger control' was ever partially achieved by the Federal Cartel Office) risk offending against the basic rights enshrined in Article 5 of the Basic Law, notably those relating to 'information and press freedom'. In West Germany, any questioning of the private commercial organisation of the press and any initiative that might be interpreted as an attempt at state intervention inevitably invites serious examination in the light of constitutional law. In the case of the press (if not broadcasting), the weight of constitutional legal authority has seemed to be on the side of the publishers.[47]

The Debate About 'Internal Press Freedom'

The public concern and debate about press concentration fuelled

---

46. See Kepplinger, *Massenkommunikation*, p. 74.
47. On the legal debate see P. Lerche, *Verfassungsrechtliche Fragen zur Pressekonzentration*, Berliner Abhandlungen zum Presserecht, Heft 14, Berlin: Duncker und Humblot, 1971; and H. Schneider, *Verfassungsrechtliche Grenzen einer gesetzlichen Regelung des Pressewesens*, Berliner Abhandlungen zum Presserecht, Heft 15, Berlin: Duncker und Humblot, 1971.

another of the major media debates of the late 1960s and 1970s, namely the controversy over reforms of the internal organisational and decision-making structures of the publishing houses themselves. This debate was conducted under the slogan of 'internal press freedom' ('innere Pressefreiheit'). It actually originated during the immediate post-war period in demands made by the journalists' associations (the DJV and the DJU) for management participation ('Mitbestimmung') by the newspapers' staff in editorial and organisational questions. At that time, as seen, the journalists' organisations had not enjoyed a strong bargaining position and their demands had been resisted fiercely by the powerfully organised publishers and generally ignored by the political decision-makers.

While the CDU/CSU had remained the dominant force in West German politics throughout the 1950s and much of the 1960s the political environment for such a drastic reform had seemed to be exceedingly unfavourable. But as seen, by the 1970s the political situation had radically changed. The SPD was actually in power (in coalition with the Liberals). In addition, the shock waves of the 1968 movement had radicalised many journalists. Under these new circumstances the journalists' organisations gained new confidence and the publishers were compelled to face up to the need to enter into collective bargaining on the issue in the years that followed.

The Journalists' Demands for Codetermination Rights and an Amendment of the 'Tendenzschutz'

The demands for 'internal press freedom' placed full-square on the political agenda the thorny question of the rights of a publisher to set the general ideological and philosophical orientation of a publication in order to interfere with specific editorial questions. As seen, in 1952 the federal government had anchored extensive employees' codetermination ('Mitbestimmung' or management participation) rights for most areas of industry in a 'works constitution law' ('Betriebsverfassungsgesetz'). However, this law had restricted management codetermination rights of employees in so-called 'Tendenz' concerns (the 'Tendenzschutz'). This restriction applied to firms which had a distinct moral, philosophical or political vocation, and it included the publishing houses. In the late 1960s, the journalists' organisations now demanded that the provisions of the general 'Mitbestimmung' laws should henceforth apply in an unrestricted and total fashion to publishing houses as well. They argued that the press should no longer be exempted in any way from existing general regulations for employees' codetermination within the firm. As well as seeking a greater say in editorial policy, the journalists also aimed to gain codecision-making rights in all matters of editorial staff policy and even in the economic affairs of the firm. In particular, the journalists' associations sought an explicit demarcation or delineation of competences ('Kompetenzen') between publishers and editorial units. Moreover, the journalists called for a new federal legislative ruling for the press which would anchor their specific demands in law. Although there was some difference between them over the details of policy, the journalists' organisations, the DJU and the DJV, and the print workers' union IG Druck und Papier, were all united in the fundamental demand for the development of management participation for editorial staff in all important areas of their newspapers and magazines.[48]

The Policy Statements of the Political Parties

Mindful of the public concern over press concentration and the evident tendency towards concentration of media power, the first special 'media policy' ('medienpolitisch') statements of the SPD and the FDP coalition parties drawn up in the early 1970s emphasised the connection between 'internal press freedom' ('innere Pressefreiheit') and the proper functioning of the pluralist press system. During this period, both parties committed themselves to the principle of introducing measures to strengthen 'internal press freedom' in both the press and broadcasting sectors. In particular, they appeared to be prepared to

---

48. For very detailed information on the background to the journalists' campaign see K.-D. Funke, *Innere Pressefreiheit – zu Problemen der Organisation von Journalisten*, unter Mitarbeit von W. Brede von der IG Druck und Papier zur Mediengewerkschaft, Pullach/Munich: Verlag Dokumentation, 1972; on the specific demands of the DJV for legislation on 'internal press freedom' see *Media Perspektiven. Dokumentation*, no. 1, 1978, p. 36.

introduce legislation which would anchor a number of extensive management participation rights for journalists in law. On the other hand, the CDU/CSU remained highly sceptical about the introduction of management participation rights for editorial staff.[49]

The Position of the Publishers' Associations

The publishers' associations were fiercely opposed to any attempt to curtail the rights of management in the affairs of the publishing concerns, and more particularly, the rights of the proprietors effectively to determine general editorial policy. They argued that management participation for editorial staff would endanger the 'free' functioning of the press system. Somewhat ironically, they also held that it would infringe the constitutionally enshrined principle that organs of the media should be kept free from any special interests. The BDZV had always continually emphasised that 'press freedom' must be taken to include the freedom of organisation of the newspaper publishing houses. Accordingly, the line of the BDZV was that a standardisation of the organisational and decision-making structures in newspaper publishing houses would be against the principles of the Basic Law and therefore unconstitutional ('grundgesetzwidrig').[50]

All the same, in view of the new political salience of the issue, by the end of the 1960s the publishers had come to accept the necessity of being seen to engage in negotiations with the journalists' organisations. In particular, the BDZV was concerned to preempt the possibility of state intervention and the enactment of federal legislation. In order to avert this threat, the BDZV was prepared to give consideration to the alternative policy of arriving at some kind of collective agreement ('tarifvertragliche Vereinbarung') about the cooperation be-

49. See, for example, the FDP *Liberale Leitlinien zur Medienpolitik*, section III on 'Innere Pressefreiheit'; also see the media policy decisions of the 1971 SPD party conference, namely 'Die Massenmedien. Beschlüsse des Parteitages 1971 zur Medienpolitik', partly reproduced in *Media Perspektiven*, 1971, pp. 297–306; and the decision of the 'mass media commission' of the SPD's party executive committee of February 1974, the 'Beschluß der Massenmedien-Kommission beim SPD Parteivorstand'.

50. See Schulze, *Der Bundesverband Deutscher Zeitungsverleger*, p. 56.

tween publishers and editors. By this means, they aimed to retain a greater degree of control of the situation.

The Negotiations Between the Publishers and the Journalists' Organisations

From 1969 onwards the BDZV and the journalists' associations entered upon a series of difficult negotiations about the introduction of a standardised formula for cooperation between publishers and editorial staff throughout the Federal Republic. Negotiations ebbed and flowed, punctuated by frequent breaks, throughout the 1970s, but no progress was made. Throughout this process, there was much to suggest that the two sides were not very seriously prepared to reach a consensus. In particular, the BDZV deliberately tried to create the impression that the trade unions were uninterested in productive cooperation and were more intent on undermining the foundation of the present press structure. The representatives of the publishers' associations even went as far as to question the loyalty of the unions to the constitution ('Verfassungstreue'). One executive member of IG Druck und Papier, Detlev Hensche, became a very special target of the publishers' venom: he was projected almost as an 'enemy' of the constitution. Moreover, as a basic condition of entering into the negotiations, the BDZV demanded that the existing structures of the press should not be called into question.[51]

The Question of a Federal 'Press Framework Law'

Meanwhile, the government appeared to vacillate and eventually retreat from the affair. When first elected, the SPD-led 'social-liberal' government had immediately announced its intention to enact a federal 'press framework law' ('Bundespresserahmengesetz'). The SPD government of Willy Brandt had been carried away by a wave of reforming zeal and had promptly begun to work towards drafting the promised law which was to contain the core of all future regulations concern-

---

51. W. Hoffmann-Riem, *Innere Pressefreiheit als politische Aufgabe*, Neuwied und Darmstadt: Luchterhand, 1979, pp. 17–19.

ing the relationship of publishers and editors. Over the next few years a number of preliminary drafts for such a law were indeed produced and circulated among the policy makers by the Interior Ministry. The resultant draft law ('Referentenentwurf') produced at the beginning of August 1974 gave an indication of the way the government's own thinking had developed.[52]

It was immediately clear that were this draft law to be duly enacted it would have the consequence of reducing drastically the influence which the newspaper proprietors had hitherto enjoyed on the final shape of their newspapers. It contained important provisions for the election of 'editorial staff representatives' with considerable 'Mitbestimmung' rights. While the law continued to reserve to the publishers the theoretical right to decide the fundamental stance of the newspapers (paragraph 10), it so extended the rights of the editors and journalists that the publishers would in practice encounter serious obstacles to determining the future line of editorial policy. In particular, paragraph 13 stipulated that:

> within the framework of the general editorial policy of his newspaper or periodical . . . the journalist shall enjoy freedom in regard to shaping the content of his individual journalistic contributions; to this extent, individual instructions by the publisher are inadmissible. No journalist shall be required, in any published work, to represent an opinion which, taking due account of all personal considerations, is irreconcilable with his conscience.

Moreover, the publishers' ability to influence editorial policy by means of their powers of appointment to the newspapers' staff was also to be severely curtailed by the extension of the 'Mitbestimmung' rights of editors and journalists. In particular, 'editorial staff representatives' were to be given consultation rights in matters relating to the appointment and dismissal of chief editors (paragraphs 14 and 15). In turn, in the crucial matter of the appointment and dismissal of individual journalists the

---

52. This draft and earlier drafts are reproduced by W. Hoffmann-Riem/N. Plander in *Rechtsfragen der Pressereform. Verfassungsrechtliche und betriebsverfassungsrechtliche Anmerkungen zum Entwurf eines Presserahmengesetzes*, Baden-Baden: Nomos, 1977; also see *Press Laws. Documents on Politics and Society in the Federal Republic of Germany*, Bonn: Inter Nationes, 1980, pp. 9–12.

agreement of the chief editor was required (paragraph 16). In fact, the draft foresaw such a heavy degree of regulation that Helmut Schmidt (SPD) was supposed to have described it as an example of 'typically German superperfection'.[53] Indeed, after Helmut Schmidt became Chancellor in 1974, following Willy Brandt's resignation over the Guillaume spy scandal, the draft law was suddenly dropped in the face of the immediate forceful opposition that it had meanwhile provoked from the publishers. For their part, the journalists' organisations, and the left more generally, saw this retreat as a hugely symbolic capitulation to economic and media giants. A leading West German media expert, who was involved in the debate, Wolfgang Hoffmann-Riem, concluded that the developments of these years: 'hardly awaken the impression of a strong political will to undertake the political task of building up press freedom. . . . Presumably, the political pressure in favour of the law was estimated to be less strong or less explosive than the potential pressure against it.'[54]

State of Progress on Editorial Statutes

By the end of the decade, the political zest for combating press concentration and extending management participation rights to editorial staff within the press sector (and indeed also broadcasting – see following chapter) had all but expired. Ever since the mid to late 1960s, the evident degree of press concentration and the power of the publishers in the Federal Republic had occasioned much alarm. As a result, the need for political action had been much discussed. However, apart from the introduction of legislation to subject mergers in the press sector to greater control (the 'Pressefusionkontrolle' of 1976), which as suggested was distinctly limited in its practical effects, no other concrete political action had actually been taken.

There were a few individual cases in which in-company agreements ('Statuten') had been drawn up between publishing concerns and their editorial staff, granting the latter limited rights of consultation and involvement in policy decisions. One notable success was the negotiation by IG Druck und Papier of fairly

---

53. See Schulze, *Der Bundesverband Deutscher Zeitungsverleger*, pp. 55–6.
54. See Hoffmann-Riem, *Innere Pressefreiheit*, pp. 17–18.

extensive codetermination rights for the editorial staff and the works council ('Betriebsrat') within SPD-owned printing and publishing concerns, principally the party newspaper *Vorwärts*. In several other newspaper and periodical editorial departments, the representatives of employees and editorial staff had managed to negotiate editorial statutes providing for a more limited degree of management participation. For example, in-company statutes of this kind had been introduced by *Stern*, the *Mannheimer Morgen Zeitung*, the *Abendzeitung*, the *Rhein-Zeitung*, the *Saarbrücker-Zeitung*, the *Süddeutsche Zeitung*, the *Kölner Stadtanzeiger*, the *Südwestpresse*, the weekly *Die Zeit* and the monthly *Capital*.[55]

However, by the turn of the decade (1979/80) the question of editorial management participation by editors and journalists was no longer a major theme of public policy making. On the side of the journalists' associations resignation and indifference reigned, on the side of the publishers there was great relief and satisfaction at the return of peace and quiet. By the time of the collapse of the 'social-liberal' coalition in late 1982, there was still no federal press framework legislation on the statute book. Moreover, many of the 'editorial statutes' ('Redaktionsstatuten') had, in the meantime, collapsed. Of the relatively small number that had been signed, fewer still survived. Besides which, most journalists had meanwhile come to concentrate upon more pressing problems, notably the state of the labour market in the depressed 1980s and, in particular, the controversy over the introduction of new technologies in both the press and broadcasting sectors.[56]

The Conflict Over the Introduction of New Technologies

During the 1970s, the focus of public controversy shifted from the question of 'internal press freedom' to the effects of a technological revolution, which was bringing momentous

55. See Haler, *Basic Law Guarantees Freedom of Opinion*, p. 28.
56. See Hoffmann-Riem, *Innere Pressefreiheit*, pp. 14–15; also on the theme of 'editorial statutes' ('Redaktionsstatuten') see C. Holtz-Bacha, *Mitspracherechte für Journalisten – Redaktionsstatuten in Presse und Rundfunk*, Cologne: Studienverlag Hayit, 1986. Serie Kommunikation.

Media and Media Policy in West Germany

consequences for the press sector. Traditional typewriters and typesetting machines were being increasingly replaced by 'telematic' terminals and computers.

On the one hand, the BDZV argued that the introduction of computerised text systems now offered small and medium-sized publishing houses new opportunities for survival. In the view of the publishers at least, the new technologies would contribute to the maintenance of a diverse and pluralistic press. The BDZV argued that the introduction of new newspaper technologies was not dependent on the size of the publishing houses, and, indeed, the small publishers had the most to gain from them. The new technologies were now even presented by the BDZV as the very prerequisite for the continuing competitiveness of many publishers. In particular, photocomposition, it was argued, lent itself to cost-cutting by small and medium-sized publishers. Accordingly, the BDZV was able to argue a powerful case that electronic systems worked against concentration tendencies.[57]

On the other hand, during the 1970s trade union concern over the new technologies steadily mounted. The trade unions pointed to the danger of increased press-concentration, arguing that small firms would simply not be able to afford the costs of modernisation and would therefore not be able to compete. Moreover, they drew attention to the obvious threats of unemployment and deskilling. In addition, they feared the effect of the new technologies on the base of union power itself. The direness of the situation was vividly summarised by Erwin Ferlemann, the Chairman of the IG Druck und Papier, in 1985 when he stated that 'the new editorial systems are the worst strike breakers of all'. The unions now feared that the new technologies would allow the publishers to continue to produce newspapers even when strikebound.[58]

It should be explained that the print workers have a very special place in the history of the German labour movement. German printworkers had been the first workers in the country

---

57. For a summary of arguments representative of this position in favour of the new technologies see C. Mast, 'Der Einzug der Elektronik in das Pressewesen', in *Der Presse in der deutschen Medienlandschaft*, Bundeszentrale für politische Bildung, 1985, pp. 44–5.
58. Ibid., p. 44.

112

to organise themselves into a union, in 1866. As a result, the IG Druck und Papier was rather inclined to perceive itself as having a 'vanguard' role in the post-war German labour movement. During the 1970s and 1980s, the IG Druck engaged in three major episodes of industrial action: in 1976 over wages, in 1978 in order to obtain safeguards against new technology-induced rationalisations and, linked to this latter campaign, in 1984 in order to obtain a 35-hour working week. It has been suggested that an important factor for the more aggressive stance adopted by IG Druck during the late 1970s and 1980s was the increasing influence within the union of Detlef Hensche, one of a new generation of more left-wing union leaders who had come to occupy important positions within the trade union movement by this time. The publisher of *Die Zeit*, Gerd Bucerius, described him in 1976 as the 'Ludendorff' behind IG Druck leader Mahlein's 'Hindenburg'.[59]

The 1978 Strike Over New Technology in the Print Industry

The most serious strike occurred in 1978 as a result of the union's demand for safeguards against the adverse effects of rationalisations arising from the introduction of new technologies in the newspaper industry. The print workers' union had called for no less than a written guarantee of jobs: IG Druck demanded a 'Rationalisierungsschutz', namely 'protection' for all those in the industry who would be adversely affected by rationalisation. The employers were prepared to provide retraining for some of the technical workforce but they also wanted to be able to make large numbers redundant. The unions were unimpressed by the employers' suggestion that the victims of redundancy plans would be helped by means of legally prescribed 'social plans'. In essence, the employers wanted the journalists themselves to perform many of the technical functions previously performed by other categories of the workforce (e.g. feeding material, correcting it, etc.). However, the IG Druck und Papier and the main journalists' associa-

59. P. Klemm, *Machtkampf einer Minderheit; der Tarifkonflikt in der Druckindustrie*, Cologne: Informedia Verlags GmbH, 1984, p. 17. This is an account of the series of industrial actions by the printworkers in the late 1970s and early 1980s written from a pro-business viewpoint.

tion, the DJV, proceeded from the principle of securing a fixed period of job security for technical personnel and a clear-cut formula for the demarcation of responsibilities between the technical production work and the editorial work. In particular, they demanded that text composition (preparation and formation as well as correction) should remain a task of the technical personnel. On the other hand, these suggestions were categorically rejected by the employers, the newspaper and magazine publishers.

On 8 February IG Druck launched a series of limited ('temporary' or 'befristet') protest strikes which affected a total of 21 newspapers with a circulation of 4 million, mainly in the country's larger cities and regional capitals. As the action escalated, a number of indefinite ('unbefristet') selective strikes ('Schwerpunktstreiks') began. On 5 March over 100 newspaper publishing houses then staged a 48-hour lockout in solidarity with the strike-bound firms.[60] According to the account of the strike subsequently given by the 'Medienbericht der Bundesregierung', in the end the strikes affected around 2,300 workers. On the other hand, the lockouts affected around 40,000 workers in around 600 concerns. After the continued failure of negotiations, on 14 March 1978 the employers' side called for a nationwide lockout of technical personnel. As the result, no less than 327 of the around 400 West German daily newspapers failed to appear from 15 March onwards. By this time, the journalists had added their active support to the striking printworkers, by refusing to produce 'emergency' papers. This situation was quite unique in the history of the German press. Chancellor Helmut Schmidt himself made a public televised appeal to the two sides to make every effort to produce a speedy settlement.[61]

The Collective Agreement on the Introduction of New Technology

Not until the dispute had involved official arbitration did the two sides at last reach agreement on a 'Collective Contract over the Introduction and Application of Computerised Text Systems' ('Tarifvertrag über die Einführung und Anwendung

60. Ibid., p. 16.
61. See Giebel, *Mediendschungel*, pp. 217–18.

Controversies Over the West German Press System

rechnergesteuerter Textsysteme'). This contract recognised the undesirability of obstructing technical progress but it also took into account the need for social safeguards. In fact, this collective agreement formed the model for similar regulations in neighbouring European countries such as Denmark, Austria, Italy and Switzerland.

The agreement was a considerable victory for the printworkers, in that the latter had managed to wring a sizeable number of important concessions from the employers' side. Many of their original demands had been met, if not in entirety at least to a very important extent. The agreement contained a large measure of protection for workers displaced by the new technologies. To be more precise, it stipulated that design, composition, printing and correcting work should be carried out exclusively by skilled printers for a period of eight years after the introduction of the new technology. The continued employment of skilled printers should be guaranteed by an agreed standardised system of advertising vacancies and hiring labour. Printworkers who were not skilled sufficiently to be able to work with new equipment were to be retrained for new occupations, preferably within the same plant. If this were not possible, financial assistance was to be given where labour mobility was required. The settlement also gave to skilled printers a six-year guarantee of wages comparable to their former status, so as to avoid downgrading. It included generous provisions for compensation in cases of redundancy, including a range of social security measures. It also laid down health and safety standards for work with visual display units (VDUs) (breaks, medical checks, etc.). In this aspect, the agreement was a forerunner in many respects of the fairly widespread VDU agreements concluded in the Federal Republic at works council and company level in a number of industrial sectors.[62] It was also agreed that the introduction of computerised text systems and their programming should not impair journalistic work, especially the 'creative freedom' of the editorial staff. VDU terminals were only to be used by journalists for reading and writing texts.

---

62. European Trade Union Institute, *Negotiating Technological Change – A Review of Trade Union Approaches to the Introduction of New Technology in Western Europe*, ETUI, 1982, p. 44.

They could only be called upon to work on them if their previous written permission had been obtained. Journalists were thus given the right not to have to work with VDU terminals, if such work did not suit them or if a medical certificate suggested that they were ill-advised to do so.[63]

The employers' side consoled themselves with the knowledge that the unions had admitted the principle of the need to introduce the new technologies and that, after the stipulated period of time, they would be able to proceed with rationalisation with much greater freedom. They also resolved to take important steps to prepare for any future industrial action. Accordingly, the BDZV decided on 17 October 1978 to establish a support fund to help the publishers most hurt by the strike and also to prepare a special support system for similar industrial disputes in the future. Provision for this fund was then entered into the statutes of the BDZV.[64]

The Question of the Right to Strike in the Newspaper Industry

After this serious outbreak of industrial action, a legal debate predictably took place in the Federal Republic about the question of whether the fundamental right of 'information and press freedom' enshrined in constitutional law ('Grundrecht der Informations- und Pressefreiheit' – Article 5 of the Basic Law) had been infringed by the industrial action in the print industry. The matter was settled by a key ruling of the Federal Court of Justice (Bundesgerichtshof). The latter judged that strikes against newspaper concerns generally did not infringe the fundamental right of press freedom and were fundamentally permissible. In the Court's view, the right of the general public to information had to be accorded a very high value, but this view was qualified by the statement that no such rights could be considered infringed if a certain newspaper simply failed to appear over a limited period of time. The court also suggested that a key labour law banning strikes in essential services ('lebenswichtige Betriebe') was also inapplicable in the case of newspapers.

63. See Giebel, *Mediendschungel*, pp. 219–20.
64. See Schulze, *Der Bundesverband Deutscher Zeitungsverleger*, p. 57.

However, the Bundesgerichtshof left open the possibility that certain forms of industrial action in the newspaper industry might go so far in scale, endurance, form or aims as to be considered to affect the core and substance of a free press. Conceivable cases of illegality were strikes aiming to prevent the appearance of the totality of newspapers and also strikes targeting specific areas of the press, such as newspapers with a certain political orientation (e.g. the 'Springer press'). In this debate, the publishers' case had been gravely weakened by the fact that the lockouts which they had initiated in response to the printworkers' strike action had actually prevented the appearance of far more newspapers than had the strikers themselves.[65]

The 'Alternative' Press

Finally, no overview of the West German press system would be complete without a mention of the spontaneous and prolific flowering of 'alternative' newspapers during the 1970s and 1980s. In probably the most detailed study of this phenomenon to date, Kurt Weichler suggests that the initial spark was the distribution of a pamphlet by a Cologne 'citizens' initiative group' ('Bürgerinitiative') in 1973. By the mid-1970s a veritable explosion of 'alternative' publications had occurred, carrying such flamboyant, pretentious and often bizarre titles as *Flaschenöffner* (Recklinghausen), *das Ruhr Volksblatt* (Gelsenkirchen), the *Stadtstreicher* (Mannheim) and Daniel Cohn-Bendit's *Pflasterstrand* (Frankfurt). Other well-known titles were the *Münchner Stadtzeitung* (Munich), the *Hamburger Rundschau* (Hamburg), and *die tageszeitung* (Berlin). As already mentioned, the latter publication has become so successful that it now numbers among the few truly national newspapers or 'überregionale Zeitungen' in the country.[66]

In fact, the genre covers a wide and diverse range of publications. Some, known as 'Stadtzeitungen' and 'Stadtteilzeitungen' reflected the attempt to promote a sense of local community, to

---

65. See Giebel, *Medienschungel*, p. 220.
66. K. Weichler, *Gegendruck. Lust und Frust der alternativen Presse*, Reinbek/ Hamburg: Rowohlt Verlag, 1983, p. 22, and p. 31.

act as a new forum for citizens' action, and to focus on local social and political issues. 'Stadtmagazine', such as the highly successful West Berlin equivalents of *Time Out* called *Tip* and *Zitty*, differed from 'Stadtzeitungen' in that they contained more cultural information such as cinema and theatre programmes and they tended to carry more local advertising. Others, such as the well-known Bavarian anti-nuclear magazine *radioaktiv* or the West Berlin-based *Zeitschrift für Lärmbekämpfung* ('journal for noise abatement'), concentrated on single issues and could be described variously as 'Initiativenzeitungen' or 'Initiativeblätter'. Even more esoterically, the so-called 'Scene-Blätter' pointed to 'alternative' lifestyles, were even 'ghetto-oriented', and self-consciously aimed at fringe groups ('Randgruppen') and minorities (a good example being the West Berlin *Instandbesetzer Post* or 'squatters' post'). Many were highly political, such as the symbolically named Frankfurt-based *Informationsdienst zur Verbreitung unterbliebener Nachrichten* or *ID* (literally 'Information Service for Disseminating Unreported News') and the Marburg-based *Antiimperialistische Informations Bulletin* or *AIB* ('Anti-Imperialist Information Bulletin'). Although it is difficult to generalise about such a multifaceted phenomenon, the 'alternative' press has perhaps been best defined as a general reaction against the highly profit-motivated, professionally organised and general information- and entertainment-based 'established' press. Beywl and Brombach have suggested that the 'alternative' press can most usefully be distinguished from the 'established' press according to four main criteria: the attempt to construct a new relationship between the economics and the aims of the publications; the attempt to pioneer a new organisation of the work and production process; the search for a new model of communication; and, last but not least, the new 'conception of politics' ('Politikverständnis') of the 'alternative' press.[67]

Like the journalists' movement for 'internal press freedom', the 'alternative' press had its roots in the 'extra-parliamentary opposition' ('außerparlamentarische Opposition') movement of the 1968 era. As with the increased trade union militancy of the

---

67. W. Beywl and H.B. Brombach, 'Kritische Anmerkungen zur Theorie der Alternativpresse', *Publizistik*, no. 4, 1982, pp. 551–69.

Controversies Over the West German Press System

1970s and 1980s, the 'alternative' press also bore witness to the greater political polarisation of these decades, but over 'postmaterialist' or 'new politics' issues rather than those with a 'materialist' concern. Its theoretical mentors were the radical, 'new-wave', neo-marxist film producer, Alexander Kluge, the left-wing academic doyen of the students, Jürgen Habermas, and the left-radical poet and critic, Hans Magnus Enzensberger, all of whom had attacked the 'established' media for being little more than an 'industry for manufacturing the people's consciousness' (a 'Bewußtseinsindustrie'). The 'alternative' press originally sprang to life seeking to create a radical and critical counterweight or 'alternative public sphere' ('Gegenöffentlichkeit') to what Habermas called the 'false public sphere' ('Scheinöffentlichkeit') of the 'established' media. The general aim was 'systemic change' ('Systemveränderung'), usually in a vaguely specified 'socialistic' direction. More specifically, these 'alternative' publications represented a general youthful rebellion against the putatively manipulative, threatening, managerial, technocratic and even repressive trends in conventional politics and social life, summarised in the emotive term 'Technisierung des Alltags'. Life was breathed into the phenomenon by enthusiastic young 'lay-journalists' seeking an 'alternative media world' ('alternative Medienwelt'). During the 1970s and 1980s, the 'alternative' press increasingly embraced the concerns and often confusing variety of 'new social movements', such as feminism and the environmentalist and peace movements. The political spectrum now ranges from 'new left', through 'left-liberal' ('linksliberal'), to overtly 'green' and 'alternative' publications. Some 'alternative' publications have even appeared to take pride in giving themselves a carefully stylised kind of 'subversive' character.

Nowhere has the 'alternative' press flourished as much as in West Berlin, where the 'alternative' movement itself is at its strongest, particularly areas such as the Kreuzberg district. Otherwise, they are mainly a phenomenon of the 'big cities' ('Großstädte'), where the radical young (mainly students) congregate in large numbers and where a vibrant 'counter-culture' has grown up. 'Alternative' publications are generally local, mainly urban papers with a restricted, mainly young audience, mostly also appearing on a highly irregular basis. However, some have achieved a wider audience and a fairly impressive degree of professionalism and regular appearance. The exact number of 'alternative' publications is difficult to specify. Weichler talks about 35 'Stadtmagazine' with a total sold circulation of around 650,000. According to Weichler, the vast majority have a circulation of only between 500 and 3,000 copies, although he notes that the very successful West Berlin *Tip* has achieved the impressive figure of around 100,000 and *die tageszeitung* sells around 45,000 copies per edition nationwide.[68] Jorg Mettke has suggested that the figure for the total circulation might be as high as 1.6 million copies if every conceivable kind of 'alternative' publication is counted.[69] Another estimate has put the total circulation of the 'alternative' press as high as 300,000.[70] In 1982, the 'Arbeitsgruppe Alternativpresse' of Bonn University provided a very useful index and classification of 'alternative' publications currently in print all over the Federal Republic. They listed no less than 529 'Alternativzeitungen', at least 200 of which fell under the rubric 'Stadtzeitungen, Volksblätter, Stadtmagazine, Dorf- und Provinzzeitungen'. Altogether they enumerated 17 different types of 'alternative' publication, including 'women's papers' ('Frauenzeitungen'), 'peace movement publications ('Friedens- und Antikriegszeitungen'), 'ecological publications' ('Umweltzeitungen'), 'anarchistic papers' ('Anarcho- und Spontiblätter'), 'papers for the underprivileged' ('Zeitungen für benachteiligte Gruppen') and 'internationalist papers' ('Dritte Welt/Internationalismus Zeitungen').[71]

On a few rare but noteworthy occasions, the state has responded with repressive measures including raids leading to the confiscation of material and equipment. The pretext for such

---

68. See Weichler, *Gegendruck*, p. 32.
69. J. Mettke, 'Selbstbespiegelungen. Über die Gegenöffentlichkeit der alternativen Presse', in Michael Haller (ed.), *Austeigen oder rebellieren. Jugendliche gegen Staat und Gesellschaft*, Hamburg: 1981.
70. F. Brüseke and H.-M. Grosse-Ötringhaus, *Blätter von unten: Alternativzeitungen in der Bundesrepublik*, Offenbach: Verlag 2000 GmbH, 1981, p. 13. This interesting 'insider account' documents the story of one particular 'alternative' newspaper, namely the *Knipperdolling* in Münster. The authors were closely involved with this publication from its establishment for a period of five years.
71. See Arbeitsgruppe Alternativpresse, *Riesengroßes Verzeichnis aller alternativen Zeitungen*, Bonn: 1981. In particular, the 'Extra-Ausgabe' of 1982.

Controversies Over the West German Press System

action has been alleged subversion, in particular the accusation that certain publications have been guilty of incitement to violence and terrorism. The legal mechanisms thus brought into play have been paragraph 129 of the Criminal Code ('Strafgesetzbuch'), which bans membership of a criminal group. This particular legal instrument had been extensively used during the Imperial period and the Weimar Republic to control the press. Other relevant legal clauses are paragraphs 88a (anticonstitutional support of criminal acts or 'verfassungsfeindliche Befürwortung von Straftaten'), 90a (disparagement of the state and its symbols or 'Verunglimpfung des Staates und seiner Symbole'), 111 (public incitement to criminal acts or 'öffentliche Aufforderung zu Straftaten') and 140 (rewarding and condoning criminal acts or 'Belohnung und Billigung von Straftaten').[72]

Such actions have, however, been exceptional. Generally, the 'alternative' press has been tolerated, even incorporated into the mainstream political/media culture of the Federal Republic. Some academic observers of the phenomenon have even gone so far as to imply that the real 'threat' to the genre is its own propensity to become, over a period of time, increasingly quasi-respectable and socially acceptable. It has been suggested that the 'alternative' press itself has shown signs of press-concentration and, worse still, that it has been imitated by the 'established' press. Allegedly the most established middle-class women's magazine, *Brigitte*, published by Gruner und Jahr, has increasingly drawn inspiration from 'alternative' feminist publications. The subject of the 'alternative' press has even been incorporated into the curriculum of some vocational courses in journalism. Rather than creating a 'Gegenöffentlichkeit', the reality may be that the 'alternative' press has merely plugged a gap left by the 'established' press. For all its pretensions to be about realising 'alternative' ideas and forms of work and production, the practice has been more prosaic: 'alternative' journalists have discovered careerism and the 'established' press has even begun to recognise that the genre is a useful recruiting-ground. The highly successful *tageszeitung* is not the only 'alternative'

72. K. Peters, *Die periodische Alternativpresse in der Bundesrepublik Deutschland und ihr Anspruch 'Gegenöffentlichkeit' herzustellen – Zur Kritik einer 'konkreten Utopie'*, Diplom-Arbeit an der Universität Göttingen, presented 24 November 1987, pp. 52–5.

publication to have introduced elements of traditional internal authority relations into the production process (e.g. chief editors, etc.). This kind of critique argues that, like the new social movements and the Green Party, the 'alternative' press is prone to be integrated and socialised into the 'system', its themes increasingly being adopted by the 'established' media. Such signs, it has been suggested, indicate a 'crisis of the alternative press'.[73]

No doubt there is some substance in this critique. However, when everything is taken into account, this view presents an over-cynical evaluation of the 'alternative' press. The 'alternative' press has pioneered new forms of expression and content. Behind its often colloquial, group-specific and occasionally highly iconoclastic language, the content of the 'alternative' press has tended to centre on serious and very real social problems. It has created a forum for the articulation of interests not generally represented by the corporatist 'elite cartel' of conventional West German politics. Moreover, it has typically slanted its 'message' towards the 'Betroffenen' (i.e. those on the 'receiving end'). Generally, the 'alternative' press has deliberately tackled themes which would otherwise have remained taboo subjects and it has unquestionably given expression to groups which would otherwise be in danger of being marginalised by conventional West German society and media. The original revolutionary spirit of 1968 has certainly mellowed somewhat. However, that would hardly seem to provide a sensible pretext to belittle the contribution of the post-'68 generations to opening up West German society and making it more participatory. The 'alternative' press has certainly contributed greatly to expanding the degree of pluralism and diversity in the West German press landscape beyond the 'limited pluralism' hitherto achieved by the 'established' press. To this extent, it has presented a positive challenge to the dominance of the giant concerns in the process of political 'Meinungsbildung' and can

---

73. Ibid., pp. 8–9. Also R. Niemcyk, 'Subkultur mit goldenem Boden. Vom alternativen Szeneblatt zur Hochglanzpostille: Die Stadtmagazine werden gesellschaftsfähig', *Das Parlament*, no. 49, 6.12.1986.

be seen as a healthy reaction to the process of press-concentration and the values of the Springer press.[74]

74. Further useful and informative works on the 'alternative' press are: W. Herminghaus, 'Stadtteilzeitungen – Keine Alternative, aber ein Ansatz zu einem neuen Lokaljournalismus', *Media Perspektiven*, 8/1980, pp. 558–60; W. Beywl, 'Lokale Alternativpresse – Eine erste Bestandsaufnahme', *Media Perspektiven*, 3/1982, pp. 184–90; W. Beywl, 'Die Alternativpresse – Ein Modell für Gegenöffentlichkeit und seine Grenzen' *Aus Politik und Zeitgeschichte*, Beilage zum *Parlament*, no. B 45/82, 13 November 1982.

3
The Historical Origins and Early Development of the West German Broadcasting System

The Weimar Republic

German broadcasting commenced in the 1920s, in parallel with other comparable industrial societies such as the USA and Britain. As elsewhere, the radio industry had received a great stimulus from the use of radio during the Great War of 1914–18. Civil radio broadcasting actually began operations in 1923. Unlike in the Anglo-Saxon countries, however, in Germany the state played a leading role in the development of the new medium right from the start. In particular, the PTT – post, telegraph and telecommunications authority or 'Reichspost' – exercised very considerable control over the early radio stations. Broadcasting regulation was, in the words of one expert, 'the uncontested domain of the executive'.[1] In great contrast to the present situation in the Federal Republic of Germany, there was no broadcasting constitution of any kind. The Weimar Constitution did not mention broadcasting at all, there were no broadcasting laws as such, there was in fact only a complex web of regulations, franchises, conventions, contracts and other kinds of legal agreements between central and regional government ministries, the ministerial bureaucracies and private interests.[2]

The early years of broadcasting in Germany were associated

---

1. D. Ross, 'Der Rundfunk in Deutschland', in Hans-Bredow-Institut/ Hamburg (ed.), *Internationales Handbuch für Rundfunk und Fernsehen*, Baden-Baden: Nomos Verlagsgesellschaft, 1986, p. B58; also see H. Pohle, *Der Rundfunk als Instrument der Politik. Zur Geschichte des deutschen Rundfunks von 1923–28*, Hamburg: Verlag Hans-Bredow-Institut, 1955.

2. See Ross, 'Der Rundfunk in Deutschland', p. B58.

Historical Origins of the West German Broadcasting System

with the overwhelming influence of one man, Hans Bredow. In 1921 Bredow was appointed Under-Secretary of State in the Imperial Post Ministry (Reichspostministerium) and in 1926 he was granted more or less complete authority over the new medium in the capacity of Broadcasting Commissioner of the Imperial Post Minister (Rundfunkkommissar des Reichspostministers). The Reichspost owned and governed all the broadcasting transmission facilities in the Reich, allocated franchises and broadcasting licences and gained a very considerable influence even within the individual broadcasting stations. In 1925 control by the central state was tightened even further by the establishment of the Imperial Broadcasting Company (Reichsrundfunkgesellschaft – RRG) in order to coordinate the organisation of broadcasting between the different Länder, which meanwhile developed their own regional stations. The Reichspost retained a 51% controlling stake in the RRG and it was immediately placed under the complete control of Hans Bredow. At the same time, the Imperial Interior Ministry (Reichsinnenministerium or Home Office) managed to win a certain amount of influence as well, particularly over the content of broadcasting. It exercised this control through its tutelage over a central information office upon whom the broadcasting stations were required to rely for their all news and information bulletins. The broadcasters themselves concentrated entirely on artistic and entertainment programming, political expression remained taboo.[3]

Thus, during Germany's ill-fated and short-lived first experiment with liberal democracy, broadcasting was treated as an important function of public administration rather than as an independent self-regulating social activity. Throughout the Weimar period, broadcasting regulation remained the preserve of state officials, who were generally unschooled in democratic theory and practice. On the other hand, many of these officials, best exemplified by Hans Bredow himself, were at least imbued with a specifically German kind of 'public-service ethos' and steeped in the Hegelian concept of the civilising mission of the state. The state was seen as a progressive force standing above the 'egotistical confusion' of society.[4] Accordingly, worthy fig-

---

3. H. Kleinsteuber, *Rundfunkpolitik in der Bundesrepublik*, Opladen: Leske Verlag & Budrich GmbH, 1982, pp. 18–19.
4. On the German state tradition see K. Dyson, *The State Tradition in Western*

ures such as Hans Bredow were concerned above all to use the new medium as a kind of instrument of civilisation ('Kultur') and to keep it above party politics, widely perceived to be in a state of irresponsible degeneration. Unwittingly, however, these undemocratic elites actually prepared the way for the usurpation of the state apparatus by the National Socialists. Ironically, very many of the old elites subsequently fell victim to the new wave of Nazi careerists that swept into power after 1933.

In 1932, during the Chancellorship of von Papen, a major reform of broadcasting brought the new medium even more under the influence of the state. Alongside Hans Bredow a second broadcasting commissioner was appointed by the Reichsinnenministerium. At the same time, the broadcasting companies were subjected to the supervision of a number of regional state commissioners appointed by the Land governments in consultation with the Reichsinnenministerium. The broadcasting companies themselves now fell under the complete ownership, as well as control, of the state – 51% of the shares falling to the RRG and the remaining 49% being distributed between the Länder. Thus, even before the collapse of the Weimar Republic, state influence over programming had become absolute. Papen was no democrat and worse still, in the words of Hans Kleinsteuber, 'this "reform", which was already considerably influenced by the National Socialists' plans for broadcasting, prepared the way for a rapid coordination ['Gleichschaltung'] of broadcasting by the NSDAP at the beginning of 1933'.[5]

The Third Reich

The structure of broadcasting created by this latter reform during the last days of the Weimar Republic bequeathed a ready-made instrument of state control to the new Nazi regime. The Reichsrundfunkgesellschaft now fell under the direct and highly

---

Europe, Oxford: Martin Robertson, 1980.
5. See Kleinsteuber, *Rundfunkpolitik in der Bundesrepublik*, p. 18. For a very detailed general history of broadcasting during the Weimar Republic see W. Lerg, *Rundfunkpolitik in der Weimarer Republik*, Vol. I of the series *Rundfunk in Deutschland*, ed. by H. Bausch, Munich: Deutscher Taschenbuch Verlag (dtv.), 1980.

centralised state control of Josef Goebbels' Reich Propaganda Ministry (Reichsministerium für Volksaufklärung und Propaganda), within which a new central information office was quickly set up. Following the abolition of the Länder, the regionalised nature of broadcasting all but vanished: individual regional stations all became 'Reichssender'. In addition, there were thorough purges of the personnel of the radio stations as broadcasting fell victim to Nazi 'coordination' or 'Gleichschaltung'. The authoritarian traits of Weimar were now replaced by the thoroughgoing totalitarian features of the Nazi regime.

During the Third Reich the immense power of broadcasting over the formation of public opinion ('Meinungsbildung') became terribly obvious. Radio very quickly became the most important propaganda instrument of the Nazi state. Goebbels considered it to be the most modern and most important instrument of influence over mass opinion. News and current affairs programmes were used as a vehicle for presenting the Führer's pronouncements and 'achievements' and little else. Foreign coverage was filtered carefully to protect the German people from the outside world. As with the press, Jewish 'influence' was purged from the medium, indeed broadcasting became a powerful weapon for expounding the Nazi views on 'racial purity'. Particularly during the latter half of the war, when Germany's defeat became increasingly inevitable, broadcasting was used as a potent means of conducting mass-deception on a huge scale about the country's precarious military situation. Finally, a massive dose of anodyne and sanitised entertainment was deployed in order to further demobilise critical reflection and to lull the Germans into a false sense of spiritual and moral contentment.

Interestingly, a few major experiments with television were conducted. For instance, the 1936 Olympiad was turned into a televisual spectacular to the glory of the Third Reich. Although the development of mass television was interrupted by the war, wireless sets, the well-known 'people's radio' ('Volksempfänger') became a mass consumer durable. By the outbreak of the Second World War, Germany had the highest number of radio sets in Europe. However war damage inevitably took its toll. By the end of hostilities, Germany had actually less radio sets than at the outbreak of the war, and the resurrection of German broadcasting was more or less totally dependent upon the Allied powers. Many of the studios and transmission facilities duly requisitioned by the Allied powers lay in various degrees of ruin or disrepair. Nevertheless, with the aid of imported equipment and trained military and non-military personnel, the Allied military governments managed quickly to restore a network of their own special radio stations to the air more or less immediately after the Nazi capitulation. As will now be seen the policies of the Allied occupation powers were informed by the fact that during the Third Reich broadcasting had been become the most effective way of disseminating the ideas of the Führer and controlling the information available to the German people.[6]

The Allied Occupation

After 1945 broadcasting in the Soviet occupied zone, later the German Democratic Republic, was destined to remain in the control of the state, this time a communist one. In the Western occupation zones, however, the occupation authorities regarded broadcasting, like the press, as an important instrument for the 'reeducation' of the Germans towards liberal democracy. Moreover, broadcasting was now to be kept free from the influence of German politicians, the state and all other sectional interests in society. When the West Germans received back state sovereignty, they were to inherit this key concern of the Allies about the independence of broadcasting. If the memory of the National Socialist years was not poignant enough, the German Democratic Republic in the East served as a living exemplar of the threat to 'freedom of opinion'.

In one very important respect, the British model of public-service broadcasting was the main influence on the new German broadcasting system. The new broadcasting organisations were to be neither privately owned, as was overwhelmingly the case

---

6. J. Sandford, *The Mass Media of the German-Speaking Countries*, London: Oswald Wolff, 1976, pp. 67–70. For a detailed general account of broadcasting under the Third Reich see J. Wulf (ed.), *Presse und Funk im Dritten Reich. Eine Dokumentation*, Gütersloh: S. Mohn Verlag, 1964; and A. Diller, *Rundfunkpolitik im Dritten Reich*, Vol. II of the series, *Rundfunk in Deutschland*, ed. by H. Bausch, Munich: Deutscher Taschenbuch Verlag (dtv.), 1980.

Historical Origins of the West German Broadcasting System

in the United States, nor state owned and controlled, as in France. Instead, according to the aims of all of the Western occupiers, the broadcasting organisations to be duly handed back to the Germans were to be 'public-service' bodies. Neither state nor privately owned, they were to be 'corporations under public law' ('Anstalten des öffentlichen Rechts').

Apart from these central principles, the other main legacy of the occupation was the very diverse regional structure of broadcasting organisation which reflected the different conceptions of the British, French and Americans. The Allied powers had agreed at Potsdam the need for a widespread administrative and economic decentralisation of the defeated Germany. This principle of decentralisation of power immediately found its expression in the broadcasting system (as well as in the federal nature of West Germany more generally). However, the Western Allies varied very markedly in their degree of enthusiasm for decentralisation. The Americans considered federalism to be self-evidently a superior system, while the British and French were in many respects unrepentant centralisers. These different attitudes profoundly influenced the establishment of the postwar German broadcasting system.

The British constructed a single corporation, the North West German Broadcasting Service (Nordwestdeutscher Rundfunk – NWDR), to serve all four Länder in their occupation zone, namely Schleswig-Holstein, Hamburg, Lower Saxony (Niedersachsen) and North-Rhine Westphalia (Nordrhein-Westfalen), and also their sector of Berlin. The NWDR was a very centralised organisation, based in Hamburg, and modelled upon the BBC. By contrast, the Americans created a decentralised broadcasting structure, according to the principle of federalism. They established a number of broadcasting stations in their zone: Radio Bremen (RB), Radio Frankfurt, which subsequently became the Hessen Broadcasting Service (Hessischer Rundfunk – HR), Radio Stuttgart, which similarly became the South German Broadcasting Service (Süddeutscher Rundfunk – SDR) for the Land of Württemberg-Baden (later to become part of Baden-Württemberg), and Radio Munich (Radio München), which evolved into the Bavarian Broadcasting Service (Bayerischer Rundfunk – BR) for Bavaria. The French founded yet another broadcasting corporation for their part of Baden-Württemberg and the Saarland, namely the South West German Broadcasting Service (Südwestdeutscher Rundfunk) which was soon renamed South West Broadcasters (Südwestfunk – SWF). As will be seen, the differing concepts of the Western Allies found expression, above all, in the arrangements for the internal organisation of these broadcasting corporations. An important element of the new broadcasting structures was the creation of bodies called 'broadcasting councils' ('Rundfunkräte') within these corporations. The purpose of these broadcasting councils was to give the public representation within the new broadcasting corporations and to provide an instrument for assuring public accountability and control. Alongside these broadcasting councils were established two other significant bodies, namely the 'administrative council' ('Verwaltungsrat'), which was responsible for the day-to-day management of the corporation, and the 'Director-General' ('Intendant'), the chief executive who was responsible for the overall general management of the corporation and the whole programme content. The Intendant and the administrative council were chosen by the broadcasting council, which was effectively the sovereign body within the corporations.

In the broadcasting corporations founded by the Americans the broadcasting councils were to be composed of representatives autonomously chosen by the so-called 'socially significant groups' ('gesellschaftlich relevante Gruppen'). By this term was meant the pluralistic elements of German society, such as the trade unions, the employers' and business organisations, the churches, the universities, local associations and so on. The composition of the broadcasting councils in the broadcasting corporations influenced by the Americans thus followed the 'corporate principle' ('ständisches Prinzip'). By contrast, in the NWDR, founded by the British, election to the broadcasting council followed the 'parliamentary principle': the members were elected by the Land parliaments. In the latter case, though, the number of Land politicians within the broadcasting council was still to be limited. In both models the principle of democratic pluralism was thus to find its expression.[7]

While the early broadcasting corporations were creations of

---

7. See Kleinsteuber, *Rundfunkpolitik in der Bundesrepublik*, pp. 19–20.

Historical Origins of the West German Broadcasting System

the Allied occupation powers, the West German Länder soon enacted legislation which gave them their legal definition and established the regulatory structures and principles by which they were bound. General practical responsibility for broadcasting was returned to the Germans with surprising alacrity. During a short period of initially strict military control, information officers of the Allied powers sought out reliable and 'Anti-Fascist' German journalists and granted them increasing responsibilities for the running of the new stations. By the end of 1947 all stations, except the NWDR in the British zone, had German 'Intendanten'. On the other hand, the NWDR was actually the first to be returned to German ownership by law on 1 January 1948. During 1948 this pattern was repeated for all the broadcasting corporations, although a press and broadcasting law of September 1949 did allow the Allied High Commission to retain reserve powers of intervention until the occupation officially ended in 1955. Nevertheless, the fact remains that the broadcasting system was returned to German control very rapidly indeed.

Yet, the Allies had clearly played an important and decisive role. They had effectively determined the characteristic value-system and overall structure of the West German broadcasting system. As seen, the distinctive pattern of variation in size, structure and internal organisation of the broadcasting organisations also clearly reflected the period of Allied occupation. Moreover, it was a pattern that could not easily be rationalised by the subsequent unification of the three Western occupation zones into the Federal Republic in 1949. Once established, the regional authorities were naturally jealous to protect and preserve their individual broadcasting corporations. Above all, however, the major legacy of the occupation was the complete break with the past structures, values and practices of Weimar and the Third Reich. This was the major contribution of the Allies to the West German broadcasting system. At least as far as broadcasting was concerned 1945 was clearly 'Stunde Null'.[8]

---

8. For a detailed account of this period and the foundation of the broadcasting system see W. Schütte, 'Der deutsche Nachkriegsrundfunk und die Gründung der Rundfunkanstalten. Eine Chronik', in W. Lerg and R. Steininger/ Studienkreis Rundfunk und Geschichte e.V. (eds.), *Rundfunk und Politik 1923–73*, Berlin: Wissenschaftsverlag Volker Spiess, 1975, pp. 217–41; also B.

The Broadcasting 'Constitution'

Apart from the direct influence of the Western Allies and the key part they played in determining the structures and values of broadcasting in the Federal Republic, West German constitutionalism also played a very major role in the early establishment and subsequent evolution of the broadcasting system. From the general guidelines and principles contained in the Constitution, or to be more accurate the 'Basic Law' ('Grundgesetz'), of the young state, a kind of broadcasting 'constitution' has been derived.

The Role of Broadcasting in a Democratic Society

The basis for the 'broadcasting constitution' is to be found in Article 5 of the Basic Law (quoted earlier in this volume).[9] By directly and explicitly incorporating the freedom of broadcasting into the Constitution – in addition to the freedom of the press – the fathers of the Basic Law of 1949 bore witness to the extraordinary power of broadcasting over the formation of public opinion ('Meinungsbildung'). After all, the National Socialist regime had abused this power with very terrible effect. The fathers of the Constitution determined that broadcasting was henceforth to be conducted as a properly regulated public service. This principle of 'public-service' regulation conformed entirely with the intentions of the Allies, who, as seen, had established the embryonic broadcasting institutions as public bodies sustained by all relevant social forces independent of the state or individual pressure groups.

Therefore, Article 5 of the Constitution provided for freedom of opinion, freedom of information and freedom of the media, including the prohibition of censorship. In fact, the Constitution made no further explicit reference to broadcasting whatsoever.

Mettler, *Demokratisierung und Kalter Krieg. Zur amerikanischen Informations- und Rundfunkpolitik in Westdeutschland 1945–49*, Berlin: Wissenschaftsverlag Volker Spiess, 1975; also Chapter 1 'Unter der Kontrolle der Besatzungsmächte' in H. Bausch, *Rundfunkpolitik nach 1945. Erster Teil 1945–62*, Vol. III of the series *Rundfunk in Deutschland*, ed. by H. Bausch, Munich: Deutscher Taschenbuch Verlag (dtv), 1980, pp. 13–164.
9. See Chapter 1, p. 53 above.

Historical Origins of the West German Broadcasting System

The fathers of the Constitution were all representatives of the Länder and the majority of them clearly intended broadcasting to be a matter for detailed legislation by the individual regional authorities. However, the Constitution did contain some general guidelines about the nature of democracy from which important lessons could be easily derived for the specific field of broadcasting. In particular, it stressed that the Federal Republic was a parliamentary democracy. In a parliamentary democracy, broadcasting could be said to have three very political functions: to disseminate information; to assist in the process of formation of public opinion ('Meinungsbildung'); and to exercise a critical and control function. Accordingly, by common understanding, the definition of 'public-service' broadcasting came to include the notion that broadcasters had an obligation to be objective, to enable the population to understand public affairs, and to help the public to make full use of its constitutional right of having an important say in the management of the new state. Moreover, as will be seen, constitutional law buttressed the idea that broadcasting in a free and pluralist democracy should represent the public interest and seek to prevent individual groups or certain economic interests from exercising excessive influence on government decisions.[10]

The Constitutional Division of Powers over Telecommunications and Broadcasting

A further constitutional provision was also very important. The Basic Law provided for a kind of functional division of powers in the field of mass communications between the Federation (the 'Bund') and the constituent states ('Länder') of the Federal Republic. The Constitution assigned responsibility for, and ownership and control of, all telecommunications networks to the state at the federal level, more precisely to the Post and Telecommunications ('Bundespost') Ministry (Article 73). On

---

10. Hessischer Rundfunk, *Radio und Fernsehen in der Bundesrepublik Deutschland*, Frankfurt/Main: Hessischer Rundfunk, June 1980, pp. 6–9. For a more detailed discussion of the constitutional framework see J. Engler, 'Das Rundfunksystem der Bundesrepublik Deutschland', in Hans-Bredow-Institut/ Hamburg (ed.), *Internationales Handbuch für Rundfunk und Fernsehen 1988/89*, Baden-Baden: Nomos Verlagsgesellschaft, 1988, pp. B70–87.

the other hand, the individual Länder were left responsible for culture and it was generally accepted that they had 'cultural sovereignty' ('Kulturhoheit'). It was immediately widely interpreted that the Länder therefore had jurisdiction over broadcasting ('Rundfunkhoheit'). Accordingly, there was a fairly general feeling that the individual Länder had the constitutional right to frame their own broadcasting laws, so long as these laws respected the guidelines laid down by the Constitution itself.

The fact that the establishment of the broadcasting corporations actually predated the Constitution explains an interesting anomaly of the West German broadcasting system: the fact that the function of broadcasting transmission is shared between the broadcasters, in the case of certain channels, and the Bundespost, in the case of others. When the occupation powers returned responsibility for broadcasting to the Germans during 1948, they also returned ownership of all existing studio and transmission facilities to the new broadcasting corporations which they had established. The Allies took this precautionary measure in order to insure the broadcasters against potential government interference. As seen, during the Weimar Republic as well as the Third Reich all transmission facilities had been in the hands of the state in the form of the Reichspost and this had resulted in overweening state control over broadcasting.

However, because this Allied measure had been taken before the Constitution was passed, all transmission stations broadcasting the radio channels of the state broadcasting corporations and also the first national television channel, mounted by the ARD (the network of public-service broadcasting corporations – see p. 148), were destined to remain the property of the broadcasting corporations, singly, or in the case of the ARD, collectively. Only later, with the establishment of a second national channel, the ZDF (Zweites Deutsches Fernsehen), and the establishment of the so-called 'third' or regional television channels of the individual Länder, were the transmission facilities supplied by the Bundespost, in accordance with the federal Post Ministry's constitutional jurisdiction for telecommunications. In other words, since this constitutional division of powers did not exist as such before 1949, the broadcasting corporations were able to retain their own transmission facilities for some, but not all, of their services. Nevertheless, the Bundespost was thenceforth unambiguously solely responsible for the supply of any new frequencies and also for any new technological developments. As will be seen (in Chapters 5 and 6), this dealt the Bundespost a potential 'trump card' in broadcasting policy-making and later – under the impact of technological change – it was able to play a very powerful role within the broadcasting policy community.

The Lack of Constitutional Detail Concerning Broadcasting

Beyond the above-mentioned basic guidelines, the Constitution actually made no detailed specification about the structures of broadcasting, for a number of obvious reasons. Firstly, as seen, the broadcasting organisations were actually established by the Allied occupation powers. In 1949, when the Germans drew up the constitution of the new state, they had very little scope to alter the basic structures already in place. Secondly, public-service broadcasting was completely alien to the German tradition. The Germans had very little to guide them other than the traditions now taken over from the Allies. Finally, as suggested, the fathers of the Constitution were all representatives of the Länder: they were keen to see broadcasting made the subject of specific Land legislation and therefore were largely silent about it in the Constitution itself. As a result, the Constitution was non-committal, at least in a direct sense, about precisely *who* was to broadcast.[11]

As will be seen, the fact that the Constitution did not explicitly rule out the possibility of private commercial broadcasting – in that it did not explicitly call for a public-service *monopoly* – was to be a constant source of political debate in the Federal Republic until the matter was finally resolved towards the end of the 1980s. In fact, it was precisely this lack of detailed specification by the Constitution that explained the subsequent crucial importance and centrality of regulatory interpretation by the Federal Constitutional Court (Bundesverfassungsgericht). In years to come the Constitutional Court was actively to intervene on numerous occasions to guide the subsequent evolution of the broadcasting system, not least in settling the thorny question of

11. See Kleinsteuber, *Rundfunkpolitik in der Bundesrepublik*, p. 25.

commercial broadcasting.

The Legal Basis of Broadcasting as Laid Down by Legislation of the Länder

From the preceding description, it is clear that broadcasting in Germany has had two interlocking foundations: the political decisions taken by the Western Allies in their respective occupation zones immediately after the end of the war; and the guidelines and ethos of the Constitution which the Germans themselves had the major part in shaping. However, the individual Länder themselves now came to play the leading role in giving the present West German broadcasting system its characteristic dimensions and character. Over the period 1948–56, the Länder enacted a series of laws formally and legally endowing the broadcasting corporations with detailed constitutions and regulatory guidelines. Moreover, several new broadcasting corporations were added to the original six established by the Allied powers. In approaching the business of broadcasting policy, the Länder were motivated by a mixture of provincialism and an evolving commitment to 'cooperative federalism'. This subtle combination was to become the hall-mark of the system for years to come.

The Anomalous Geography of the West German Broadcasting System

As a result of the manner of its genesis, the public-service broadcasting system has a rather anomalous character, which goes a long way towards explaining its current imbalances and problems. On the one hand, the early broadcasting system contained the giant NWDR, founded by the British, which had nearly half the population in its catchment area. On the other hand, the system contained tiny stations such as Radio Bremen (RB), which just served the two cities of Bremen and Bremerhaven. The latter cities had been placed under American jurisdiction during the occupation in order to provide the US forces with access to the sea. Therefore, although finding itself in the middle of the catchment area of the NWDR, RB had become an island of American influence in the north of Germany. The tiny

Historical Origins of the West German Broadcasting System

size of the station was quite simply a legacy of the occupation, it had no other rationale.

Moreover, in southern Germany, the French zone of occupation had been carved out of the south-western corner of the American zone (the two former states of Baden and Württemberg-Hohenzollern) and the southern extremity of the British zone (the state of the Rhineland-Palatinate or 'Rheinland-Pfalz').

The French had established the rather small South-West Broadcasters (Südwestfunk – SWF) for their zone, while the American part of south-western Germany was served by a similarly small station, the South German Broadcasting Service (Süddeutscher Rundfunk – SDR). In 1952, the modern Land of Baden-Württemberg was created from the southern part of the French zone and a significant south-western part of the US zone. However, the radio stations did not then become the subject of an appropriate and equivalent rationalisation – once established a potent mixture of inertia and local pride dictated that they remained *in situ*. Finally, in 1957 the Saarland was finally returned to the Federal Republic, leading to the establishment of yet another radio station, the tiny Saarland Broadcasting Service (Saarländischer Rundfunk – SR). Thus, by 1956 south-western Germany had been endowed with no less than three small or tiny radio corporations, Baden-Württemberg being served by two. One of these was also shared by the neighbouring Land of the Rhineland-Palatinate, namely the SWF. Accordingly, the SWF duly became the subject of an inter-state treaty ('Staatsvertrag') between its two 'host' Länder.

The only sensible rationalisation which did occur was the break-up of the giant NWDR over the period 1953–6. This huge and unwieldy station set up by the British was progressively broken into three. First of all, in 1953, its Berlin service was taken over by another small corporation, the Free Berlin Broadcasting Service (Sender Freies Berlin – SFB). Then, in 1954 the Land government of North-Rhine Westphalia detached itself from the catchment area of the NWDR and established in its place the West of Germany Broadcasting Service (Westdeutscher Rundfunk – WDR). In 1955, the Land parliaments of Hamburg, Lower Saxony and Schleswig-Holstein duly enacted an inter-state treaty to found the North German Broadcasting Service (Norddeutscher Rundfunk – NDR) from what remained

137

of the NWDR.

Significantly, there was an element of party politics in the break-up of the NWDR, which was a premonition of the shape of things to come. The NWDR was very suspect in the view of the CDU/CSU. Chancellor Konrad Adenauer (CDU) repeatedly accused it of being 'red' ('rot', i.e. SPD-orientated). At this time, North-Rhine Westphalia, the area of coverage of the WDR, was governed by the CDU. The establishment of the 'breakaway' WDR can therefore be seen, at least in part, as an early political gambit by the CDU to counter an alleged SPD bias in north German broadcasting. Already, the politicians were behaving in a manner that portended a certain politicisation of the broadcasting system.[12]

By 1956, the Federal Republic had been endowed with no fewer than nine regionally decentralised broadcasting stations, varying in size in what seems to an outside observer to be a very arbitrary and random fashion. Despite the break-up of the giant NWDR, two of its 'offspring', namely the North German Broadcasting Service (NDR) and the West of Germany Broadcasting Service (WDR), still remain huge by the standards of the rest of the stations in the Federal Republic, with the exception of the Bavarian Broadcasting Service (Bayerischer Rundfunk – BR), which is also a very large station indeed covering the whole of Bavaria. At the same time, as seen, Radio Bremen (RB), the Free Berlin Broadcasting Service (SFB), the Saarland Broadcasting Service (SR) and South West Broadcasters (SWF) were all small corporations.

Each of the West German public-service broadcasting corporations currently produces at least three, and sometimes four, radio services and also a regional television service. In addition, they cooperate in producing a national television service (some cooperate in regional television as well). Furthermore, an American radio station (RIAS, Rundfunk im Amerikanischen Sektor, Berlin) continues to broadcast from Berlin. Finally, two national German radio stations, the Deutsche Welle (DW) and Deutschlandfunk (DLF), were established in 1961 by federal, not Land, legislation (see p. 159). Both based in Cologne, these stations supply national and external radio services.

12. Ibid., p. 21.

Historical Origins of the West German Broadcasting System

Land Laws and 'Staatsverträge'

The corporations that serve a single Land only were all established by the enactment of simple Land legislation. On the other hand, as seen, some corporations cover more than one Land, or parts of several Länder, and these were the subject of 'inter-state treaties' ('Staatsverträge'). Even though the broadcasting corporations constituted after 1949 were established without direct Allied assistance, they remain guided by the very same public-service principle that had been inspired by the Western Allies. By these various Land laws and 'Staatsverträge', the federal system of broadcasting, originally provided by the Western powers in their occupation zones, was completely taken over by the individual Länder (with the exception of the Deutsche Welle, Deutschlandfunk and RIAS Berlin – the first two of which remain the responsibility of the central state, the Bund, and the latter of which remains under American 'tutelage').[13]

These Land laws and 'Staatsverträge' were all very similar in most of their main provisions. They all adopted the fundamental premise bequeathed to the West Germans by the Western Allies, namely the 'public-service' nature of broadcasting. Rather than choosing a private law form of broadcasting organisation, instead the Land governments all opted in favour of keeping them non-profit-making, self-administered 'corporations governed under public law' ('Anstalten des öffentlichen Rechts'). This legal form guarantees the legal autonomy, independence of programme planning, budgeting and production, and financial self-sufficiency of the broadcasters. Financial self-sufficiency and self-administration were to be the principal insurance against capture by the state or by sectional interests. At the same time, the editorial independence of the broadcasters was assured: governments were not to direct broadcasters, nor to intervene in the broadcasting of programmes, except in the case of contravention of broadcasting laws or other legislation.

---

13. Inter Nationes, *Broadcasting Laws*. Series: *Documents on politics and society in the Federal Republic of Germany* (2nd edn), Bonn: Inter Nationes, 1984. Also see W.-D. Ring (ed.), *Deutsches Presse-und Rundfunkrecht. Textsammlung mit Anmerkungen, Verweisungen und Sachregister* Munich: Franz Rehm Verlag für Verwaltungspraxis, 1986; and, W. Lehr and K. Berg, *Rundfunk und Presse in Deutschland – Rechtsgrundlagen der Massenmedien – Texte*, Mainz: von Hase und Koehler Verlag, 1971.

Fig. 3.1

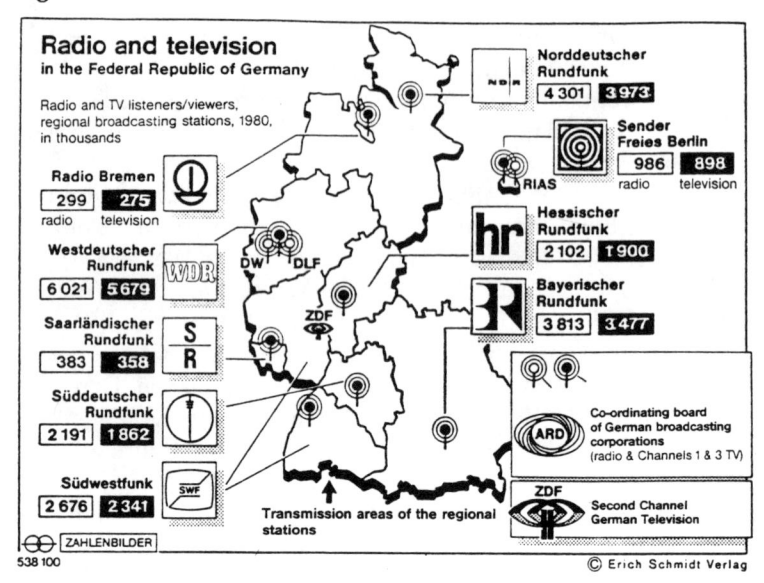

Radio and television in the Federal Republic of Germany

Radio and TV listeners/viewers, regional broadcasting stations, 1980, in thousands

- Radio Bremen: radio 299 | television 275
- Westdeutscher Rundfunk (WDR): 6 021 | 5 679
- Saarländischer Rundfunk (SR): 383 | 358
- Süddeutscher Rundfunk: 2 191 | 1 862
- Südwestfunk (SWF): 2 676 | 2 341
- Norddeutscher Rundfunk (NDR): 4 301 | 3 973
- Sender Freies Berlin / RIAS: radio 986 | television 898
- Hessischer Rundfunk (hr): 2 102 | 1 900
- Bayerischer Rundfunk: 3 813 | 3 477
- ARD: Co-ordinating board of German broadcasting corporations (radio & Channels 1 & 3 TV)
- ZDF: Second Channel German Television

Transmission areas of the regional stations

538 100 © Erich Schmidt Verlag

However, while the public broadcasting corporations were to be independent of the state, they were to remain subject to Land legislation, to a certain degree of Land budgetary control and also to a certain amount of Land lawful supervision (the two radio stations constituted under federal law, namely Deutsche Welle and Deutschlandfunk were to remain subject to lawful supervision by the federal government). Lawful supervision ('Rechtsaufsicht') meant that the Land governments retained the authority to intervene in the event of an infringement of the relevant Länder broadcasting legislation by any part of the broadcasting corporation. In such an event, the public authorities could demand that the offending corporation take appropriate corrective action. For its part, the corporation was empowered to take any such government demand to the relevant administrative court and, if need be, as far as the Constitutional Court system. Nevertheless, this supervisory function of the state was intended to be a 'hands-off' kind of residual regulation, which was not to contravene the constitutionally guaranteed principle of freedom of broadcasting, and in particular the related principle of independence from the state ('Staatsferne').

Historical Origins of the West German Broadcasting System

As suggested, the rules of the various Land broadcasting laws or state treaties were all guided by the overriding principle of the public-service nature of broadcasting. Accordingly, all the laws deemed broadcasting to be an independent medium committed to democratic freedom and truth as its supreme objectives and ideals. All the laws provided for broadcasting to reflect and to discuss the diversity of different and divergent ideological, political, scientific and cultural convictions, views and opinions in society (the principle of pluralist diversity or 'Vielfalt'). Regional and ethnic divisions in society were to be fully catered for and respected. Public-service broadcasting had a duty to promote international understanding, peace and social justice. In fulfilling all of these functions, broadcasting was to remain strictly impartial and balanced. Public-service broadcasting was not to serve a single political party or group, pressure group, religious confession, or ideology. Moreover, all democratic views and opinions held throughout society had to be adequately expressed *within* the channels of the various broadcasting corporations.

The Land governments were mindful of one particular feature of broadcasting, which was later to be made far more explicit by subsequent rulings of the Federal Constitutional Court, in particular by the so-called 'First Television Judgement' of 1961 ('Erstes Fernsehurteil' – see p. 161). This was the underlying difference between broadcasting and the press, leading to the requirement that the former be far more regulated than the latter. The Constitution of the Federal Republic was, above all else, a paean and a pledge to the concept of pluralism. Thus, the backbone of the subsequent legislation by the Länder reflected a firm commitment to pluralism in practice. As seen, it was widely held by the policy-making elites of post-war West Germany that pluralism could be adequately provided by a private commercial press sector, by virtue of the large number of competing views supposedly supplied by a range of newspapers reflecting different 'tendencies' ('Tendenzen'). However, the scarcity of broadcasting frequencies and the very high cost of broadcasting meant that a similar multiplicity of channels was neither technically nor economically feasible. Therefore, the Land legislators decided that 'internal pluralism' *within* each channel ('Binnenpluralismus') had to be supplied by other means, namely 'internal control' ('Binnenkontrolle') within each broadcasting corporation.

The Internal Organisation of the Broadcasting Corporations

In order to fulfil this all-important condition, namely, the provision of internal pluralism, the Land legislation provided for pluralistically composed supervisory bodies – the broadcasting councils ('Rundfunkräte') – *within* the individual broadcasting corporations to ensure a balance and diversity of opinion and to safeguard against the abuse of power by individual groups. These supervisory bodies were also to ensure that broadcasting promoted the principles of a free and democratic basic order and that it would not be turned against these principles. The broadcasting stations were thus organised so as to provide the public with a deliberately balanced diversity ('Vielfalt') of information and comment, thereby contributing to the all-important process of public opinion forming ('Meinungsbildung'). The 'internally pluralistically controlled' self-regulating public corporations were to serve the purpose of plurality just as, in theory at least, the relatively large number of independent newspapers and periodicals competing with each other in terms of their political views and ideological alignment satisfied the principle of plurality of the German press.

All the Land laws and 'Staatsverträge' provided for a multi-layered (though not in the strictest sense of the word 'hierarchical') internal organisation of the broadcasting corporations. The base of the structure was the broadcasting council, which represented the public in broadcasting. The broadcasting council was the sovereign body or 'parliament' of the broadcasting corporation, with the task of deliberating on all matters of internal policy. It advised the Intendant on fundamental editorial questions, ensured adherence to editorial principles and had the final say over programming regulation and any complaints arising therefrom. In addition, it had a number of lesser functions such as approving the budget, annual accounts and annual report. Importantly, in most cases, though not all, the broadcasting council also actually chose the Intendant (see Fig. 3.2).

Unlike the broadcasting council, the administrative council fulfilled no representative function; it was, as its name suggests, purely an administrative organ. In particular, it was responsible for the day-to-day running of the corporation, supervising the Intendant's general management and the auditing of the budget

Historical Origins of the West German Broadcasting System

Fig. 3.2

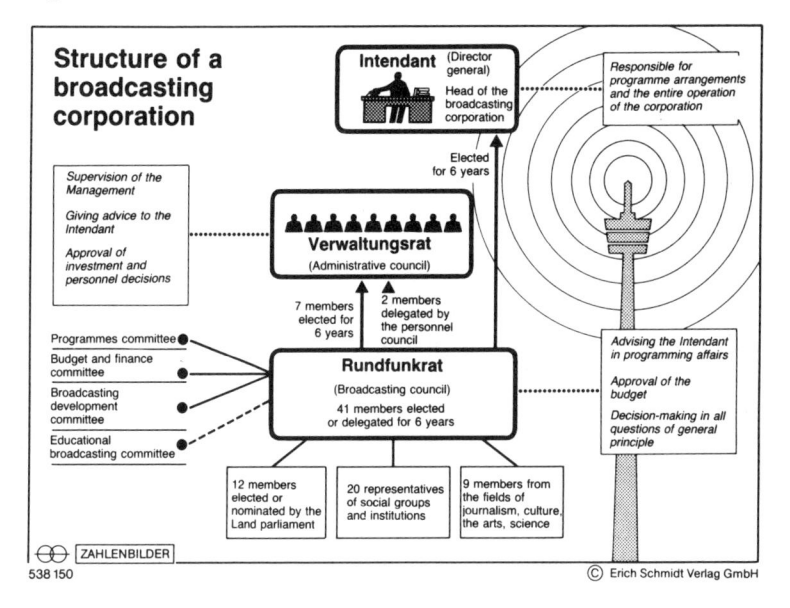

Structure of a broadcasting corporation

- **Intendant** (Director general)
  - Head of the broadcasting corporation
  - Responsible for programme arrangements and the entire operation of the corporation
  - Elected for 6 years

- Supervision of the Management
- Giving advice to the Intendant
- Approval of investment and personnel decisions

- **Verwaltungsrat** (Administrative council)
  - 7 members elected for 6 years
  - 2 members delegated by the personnel council

- Programmes committee
- Budget and finance committee
- Broadcasting development committee
- Educational broadcasting committee

- **Rundfunkrat** (Broadcasting council)
  - 41 members elected or delegated for 6 years
  - Advising the Intendant in programming affairs
  - Approval of the budget
  - Decision-making in all questions of general principle

- 12 members elected or nominated by the Land parliament
- 20 representatives of social groups and institutions
- 9 members from the fields of journalism, culture, the arts, science

ZAHLENBILDER 538 150 © Erich Schmidt Verlag GmbH

Note: As indicated in the text, the precise pattern varies between the different corporations. This model approximates to the 'corporate model' rather than the 'parliamentary model'. The former had become standard by the 1980s.

estimate, the annual report and the annual account. It controlled the corporation's general conduct of business. In most cases, the members of the administrative council were once again chosen by the broadcasting council. In certain cases, some members came from the ranks of the 'great and the good', namely local notables (e.g. presidents of the relevant Landesbank, the Oberlandesgericht, leading university figures, etc.). The administrative council also contained experts from the fields of finance, law and engineering. In some cases, such as Hessischer Rundfunk (HR), the station's staff also participated in the election of the administrative council. Generally, the members of the administrative council were not to be employees of the station nor simultaneously to belong to the broadcasting council. In the routine management of the stations, members of the administrative council could exercise a high degree of discretion. The

143

only exception to this system was the Land Broadcasting Act of Sender Freies Berlin (SFB), which did not provide for an administrative council.

The pinnacle of the structure was the Intendant (or 'Director General' in British broadcasting parlance). The Intendant combined the functions of the chief executive organ and chief administrative officer of the corporation and was in full charge of its programme. Power was collected in his hands in order to give the corporation effective leadership and to avoid the paralysis that might follow from too much collegiality. Nevertheless, it was generally assumed that the countervailing powers of the other main organs, in particular the ultimate 'sovereignty' of the broadcasting council, would prevent an undue concentration of power or indeed the irresponsible abuse of power by 'rogue' Intendanten. In most cases, the Intendant was appointed by the broadcasting council by a majority vote. He remained in office for a term of between five and nine years, and he remained 'responsible' to the broadcasting council. The Intendant was to represent the corporation in and out of court. He generally required the approval of the administrative council in the sphere of administrative and technical appointments and dismissals as well as for legal acts of major financial scope. The Intendant was also responsible for programming, although he remained bound by the ultimate 'sovereignty' of the broadcasting council in this crucial matter. The Intendant represented the corporation in the ARD (the 'network' of public-service broadcasters in the FRG – see p. 148).

In addition to these three layers, the 'Staatsvertrag' providing for the establishment of NDR and the Land Broadcasting Act of WDR provided for an additional advisory programme council (Programmbeirat), elected by the broadcasting councils of the corporations on the recommendation of the various 'socially relevant groups'. As its title suggests, this council's powers were limited to a purely advisory role on programming policy *vis-à-vis* both the broadcasting council and the Intendant. As will be now explained, this was the only means by which the 'socially significant groups' gained immediate representation within the latter two broadcasting corporations, until their internal organisation was reformed in the early 1980s to bring them into line with the other broadcasting corporations.

Historical Origins of the West German Broadcasting System

The Different Modes of Selection of Membership to the Supervisory Boards

This basic general uniformity of the overall structures of the broadcasting corporations, however, should not obscure the fundamental variation in the mode of selection of the supervisory bodies. As will be seen, this delicate issue was to become a matter of very considerable controversy in later years. In view of the 'sovereign' nature of the broadcasting councils – and their ultimate centrality in the fields of internal self-regulation and policy making of the corporations – the manner in which their membership was selected is clearly a matter of great significance.

As suggested already, basically two different patterns were inherited from the occupation period. The broadcasting corporations influenced by the Americans had favoured the so-called 'corporate model' ('ständisches Modell') where the greater part of the membership of the broadcasting council was determined by the 'socially significant groups' in West German society, with only a smaller part chosen by the Land parliaments (as in Fig. 3.2). However, in the case of the WDR and the NDR, which inherited the 'British way of doing things' within the NWDR, the pattern reflected the so-called 'parliamentary' model, where the Land parliament ultimately determined the membership of the broadcasting council.

The Hessen law is a good example of the former method, namely the 'corporate model'. The broadcasting council of HR was to be composed of a representative of the Land government and five members of the regional parliament nominated according to the characteristically German 'Proporz' principle (i.e. in proportion to the strength of the parties in the Land parliament). However, all the other members were to be chosen by specific groups and organisations: the universities, the Protestant church, the Roman Catholic Church, the Jewish cultural communities, teachers' associations, employers' associations, trade unions, the association of adult education classes, and even both the University of Music and Interpretive Arts and the Academy of The Freies Deutsches Hochstift of Frankfurt. In addition, the broadcasting council was to include three women members, who were able to be coopted by the broadcasting

145

council itself in agreement with women's organisations. Every two years, one-third of the council members were to be replaced by rotation, reelection being permitted. In theory, at least, the members of the broadcasting council were not to be bound by any mandate. However, no rule prevents the socially significant groups from choosing sympathisers of a particular political party as their representatives. In practice, the latter can hardly be prevented from acting politically.

In the case of the WDR and the NDR by contrast, all members of the broadcasting council were elected by the Land parliament, according to the 'Proporz' principle. Both laws did place a certain limitation on the number of serving politicians in the broadcasting council, eight in both cases. Nevertheless, through party patronage the composition of the broadcasting councils could easily come to reflect the political balance of the Land parliaments at any given time. The members of the broadcasting council were elected for a period of five years and simultaneous membership of the administrative council and the broadcasting council was ruled out in both cases. Significantly, in these two examples of the 'parliamentary model' the only reference to the 'socially significant groups' was for the composition of the programme advisory councils, selected by the broadcasting council from nominees of these groups. However, as seen, these programme advisory councils were not 'sovereign' supervisory organs, merely rather ineffectual advisory bodies.

The fact that the NDR served three different Länder led to one important difference from the WDR. The membership of the broadcasting council (and indeed of the administrative council too) had faithfully to reflect a balance between the three signatory Länder of the NDR 'Staatsvertrag'. Accordingly, membership was weighted according, though not in direct proportion, to the size of these Länder. Thus the parliament of the populous Land of Lower Saxony nominated twelve members to the broadcasting council while the parliaments of the less populous state of Schleswig-Holstein and the city-state of Hamburg elected six each.

As will be seen, neither model was to prevent the practice of politicisation by stealth which came to afflict the broadcasting councils. The parliamentary model seemed to offer the least defence against this practice, with the obvious scope the 'Proporz' system (i.e. through the parliamentary model of selection of members of the supervisory bodies) opened to political patronage. The NDR soon came to be widely regarded to be a broadly SPD-oriented station (so too did the WDR from the 1960s onwards). Nevertheless, the range of 'socially significant groups' in the 'corporate model' gave ample scope for more subtle but nevertheless very real politicisation processes to work there as well. Arguably, the range of such groups was such as to reflect a certain 'establishment' bias and, in turn, the post-war 'establishment', at least in CDU/CSU Länder, could be said to reflect a CDU/CSU bias. The trade unions, in particular, felt themselves to be distinctly marginalised in the southern German stations. Moreover, neither system was designed to give much expression, if any, to groups that existed beyond the centrist consensus – for example, the Greens and 'Alternatives', the environmentalists and the peace movement of the late 1970s and 1980s.

An Open Policy Community?

Despite this significant difference between the various Land laws, the broadcasting legislation of the Länder enacted in the early post-war period had one overriding aim. All the laws commonly sought to overcome the undemocratic and non-pluralist features of the German tradition. In the past, broadcasting policy in Germany had always been confined to a tightly circumscribed body of elites. It had been governed by a quintessentially closed policy community. The post-war opening up of the broadcasting policy community to a range of 'socially significant groups' on the one hand, or at least to the principle of democratic representation (via the parliamentary model) on the other, bore witness to the intention of the post-war elites to remedy the faults of the German tradition. As will be seen, the reality did not entirely match up to the noble ideal. The elite groups of the Federal Republic – in particular the political parties – were destined still to predominate in broadcasting policy. Nevertheless, the very much greater breadth and plurality of elites in post-war West Germany was to become one of the major characteristics of the developed liberal democratic state, standing in stark contrast to the German historical experience.[14]

14. Kleinsteuber talks about the 'corporate' and 'parliamentary' models,

The ARD

Although the broadcasting corporations had been brought into existence by a combination of the Allies' concern for decentralisation and legislation by individual Länder jealous to establish their jurisdiction over what they argued to be patently a cultural activity, the decentralised and federal nature of the new broadcasting system was not completely safeguarded from powerful centralising tendencies. During the formative years of the broadcasting system, the threat of the development of a central broadcasting authority, or the intervention of the federal authorities themselves, was never far away. As a result of this and other factors, the broadcasting corporations had a powerful incentive to cooperate.

Inevitably, German tradition weighed heavily on the young republic. Eminent figures from the broadcasting system of the Weimar Republic were still influential, none more so than Hans Bredow himself, the 'Grand Old Man' of German broadcasting. Bredow had been dismissed by the National Socialists, as a result of which his immense stature had survived the Nazi period more or less intact. In the post-war period he soon became chairman of the administrative council of Hessischer Rundfunk (HR) in Frankfurt. From this base, Bredow immediately attempted to exert a strong influence over the future development of the infant West German broadcasting system. In particular, he retained his traditional commitment to the civilising mission of public officialdom. Bredow also sought a speedy 'unification' (i.e. centralisation) of the broadcasting authorities.

In order to achieve these goals, Bredow energetically masterminded the organisation of a 'policy network' composed of the

---

others refer to 'pluralistic' and a mixture of 'state-political', 'parliamentary' and 'parliamentary/bureaucratic'. Also see H.-M. Kepplinger, *Massenkommunikation*, Stuttgart: Teubner Studienskripte, 1982, pp. 80–3. Also see K. Jank, *Die Rundfunkanstalten der Länder und des Bundes. Eine systematische Darstellung ihrer organisatorischen Grundlagen*, Berlin: Duncker und Humblot, 1967; and, Chapter 7, on 'Control in the West German Broadcasting System', in A. Williams, *Broadcasting and Democracy in West Germany*, London: Bradford University Press/Crosby Lockwood Staples, 1976, pp. 95–119; and finally, Gunther Herrmann, 'Zur Entwicklung der Rundfunkorganisationen in der Bundesrepublik Deutschland', in H. Brack, G. Herrmann and H.-P. Hillig, *Organisation des Rundfunks in der Bundesrepublik Deutschland 1948–62*, Hamburg: Verlag Hans-Bredow-Institut, 1962.

chairmen of the administrative councils of the broadcasting corporations. It was his full intention, in so doing, to shift the balance of control of the broadcasting corporations irrevocably in the favour of the administrators and away from the Intendant system which was based, at least formally, on a high degree of democratic control by the broadcasting councils. According to Hans Bausch, Bredow did not like the Intendant system, he suspected the Intendanten of being too 'political'. It was Bredow's ultimate aim to see established an association ('Arbeitsgemeinschaft') of the chairmen of the administrative councils significantly to be called the German Broadcasting Service (Deutscher Rundfunk). In this way, Bredow sought speedily to resurrect and reassert, be it in a new shape, the traditional primacy of public administration that had been the hall-mark of the Weimar broadcasting system.[15]

Bredow's activism caused a great amount of concern, especially among the Intendanten themselves, whose sense of their own independent power and importance was never greater than during this early phase of the West German broadcasting system. Nevertheless, the Intendanten were not heedless of the imperatives to cooperate. In fact, they had been meeting intermittently throughout the occupation period. In 1949, the first major conferences of programme and technical directors took place. Cooperation between the broadcasting corporations was further promoted by the need to answer such questions as how the German broadcasters should be represented within the European Broadcasting Union (EBU). Even more pressing was the need to establish their own collective power in their relations with the central government, which was then developing its own plans to enact a federal broadcasting law, as will be seen shortly. Bredow's interventions gave an added spur to the Intendanten to respond by giving positive consideration to the issue of some kind of future cooperation between the broadcasting corporations. Moreover, there were sound economic and cultural reasons why the individual broadcasting corporations should produce some kind of cooperative arrangement. Not least, the imminent arrival of television in the early 1950s provided a powerful incentive for future cooperation between

15. Bausch, *Rundfunkpolitik nach 1945, Erster Teil 1945–62*, pp. 252–7.

the broadcasting corporations. The production of television programmes was an expensive business, far exceeding the cost of radio. The broadcasting corporations, especially the smaller ones, realised that individually they were incapable of financing the start-up and running costs of a comprehensive television service of their own.

Therefore, the Intendanten felt compelled to run with the tide and themselves take charge of the business of establishing a public-service broadcasters' association. As the result, on 5 August 1950 in Munich, the six original public-service broadcasting corporations founded an association called the Association of Public Broadcasting Corporations in West Germany (Arbeitsgemeinschaft der öffentlich-rechtlichen Rundfunkanstalten in der Bundesrepublik Deutschland – ARD). In coming together in the ARD, the broadcasting corporations retained their individual organisational independence but at the same time laid the basis for an important measure of future financial cross-subsidisation and networking of the member institutions. Soon no fewer than 11 broadcasting corporations were joined together in the ARD: the 9 regional broadcasting corporations (i.e. the original 6 plus the 3 that were established subsequently); and the 2 broadcasting corporations under federal law, namely Deutsche Welle and Deutschlandfunk. In addition, it quickly became customary for RIAS Berlin to take part in the ARD as a 'guest'.[16]

The four major tasks of the ARD were established by Article 2 para. 1 of its very short constitution. They were:

i) to protect the common interests of the broadcasting corporations in the exercise of their sovereign rights in the field of broadcasting;
ii) to protect other common interests of the broadcasting corporations;
iii) to attend to common questions of programming and common legal, technical and commercial questions;
iv) to furnish expert reports on questions arising from the interpretation and application of regulations pertaining to the individual corporations which have a general rel-

16. On the origins of the ARD see ibid., pp. 249–59.

Historical Origins of the West German Broadcasting System

evance.[17]

The ARD constitution itself was a quintessentially flexible and liberal 'framework document' – very different from the customary West German legal texts – and as such it reflected the overriding concern of the broadcasting corporations to safeguard their new-found independence. However, the constitution has since been supplemented by a whole panoply of additional agreements and conventions between the corporations over an extensive range of matters (e.g. cooperation with the second 'national' television channel, ZDF – see next chapter).

The ARD quickly gained importance during the early 1950s with the introduction of television in the Federal Republic. In fact, the operation of a common television channel on a cooperative basis soon became the main function of the ARD. On 27 March 1953, the members of the ARD concluded an agreement to 'operate a joint network consisting of programmes provided by the broadcasting corporations' ('Vereinbarung der Landesrundfunkanstalten über die Zusammenarbeit auf dem Gebiet des Fernsehens' ["Fernsehvertrag"]). In 1953, West Germany's first 'national' channel, German Television (Deutsches Fernsehen – DFS), was duly founded (DFS is often referred to as the 'First Programme' or simply 'ARD'). Coordination and planning of the joint ARD 'network' became the business of a 'permanent programme conference' ('Ständige Programmkonferenz') in which all regional stations were represented by their Intendant or, on the latter's behalf, by the television programme directors. This conference was in turn chaired by the director of programmes of DFS, whose office was based in Munich and whose work was assisted by a number of coordinators for various programme fields. The new channel had a kind of collective broadcasting council, in this case called 'advisory council' ('Fernsehbeirat'), which advised the permanent programme conference. This advisory council was composed of members of the supervisory bodies of all the member broadcasting corporations.

The DFS agreement specified carefully the programme contri-

17. Hans-Bredow-Institut/Hamburg (ed.), *Internationales Handbuch für Rundfunk und Fernsehen 1988/89*, Baden-Baden: Nomos Verlagsgesellschaft, 1988, p. C1.

151

butions to be made by each individual station according to its financial strength and programme- making capability. Throughout the life of the ARD, the main burden has been carried by the three largest stations, namely BR, NDR and especially WDR. In 1986, for example, no less than 27.8% of the total DFS programmes supplied individually by the various corporations were provided by the WDR and a further 19.3% and 15.5% by the NDR and BR respectively. HR, SDR and SFB each provided 8.1%, 8.0% and 7.9% respectively. The two tiny stations in the 'network', namely RB and SR, supplied a mere 2.5% and 3.0% respectively.[18] The ARD members also produce programmes jointly and in 1986 this kind of common production accounted for 42.8% of the total, the remaining 57.2% being provided by the corporations on an individual basis. In addition to television, each member corporation produces three or four radio programmes on AM or FM and a regional television programme every weekday between 18.00 and 20.00 hours (on Saturdays between 19.00 and 20.00 hours).

In accordance with its original brief, the ARD has continued to represent the common interests of the public-service broadcasting corporations throughout the history of the Federal Republic, generally settling joint programming concerns and coordinating joint technical, legal and commercial arrangements. In addition, it has occupied itself with tackling any new developments in broadcasting, such as the subsequent establishment of a second national television channel, called ZDF, or the much more recent arrival of satellite television in the 1980s.[19]

The Significance of 'Stunde Null'

Just as in the case of the press, perhaps even more clearly so, 'Stunde Null' marked a new beginning for the (West) German broadcasting system. During the Weimar Republic the broadcasting system had been treated like a department of public administration, dominated by conservative elites who had little

---

18. Data from ibid., pp. C96–7.
19. A detailed account of the ARD is given by Bausch, *Rundfunkpolitik nach 1945, Erster Teil 1945–62*, pp. 239–304.

Historical Origins of the West German Broadcasting System

understanding of, or sympathy for, the liberal democractic system. Subsequently, under the National Socialists the medium had been thoroughly transformed into the main propaganda instrument of the fascist state. In the light of this inauspicious record, the Western Allies had been mainly concerned to start wholly afresh and establish a completely new broadcasting system which would be genuinely independent of the state and other powerful social forces. In particular, the principle of independence from the state ('Staatsferne') had informed their unambiguous choice in favour of a public-service model characterised by an organisational and legal structure making broadcasting the responsibility of largely self-regulating, independent and public corporations. In this respect, the model which had been adopted was far more akin to the British conception than that of either the Americans (who had toyed with the idea of a commercial system resembling their own and such as they had established in Japan) or the French (who themselves had a state-run system). Moreover, from the very outset, partly reflecting the Western Allies' preference for a federal political system, but in large part as the inevitable result of the effect of the division of Germany into occupation zones, the broadcasting system had acquired a regional structure. In this latter respect, the federal pattern had been more the result of American, than British or French, influence. The West German elites, who had very quickly assumed responsibility for broadcasting, had themselves been predominantly disposed towards the federal structure and thus it had fallen upon the Länder to enact the laws governing broadcasting. The resultant system seemed immediately to bear witness to a considerable degree of regional parochialism. In an important sense, this was a positive feature. Unlike Britain, where London is preeminent (despite a certain degree of regionalised production), or France, where Paris clearly dominates broadcasting production, in West Germany a number of West German cities aspired to be considered important 'media centres' ('Medienzentren'): behind Hamburg came Munich, Mainz, West Berlin, Stuttgart and Cologne, not to forget Saarbrücken and Bremen. Yet at the same time, the fairly rapid establishment of the ARD 'network' testified to the development of the countervailing principle of 'cooperative federalism' ('kooperativer Föderalismus'), which as with the broader political system itself acted as a necessary unifying force. Indeed, in few other fields of policy-making was this principle of 'cooperative federalism' more fundamental to the smooth functioning of the system. By the same token, it was also a potential 'Achilles Heel' (as Chapters 5 and 6 will describe).

The most striking innovation, however, was the extent of the 'democratisation' of the broadcasting system. As seen, the regulatory model which had been chosen reflected a mixture of the Allies' concern to make the broadcasters publicly accountable and the Germans' own respect for corporatism and proportional representation ('Proporz'). As with federalism, strong elements of both of these latter concepts were to be found in the German tradition, it had merely remained to implement them in an unreservedly democratic manner. In the context of 'Stunde Null' this had been, at least in formal terms, a fairly straightforward affair. Thus, the broadcasting corporations had been deliberately opened up to a range of 'socially significant' influences, such as interest groups and associations, the churches and, of course, the liberal-democratic political parties. The main object of this exercise had been to ensure that the broadcasting fare produced by the new public-service corporations should reflect a pluralistic and balanced diversity of opinion and information as well as entertainment. In striking contrast to the new West German press system, the broadcasting system was to be both heavily regulated by detailed broadcasting laws and strictly supervised by pluralistic 'broadcasting councils' (Rundfunkräte) *internal* to the broadcasting corporations. In view of high 'entrance threshold requirements' for broadcasting, in terms of finance and technological resources, as well as in recognition of the extraordinary power of the medium, this kind of regulation was considered vital in order to safeguard pluralism. Unlike the Board of Governors of the British Broadcasting Corporation, which this regulatory model superficially resembled, the business of supervision was not to be left solely to the 'great and the good', but instead it was to be the responsibility of a wider range of outside influences. In fact, the range of bodies thus 'incorporated' into the broadcasting policy community remained fairly elitist, but there could be no doubting that, in the wake of 'Stunde Null', the authoritarian conservative and totalitarian demons had finally been exorcised.

4
Controversies Over the Public-Service Broadcasting System

The Attempts to Centralise Broadcasting

The strength of purpose and unity of the ARD was immediately and powerfully reinforced by the manoeuvres of central government. The first CDU/CSU federal government of Chancellor Konrad Adenauer (CDU) immediately made clear its aim to subject West German broadcasting to a far greater degree of central government influence than had been envisaged by either the Allies or by the system's founding legislators in the Länder. As seen, Adenauer had bitterly attacked the NWDR for being 'red' and he now professed his determination to transform the system. Adenauer's ill-disguised ambition to gain control of the medium of broadcasting was shared by many other influential figures in the CDU/CSU, at the federal level at least. On the other hand, the SPD, as the party of opposition at the federal level, was quite naturally anxious to prevent any extension of the federal authorities' power into the sphere of broadcasting. The SPD had retained significant bastions of power at the Land level and was therefore very happy with the decentralised nature of the broadcasting system inherited from the occupation period. The 1950s was a decade of struggle between the Länder and the Bund. It soon became very clear that to gain influence over broadcasting was becoming a prized goal of the politicians.

The Adenauer Government's First Foray into Broadcasting Policy

In 1952 the Interior Ministry drafted a bill with the putative aim of seeking to 'rationalise' the haphazardly unbalanced broadcasting system into five 'broadcasting regions' plus West Berlin. The draft legislation, if successful, would have dismantled the intricate system carefully established by the Länder and the Allies and replaced the NWDR, SWF and RB entirely. Significantly, the draft foresaw the establishment of a federal broadcasting station in Bonn, to be called simply the German Broadcasting Service (Der Deutsche Rundfunk). The Länder were further incensed by the suggestion that, although intended to be a centralised Bonn-directed national channel, Der Deutsche Rundfunk should actually be financed by contributions from them. The government deployed several persuasive arguments in favour of a more centralised broadcasting system. It was argued that the financial disparities between the existing stations were an unnecessary and costly disadvantage of the present system. It was also suggested that the decentralised system weakened the 'voice of Germany' on the international stage and in particular *vis-à-vis* the GDR. It was even argued that a more centralised, Bonn-centred broadcasting system was likely to be less vulnerable to politicisation!

Legislation for a federal law was prepared and duly presented to the Bundestag in March 1953. However, the bill immediately generated very considerable opposition from the SPD, from the public-service broadcasters and from the Länder, including those controlled by the CDU/CSU. The 'Draft Law on the Fulfilment of Common Tasks in the Field of Broadcasting' ('Gesetzentwurf über die Wahrnehmung gemeinsamer Aufgaben auf dem Gebiete des Rundfunks') was subsequently passed on to the Bundestag committee which was specially responsible for the press, broadcasting and film. However, by the end of the legislative period it still had not received a second reading. At this stage, it was swamped by the onrush of the federal election campaign of the summer of 1953. In any case, the prospect of the bill being passed in the Bundesrat (the second chamber of the federal parliament which was entirely composed of delegates of the Land governments) had been very unlikely in view of the opposition, not only of the SPD, but also of many CDU/CSU Land politicians. Moreover, until 1955, the Allied High Commission still retained the right to intervene in the affairs of the West German broadcasting system. It is quite likely that the passage of the projected legislation would have brought about such an intervention in order to protect the independence of West German broadcasting from the state (the principle of 'Staatsferne').

However, the significance of the bill was not lost on the

broadcasters or on the Länder governments: there existed a very real danger that broadcasting might be usurped by the federation (the Bund). This threat to the broadcasting sovereignty ('Rundfunkhoheit') of the Länder stemmed from the vagueness of the Constitution which, as the last chapter has explained, had merely specified that 'culture' was an area of Land sovereignty and which had not explicitly mentioned broadcasting in this connection. The struggle over the law about 'the common tasks' in the field of broadcasting had been no less than a premonition of a far more serious attempt of the federation to impinge on the jurisdiction of the Länder in broadcasting affairs.

In 1957 the CDU/CSU parties gained an absolute majority in the Bundestag. At this time, television was really taking off. There were already over one million television sets in the Federal Republic and within a decade there would be over ten million. Chancellor Adenauer was more determined than ever to gain mastery over the medium and, given new confidence by his absolute majority in the Bundestag, he immediately launched a second attempt to gain federal jurisdiction over broadcasting. This time the controversy was brought about by a dispute between the government and the Länder over proposals to establish a second 'national' television channel with direct federal government involvement.

The Second National Television Channel: 'Adenauer TV'

The issue of a second national television channel was actually placed on the policy agenda by a number of diverse interests. Firstly, the Bundespost was anxious to gain a broadcasting transmission service in order to establish its competence for all areas of telecommunications, and specifically its powers of frequency allocation. Secondly, a coalition of powerful economic interests was pressing for the introduction of a commercial television channel. These interests pointed to the recent example of the introduction of ITV in the United Kingdom. This coalition embraced the advertisers' lobby, the electronics industry and, very significantly, also the newspaper and magazine publishers' associations. Thirdly, the ARD broadcasters themselves were interested in launching a second national television channel and had already asked the Bundespost for frequencies. Then, in July

1958, following a CDU motion to the Bundestag calling for the introduction of an 'independent' national television station, the CDU/CSU government commissioned the Interior Minister to prepare suitable legislation and at the same time commanded the Bundespost to make the necessary technical preparations for a second national channel. In turn, certain commercial interests, mainly publishers, were now encouraged to establish a company called the Free Television Company Ltd (Freies Fernsehen GmbH – FFG) in confident anticipation of the aforesaid government action.

Events now moved fast. In April 1959 the FFG approached the Interior Ministry to announce its state of preparedness, both from a financial and a programming point of view, to commence operations (the FFG aimed mainly to buy in cheap programmes from the film studios, both home and abroad). It quickly became apparent that a distinct 'policy network' was forming between the federal government, the Bundespost and the FFG around the issue of the second national channel. This 'policy network' was circumventing the wider 'policy community' and excluding the public-service broadcasting corporations and the Länder authorities. In December 1959, the federal government actually directed the FFG to prepare its programming schedule. The CDU/CSU Bonn government even guaranteed to provide surety against the collapse of the project to the tune of DM 20 million, later raised to no less than DM 120 million. All this occurred behind the scenes. No formal franchising procedure had taken place. As indicated, no attempt to involve the established broadcasting 'policy community' had been made. Worse still, parliament had not been informed.[1]

The CDU and SPD Ministerpräsidenten (prime ministers of the 'Länder') alike now reacted sharply. They bitterly resented the idea that broadcasting frequencies might be allocated to new commercial operators. They also challenged the constitutionality of the federal government's proposed enacting of broadcasting legislation. The CDU/CSU Ministerpräsidenten expressed their concern to their party colleagues in the federal government in private meetings but to no avail. In a desperate attempt to

---

1. H. von Gottberg, *Initiativen zur Errichtung kommerziellen Rundfunks*, Berlin: Wissenschaftsverlag Volker Spiess, 1979, p. 214.

produce a compromise solution, the Ministerpräsidenten met at Kiel in June 1959 and put forward an alternative proposal to create by 'Staatsvertrag' a new public-service corporation to be called German Television (Deutsches Fernsehen). This channel, it was suggested, should be a member of the ARD, financed by the licence-fee and placed under the control of a supervisory board composed of representatives from the Bund (the federal authorities), the Länder, the existing broadcasting organisations and the public (i.e. the 'socially significant groups').

However, Adenauer immediately disregarded this suggestion, with its implication of the involvement of the wider 'policy community', and instead produced a 'Draft Federal Broadcasting Law' ('Entwurf eines Gesetzes über den Rundfunk').[2] This draft law envisaged the creation of three new stations: the two radio stations established by federal law which have already been mentioned, namely Deutsche Welle and Deutschlandfunk; and the promised second national television channel to be called Germany Television Company Ltd (Deutschland Fernsehen GmbH) and operated from Frankfurt. In fact, Deutschland Fernsehen GmbH was to be little more than a commissioning company for private commercial programming companies such as the FFG. On 29 June 1960 the law was passed in the Bundestag against the opposition of the SPD.

It was, however, clear that, apart from being a riposte to the Länder authorities, the law was a considerable disappointment for the FFG. In the first place, the latter had wanted to receive an exclusive licence to be solely responsible for broadcasting the new channel, whereas it now saw itself faced with the distinct possibility that it might be merely one of several programming companies (although it appeared to face very little real competition). In the second place, the federal government's prime motivation was to gain federal influence over broadcasting, not to hand the new channel entirely over to private enterprise to do with as it pleased. Very clearly, Adenauer was prepared to let business serve his interests, rather than vice versa. The government would be powerfully represented on the supervisory body of the new channel. There can be no doubting that Adenauer

2. *Entwurf eines Gesetzes über den Rundfunk*, Bonn: Deutscher Bundestag, 3. Wahlperiode, Drucksache 1434 of 26.11.1959.

intended the new channel to be 'Adenauer TV'.

By now, Adenauer was unwilling to waste any more time continuing the difficult negotiations with the Länder. Above all, he was eager to have the new channel operating before the federal elections of 1961. He, therefore, simply 'decided' unilaterally to proceed with the founding of the channel as a joint venture between the Bund and the Länder – if need be, without their active assent. The Chancellor's determination that the new channel would amount to 'Adenauer TV' was now made even more clear by the fact that the Bund would take a DM 12,000 direct majority share in the basic capital. The remaining DM 11,000 stake was to be held by the Federal Minister of Justice on behalf of the Länder until they came forward and actively joined the project. In an astonishingly high-handed and authoritarian manner, Adenauer ordered the Federal Minister of Justice to sign the related contract on behalf of all the Länder in anticipation of their eventual compliance. This remarkable act of attempted political *force majeure* actually occurred before the assembled cameras of the public-service broadcasters on 25 July 1960.[3]

Any doubts that Deutschland Fernsehen GmbH was intended to be 'Adenauer TV' were dispelled when the membership of the supervisory body ('Aufsichtsrat') of the new channel became known. It contained a suspicious number of loyal supporters of the Chancellor, including his doctor and a neighbour. The post of business manager went to a ministerial director in the Federal Chancellor's Office. Even CDU politicians expressed some reservations about this kind of 'Personalpolitik'.[4] Moreover, when the Länder declined to accept the shares in Deutschland Fernsehen GmbH which Adenauer had intended for them, these shares were duly taken over directly by the Bund. By now, in the words of Hans Bausch, the Federal Chancellor 'practically personally embodied the company's entire shareholder meeting' ('Gesellschafterversammlung').[5]

3. See von Gottberg, *Initiativen zur Errichtung kommerziellen Rundfunks*, pp. 238–9.
4. Ibid., pp. 241–2.
5. H. Bausch, *Rundfunkpolitik nach 1945. Erster Teil 1945–62*, vol. III of the series *Rundfunk in Deutschland* ed. by H. Bausch, Munich: Deutscher Taschenbuch Verlag (dtv.), 1980, p. 420.

Controversies Over the Public-Service Broadcasting System

The SPD Länder of Hamburg, Hessen, Bremen and Lower Saxony now responded promptly by taking the federal government to the Federal Constitutional Court. In this action, they were tacitly supported by the CDU/CSU Länder. Nevertheless, there was still a real danger that Adenauer would be able to steamroller the development through while the matter was *sub judice*. In the nick of time, the combined Länder, led by Hamburg, managed to obtain an injuction to prevent Deutschland Fernsehen GmbH from starting operations.

The 'First TV Ruling' of the Federal Constitutional Court

The resultant 'First TV Ruling' ('Erstes Fernsehurteil') of 28 February 1961 became a kind of 'Magna Carta' for the broadcasting system of the Federal Republic (see Appendix 2(a)). The Federal Constitutional Court ruled that, in founding Deutschland Fernsehen GmbH, the federal government had offended against the articles in the Basic Law which delineated the spheres of federal and Land jurisdiction. The government's action was therefore contrary to the Constitution ('verfassungswidrig'). The Court confirmed quite unequivocally that according to constitutional principles broadcasting policy was the sole responsibility of the Länder. On the matter of the commercial nature of the proposed channel, the Court's ruling was rather more ambiguous. The Court suggested that constraints of technology and finance meant that broadcasting did not permit a similar degree of plurality of broadcasting channels as resulted from the wide range of newspapers and magazines on offer in the press sector. As a result, broadcasting had to remain subject to public-service regulation in order to ensure that pluralism was provided by other means (i.e. control by the internal supervisory organs of the broadcasting houses etc.). However, the Court did not entirely rule out the possibility of private companies running broadcasting services. Instead, it stipulated that broadcasting by a 'legally established private company' would require the same kind of public accountability and be required to 'allow free expression to all socially significant groups' as the public-service stations. At the time, the ruling was widely interpreted as a rejection of the possibility of private commercial broadcasting and a very serious setback for those interests seeking its

161

introduction. Above all, the ruling clearly amounted to a very clear defeat for Chancellor Adenauer himself and also for the attempt by the CDU/CSU-controlled federation to gain a direct political influence over broadcasting.[6]

At the same time, the Länder, irrespective of their individual political incumbency, had been thrown into a collective defence of their Land prerogatives. On this memorable occasion, the CDU/CSU Ministerpräsidenten had actually opposed, or at least not supported, their own Federal Chancellor. The whole affair ushered in the next phase in the establishment of a distinctive pattern of 'cooperative federalism' in the field of broadcasting. In collaboration with the Intendanten of the public-service broadcasters within the ARD, the Ministerpräsidenten of all of the Länder, regardless of political orientation, now drafted another 'Staatsvertrag' as the legal basis for a second federal-wide television channel. It was to be another public-service broadcasting organisation, the 'Second German Television' service (Zweites Deutsches Fernsehen – ZDF). However, before examining the ZDF, it is more appropriate to recount the sequel to the 'Adenauer TV' affair which was likewise adjudicated by the Federal Constitutional Court.[7]

The So-called 'VAT Ruling' of the Federal Constitutional Court

In July 1971 the Constitutional Court was compelled to intervene once again to reject yet another attempt by the federal authorities to gain a measure of control over broadcasting and confirm the principle of Land competence in broadcasting affairs.

During the so-called 'Grand Coalition' of the SPD and the CDU/CSU (1966–9), this time it was the right-wing Finance Minister Franz Josef Strauss (CSU) who attempted to subject the broadcasters to the influence of the federal government. On this

---

6. *Das Rundfunkurteil ('Erstes Fernsehurteil') vom 28. Februar 1961*, BVerfGE, 12/205. This law is reproduced in W. Lehr and K. Berg, *Rundfunk und Presse in Deutschland – Rechtsgrundlagen der Massenmedien – Texte*, Mainz: von Hase und Koehler Verlag, 1971, pp. 221–56.

7. On the various attempts by the Adenauer CDU/CSU governments to gain control over broadcasting see Bausch, *Rundfunkpolitik nach 1945. Erster Teil 1945–62*, pp. 385–446; also see von Gottberg, *Initiativen zur Errichtung kommerziellen Rundfunks*, pp. 177–254.

occasion, the tactic was indirect and more subtle. By making the licence-fee of the public-service broadcasting system eligible for a VAT levy by the central authorities, Strauss hoped to gain for the federal government in Bonn a very significant, yet hidden, degree of political leverage on the public-service broadcasters. However, like the 'Adenauer TV affair', the 'Strauss VAT affair' quickly led to litigation. First the SPD Land government of Hessen, then the public-service broadcasters themselves appealed to the Federal Constitutional Court against the federal government's policy. Subsequently, the judges ruled four against three in favour of the plaintiffs. In its so-called 'Second TV Judgement' - also known as the 'Value Added Tax Ruling' ('Mehrwertsteuerurteil') - the Federal Constitutional Court specified that the payment of a broadcasting licence-fee was not a commercial transaction, but a contribution to a public fund in return for a public service. It could not therefore be subject to a value added tax (see Appendix 2(b)).

The 'Second TV Judgement' did have a special significance. In common with many of the Court's interventions in the field of broadcasting, its deliberations in reaching its verdict ranged beyond the immediate legal problem to dwell upon broad questions of broadcasting as a social institution. In fact, the various rulings of the Court - and there have been several very important ones over the course of the forty-year history of the Federal Republic - each brought a considerable layer of enlightenment to the general understanding of the nature of public broadcasting. In arriving at its 'Second TV Judgement' in 1971, the Court gave new consideration to the concept of public service. It reaffirmed the principle of the sovereignty of the pluralistic groups in society and determined that neither the state nor the broadcasters themselves in any sense had a proprietary role within the system. Moreover, one particular passage seemed to confirm the non-commercial nature of broadcasting: 'the activity of the broadcasting organisations takes place in the public domain. The broadcasting organisations are publicly accountable; they perform tasks of public administration; they fulfil an integrating function for the whole of the state. Their activity is not of a commercial kind.'[8]

8. *Mehrwertsteuer Urteil vom 27. Juli 1971*, BVerfGE 57/295.

Media and Media Policy in West Germany

In common with the 'First TV Judgement' of 1961, the 'Second TV Judgement' thus rejected attempts, even indirect ones, by the federal authorities to enter into the broadcasting 'policy community'. The central state's sphere of activity in communications remained limited to the Bundespost Minister's competence for telecommunications policy. However, as will be seen in Chapter 6, it was precisely the latter area of state activity that was destined, in the end, to allow the federal authorities finally to achieve a considerable measure of influence over broadcasting policy during the 1980s. In the meantime, however, the strict delineation of jurisdictions by the Constitutional Court seemed to be an end to the matter.

ZDF

Following the government's abortive bid to establish 'Adenauer TV', the Ministerpräsidenten of the Länder grasped the initiative. They were eager now to demonstrate their ability to cooperate with each other according to the principle of 'cooperative federalism' ('kooperativer Föderalismus') in order to discharge their recently confirmed constitutional responsibility for broadcasting. Moreover, they were aware that the ARD itself was also keen to establish a second channel and wanted to get in first. On 17 March 1961 the Ministerpräsidenten met and decided not to leave the matter in the hands of the broadcasters but to establish their own independent second channel. On 6 June 1961 they therefore produced a 'Staatsvertrag', bringing the Zweites Deutsches Fernsehen (ZDF) into existence. The ZDF 'Staatsvertrag' was duly ratified by all eleven Länder and it came into force on 1 December 1961.[9] The fact that the channel had been brought into existence by politicians, if at the Land level, said something about the nature of the link that was developing between broadcasting and politics.

Nevertheless, the ZDF was founded as a public-service cor-

---

9. *Staatsvertrag über die Errichtung der Anstalt des öffentlichen Rechts 'Zweites Deutsches Fernsehen' vom 6. Juni 1961*. This is reproduced in Lehr and Berg, *Rundfunk und Presse in Deutschland*, pp. 161–9 (and the ZDF constitution or 'Satzung' is provided by pp. 170–6); also on ZDF see E. Fuhr, *ZDF Staatsvertrag*, Mainz: von Hase und Koehler, 1972.

Controversies Over the Public-Service Broadcasting System

poration, with all the customary public-service principles written into its constitutional make-up. The 'Staatsvertrag' contained a section laying down such noble aims as a commitment to truth, impartiality, and balance and diversity of opinion. In addition, however, it stipulated that the station had a national, rather than purely regional, vocation. Contrary to ARD television and its federal structure, ZDF was accordingly organised on a centralised basis. Its programmes were to be broadcast from its headquarters in Mainz and it provided only a new nationwide television service but no radio programmes. The 'Staatsvertrag' intended ZDF to be a new service in complete independence from the existing ARD network.

None the less, the Intendant of ZDF was also obliged under the terms of the 'Staatsvertrag' to ensure, through coordination with those responsible for the ARD network, that television viewers in West Germany would be able to choose between two quite distinct programmes. The final protocol of the 'Staatsvertrag' laid a similar obligation upon those responsible for DFS, the 'first channel'. As a result, it became customary for the ARD and ZDF to conclude a coordination agreement for a two- to three-year term, the most important element of which was a programme scheme which was binding on programme-makers in both channels and from which they could deviate only for 'important reasons'. Accordingly, a coordination committee composed of an equal number of representatives from each national television channel met every six months to discuss and vote on potential changes to the programme schedule. In addition, representatives of ARD and ZDF soon became accustomed to meet once a month for a detailed discussion on both channels' programmes before they were published. The coordination agreement of ARD and ZDF also provided for a joint media commission of the two channels to study developments in viewing trends so that the programme schedule could be adapted accordingly if necessary.

The Internal Control of ZDF

The ZDF 'Staatsvertrag' established a 'television council ('Fernsehrat') analogous to the broadcasting councils of the ARD stations. In addition, it provided for an administrative council

165

and an Intendant. The functions of these bodies followed closely the pattern already established in the other public-service corporations. The obligations of the television council consisted mainly of advising the Intendant on fundamental issues of policy and of ensuring that the legally constituted editorial principles and guidelines were observed. In addition, the television council was to approve the budget and appoint the Intendant. The administrative council was to be responsible for the routine management of the station and support and supervise the Intendant primarily in budgetary matters. The Intendant himself was to represent ZDF in and out of court and to be responsible for all the corporation's main business including programme making. Although, in practice, the Intendanten of the ZDF have delegated much of their actual work to departmental directors, they remain ultimately responsible for the delicate business of programming policy, subject only to the ultimate authority of the television council.

As with the ARD stations, the manner of selection of the television council, and also the administrative council, is of great significance in respect of the direction of the station. In the case of the television council, the 'Staatsvertrag' opted for 'corporate' representation with a strong element of 'Proporz'. It testified to the contradictory pressures which by now quite evidently at work in the field of broadcasting policy. A commitment to the constitutional principle of pluralism, and giving free and independent representation to the 'socially significant groups', combined rather uneasily with the politicians' scarcely disguised desire to gain more than a toehold within the regulatory body of the new station.

On the one hand, the majority of the 66 members of the ZDF television council were to be independent representatives of 'socially significant groups'. Accordingly, they represented the interests of the public towards the ZDF. They included, for example, no less than ten representatives from the fields of education, science and the arts, five representatives of the churches, and further representatives from bodies as diverse as the central council of Jews in Germany, the trade unions, the employers' associations, the newspaper publishers, the German journalists' association, women's groups, youth groups and other organisations. On the other hand, the television council also contained no less than 11 representatives of the Länder, 3 from the federal government, and as many as 12 from the political parties in 'Proporz' to the balance of party power nationally. As the result, many prominent politicians, including ministers and members of parliament, have featured as members of the ZDF television council over the years. If this did not give enough scope for politicisation, some of the representatives of the 'socially significant groups' were directly appointed by the Ministerpräsidenten. In the majority of cases, the 'socially significant groups' nominated three candidates and the Ministerpräsidenten made the final choice between them, again giving scope for the 'Proporz' principle to be applied. According to Bausch, only the representatives of the churches could be said to be entirely beyond the scope of the party 'Proporz' effect.[10]

The administrative council of the ZDF consisted of 5 representatives appointed by the broadcasting council, 3 representatives delegated by the 11 Ministerpräsidenten of the Länder and 1 representative appointed by the federal government. The supervisory organs of the ZDF were thus exposed to the danger of politicisation through party patronage, in a similar way to, and even more obviously so than, the practice in most of the other broadcasting corporations. However, rather than reflect the balance of power within a single Land (or as in the case of NDR within several Länder), the politicisation of the ZDF tended to reflect the balance of power relations among all the Länder. Incumbency in Bonn was a factor of very much less significance.

Political Influence Within the ZDF and the Other Public-Service Broadcasting Corporations

Arthur Williams has drawn attention to the existence of 'circles of friends' ('Freundekreise') which quickly grew up around the ZDF, and indeed also the other broadcasting corporations, to denote the groups of politicians and closely related interest groups (i.e. unions in the case of the SPD, business associations in the case of the CDU/CSU) which now began to meet very

---

10. Bausch, *Rundfunkpolitik nach 1945. Erster Teil 1945–62*, pp. 477–80. Also see *Politics, Society and Government in the Federal Republic of Germany, Basic Documents*, ed. C. C. Schweitzer et al., Leamington Spa: Berg, 1984, pp. 256–7.

Media and Media Policy in West Germany

regularly to discuss broadcasting policy. These groups met in different party haunts in advance of sittings of the ZDF television council, or the broadcasting councils of the ARD corporations, in order to 'mandate' the different parties' representatives and sympathisers within the councils. In this way independent decision-making by the councils came to be preempted by the political parties and the pluralistic system of internal regulation came to be reduced substantially to party political and powerful interest group influence.[11]

In this connection, it is interesting to note that later, during the late 1970s and 1980s, when the CDU/CSU came to mount a full-scale attack on public-service broadcasting (see Chapters 5 and 6), the ZDF was to incur much less of their hostility than the ARD. The reason is simple. The ARD gave national coverage to politically suspect (to the CDU/CSU) programmes of the NDR and WDR. On the other hand, after its establishment in 1961 the CDU/CSU soon gained a substantial influence within the ZDF. During much of the 1960s, 1970s and 1980s the balance of political power in the Länder (collectively) lay in favour of the CDU/CSU, and this was translated directly into influence within the ZDF.

The 'Third Channel'

With the introduction of ZDF, the energy which the public-service broadcasting corporations themselves had been devoting to plans for a second ARD channel was now diverted into a new project. They now began to draw up plans to operate a third television service, the so-called 'Third Channel'. This 'Third Channel' was to be operated by the individual corporations of the Länder themselves and composed of 'third programmes', which were effectively regional channels.

These 'third programmes' (as they generally came to be re-

---

11. A. Williams, *Broadcasting and Democracy in West Germany*, London: Bradford University Press/Crosby Lockwood Staples, 1976, pp. 124–7. Also see K. Sontheimer, 'Zum Problem der gesellschaftlichen Kontrolle des Rundfunks und seiner Organisation', in Gemeinschaft der Evangelistischen Publizistik (ed.), *Herrschaft und Kritik: Probleme der Rundfunkfreiheit*, Frankfurt/Main: Verlag Haus der Evangelischen Publizistik, 1974, pp. 48–77.

Controversies Over the Public-Service Broadcasting System

ferred to) were introduced progressively during the mid- to late 1960s. The first to open was the 'third programme' of BR, shortly followed by that of HR, both in the autumn of 1964. These were followed by a joint 'third programme' resulting from an agreement, in order to share costs (as well as general SPD political orientation), by the NDR, the RB and the SFB in northern Germany. This station, called 'Nord 3', opened in early 1965. Next came the 'third programme' of the WDR at the end of that year. WDR was large and powerful enough to eschew any cooperation and, unlike the NDR, was disinclined to help any of its smaller ('CDU') neighbours. Finally in the spring of 1969, the joint service of the three small corporations in south-western Germany (all 'CDU') was established as 'Südwest 3'. Until very recently, they have only been received regionally. As will be seen, satellite broadcasting has now brought the Land stations the option of 'going national'. When it first appeared, however, the 'Third Channel' became in reality a 'Third Network' of distinctly regional channels. The 'Third Channel' broadcasts at the same time as the joint programme of the ARD after 20.00 hours (although some also broadcast in the morning and afternoon).

The 'third programmes' were devised originally as 'highbrow' regional channels appealing to viewer minorities (comparable to BBC2 and Channel 4 in the United Kingdom). Over the passage of time, however, they tended to become more orientated to mass audiences within the Länder, broadcasting an increasing amount of popular programming such as feature films, drama or light entertainment. While they still offer venues for 'alternative' programming, they now compete with the two national channels for a wider audience. At the same time, as regional channels they have also become vehicles for sometimes directly, sometimes less directly, political programming reflecting the incumbency of the main political parties in different Länder and the respective pattern of political influence within the broadcasting corporations. As John Sandford has put it, 'many programmes that might well cause an outcry were they to appear on the ARD or ZDF networks are broadcast with impunity on the third channels'.[12]

12. J. Sandford, *The Mass Media of the German-Speaking Countries*, London: Oswald Wolff, 1976, p. 109.

The Financial Basis of West German Broadcasting

The 'VAT affair' has already demonstrated the 'political' nature of the question of financing broadcasting. Furthermore, the fact that politicians are ultimately responsible for determining the licence-fee (and indeed the amount of advertising) has always been another point of intersection of broadcasting and politics. Public-service broadcasting in West Germany is financed primarily by the licence-fee, which is set at exactly the same level for all Länder at any given time. The amount of the monthly licence-fee for broadcast receiving licences is fixed by the Ministerpräsidenten subject to approval by the Land parliaments. In addition, this fee is supplemented by advertising on both radio and television. The Länder have an indirect say on the revenue from television advertising since, unlike radio, advertising time on television is limited by law. There are, however, certain exceptions to this dualistic model of finance. Deutsche Welle and Deutschlandfunk, the two federal radio stations, carry no advertising at all: Deutsche Welle is exclusively financed from the federal budget; Deutschlandfunk is part financed by the ARD stations collectively and part financed by the federal government. In addition, RIAS Berlin is exclusively financed by the United States government. Finally, it should be mentioned that, until recently, neither NDR nor WDR have sought to carry any advertising at all on their radio networks.[13]

The Licence-Fee

Until the late 1960s and early 1970s, broadcasting enjoyed an extended period of financial stability based on a surprisingly low basic radio licence-fee ('Grundgebühr'). For a long time, this was fixed at monthly fee of DM 2.00 for each family (in West Germany, interestingly, low income families and recipients of national assistance are exempt from licence-fees). After the introduction of television in the early 1950s, an increment of DM 5.00 was added to the 'Grundgebühr' to cover the cost of

---

13. On the finance of the public-service broadcasting system see J. Engler, 'Das Rundfunksystem der Bundesrepublik Deutschland', in Hans-Bredow-Institut/Hamburg (ed.), *Internationales Handbuch für Rundfunk und Fernsehen 1988/89*, Baden-Baden: Nomos Verlagsgesellschaft, 1988, pp. B96–100.

Table 4.1 Development of licence-fees (Deutsche Mark): cost per month

	Licence-fees Radio ('Basic Fee' or 'Grundgebühr)	Television ('TV Fee' or 'Fernsehgebühr')	Both
up to 1969	2,–	5,–	7,–
1970	2,50	6,–	8,50
1974	3,–	7,50	10,50
1979	3,80	9,20	13,–
1983	5,05	11,20	16,25
1988	5,16	11,44	16,60

television broadcasting. For a long time to follow, these duties remained unchanged as rises in expenditure were covered by the enormous increase in the number of broadcasting receiving licences. However, at the end of the 1960s, the television market began to reach saturation level. From this point onwards, the number of viewers and listeners rose only slightly. As a result, the corporations have been periodically forced ever since to appeal to the politicians to raise the monthly licence-fees. In 1970 the Ministerpräsidenten of the Länder granted the broadcasters the first of what was to become a regular series of increases in the licence-fee. By 1983 the 'Grundgebühr' had been raised to DM 5.05 and the television duty to 11.20 making the total 'licence-fee' DM 16.25 per month.

Unsurprisingly, from the moment when the broadcasters first turned to the politicians for an increase in the licence-fee, the level of the fee became a pawn in the political game to influence or control the broadcasting system. In 1971, during the VAT controversy, three judges of the Federal Constitutional Court pointed out that the constitutional principle of non-interference by the state in broadcasting affairs would be better served by removing the authority over the licence-fee from the hands of the state, namely the conference of Ministerpräsidenten of the Länder, and perhaps placing it in the hands of the broadcasters themselves. They suggested that the present situation could be tolerated 'only so long as the state did not abuse its competence in this matter in order to exert influence on the broadcasters and only so long as the public-service broadcasters were thereby assured of sufficient funding'. However, this has not been the case.[14] Raising the licence-fee has always been a protracted and difficult affair at the best of times. Public controversy has tended to focus on the question of the efficiency and cost-effectiveness of the broadcasting corporations. As a highly visible 'tax' the licence exposes the broadcasters to criticism about the expenses they incur – for example, the salaries paid to broadcasting personnel and senior positions in particular. Political oppositions can use such arguments to great effect in order to delegitimise public-service broadcasting corporations deemed to be biased against them, and indeed to seek to delegitimise the public-service broadcasting monopoly itself. As will be seen, after 1983 the CDU/CSU Ministerpräsidenten effectively used their ability to block incremental revision of the licence fee in order to pressure the SPD Ministerpräsidenten into accepting their terms for the introduction of a commercial broadcasting sector. Only after the 1987 signing of a comprehensive 'Staatsvertrag' on the reform of the broadcasting system between the Ministerpräsidenten of all the Länder, providing for a 'dual' (i.e. public/private) broadcasting system, was the licence-fee raised to its present level of DM 16.60 per month and provision made against political delaying tactics (see Chapter 6 and Table 4.1 above).

Until the mid-1970s the Federal Post Office (Bundespost) collected the licence fees and redistributed them to the broadcasting organisations. Since 1976, the licence has been collected and allocated to the broadcasting corporations by a new institution, the Licence Fee Office (Gebühreneinzugszentrale – GEZ). The GEZ is a fully-automated service based in Cologne jointly operated by the ARD and the ZDF. It provides for the collection and subsequent redistribution of the total licence-fee revenue to the individual broadcasting corporations. This innovation rationalised the previously cumbersome process of licence-fee collection by agents of the Bundespost. The ZDF is

---

14. W. La Roche and L. Maassen, *Massenmedien – Fakten – Formen – Funktionen in der Bundesrepublik Deutschland*, Heidelberg: C. F. Müller Juristischer Verlag, 1983, pp. 60–3, esp. p. 61.

apportioned 30% of the total licence revenue and about 50% goes to the nine ARD corporations according to a ratio based on the number of licence-holders in each corporation's area. The Bundespost receives the remaining 20% of the licence-fee revenue in return for its provision of the transmission facilities for the ZDF and the 'third programmes'.

Revenue from Advertising

In addition to the licence fees, all public-service broadcasting corporations have gained supplementary revenues from advertising. According to the ARD 'Jahrbuch' of 1985, in 1984 the ARD corporations received about 20% of their total budget from advertising, and the ZDF about 37%.

The SWF and the BR began broadcasting advertising on their radio programmes as early as 1948. Very quickly, the practice was followed by the other corporations. Similarly, in 1956 the BR was the first to introduce commercials on its television service and within three years all the other ARD corporations had followed suit. Advertising on radio has not been the subject of detailed legal regulation. With the exception of the NDR and WDR, all regional broadcasting corporations carry advertising programmes at least in one of their radio services, usually in the morning. These programmes essentially consist of spot advertising incorporated in a programme of light music. Advertising on radio is broadcast daily with the exception of Sundays and holidays.

Contrary to advertising on radio, advertising on television is subject to very specific legal requirements. When the Länder governments established the ZDF in 1961, they enacted some common regulations for all television advertising. Accordingly, advertising on public-service television had to be broadcast only between 18.00 hours and 20.00 hours as a block, in the case of the ZDF between 18.50 and 19.30 hours. In addition, all advertising had to be clearly separated from the programmes. This means that commercials are broadcast in several individual spots, about five to ten minutes in duration, interrupted by short cartoons. The blocks are usually inserted in between light entertainment programmes. Moreover, television advertising is limited to 20 minutes per day averaged throughout the year and to a daily maximum of 25 minutes. In addition, as with radio, there is no television advertising on Sundays or national holidays. Whereas the regional broadcasting corporations carry their advertising programmes in their regional programmes, the ZDF broadcasts its advertising programmes nationwide like all its other transmissions.

The advertising business of the regional broadcasting corporations is managed by private firms, which are in fact subsidiaries owned by the broadcasting corporations. This reflects the attempt to keep at least a respectable degree of separation of commercial operations from public-service broadcasting services. On the other hand, the ZDF remains responsible for its own advertising, which is managed by a division of the corporation's own administration. Due to these strict limitations, television has accounted for only a minor share of total West German advertising expenditure. In 1983, for example, television advertising accounted for a mere 9.0% of net receipts from advertising. This placed West German television's percentage of total national adspend far behind that of countries such as Ireland (32.9%), Italy (32.0%), Austria (27.8%), the United Kingdom (25.1%) and France (15.5%), and also way behind the European average (16.3%).[15]

During the 1970s and 1980s, the existence of a massive unsatisfied demand for television advertising in West Germany became increasingly conspicuous. Indeed, as will be seen, it became one of the main arguments deployed in favour of the introduction of a commercial broadcasting sector. The advertisers had long had to pay inflated rates for their commercial slots and they had had to, sometimes humiliatingly, kowtow to the moral judgements of those broadcasting corporations' officials responsible for selecting commercials. During the 1970s the advertisers therefore joined a mounting political campaign for the introduction of a commercial sector, in order to reap the benefits of increased competition in the advertisement-carrier market and to escape the public-service bind. Since the politicians remained responsible for legislating the rules governing the distribution of advertising time (therefore revenue) between

15. Euromonitor Publications Ltd, *Advertising In Western Europe*, London: Euromonitor, 1984.

Controversies Over the Public-Service Broadcasting System

the public-service and the commercial broadcasters, the conference of Ministerpräsidenten was destined to become a battleground over this issue as well as that of the licence-fee. This conflict flared up in the 1980s (see Chapter 6).

Revenue Equalisation Scheme

However, until the 1980s the central problem in the financial structure of the West German broadcasting system arose from the vast disparities in size and wealth of the different broadcasting stations – the WDR and the NDR are two of the world's largest broadcasting organisations, while RB, the SR and the SFB are three of the tiniest. There is also an enormous difference in both the number of licences payable in each of the nine areas covered by the regional corporations and in the advertising revenues generated by them. In order to compensate for these inequalities, a cross-subsidisation ('Finanzausgleich') was soon established by the members of the ARD. As a result, the 'poorer' corporations – RB, the SR and the SFB – have been accustomed to receive as much as 30% of their budget from the 'richer' ones. Without such a scheme, the smaller and 'poorer' ARD corporations would have been unable to meet their commitments within a joint ARD television channel.

In 1959, the ARD corporations therefore produced a formula, codified in the 'Agreement on Revenue Equalisation between Broadcasting Corporations' (Abkommen über einen Finanzausgleich zwischen den Rundfunkanstalten'), to organise a financial equalisation scheme enabling the various corporations to meet their public-service obligations to produce and broadcast an adequate schedule of their own. This agreement was subsequently ratified by all the Länder. The main provision of the 'Finanzausgleich', which has operated ever since, is that corporations with fewer than 650,000 listeners and 75,000 viewers are eligible for substantial revenue equalisation payments from the rest of the membership of the ARD. In practice, the beneficiaries have been the SFB, the SR and RB, while the main contributors have been the BR, the NDR and especially the WDR. The equalisation fund is managed by an ARD committee (the Finanzausgleichsgremium), in which the three major ARD stations – the BR, the NDR and the WDR – have three votes and

175

the rest (including DW, DLF and RIAS) have one each. The equalisation agreement did not, however, include the ZDF. According to the revenue equalisation settlement for 1981, DLF received DM 41.70 million, SFB DM 38.98 million, SR DM 27.62 million, and RB DM 23.02 million. This amounted to a total sum of DM 131.32 million, put up by the other six regional broadcasting corporations.[16] The 'Finanzausgleich' testifies to the centrality of the concept, and indeed the vital importance of adhering to the practice, of 'cooperative federalism' ('kooperativer Föderalismus') in the field of broadcasting policy. So too does the manner by which the Länder adjust the licence-fee. The whole financial underpinning of the public-service broadcasting system evolved through, and significantly continued to depend upon, a high degree of accommodation and agreement between the Länder. However, as will be seen, the late 1970s and in particular the 1980s were to produce a dangerous degeneration of this consensus, which in turn was gravely to jeopardise the future of the entire broadcasting system (see Chapters 5 and 6).

Party-Political Pressures on Broadcasting

As seen, since its very beginning, the West German broadcasting system has been exposed to political pressure from the parties. Apart from the blatant attempt by the CDU/CSU federal governments to gain control of the second channel, a marked discrepancy soon became apparent between the constitutional juridical theory of broadcasting, stressing its independence, and the actual practice of the internal organs of control of the ARD broadcasting corporations. The latter had, it seemed, quickly fallen prey to a process of considerable politicisation.

The most obvious cases of party politicisation of the broadcasters were those broadcasting corporations in which the membership of the supervisory bodies was elected according to the 'parliamentary model' – namely, the NDR and the WDR. As seen, the ZDF was another very obvious case, because it gave

16. *Radio und Fernsehen in der Bundesrepublik Deutschland*, Frankfurt/Main: Hessischer Rundfunk, 1980, p. 28.

very similar scope for the party influence by 'Proporz'. However, 'politicisation by stealth' came to afflict all the broadcasting corporations in the FRG to the extent that by the 1970s it had become a rule of thumb that the broadcast media in the north of the country (NDR, WDR, SFB, RB, HR) customarily reflected a distinct SPD bias, while in the south (SR, SWF, SDR, BR) a CDU/CSU orientation usually prevailed. In the broadcasting councils elected by the 'corporate' (otherwise known as 'pluralistic') model the influence of the political parties remained, in practice, hardly less considerable due to the fact that the representatives of the 'socially significant groups' were usually swayed by the positions of the parties to which they often belonged or with which they sympathised. In the 'post-'68' decades this state of affairs was exacerbated by a significant polarisation of politics in the Federal Republic. In turn, this polarisation was inevitably reflected within the broadcasting system. Two major controversies were highly illustrative of the degree of its extent during the 1970s.[17]

The 1972 Controversy in Bavaria

The first major controversy broke out in 1972, during the first legislative period of the 'social liberal' (SPD/FDP) government in Bonn. On this occasion, the cause of the conflict was a blatant attempt by the CSU state government of Bavaria to increase its political influence within the BR, the regional broadcasting corporation of CSU-dominated Bavaria.[18]

17. J. Seifert, 'Probleme der Parteien und Verbandskontrolle von Rundfunk- und Fernsehanstalten', in D. Prokop (ed.), *Massenkommunikationsforschung: 1 Produktion*, Frankfurt/Main: Fischer Taschenbuch Verlag, 1972, pp. 301–30; also on the influence of the political parties within the broadcasting system see H. Kleinsteuber, *Rundfunkpolitik in der Bundesrepublik*, Opladen: Leske Verlag & Budrich, 1982, Chapter IX, 'Rundfunkpolitik als Aktionsfeld von Regierungen, Parteien, Verbänden', pp. 95–112. Also see Sontheimer, 'Zum Problem der gesellschaftlichen Kontrolle des Rundfunks und seiner Organisation'.
18. On the background to this conflict see L. Maassen, *Der Kampf um den Rundfunk in Bayern. Rundfunkpolitik in Bayern 1945 bis 1973*, Berlin: Wissenschaftsverlag Volker Spiess, 1979; for detail on the conflict see Harald von Gottberg, *Initiativen zur Errichtung kommerziellen Rundfunks*, Chapter Four, 'Bestrebungen zur Errichtung kommerziellen Rundfunks in Bayern', pp. 367–447; also see M. Crone, 'Freiheit oder Kontrolle. Der Kampf um die Rundfunkfreiheit in Bayern 1972/73', in W. Lerg and R. Steininger (eds.), *Rundfunk und Politik 1923–73*, Berlin: Wissenschaftsverlag Volker Spiess, 1975, pp. 439–61.

By seeking to amend the original Bavarian broadcasting law of 10 August 1948, the CSU state government suddenly attempted significantly to increase the representation of the political parties on the broadcasting council of the BR. The 1948 law had followed the 'corporate model' and accordingly the ratio of broadcasting council members directly elected by the socially significant groups to those chosen by the political parties was heavily weighted in favour of the former. In total, not more than one-third of the broadcasting council could be allocated to political representatives. However, the new law now sought measurably to increase the influence of the politicians, a move that would have undoubtedly strengthened the influence of the ruling CSU Party, the dominant party in Bavaria. At the same time, the proposed amendments to the 1948 law sought to pave the way for the introduction of commercial broadcasting, at least partly because private sector broadcasting was assumed to be likely to be more favourable to the CSU. The amendments were easily passed by the 'in-built' CSU majority in the Bavarian state parliament and the bill became law on 1 March 1972. However, the SPD reacted immediately in a manner that was, as seen already, highly characteristic of the legalistic political culture of the Federal Republic. The SPD appealed against the law to the Bavarian Constitutional Court. At the same time, this barefaced political intervention triggered an immediate protest among the Bavarian public that even spilled over onto the national scene. During the 1970s more and more social interests had begun to press – often by means of 'unconventional participation' – for a greater say in the policy process. West Germany provided perhaps the best example of this phenomenon in Western Europe, and the field of broadcasting was no exception. The 'citizens' initiative groups', the 'Greens' and 'Alternatives', and the 'Young Socialist' radicals on the left-wing of the SPD were all part of a wider reaction against the pervasive influence of the political parties (the so-called 'Parteienstaat') and the corporatism of West German politics, which was held to disfigure much of public life, including the sphere of broadcasting.[19]

Unsurprisingly the countervailing influence of the law (the

19. On the effects of this phenomenon on public policy making generally see Jeremy Richardson et al., 'The Concept of the Policy Style', in Jeremy Richardson, *Policy Styles in Western Europe*, London: Allen and Unwin, 1982, pp. 1–16.

Controversies Over the Public-Service Broadcasting System

'Rechtsstaat') in West German social and political life and the system of intricate checks and balances built into the constitutional structure through the separation of powers quickly came to play an important role in the unfolding drama. The Bavarian state constitution allowed for the possibility of a popular request ('Volksbegehren') for a plebiscite ('Volksentscheid') on matters of controversial legislation. The demand for a plebiscite to protect BR from this political assault and to ban commercial broadcasting now became the major focus of the mass mobilising activities of a newly-constituted Citizens' Committee for Broadcasting Freedom (Bürgerkomitee Rundfunkfreiheit), organised by SPD politicians, journalists and broadcasters. At the same time, the 'upper house' of the Bavarian state parliament ('Senat') intervened to criticise implicitly the attempt to politicise broadcasting. When in response the CSU majority in the lower house of the parliament attempted to bulldoze an amendment to the Bavarian state constitution in order to facilitate its legislation, the FDP also joined forces with the SPD to take the appeal as far as Bavarian constitutional court.

In the event, this combined pressure of the official SPD opposition, the small but pivotal FDP, the highly vocal citizens' initiative group, the 'Senat' and, ultimately, the threat of intervention of the 'Rechtsstaat' itself proved to be too much for the single political force of the CSU, singularly mighty though it was with its overwhelming dominant party status in Bavaria. It was clear to all that a typically West German compromise solution was the only way out of the impasse. Consequently, in January 1973 representatives of all three political parties met up with the leaders of the citizens' initiative group, Bürgerkomitee Rundfunkfreiheit, to formulate a mutually acceptable solution.

As a result, an amendment to the Bavarian state constitution was soon drawn up which introduced a new article (111a) guaranteeing the publicly accountable and pluralistic control of broadcasting and limiting direct political representation on the broadcasting council of BR to no more than one-third, with the remaining 'socially significant groups' nominating their own representatives themselves. Thus, the 'corporate model' of broadcasting regulation, with the central role it gave to the 'socially significant groups', stood powerfully confirmed by popular demand as a result of the CSU's ill-judged attempt to replace it with the 'parliamentary model' more characteristic of the north German 'SPD' corporations, the NDR and the WDR. The role of the SPD in the affair merely pointed to a paradox that was itself shortly to become the focus of national debate. Significantly, the possibility of the introduction of commercial broadcasting was not ruled out, but, no less significantly, the 'corporate' model of public accountability was to be upheld for all conceivable future forms of broadcasting in Bavaria. This arrangement received popular legitimacy by a plebiscite which was duly conducted on 1 July 1973. Thus, a blatant attempt by ruling politicians to increase their grip on broadcasting received a dramatic popular rebuff. More to the point, however, the practice of political interference was by no means done away with, but merely established within certain limits. The BR continued to be one of the most politicised of the public-service broadcasting corporations.

The Controversy During the 1970s over the NDR

After the Bavarian drama, the question of the politicisation of broadcasting next came to focus on a major controversy over the NDR. This particularly bitter controversy over broadcasting had its roots in the early post-war period.[20]

As seen, the British occupation authorities had favoured the so-called 'parliamentary model' of control of broadcasting, whereby the members of the pluralistically composed supervisory bodies of public broadcasting corporations were selected directly by the Land parliaments. When the NWDR had been split up in the period 1953–5, this system had been retained for the NDR by the 'Staatsvertrag' between the Länder of Hamburg, Lower Saxony and Schleswig-Holstein: on the one hand, the allocation of NDR broadcasting council seats was divided between each of the three north German states that the station served; on the other hand, according to the traditional German principle of 'Proporz', these allocations were then shared out

---

20. A very detailed account of the NDR controversy in English is provided by A. Williams, 'West German broadcasting in the eighties *plus ça change* . . .?', *ASGP Journal, the Journal of the Association for the Study of German Politics*, Spring 1984, pp. 3–35, esp. pp. 5–23; also see Kleinsteuber, *Rundfunkpolitik in der Bundesrepublik*, pp. 102–10.

Controversies Over the Public-Service Broadcasting System

among the major political parties according to their respective parliamentary strengths. As suggested this method presented an obvious opportunity for the direct politicisation of appointments to the supervisory boards.

That the NDR should become the focus of a bitter controversy is explained by two main factors. First and foremost, the NDR had inherited from the NWDR a crucially strategic position within the whole ARD system. Hamburg, the SPD's northern citadel, had enjoyed a central importance both within the NDR itself and also in the wider development of the public-service broadcasting system during the post-war period. Indeed, it had taken the lead in the foundation of the ARD. A major legacy of this dominance of SPD Hamburg during the formative years of the broadcasting system, was that the main news programme of the ARD system, the 'Tagesschau', was produced by the NDR studio in Hamburg. This single fact was bound to fuel CDU/CSU complaints of political bias in the ARD system. As seen, Hamburg had also played a key role in resisting the attempts by the central federation, under Adenauer (CDU), to become involved in broadcasting in 1961. Moreover, the NDR was the second largest broadcasting corporation in the FRG, after the WDR in which an SPD bias was also evident from the 1970s onwards. As seen, between them the NDR and WDR made by far the largest contribution to DFS, the first television channel. They made a similar contribution to the financial equalisation fund, which offset the differential financial strengths and production capabilities of the various regional broadcasting corporations. Therefore, the NDR and WDR, both corporations with an SPD bias, occupied a key pivotal position within the overall public-service system.

The second factor relates to the non-unitary character of the NDR itself. While the WDR remained a unitary station for the state of North-Rhine Westphalia, and as such the practice of politicisation by 'Proporz' remained largely uncontested, the NDR was, by contrast, a corporation serving three states and the product of a 'Staatsvertrag' between these three states. As a result, the political interests of all three states had to be reconciled within the NDR and respected in the composition of its broadcasting and administrative councils. In 1978, the 'fragile truce' within the NDR was dramatically broken. For most of the

1960s and 1970s Lower Saxony had been ruled by the SPD in coalition with the FDP, and Hamburg was very much an SPD stronghold. By contrast, Schleswig-Holstein had for many years been CDU, but the balance of power within the NDR had long reflected SPD strength in the other two states. As suggested, Hamburg's voice, in particular, had seemed to predominate within the NDR. However, in 1978 control of Lower Saxony passed to the CDU, for a brief period of months in coalition with the FDP, then in 1979 by itself. This change in the balance of power in northern Germany was to have immediate repercussions within the NDR. The new CDU Ministerpräsident of Lower Saxony, Ernst Albrecht, gave immediate warning of the shape of things to come: 'the completely biased appointments and personnel policies within the NDR were hitherto impossible to change. Now, however, everyone will have to realise that the majority of the north German population has voted in the CDU.'[21]

At the same time, during the 1970s the two major political groups in the Federal Republic, the CDU/CSU and the SPD, had entered into what Gordon Smith has described as a state of 'balance' at the national level. A clear polarisation of politics had occurred and there were 'comparable chances for either to come to power'.[22] The result was a concomitant increase in the fierceness of party competition nationally. This competition was given an added twist by the central importance that the parties had meanwhile come to attach to the electoral effects of broadcasting. During the 1970s, the CDU/CSU increasingly blamed the 'red' public-service broadcasting corporations, and the fact that the 'red' NDR furnished the ARD with its main national news service, for the series of electoral defeats that had seemingly reduced them to a state of permanent opposition in national politics (1972, 1976 and 1980). By the early 1980s, the CDU/CSU were being powerfully supported by a series of conservative-inspired academic research documents about the political influence of broadcasting.[23]

21. See Kleinsteuber, *Rundfunkpolitik in der Bundesrepublik*, p. 103.
22. G. Smith, *Democracy in Western Germany*, London: Heinemann, 1979, pp. 116–19.
23. Hans-Seidel-Stiftung e.V., *Wahlkampf und Fernsehen*, Munich: Akademie für Politik und Zeitgeschehen der Hans-Seidel-Stiftung e.V. 1980; P. Radunski,

Controversies Over the Public-Service Broadcasting System

Moreover, in 1978 important federal elections were fast approaching; they were scheduled for 1980. In the north German state of Lower Saxony, the CDU had tended to register worse results in national than in regional elections.[24] However, the Land elections of 1978 had brought the CDU great encouragement, Lower Saxony was now a distinctly 'marginal' state. As a result, the new CDU Ministerpräsident of Lower Saxony, Ernst Albrecht, became obsessed with the idea of consolidating his position, and boosting the CDU's chances nationally as well, by wresting political influence over broadcasting in his part of northern Germany from the SDP. Against this background, Albrecht promptly produced a proposal to introduce commercial broadcasting within Lower Saxony and let it be known that he was prepared to see a new 'independent' broadcasting organisation established in his Land. In the summer of 1979, Lower Saxony duly withdrew from the NDR 'Staatsvertrag'.

There immediately followed an enormous political controversy. Gerhard Stoltenberg (CDU Ministerpräsident of Schleswig-Holstein) immediately swung his support behind Albrecht and in the autumn of 1979 a joint proposal was produced to establish a 'CDU' NDR serving Schleswig-Holstein and Lower Saxony alone. Such a development would have suddenly left ('SPD') Hamburg with a much depleted 'rump' corporation which would probably have ended up being as tiny as that of Bremen, Berlin or the Saarland.[25] Faced with this threat, the SPD adopted the characteristic West German line of defence, namely recourse to the law (the 'Rechtsstaat'). The SPD state government of Hamburg now appealed to the Federal Administrative Court (Bundesverwaltungsgericht). This was a serious escalation of the controversy, which might eventually have led all the way up to the Federal Constitutional Court, if its result had not exerted sufficient pressure on the CDU Minister-

---

Wahlkämpfe. Moderne Wahlkampfführung als politische Kommunikation, Munich/Vienna: Olzog, 1980, especially pp. 60 ff. E. Noelle-Neumann, *Die Schweigespirale. Öffentliche Meinung – Unsere soziale Haut*, Munich: Piper, 1980. See also Chapter 5, pp. 202 f. below.
24. See Smith, *Democracy in Western Germany*, p. 143.
25. 'Staatsvertrag über eine Gemeinsame Rundfunkanstalt der Länder Niedersachsen und Schleswig-Holstein – Entwurf', *Media Perspektiven*, 1/1980, pp. 51–70.

präsidenten to compromise. In fact, the ruling of the Federal Administrative Court upheld the main complaints of the state government of Hamburg about the illegality of Albrecht's withdrawal from the 'Staatsvertrag'. Such 'Staatsverträge', it was ruled, could only be terminated by mutual agreement of all the signatories. As the result, the 'unitary' NDR was saved.[26] Once again, the intervention of the 'Rechtsstaat' had prepared the way forward, repeating the pattern already established by the 1961 'First TV Judgement' against 'Adenauer TV'. During the summer of 1980, the three original signatory states of the NDR 'Staatsvertrag' found their way towards a new compromise. A new 'Staatsvertrag' was drafted, duly ratified and passed into law, becoming effective from 1 January 1981. The 'Staatsvertrag' introduced some major new provisions to decentralise the NDR's operations, giving a greater voice to Lower Saxony and Schleswig-Holstein, each of which would now have a studio with its own director and programme controller (in Kiel and in Hanover) which would be on an equal footing with the previously main Hamburg studio. Undoubtedly, the most significant development to arise from the controversy and to be introduced by the resultant 'Staatsvertrag' of 1980 was the move away from the former 'parliamentary model' of selection for the broadcasting council and the administrative council of the corporation. The controversy itself had patently been produced by the ambitions of the political parties either to gain, or to safeguard, the level of their respective political influence within the NDR which the 'Proporz' system had presented to them. In fact, the controversy had actually exposed the weakness of this particular system of organising the supposedly pluralistic internal control structures of broadcasting corporations. Moreover, the outcome of the Bavarian controversy of 1972–3 had seemed to point to the greater desirability of the 'corporate model' ('ständisches Modell'), or at least a mixed model with much stronger representation allocated to the 'socially significant

---

26. 'Bundesverwaltungsgerichtsurteil zur Kündigung des NDR-Staatsvertrags', *Media Perspektiven* 6/1980, pp. 407–8. This issue of *MP* also contains statements on the NDR crisis by Ministerpräsidenten Stoltenberg and Albrecht and the Hamburg Senate. See also 'Bundesverwaltungsgerichtsurteil zum Norddeutschen Rundfunk (Urteil vom 28 Mai 1980 – BVerwG 7A 2.79)', *Media Perspektiven*, 7/1980, pp. 503–14.

groups' than to the appointees of the political parties. The Bavarian controversy had seemingly implied little less than a wholesale public rejection of the 'parliamentary model' of the NDR (and the WDR). The 1980 NDR 'Staatsvertrag', therefore, limited the number of political appointees on the broadcasting council to one-third of its total (i.e. no more than ten in a thirty-seat council). The remaining seats were to be allocated to nominees of the 'socially significant groups'. As was normal, most of these groups were explicitly named in the treaty – for example, the churches, the trade unions, the employers' associations, educational institutions, etc. However, the 'Staatsvertrag' did introduce a very significant innovation to the established pattern of 'corporate' representation. It reserved no less than nine seats to be allocated proportionally by the three Land parliaments to unnamed interest groups. This latter provision was intended to accommodate new social interests which were, as seen, constantly demanding more political participation. As such, it could be seen as an innovation designed to cater to one of the major political and social developments of the late 1970s and 1980s. In typically West German fashion, it was an attempt to incorporate new interests into the larger social 'consensus'. However, the chosen mechanism did still give the political parties some scope for continued political patronage. Having thus adopted a quasi-'corporate model', the NDR 'Staatsvertrag' dispensed with the rather ineffectual programme advisory council ('Programmbeirat') altogether. As seen, this had hitherto been the only body giving representation to the 'socially significant groups'. Within a short period, the WDR followed the NDR's example in adopting a 'quasi-corporate' model.[27]

An End to Politicisation?

However, these major developments during the 1970s should not lead to any general misconception that the problem of political influence within broadcasting corporations was ex-

27. 'Neufassung des Staatsvertrages über den Norddeutschen Rundfunk' (signed on 17 July 1980 in Bonn), *Media Perspektiven*, 7/1980, pp. 480–502; also see 'Entwurf eines Gesetzes zu dem Staatsvertrag über den NDR' (of the Land Niedersachsen), *Media Perspektiven*, 9/1980, pp. 633–44.

punged by the general acceptance by now of the 'corporate model' of internal supervisory organ. In the case of the corporate model, the political parties merely had to act less directly and more subtly in penetrating the broadcasting corporations. Inevitably, the range of interests represented in broadcasting councils remained circumscribed, generally being limited to the consensus that made up the West German social, economic and political establishment. Moreover, party patronage still played a role, if in a more hidden fashion, so extensive were the scope of the permeation and envelopment of other elites by the political parties in the Federal Republic (the 'Parteienstaat'), and the degree of 'Verflechtung' (interpenetration) of interests and parties.

As West Germany entered the 1980s, a decade which was to bring the political conflicts about broadcasting to an even higher, and far more dangerous, level of polarisation (see Chapters 5 and 6), all but one of the Intendanten of the public-service broadcasting corporations belonged to the party which was in power in the respective Land (or in the case of the NDR the party with the balance of power in three Länder). The exception was the 'non-party' Werner Hess, Intendant of HR, but he too was surrounded by a 'Freundekreis' connected to the ruling party of Hessen, the SPD (until 1988). In the case of the ZDF, the Intendant, Karl-Günther von Hase, was also not actually a member of a political party, but it was well known that his loyalty had lain with the CDU for years. Indeed, the influence of the CDU/CSU within the ZDF was a very conspicuous fact (reflecting the power of the CDU/CSU at Land level during the 1970s).[28]

The politicisation of the internal supervisory organs of the broadcasting corporations inevitably involved a certain penetration of party patronage deep into the corporations themselves. Politicisation of senior appointments and other posts in the programming field became fairly commonplace. In particular, the parties strove to influence the appointment of chief editors ('Chefredakteure'), the heads of programmes and sometimes even junior positions in the news and current affairs departments. The politicisation of the broadcasting houses was per-

28. Kleinsteuber, *Rundfunkpolitik in der Bundesrepublik*, pp. 99–100.

Controversies Over the Public-Service Broadcasting System

haps best symbolised by the contrast between the left/liberal and 'critical' reporting of the flagship political magazine programme 'Panorama', broadcast by the NDR, and the similar programme 'Monitor' of the WDR, and, on the other hand, the predominantly right-wing or conservative reporting of the 'ZDF-Magazin'.

The Statute Movement

At the same time, during the turbulent 1970s the broadcasting corporations, like the press, were subjected to another kind of political pressure, this time in the shape of demands for a greater say in their management from the journalists working within them. To no small extent, these demands of the journalists were related to the above-mentioned party-political pressures on broadcasting. To some extent, the journalists' activism in the late 1960s and early 1970s was also part of the wider 'liberationist' or 'participatory' spirit of 1968.

During the period 1968–70 'editorial committees' ('Redaktionsausschüsse') sprang up in every single broadcasting corporation in the country to demand the enactment of statutes guaranteeing 'internal broadcasting freedom' and 'internal democracy' for broadcasting producers and journalists. Collectively, this phenomenon was known as the 'statute movement' ('Statutenbewegung'). In 1970 the broadcasters' union, the Rundfunk-Fernseh-Film-Union (RFFU), published a draft statute as a basis for collective bargaining. The RFFU also established a codetermination commission ('Mitbestimmungskommission') which set itself the immediate task of exploring ways and means of gaining codetermination (or management participation) rights in the ZDF for broadcasting staff, including journalists, editors and producers. Like the journalists of the press, those involved in television production were seeking special safeguards for their editorial and journalistic independence. The various draft statutes which were now drawn up all contained some kind of reference to the need to defend journalists and programme producers from being compelled to broadcast material which was counter to their beliefs. On the other hand, the Intendanten pointed out that the whole concept of public-service broadcasting, unlike the press, involved the presentation of a balance of different viewpoints. The conflicts were most intense within the WDR, the NDR and the ZDF. According to Hans Bausch, there were two reasons for this: firstly, that as large corporations they were inevitably harder to 'rule'; secondly, they were the most politicised of the corporations (although, as suggested, this was by no means necessarily the case).[29]

Only in the case of the NDR was a statute for the programme workers of the NDR actually produced as a result of the statute movement. Nevertheless, over the period 1969–74 most corporations drew up some kind of document at least resembling a statute. These 'statutes' amounted to a typically German compromise. They neither granted the programme staff all that they sought, nor did they leave them entirely empty handed. The NDR statute went furthest in the former direction, whereas in other cases management declined to go very far at all. Generally, however, the attempt was made to improve the internal flow of information within the broadcasting corporations and to give the workforce a feeling of greater involvement and responsibility.

The 'statute movement' was seen by its fierce opponents on the CDU/CSU side of the political spectrum as a dangerous attempt by the 1968 inspired 'liberation movement' to infringe the constitutional principle of broadcasting freedom. Conventional wisdom accepted that the broadcasting policy community was already pluralistic enough, and any attempt by the production workers to interfere with the established edifice would upset its assumed balance, challenge the authority of the Intendant system and, worse still amount to a direct assault by a special group on the sovereignty of the broadcasting councils. As seen, the Constitution and subsequent broadcasting legislation of the Länder had ruled out the possibility of any particular sectional group in society gaining any special say in the field of the media. According to the opponents of the statute movement this would be the case were the production workers to gain extended rights in the running of the broadcasting corporations.

29. H. Bausch, *Rundfunkpolitik nach 1945. Zweiter Teil 1963–80*, vol. IV of the series *Rundfunk in Deutschland*, ed. by H. Bausch, Munich: Deutscher Taschenbuch Verlag, 1980, p. 824.

Controversies Over the Public-Service Broadcasting System

Thus, the opponents of the statute movement deployed similar legalistic arguments to those produced by their counterparts in the press sector. In both cases, the demand for 'internal democracy' was held to carry the danger of an infringement of the 'freedom of the media'.

In the end, however, the statute movement simply ran out of steam. It was undoubtedly weakened by the failure of the SPD properly to embrace it. Cynics might point to the fact that the SPD benefited from the practice of politicisation by party patronage and the 'Proporz' system. There was, therefore, little practical incentive for the SPD government to reform the system in a way that would free the broadcasters from the 'Parteienstaat'. Perhaps more importantly, the statute movement was quickly overtaken by other developments, namely the progressive switch during the 1970s of the focus of controversy – and of the concerns of the broadcasting personnel themselves – to the more pressing questions of the introduction of new technologies, the break-up of the public-service broadcasting monopoly and the impending introduction of commercial broadcasting (see Chapters 5 and 6).

Nevertheless, the statute movement was not entirely without effect. It did compel the management of the broadcasting corporations, and especially the Intendanten, to think much more seriously about the legitimate rights of the producers and journalists within the field of broadcasting. As a result, in all the stations, and especially within the NDR, the position of the broadcasting personnel was considerably strengthened. In particular, the broadcasting personnel gained greater public recognition of their contribution to broadcasting's critical control function in a living, rather than a merely formal, democracy. In sum, the controversy probably led to a somewhat greater transparency of broadcasting policy and increased public awareness of the pressures to which it was subject.

Moreover, the statute movement did contribute to the creation of a climate of popular opinion which prevented some fairly open attempts by certain politicians to constrain the freedom of reporting of the broadcasters. For instance, at the height of the controversy, the very conservative Intendant of the SWF, Helmut Hammerschmidt, seeking to counter 'left-wing' trends in broadcasting journalism (emanating from the 'SPD' northern

189

German stations), had produced a controversial paper calling for the enactment of a new set of guidelines for ARD programming. The main thrust of this paper argued for a new degree of restraint on the expression of political comment by broadcasting journalists. This blatant attempt to 'tame' broadcasting journalism met with abject failure in the face of the opposition of the other Intendanten, who had been compelled by the statute movement to reexamine the first principles of broadcasting in a parliamentary democracy. Put on the spot, they concluded that the critical control function of broadcasting could not be reduced to an anodyne reflection of the lowest common political denominator. As a result, at least in part, of the statute movement a healthy confrontation of views in German broadcasting was safeguarded.[30]

Commercial Television

Lastly, the West German broadcasting system has, almost from its very foundation, been the subject of a running political battle over the issue of commercial broadcasting. Neither the Constitution nor the early broadcasting legislation of the Länder had gone quite so far as to rule explicitly in favour of public-service monopoly. Rather there had arisen a general assumption of such a monopoly situation, flowing from the law-makers' single-minded concentration on establishing the all-important principle of public-service broadcasting, and also from general interpretations of important rulings of the Federal Constitutional Court (see Appendix 2). However, even these landmark rulings of the highest court in the land had not gone so far as to explicitly and negatively rule out the possibility of commercial broadcasting. What the court had ruled, in a positive statement, was simply that broadcasting legislation should guarantee pluralism. This element of vagueness or open-endedness seemed to

30. For a detailed discussion, in English, of this phenomenon see A. Smith, 'The German Television Producer and the Problem of Internal Democracy', Chapter 6 in A. Smith, *The Politics of Information*, London: Macmillan, 1978, pp. 54–73; also see Bausch, *Rundfunkpolitik nach 1945. Zweiter Teil 1963–80*, pp. 817–29; and, W. Hoffmann-Riem, *Redaktionsstatute im Rundfunk*, Baden-Baden: Nomos Verlagsgesellschaft, 1972.

Controversies Over the Public-Service Broadcasting System

leave the door slightly ajar to the would-be commercial broadcasters.

During the post-war period, there have been several noteworthy attempts by the publishers to become involved in broadcasting. Even before the foundation of the ARD, newspaper publishers in south-western Germany had drawn up plans to establish a television service. On this occasion, these plans did not materialise in any concrete attempt to break the public-service monopoly. Later, the publishers were to be disappointed by the failure of Chancellor Konrad Adenauer to establish a commercial national television channel in 1960/1. Then, in 1971, a private television company called the Television Company of Berlin Daily Newspapers (the Fernsehgesellschaft Berliner Tageszeitungen) demanded a franchise to broadcast in Berlin. On this occasion, the ruling SPD government of West Berlin contested the publishers' right to break the public-service monopoly of the SFB and, in line with the characteristic pattern of broadcasting policy-making, the Federal Administrative Court was quickly drawn into the affair. Once again, the commercial broadcasting lobby was frustrated by the Court's ruling against them, by reason of the technical limitations on broadcasting, namely the 'scarcity of frequencies'. Yet another disappointment followed shortly in 1972 when the hopes of the Bavarian publishers to become involved in broadcasting collapsed with the failure of the CSU majority in the Bavarian state parliament to introduce commercial broadcasting in that Land. As a result, the Bavarian publishers were thoroughly disheartened by the specific introduction of a clause in the state's constitution which explicitly stated that broadcasting should henceforth be conducted in 'public-service responsibility and by public-service bodies' (Article 111a, paragraph 2).

However, in the meantime, a chain of developments had been set in motion by a controversy in the Saarland, which was to run and run until the Federal Constitutional Court once more intervened definitively in 1981, after a period of no less than fourteen long years. The special significance of this particular controversy was that it was destined to lead to another landmark ruling of the Federal Constitutional Court, the so-called 'FRAG Judgement' (see Appendix 2 (c) and Chapter 5, p. 235 f.)

Very briefly, in 1967, the CDU Saarland state government

amended its original broadcasting law in a manner designed to enlarge the scope for commercial broadcasting. In this instance, the SPD opposition seems to have been uncharacteristically compliant over the matter. In fact, the motivation of both parties was illustrative of the extent to which the 'Parteienstaat' had become a threat to the independence of broadcasting. It appears that both major parties harboured an ambition to take a large stake each in a proposed new commercially-funded channel for the Saarland.[31] At the same time, however, this measure encouraged a group of Saarland newspaper publishers to immediately found a commercial consortium, called the Free Broadcasting Company Ltd (Freie Rundfunk AG – FRAG) and demand a broadcasting franchise. When the state government delayed and later refused to award the FRAG a franchise, there ensued a long-drawn-out chain of court cases and referrals (between the administrative and the constitutional court systems) which was eventually only settled by the Federal Constitutional Court many years later, in 1981. In the event, the Court was to rule against the original amendment of the Saarland media law, but in doing so effectively open up the legal door to commercial broadcasting, as the following chapter will describe.

31. Bausch, *Rundfunkpolitik nach 1945. Zweiter Teil 1963–80*, pp. 618–19.

5
The Controversy Over the Introduction of the New Media

During the 1970s, and especially the 1980s, technological developments – notably cable and satellite – have led to a new questioning of traditional West European assumptions upon which the need for public regulation of broadcasting had been based. Historically, a major justification of public regulation had been the 'scarcity of frequencies' for broadcast transmission. As seen, in West Germany this had been one of the central rationales behind various landmark rulings of the Federal Constitutional Court, underpinning the whole edifice of the public-service broadcasting monopoly. However, with new cable and satellite technologies this scarcity is being replaced by a potential abundance of means of transmission. Arguably, this simple fact has prompted a 'paradigm change' in the theory and practice of West European broadcasting.[1]

In West Germany, as seen, there has been a long history of pressure for the break-up of the public-service broadcasting monopoly and the introduction of private commercial broadcasting. However, legal brakes on change had been set by key judgements of the Federal Constitutional Court. Despite such restraints, with the advent of the new technologies in the 1970s, the pressures for change gradually became overwhelming. This chapter will give an account of the development of a very powerful 'coalition for change', describing the rise of a broad alliance of social and political forces clamouring for a radical

---

1. On this paradigm change see: K. Dyson and P. Humphreys, 'Regulatory change in Western Europe', in K. Dyson and P. Humphreys, *Broadcasting and New Media Policy in Western Europe: A Comparative Study of Technological Change and Public Policy*, London: Routledge and Kegan Paul, 1988; also see W. Hoffmann-Riem, 'Law, Politics and the New Media', in K. Dyson and P. Humphreys (eds.), *The Politics of the Communications Revolution in Western Europe*, London: Frank Cass, 1986, pp. 125–46.

reform of the broadcasting system. It will also show how the entrenched interests in favour of the status quo, as it has been so far described, were progressively forced very much onto the defensive.

The KtK: Kommission für den Ausbau des technischen Kommunikationssystems

Any discussion of the debate about the 'new media' has to begin with an account of the way policy was initiated by the Commission for the Development of the Technical Communications System (Kommission für den Ausbau des technischen Kommunikationssystems – KtK) in the mid-1970s. The purpose of the KtK was to explore the implications of new technological developments in the field of communications generally. It was established in February 1974 by Horst Ehmke (SPD) who was jointly responsible for the Federal Ministry for Research and Technology (Bundesministerium für Forschung und Technologie – BMFT) and the Bundespost Ministry. Characteristically, the KtK was 'pluralistically' composed of representatives of industry and commerce (51%), the government and the political parties (32%), publishers and broadcasting institutions (11%), and the churches (2%). As was customary, the commission was well serviced by experts, including specialists from the telecommunications industry and the Bundespost. It was chaired by a leading academic with close links to industry, Professor Eberhard Witte.[2]

In January 1976, the KtK delivered a unanimous report. Its recommendations were cautious. The commission came down in favour of concentrating on the extension of the telephone network, its modernisation (digitalisation) and also on the development of a number of different narrowband networks for various kinds of telecommunications services, such as telex. The KtK was sceptical about broadband cable on the grounds of cost and demand. Moreover, at this time, conflict over the future of broadcasting was growing. Therefore, the KtK adopted a compromise formula: the report recommended the establishment of

---

2. M. Schmidbauer, *Kabelfernsehen in der Bundesrepublik Deutschland*, Munich: K. G. Sauer Verlag, 1982, p. 49.

The Controversy Over the Introduction of the New Media

'pilot-projects' to test out the new modes of finance, organisational forms and content of cable systems. Nevertheless, as Hoffmann-Riem has argued, this cautious recommendation was a momentous and fateful development, since it meant that, in effect, for the first time in the history of the Federal Republic, private commercially financed broadcasters would be permitted, if only on an experimental basis. There arose the distinct possibility that once private television was introduced – even if only on an experimental basis – it would be politically difficult to do away with it later.[3]

The Group Politics of the Broadcasting Revolution

The broadcasting revolution that has occurred between the late 1970s and 1980s as the result of the introduction of new technologies has been accompanied by a very complex pattern of group politics. During the 1970s, a powerful 'coalition for change' emerged to challenge the 'coalition of forces' in favour of the status quo in broadcasting policy. Moreover, critical elements began not only to argue against the introduction of the new technologies, but also to question the premises of both sides regarding the proper organisation of the media. To a large extent, broadcasting and new media policy has been shaped by the interplay of these group political forces. The purpose of the section is to describe broadly the field of these group political forces. Firstly, it is necessary to examine the 'coalition for change'.

The Bundespost

At the centre of developments concerning the new technologies stood the Bundespost. Under Article 73 of the Basic Law, the

---

3. Kommission für den Ausbau des Technischen Kommunikationssystems – KtK, *Telekommunikationsbericht mit 8 Anlagebänden*, Bonn: Bundesministerium für das Post- und Fernmeldewesen, 1976. For a critical view of the KtK's role in paving the way for the introduction of the new media and commercial broadcasting see W. Hoffmann-Riem, 'New Media Policies in West Germany: The Politics of Legitimation', in K. Dyson and P. Humphreys (eds.), *The International Political Economy of Communication Policies*, London: Routledge & Kegan Paul (forthcoming).

Bundespost was a federal public institution, directed by the Minister of Posts and Telecommunications (Bundespostminister). During the 1970s the Bundespost became increasingly interested in the introduction of the new mass communication technologies (cable, satellite, and videotext). In the first place, its motivation was technocratic and economic in nature. The Bundespost was naturally interested in any development that affected the sphere of telecommunications. However, it also had a powerful organisational-political motivation for becoming involved in the development of new communications systems. The Bundespost enjoyed a monopoly status in all areas of the telecommunications network and was therefore very concerned to maintain this monopoly for all future forms of communication. To be involved in the development of new systems ensured its future control of all aspects of the system.

The Bundespost was a very powerful actor in the group political game. Its power derived not only from its key role in the administration but also from the fact that it was the largest economic concern in the Federal Republic. In 1987, it had over half a million employees, an annual turnover of DM 50 billion. In the period 1975–80 alone the Bundespost invested between DM 6 billion and DM 10 billion per annum, rising to DM 12 billion in 1981.[4] By 1987, the Bundespost handled an investment volume of DM 18 billion. Its political power was further strengthened by the fact that a broad section of the West German information and communications industry depended on it as their main customer. As a result, the policies of the Bundespost had a central significance for the development of economic policy more generally.

The power of the Bundespost was very considerably reinforced by the incestuous relations that it enjoyed with West German industry. It maintained very close contact with many 'client' firms. Indeed, the position of the West German electronics industry in both domestic and international markets was directly related to the Bundespost's preferential treatment (subsidies, research grants and massive state contracts). Moreover, the Bundespost's enormous powers of investment gave it very considerable scope for pressurising other actors in the group

---

4. See Schmidbauer, *Kabelfernsehen*, p. 60.

The Controversy Over the Introduction of the New Media

political game. Through the Bundespost's key role in the development of telecommunications policy, the central government was able to exercise a new degree of central control over the future development of the broadcasting system. To be more precise, the Bundestag was able to 'blackmail' other actors in the political system, most notably the Länder, who were theoretically responsible for broadcasting policy but who, in the bleak economic climate of the 1980s, were also especially anxious to attract federal investment.[5]

The Electronics Industry

Apart from the Bundespost, the electronics industry itself represented a powerful economic lobby for the introduction of the new communications technologies. There were several aspects to the industry's interest in the new broadcasting technologies.

During the 1970s the West German electronics industry began to see the new communications technologies as a golden opportunity for breaking out of a situation of market saturation for its more traditional products (indeed, this had been the pattern earlier, in the case of colour television). At the same time, foreign competition in the new markets was additional important motivation. By the mid-1970s there had arisen fairly widespread fears in West Germany that a 'technology gap' had opened up with powerful overseas competitors, most notably the United States and Japan, in the field of information and communications technologies. Export chances depended on the existence of a flourishing domestic market. A healthy domestic market was deemed to be crucial for the maintenance of low unit costs through the existence of high production capacities. In addition, a vigorous domestic market was also seen as being highly important for the demonstration effect that it provided for West German products.

The electronics industry amounted to a very powerful lobby for a number of reasons. Firstly, the West German electronics

---

5. A. Zerdick, 'Ökonomische Interessen und Entwicklungslinien bei der Durchsetzung neuer Informations- und Kommunikationstechniken', *Rundfunk und Fernsehen*, 30. Jahrgang, no. 4, 1982, pp. 485–6; and H. Kleinsteuber et al. (eds.), *Medien: Thema Kabelfernsehen*, Berlin: Wissenschaftsverlag Volker Spiess, 1980, pp. 59–64.

industry was characterised by a very high degree of concentration of resources in a few firms: notably, Siemens AG, AEG-Telefunken and Standard Elektrik Lorenz (SEL). These giant firms already received over half of the Bundespost's investment in telecommunications. In the second place, this branch of industry was very powerfully organised in the Central Association of the Electronics Industry (Zentralverband der Elektronischen Industrie – ZVEI), which in turn was an influential member of West Germany's powerful central business association, the Federal Association of German Industry (Bundesverband der Deutschen Industrie – BDI). Thirdly, due to its central role in the economy, the industry had privileged access to government.

During the 1970s, the electronics industry began to see its long-term prospects as being dependent upon the development of a national cable programme. However, the industry was torn between giving priority to traditional copper-coaxial cable, which was already easily mass-produced and relatively inexpensive, or to the new fibre-optic cable, which was technologically much more promising, because it provided greater channel capacity and the possibility of 'interactive' (i.e. two-way) communication, but was also very much more expensive. In the case of the latter, production capacity would have to be greatly developed before a national fibre-optic cable programme became a serious prospect. In short, the industrial lobby was torn between short- and long-term goals. Nevertheless, the electronics industry amounted to a very powerful lobby indeed in general favour of a broadcasting revolution. It not only stood to gain lucrative contracts for cable, but also a much wider range of new products would be required (e.g. satellite equipment, new reception equipment, etc.).[6]

The Publishers of the Press

The publishers of the press, and their trade associations the BDZV and the VDZ (for the magazine publishers), have played a very key role in the policy debate about the new media. The

---

6. Zerdick, 'Ökonomische Interessen und Entwicklungslinien', pp. 482–4; and Kleinsteuber et al. (eds.), *Medien: Thema Kabelfernsehen*, pp. 53–8; also see H. Ebinger, *Neue Medien. Strategien von Staat und Kapital*, Frankfurt/Main: Nachrichten-Verlags GmbH, 1983.

The Controversy Over the Introduction of the New Media

BDZV, in particular, has accompanied its longstanding demand for private commercial enterprise in cable television with massive attacks against the existing public-service broadcasting system.[7] The press had mixed motivations for mounting its campaign during the 1970s. On the one hand, it had always regarded broadcasting as a serious competitor for its major source of revenue, namely advertising. As seen, during the 1950s and 1960s the publishers' attempts to block advertising by the public-service broadcasting corporations had led to the establishment of the Michel Commission, which in the event had been a great disappointment to them. During the 1970s, they now came to see the new media both as a potential existential threat, if they were excluded from participation, or as a golden opportunity, if they could gain a role in their introduction. As seen, the publishers had always harboured an ambition to extend their sphere of activities to encompass commercial broadcasting and had therefore long supported the break-up of the public-sector monopoly. The debate about the introduction of new communications technologies now served to raise anew the hopes of the publishers that the constitutional obstacles to commercial broadcasting could at last be removed.

The publishers felt themselves to have been underrepresented in the KtK (in which they only had one representative out of a total of 23), so together with the trade association of the printing industry (Bundesverband der Druckindustrie) and the Deutsche Presse-Agentur (their news agency) they formed their own working party on the new technologies: the Arbeitsgemeinschaft technische Kommunikationssysteme der Presse (Atk-Presse). At the same time, individual newspapers launched a vigorous campaign, orchestrated by the BDZV, in favour of the new media. Forced to recognise the futility of their struggle to limit the steady encroachment of broadcasting into their main source of revenue, the publishers now placed all their hopes on one more major bid to enter the broadcasting sector themselves. Indeed, their economic motivation was growing.

For the greater part of the 1970s the press had registered an upward trend in both advertising revenue and circulation. In the mid-1970s, it depended upon advertising for around two-

---

7. Kleinsteuber et al. (eds.), *Medien: Thema Kabelfernsehen*, p. 38.

thirds of its income, and by 1978 it accounted for about 45.6% of total advertising expenditure in the FRG.[8] However, since 1978 the trend in the share of the press of total advertising expenditure has been downward: in 1980 the share of the press was 42.7%, in 1981 it fell to 41.6%, and in 1982 it fell again to 40.9%. This loss in advertising share was compensated to some extent by a rise in prices and a continued rise in circulation, which rose by 4% in 1982 and continued to rise in 1983. But this rise in circulation was largely accounted for by one newspaper, namely Springer's *Bild-Zeitung*, and at the same time costs increased by the roughly the same percentage as circulation (4.2% in 1982). By contrast, the share of total adspend taken by broadcasting had been steadily increasing since 1975. Between 1975 and 1980 the gross advertising revenue of radio had increased by 73% and that of television by 22%, compared to a meagre rise of 8% registered by the press.[9] The press was thus losing ground significantly to the broadcasters, even before the challenge of increased competition from the new media had materialised. Hence, the press had a powerful economic motivation for wanting to become involved in the new media sector. Therefore, during the 1970s, the major publishers all established companies through which to invest in the electronic media, notably Bertelsmann's Ufa-TV, Springer's Ullstein AV, and Burda's Burda-Scope.[10]

The Advertisers' Lobby

The advertisers' interest in the new media could be explained simply by their interest in seeing more competition between carriers of advertising. The public-service monopoly of broadcasting meant that they had to pay higher rates for broadcast advertising than they would if the public-service broadcasters were compelled to compete with commercial broadcasting outlets. Moreover, the advertisers anticipated a massive increase in

---

8. 'Daten zur Mediensituation in der Bundesrepublik', *Media Perspektiven* 1979, p. 32.
9. M. Brynin, 'A Report on Media Policy in West Germany', Manuscript, Leeds University, Centre for Television Studies, 1984, p. 37.
10. Schmidbauer, *Kabelfernsehen*, pp. 69–70; and Zerdick, 'Ökonomische Interessen und Entwicklungslinien', pp. 479–80.

and the licensing of new commercial broadcasters. The advertisers were also interested in increased broadcast advertising because, in many cases, it was deemed to be a far more effective means of communicating their message. Advertising in the press was perforce limited to verbal communication. Broadcast advertising was far more powerful because it could employ non-verbal communication: it worked through the medium of fast-moving images, striking colours and soothing or otherwise compelling tones. Moreover, the new media also brought the prospect of 'narrowcasting', namely programmes aimed specifically at special minority audiences. By this means, advertising expenditure could be rationalised to avoid the 'overkill' that was inevitably involved in mass broadcasting.

The advertising industry was collectively organised in the Central Committee of the Advertising Industry (Zentralausschuß der Werbewirtschaft – ZAW). Founded in 1949, the ZAW organised sub-associations of all areas of the industry, including those benefiting from advertising, the various branches of the media, the advertising agencies and the advertising profession itself. This body was a powerful lobbying force *vis-à-vis* government, the legislature, the public administration and other organised groups in the Federal Republic. It had its own democratic constitution, with a 'General Council' ('Präsidialrat') at the head of its forty-two sub-associations, and it could boast an impressive number of expert committees ('Fachausschüsse') to explore into all areas of specialised concern. In addition, the ZAW had its own newssheet, the *ZAW basisdienst*, and presided over its own statistics office, the Information Association to Monitor the Dissemination of Advertising Carriers (Informationsgemeinschaft zur Feststellung der Verbreitung von Werbeträgern e. V. – a very valuable source of statistics relating to the media industry). Apart from boasting this impressive degree of collective organisation, the advertisers could also fairly claim to represent a very important area of economic activity. According to their own estimate in 1979, their industry accounted for an annual expenditure in West Germany of around DM 200 million. Moreover, the industry employed around 300,000 people. In sum, the ZAW amounted to a very powerful lobby indeed.[11]

11. Zentralausschuß der Werbewirtschaft, *Der ZAW. Aufgaben, Organisation,*

The CDU/CSU

During the 1970s, as seen, the CDU/CSU mounted a vigorous campaign against the public-service broadcasting corporations, which it had become increasingly inclined to blame for the series of electoral defeats that had seemingly reduced them to a state of permanent opposition in national politics.[12] In fact, during the 1960s and 1970s the CDU/CSU parties had actually managed steadily to increase their representation in the administration of certain broadcasting corporations in the southern part of Germany, particularly Bavaria, through the characteristic system of party patronage.[13] Nevertheless, the CDU/CSU became vigorous proponents of a broadcasting revolution, designed to introduce a new commercial broadcasting sector.

At the time of the KtK, the CDU/CSU had already begun to evaluate the new technologies of broadband cable and satellite as an interesting lever to bring about a dramatic transformation of the structure of broadcasting, in particular the removal of the monopoly of the public-service broadcasters. Non-conservative media analysts detected an ulterior motivation for this interest in the new media: namely, their ill-disguised interest in 'strengthening their political position in the area of the mass media'.[14] The CDU/CSU's support for commercial broadcasting reflected, at least in part, the belief that its values and political tone would be more in tune with CDU/CSU political positions, as was clearly the case with much of the private, commercially organised press.[15]

During the mid- to late 1970s, the CDU/CSU parties began to accuse the public-service broadcasting corporations of 'red broadcasting' ('Rotfunk') and backed up their call for the introduction of private sector broadcasting with slogans claiming that the new media would bring greater 'freedom' for the 'politically

---

Mitgliedsverbände, Bonn: ZAW, 1979; see also ZAW, *Dachorganisation der Werbewirtschaft – Organisation und Arbeitsfelder*, Bonn: ZAW; also see Zerdick, 'Ökonomische Interessen und Entwicklungslinien', pp. 480–2.

12. See Chapter 4, p. 182 and footnote 23 p. 182–3 above.
13. W. Hoffmann-Riem, 'Tendenzen der Kommerzialisierung im Rundfunksystem', *Rundfunk und Fernsehen*, 32. Jahrgang, 1984/1, p. 36.
14. See Kleinsteuber et al. (eds.), *Medien: Thema Kabelfernsehen*, p. 69.
15. P. Humphreys, 'Satellite Broadcasting Policy in West Germany – Political Conflict and Competition in a Decentralised System', in Ralph Negrine, *Satellite Broadcasting and Politics*, London: Routledge and Kegan Paul, 1988, pp. 117–18.

mature and responsible citizen' ('mündiger Bürger') and that 'more programmes means more choice, not more watching' ('mehr Auswahl, nicht mehr Konsum'). The message was: 'more programmes, more choice; more competition, more freedom'. The CDU/CSU media policy statements claimed that such a reform of broadcasting would improve West German democracy![16] Finally, it seemed natural that the CDU/CSU, as the voice of business, should support the phalanx of business interests described above, notably the electronics industry, the press and the advertisers – which were increasingly anxious to see the introduction of private sector broadcasting.

The CDU/CSU Länder

At the same time, a number of individual CDU/CSU Länder governments began to seek a speedy reorganisation of broadcasting while remaining committed to the decentralised nature of broadcasting regulation. Indeed, they began to see in the new media an historic opportunity to promote the economic and industrial futures of their own regions. They quickly realised the economic as well as political advantages of deregulating the strict public-service requirements for broadcasting. Therefore, in line with national CDU/CSU policy, Ministerpräsidenten Lothar Späth (CDU, Baden-Württemberg), Franz Josef Strauss (CSU, Bavaria), Ernst Albrecht (CDU, Lower Saxony) and Bernhard Vogel (CDU, Rhineland-Palatinate) all began to launch fierce attacks on the public-service monopoly and call for an opening to private, commercial initiative.[17]

The FDP

The FDP's position did not differ greatly from that of the CDU/CSU, even while the former was a coalition partner of the SPD in Bonn (i.e. until late 1982). Although concerned to protect

---

16. CDU, *Freiheitliche Medienpolitik: 10 Thesen, Diskussionsgrundlage für den Medientag der CDU/CSU*, Bonn: CDU, 1978; CDU/CSU, *Medien von morgen: für mehr Bürgerfreiheit und Meinungsvielfalt*, Bonn: CDU, 1984.
17. P. Humphreys 'New Media Policy Dilemmas in West Germany', in K. Dyson and P. Humphreys, *Broadcasting and New Media Policies in Western Europe*, London: Routledge and Kegan Paul, 1988, pp. 191/2.

public-service broadcasting, the FDP was frustrated by the slow progress made under the SPD in introducing the new media. As a party of business, the FDP was also keenly in favour of introducing private commercial broadcasting. Nevertheless, it was careful to suggest that commercialisation should occur according to 'public-service' principles. Moreover, the FDP argued strongly that this should not lead to new concentrations of economic and media power.[18]

The SPD

The above-mentioned 'coalition for change' confronted a range of groups interested in preserving strong elements of the status quo in broadcasting policy. From 1969 until 1982, the dominant party of government in Bonn remained the SPD. The SPD was a staunch supporter of the public-service model of broadcasting and was therefore, from a cultural policy perspective, generally inclined to be very cautious about the new media. Helmut Schmidt even likened the new media issue to that concerning nuclear power: both issues had to be handled with extreme care! Indeed, Schmidt himself displayed a characteristic German 'moral conservatism' ('Wertkonservatismus') regarding the social influence of television and even went on record to advocate the introduction of a 'television-free day per week'. This suggestion reflected the widespread concern within the SPD about the negative effects of television on family and community life, a worry shared by the West German churches as well.

Along with the public-service broadcasters and the churches, the SPD was highly apprehensive about the negative effect of commercialisation on the standards and quality of broadcasting. It maintained that broadcasting standards would inevitably fall, as broadcasters eager to maximise their audience ratings under the pressure of increased competition for advertising revenue gave increasing air-time to low-quality light entertainment programmes, game-shows and such like. This competitive pressure

18. See, for example, the FDP's 'Grundsatzkatalog zu den neuen Medien', printed in FUNK Korrespondenz, no. 10, 9 March 1984, Dokumentation Medienpolitik, pp. D1–D3; or the policy statement 'Neue Medien-Thesen zur Medienpolitik' produced by the Bundeshauptausschuß der FDP in Bonn on 16 November 1984.

The Controversy Over the Introduction of the New Media

would even bring the danger of the public-service broadcasters chasing the private commercial broadcasters 'down market'. Moreover, the 'market-model' of broadcasting, the SPD argued fiercely, would undermine the public-service commitment to balanced and diverse programming, with its prime obligation to preserve impartiality and objectivity. The whole principle of integrational broadcasting ('Integrationsrundfunk') – broadcasting with a special duty to 'integrate' social groups and to 'bond' society together – would fall by the wayside. Rather than providing a broad schedule, reflecting the viewpoints of a wide range of social interests and catering for minorities and marginal groups, commercial broadcasting would inevitably end up promoting the viewpoints of those powerful interests with the financial muscle to launch and maintain private channels.

In this latter respect, the mounting campaign of the publishers to gain entry into the media sector presented the SPD with a very special and pressing motivation to develop and implement a coherent media policy programme. The SPD had always been very anxious about the concentration of media power – and in particular, the concentration of media power in the hands of hostile right-wing publishers such as the Axel Springer concern. Therefore, in a number of detailed media policy statements from the early 1970s onwards, the SPD pledged itself staunchly to defend the existing regulatory principles and mechanisms for broadcasting and to resist any commercialisation of broadcasting and media-concentration. The SPD adopted the slogan that 'the public-service broadcasting system had proven its value' ('hat sich bewährt'). Thus, it advocated the retention of the principle of a 'balance of power' in the media between the public-service broadcasting sector and the commercially organised press.[19]

The Public-Service Broadcasting Corporations

The public-service broadcasting corporations themselves had an

19. SPD, *Leitlinien zur Zukunftsentwicklung der elektronischen Medien*, Bonn: SPD, 1978; SPD, *Neue Medien. Aktionsprogramm der SPD zu den neuen Techniken im Medienbereich*, Bonn: SPD, 1981; SPD, *Neue Medien und neue Techniken*, Bonn: SPD, 1982; also see Kleinsteuber et al. (eds.), *Medien: Thema Kabelfernsehen*, pp. 66–8.

obvious interest in maintaining their broadcasting monopoly. They felt distinctly threatened by the possibility of the introduction of competition from the new media and a commercial broadcasting sector. The latter would amount to unwanted competition for audiences and for advertising revenue. Moreover, like the SPD, the public-service broadcasters had strong reservations about the effect that increased competition would have on the quality and standards of programming. In particular, they pointed to developments in the United States which seemed to demonstrate that competition in the broadcasting sector brought less, rather than more, genuine choice of viewing and to a predisposition of the broadcasters to produce massive amounts of popular light entertainment at the expense of informative and cultural programming.

Initially, the public-service broadcasters adopted an essentially defensive attitude. They sought to draw public attention to the various rulings of the Federal Constitutional Court which had seemed to uphold the principle of a public-service broadcasting monopoly. They also generally lobbied hard against the introduction of commercial broadcasting. They argued that the press was already characterised by a considerable concentration of media power and that, given the high costs of broadcasting, this situation would be further aggravated by allowing the press entrance into the broadcasting sector. The public-service broadcasters were not, however, wholeheartedly opposed to the introduction of limited pilot-projects for the new media. They admitted that the new media brought considerable scope for a greater differentiation of programming to cater for specialised audiences. At the same time, they argued strongly that they themselves were the appropriate organisations to take responsibility for these media. To the extent that this organisational principle was adopted, they held the door open to some participation by the local press and other local actors. Accordingly, the public-service broadcasters also argued for a raising of the licence-fee to cover the costs of their own major involvement in the new media. At the same time, they feared that any introduction of these media, which they did not control themselves, would delegitimise the licence-fee.

As will be seen, the public-service broadcaster's defensive orientation, and initial apprehensiveness, was progressively replaced by a more aggressive posture. The difficulties encountered by the new commercial sector, when it did arrive (see Chapter 6), greatly increased the confidence of the public-service broadcasters. They soon adopted the tactics of seeking to 'steal the wind from the sails' of the new commercial broadcasters by deploying their own massive in-built resources of finance, programming and technical expertise to launch their own new media ventures (i.e. satellite television). Nevertheless, as far as the organising principles of broadcasting policy were concerned, the public-service broadcasters were generally part of the coalition in favour of the status quo.[20]

The Unions

During the 1970s the trade unions became increasingly concerned about the negative effects of new technologies, particularly the rationalisation of jobs and deskilling. However, this concern was not confined to the printworkers (see Chapter 2). The debate about the introduction of new communications technologies, following the establishment of the KtK, was the stimulus to the development of a considerable trade union mobilisation around the theme of cable policy ('Kabelpolitik'). The establishment of the cable pilot-projects quickly became the focus of vigorous trade union involvement in the new media debate. As was the case with the political parties, this decade saw the unions evolve a close interest in the debate about the future of broadcasting. Union policy formulation likewise began in an ad hoc fashion as the unions began to grapple with the technical complexities of the issues and consciousness of the risks and opportunities grew only incrementally.

Some awareness of the potential of the new media seems to have surfaced as early as the end of the 1960s. The early stages of policy formation were, however, characterised by a significant degree of contradiction. The Bund/Länder dimensions of the impact of the new media on the future regulatory structures of the broadcasting system appeared to have been grasped immediately, when the DGB federal congress of 1969 advocated

20. See Kleinsteuber et al. (eds.), *Medien: Thema Kabelfernsehen*, pp. 50–3; also Zerdick, 'Ökonomische Interessen und Entwicklungslinien', pp. 484–5.

the establishment of an expert commission by the Ministerpräsidenten of the Länder in order to underline the regulatory jurisdiction of the Länder in the field of the new media. However, at the beginning of the 1970s, the DGB executive also began to explore the possibility of establishing a cable network with cooperative enterprises through the agency of its own 'Neue Heimat' property company. Moreover, the DGB representative to the KtK actually voted in favour of experimenting with private, as well as communal and public, forms of local cable operation.[21]

It was a combination of growing awareness of the negative effects of the new technologies with the massive campaign of the publishers in favour of private commercial broadcasting and involvement in the new media that explains the far more negative stance subsequently adopted by the unions towards the new media. In the first place, trade union concern about the rationalisation of jobs that would follow the introduction of new technologies had steadily mounted during the 1970s. At the end of the decade, union attention focused on cable. A leading trade unionist, Lothar Zimmermann, described cable as representing 'an assault on the mind, the bank account and the jobs of workers'. The unions now began to organise a general publicity campaign by means of pamphleteering, street distribution of leaflets and staging public meetings. More than one special conference was devoted to the issue, under slogans such as 'Defend Against the Dangers of the New Media!' ('Die Gefahren der neuen Medien abwehren!').[22]

In the second place, the unions now began to perceive cable as a distinct threat to the public-service monopoly of both broadcasting and telecommunications. During the discussions about the introduction of the pilot-projects the unions became the public broadcasters' fiercest defenders and at the same time, the union movement swung its support behind the German

21. See Kleinsteuber et al. (eds.), *Medien: Thema Kabelfernsehen*, p. 72.
22. DGB, *Ist die Rundfunkfreiheit bedroht?*, Medienpolitische Konferenz des DGB von 18/19. 4. 1978; DGB-Landesbezirk (LBZ) Rhineland-Palatinate (ed.), *Neue Medien – Angriff auf Kopf, Konto und Arbeitsplatz des Arbeitnehmers*, Mainz: DGB, 1983; also see DGB-Landesbezirk (LBZ) Nordrhein-Westfalen (ed.), *Die Gefahren der neuen Medien abwehren! Dokumentation Medien Konferenz 21.4.1983 in Düsseldorf*, Düsseldorf: DGB-NRW, 1983.

postworkers' union (the Deutsche Postgewerkschaft) in the latter's fight to defend the Bundespost's monopoly of the actual networks. From a certain initial neutrality, the unions' position quickly became one of unequivocal defence of maintaining a strict separation between network ownership and programming, both remaining in public control, and the financing of the new systems by means of the licence-fee not advertising.[23]

At first, the pilot-projects, recommended by the KtK, were the main terrain of confrontation. In May 1978, the Munich branch of the DGB issued a policy statement that called for responsibility for the pilot-project to be conferred upon the Bavarian Broadcasting Service (BR) and the banning of advertising on the network. By 1984, the DGB was calling for an immediate halt to the pilot-project, which by then had come to be seen as a Trojan horse for commercial broadcasting. A major concern of the union movement was the threat to pluralism and diversity represented by private commercial broadcasting. Like the SPD, the unions feared that the admission of private commercial interests would lead to a further concentration of media power in the hands of a few monopolists and exclude the participation of smaller groups.[24]

The Churches

The Catholic and Protestant ('Evangelisch' or 'Lutheran') churches adopted different positions. While the former was generally more politically predisposed to be sympathetic to CDU/CSU media policy, the latter's position was very much closer to that of the SPD, the public-service broadcasters and the unions. On the one hand, the Catholic church argued for experimentation with many kinds of new media organisation, including private commercial enterprise. At the same time, however, the Catholic position was tinged with a characteristically strong 'moral con-

23. D. Hensche, 'Neue Medien gehören in öffentliche Hand. Der Kampf um die Privatisierung', *Gewerkschaftliche Praxis*, 1977, no. 6/7, pp. 25–31.
24. 'Durch den Kopf gehen lassen: brauchen wir Kommerzfernsehen?', DGB pamphlet; also see Kleinsteuber et al. (eds.), *Medien: Thema Kabelfernsehen*, pp. 70–2; in addition see DGB-Bundesvorstand, *Stellungnahme des DGB-Bundesvorstandes zu den neuen Informations- und Kommunikationstechniken*, Düsseldorf: DGB, 8.5.1984; and *Medienpolitische Positionen des Deutschen Gewerkschaftsbundes*, Beschluß des DGB-Bundesvorstandes von 8.5.1984.

servatism' ('Wertkonservatismus'). In 1983, the Catholic church produced a set of 'Preliminary Observations and Guidelines towards the Formation of a Media Policy Position of the Catholic Church' ('Ansätze und Leitlinien einer medienpolitische Position der katholischen Kirche'), in which many of the fears expressed by the SPD and the public-service broadcasters were echoed. Moreover, grave doubts were expressed about the manner in which the new media and commercial broadcasting were being introduced to the benefit of powerful economic and political interests. Thus, despite its advocacy of commercial broadcasting, the Catholic church and the active Catholic wing of the CDU/CSU acted as a powerful restraint on any rampant commercialisation of the media. On the other hand, the Protestant church fiercely defended the principle of a public-service broadcasting monopoly and believed the public-service broadcasters to be best equipped to take responsibility for the new media. Both churches were naturally highly concerned to protect the moral standards of broadcasting and to prevent any degeneration of family and community life. Indeed, both churches sought an extension of local programming and an increase in social communication from the new media. Moreover, they were strongly against the possibility of any decisions being taken about the introduction of the new media until the results of the pilot-projects became known.[25]

The Greens and 'Alternatives'

The Greens and 'Alternatives', and indeed certain 'grass-roots' elements in the SPD, cannot properly be considered to be part of the coalition in favour of the status quo. These elements adopted a 'radical critical' position *vis-à-vis* the West German media system. They demanded a 'democratisation' of the media, arguing for much greater extension of the media 'policy community'.

25. See Kleinsteuber et al. (eds.), *Medien: Thema Kabelfernsehen*, p. 70. Also see 'Ansätze und Leitlinien einer medienpolitischen Position der katholischen Kirche', *Media Perspektiven*, 1/1984 pp. 12–20; and Evangelische Kirche in Deutschland, 'Zur Ordnung des Rundfunkwesens in der Bundesrepublik Deutschland. Stellungnahme des Rates der Evangelischen Kirche in Deutschland', *Media Perspektiven*, 7/1984, pp. 571–3.

The Controversy Over the Introduction of the New Media

Nevertheless, objectively, these elements reinforced the coalition in favour of the status quo, in that they amounted to a powerful 'grass-roots' movement against the introduction of the new media and commercial broadcasting. They were supported by various citizens' initiative groups. The Greens and citizens' initiative groups were prone to operate in their characteristic fashion of organising grass-roots meetings and distributing numerous pamphlets drawing attention to the Orwellian dangers of a cabled society by means of slogans such as 'technocrats are reducing our lives to data!' ('Technokraten verdaten unser Leben'), or, even more graphically, 'only just born, already cabled!' ('kaum abgenabelt, schon angekabelt!'), accompanied by a cartoon of a midwife holding up a new-born baby with a television in place of its head and a cable in place of its umbilical cord!

The Greens' arguments typically reflected a mixture of 'cultural pessimism', reminiscent of traditional German romanticism, and a wholly new awareness of the degree to which modern life was threatened by powerful and dangerous technocratic forces. Many Greens even argued that cable was an instrument of totalitarian control and manipulation. At a more mundane level, they maintained that it would lead to an inevitable commercialisation and Americanisation of the broadcasting system, that it represented a massive waste of scarce resources for the benefit of a few powerful economic interests, and that it would have a corrosive effect on family life and the social fabric. They also joined the trade unions – otherwise rather strange bedfellows – in pointing to the dangers of introducing 'rationalisation technologies' ('Rationalisierungstechnologien') and linked their campaign against the new media to their wider mobilisation against the West German 'surveillance state' ('Überwachungsstaat').[26]

---

26. See, for example, F. Kühn and W. Schmitt (eds.), *Einsam, überwacht und arbeitlos: Technokraten verdaten unser Leben*, Stuttgart: Die Grünen, 1984 (The editors were members of the Green Party group in the Baden-Württemberg state parliament in Stuttgart); see also W. Hippe and M. Stankowski (eds.), *Ausgezählt: Materialien zu Volkserfassung und Computerstaat. Ansätze zum Widerstand*, Cologne: Kölner Volksblatt Verlag, 1983.

The Cable Pilot-Projects

From now on, this polarisation was seriously to undermine the pattern of cooperative federalism which over the years had come to characterise West German broadcasting policy. This break-down of cooperative federalism was to reach a dramatic climax in the mid-1980s. In the meantime, however, damaging signs of the emerging dissension became apparent in the latter half of the 1970s whenever the Ministerpräsidenten of the Länder met to consider the question of the establishment of the pilot-projects which had been recommended by the KtK's report of 1976.

The cable pilot-projects actually had a long and controversial gestation. In accordance with the constitutional division of responsibilities for broadcasting and telecommunications, the aspects of the cable pilot-projects that affected the former fell under the policy-making aegis of the Länder. Accordingly decisions about their siting, finance, organisation and regulation were the business of the Ministerpräsidentenkonferenz of the Länder (conference of the heads of the state governments). From the start, the pilot-projects were seen by the SPD Ministerpräsidenten as the 'hole in the dyke' for commercial broadcasting. With the benefit of hindsight, it is clear that this was an accurate perception of the hidden motivation of the CDU/CSU Ministerpräsidenten. However, at first the latter made great public play of the 'test' nature of the projects and their corresponding 'reversability'. Nevertheless, the decision to proceed with these cable pilot-projects was a fateful one. Once started, they developed a logic of their own, which was to place SPD media policy progressively on the defensive.

The Cable 'Blockade'

At first, however, the SPD appeared to have the upper hand. While the Ministerpräsidenten deliberated over the pilot-projects, SPD opposition to cable was symbolised powerfully by the so-called cable 'blockade' of 1979. In the spring of 1979 the Bundespost had announced that it intended to proceed with the wholesale cabling ('flächendeckende Verkabelung') of eleven West German cities. This appears to have been an autonomous decision, indicative of the growing interest of Bundespost technocrats in the new medium in the period that had elapsed since the KtK. The Bundespost justified its plans by reference to the 'need to improve television reception'!

However, on 26 September 1979, Chancellor Helmut Schmidt himself intervened dramatically to produce a cabinet decision to block the Bundespost's plans. This high-level intervention was accompanied by a much publicised statement by Schmidt that 'cable was more dangerous than nuclear power'! The cable 'blockade', as it was immediately described by the CDU/CSU opposition, had almost certainly been engineered by Albrecht Müller, one of Schmidt's leading media policy advisers in the Federal Chancellor's Office and a die-hard opponent of the new media. Doubtless, Müller had also impressed upon Chancellor Schmidt the 'electoral dangers' to the SPD of any expansion of the media.[27]

Meanwhile, the SPD Ministerpräsidenten had embarked upon the first stage of a long-drawn-out delaying action of their own designed to forestall the introduction of commercial television. Thus, it took three years for the Ministerpräsidentenkonferenz to reach the necessary minimum of agreement about the siting of the pilot-projects. In the end, the old faithful, the 'Proporz' principle, came to the rescue: in 1978, the Ministerpräsidenten finally agreed to establish four cable pilot-projects, two in CDU/CSU Länder and two in SPD Länder.

The cities in CDU/CSU Länder chosen were Munich and Mannheim-Ludwigshafen. However, Baden-Württemberg quickly withdrew from the latter pilot-project, leaving Ludwigshafen alone as the second CDU site (Mannheim is in Baden-Württemberg, separated only by the river Rhine from Ludwigshafen, which is in the Rhineland-Palatinate). This move reflected the 'go-it-alone' approach of Baden-Württemberg's dynamic and technocratic Ministerpräsident Lothar Späth (CDU), who envisaged the use of already cabled towns and localities in Baden-Württemberg in his own ambitious plans for

---

27. For Müller's general reservations about the new media see A. Müller, 'Wieviel Medien braucht der Mensch?', in U. Lang (ed.), *Der verkabelte Bürger. Brauchen wir die neuen Medien?*, Freiburg/Breisgau: Dreisam Verlag, 1981, pp. 49–56.

new communications services and private broadcasting.[28] The state government of Baden-Württemberg soon established its own commission to explore the potentialities of the new media in 1980 (the so-called 'Expertenkommission Neue Medien'). The remaining two pilot-projects were to be conducted in the then SPD Länder of West Berlin and North-Rhine Westphalia at Dortmund. Then in 1981 the traditional SPD stronghold of West Berlin fell to the CDU, leaving Dortmund as the only pilot-project upon which the SPD could make its mark. According to the principle of state (Land) sovereignty for media regulation, the arrangements for the programming side of the cable projects could be shaped according to the differing preferences of the local political forces (within constitutional parameters). However, the actual telecommunications operations of the networks, that is the installation and operation of the cable systems, were to remain the responsibility of the Bundespost.

It then took another two-and-a-half years before an agreement on the financial basis and mode of evaluation of the pilot-projects was produced by the Ministerpräsidentenkonferenz in November 1980.[29] The main financial burden was to be carried by a surcharge of DM 0.20 per month to the usual licence-fee, to be paid by all television viewers in the FRG for a period of three years, the expected duration of the pilot-projects. The social research resulting from the cable projects was to be funded entirely by the Länder themselves. The results of the cable-projects were to be evaluated by a special Media Commission (Medienkommission) composed of sundry communications experts, academics and representatives from the press, broadcasting and film sectors. The commission's brief was very wide: to explore a wide range of new services including videotext and cable television; to examine the social effects of the new media (on the family, etc.); to assess the interaction of the new media on the old media of press, broadcasting and cinema; to consider the effects on the labour market (such as employment consequences, training, etc.); to explore the need for appropriate new data protection legislation; and, importantly, to explore possible

28. See L. Späth (ed.), *Das Kabel. Anschluß an die Zukunft*, Bonn: Bonn Aktuell, 1981.
29. For a text of this agreement see *Media Perspektiven*, 11/1980, pp. 756–7.

variants of regulatory and financial structure for future expanded cable operations. In actual fact, the real significance of at least the CDU/CSU pilot-projects was that they amounted to the first real foot-in-the-door for private commercial broadcasting in the history of broadcasting in the Federal Republic. In particular, the Ludwigshafen pilot-project very quickly became the key catalyst for a dramatic transformation of West German broadcasting, followed closely by Munich.

The Ludwigshafen Pilot-Project

In December 1980 a special law was passed by the Rhineland-Palatinate state parliament which explicitly made provision for the licensing of the private supply and transmission of programmes, albeit under the auspices of public-service regulation – the so-called, 'Law Concerning an Experiment with Broadband Cable' ('Landesgesetz über einen Versuch mit Breitbandkabel').[30] This law reflected the new media policy of the ruling CDU party in that Land, and in particular of its Ministerpräsident, Bernhard Vogel. Vogel was also chairman of the Broadcasting Commission of the Länder (Rundfunkkommission der Länder). A vigorous proponent of commercial broadcasting, he was very ambitious that his Land should lead the way forward and consequently reap the early bird's share of the expected economic advantages of the new media. The Rhineland-Palatinate was already the home of the ZDF, based in Mainz, and Vogel now sought to increase this already high profile of his Land in the field of the media.

To coordinate and control the pilot-project and manage the programming side, the cable head-end (the centre of the network) and the studio complex, the law established an Authority for Cable Communication (Anstalt für Kabelkommunikation – AKK). Superficially, the AKK appeared to be organised along the same traditional lines as the public-service broadcasting corporations. It was an institution of public law ('Anstalt des öffentlichen Rechts') to be governed by an 'Assembly' (a 'Versammlung' – analogous to the public broadcasters' broadcasting councils) of forty members which gave representation to the

30. For the full text see *Media Perspektiven*, 12/1980, pp. 836–43.

Media and Media Policy in West Germany

usual 'socially significant groups'. This Assembly gave representation to the political parties, local and regional government representatives, the press, trade unions, employers' associations, the churches, community groups and suchlike. It also gave some representation to the public-service broadcasting corporations, an innovation which appeared to be a necessarily appropriate concession in view of the anticipated impact of the new media on the established broadcasters. Moreover, the Assembly was to be responsible for the supervision of all of the programming, finance and administration of the pilot-project. It also elected the three-member executive committee ('Vorstand'), responsible for the day-to-day management of the pilot-project, which in turn nominally appointed the chief executive (Geschäftsführer'), though in reality the latter was nominated by the state government. According to the letter of the law, at least, the Assembly appeared to be sovereign, remaining solely responsible for ensuring that programming was balanced and diverse in accordance with constitutional principles.

Despite this superficial similarity of structure to that of the public-service corporations, the Rhineland-Palatinate's cable pilot-project actually marked a very significant rupture with the traditional model of public-service broadcasting in the Federal Republic. The real aim of the Rhineland-Palatinate's law of December 1980 was to establish the Ludwigshafen pilot-project as a model for the future shape of a mixed public/private commercial broadcasting system. To this end, the AKK was designed to be a pioneering regulatory body embracing an entirely new concept of broadcasting regulation. To be precise, the law adopted a regulatory model of 'external pluralism', according to which, unlike the past practice of the public-service broadcasters, the new programmers would be allowed to produce programmes and programme schedules which might be unbalanced or biased, so long as the overall total of programming amounted to a balance. Implicit in this model was the assumption that a greatly increased number of programme-providers would in itself provide balance and diversity. Moreover, the AKK itself represented a new form of 'external control' whereby regulation was no longer to be the function of a socially-representative governing structure, such as the broadcasting councils of the corporations, *within* each channel. Implicit within this idea was the impracticability of having internal control bodies within each of the new broadcasting operations. The AKK contained such a body, namely the Assembly, but this regulatory structure was now placed *externally* to the new broadcasters. Accordingly, this model lent itself to the promotion of a new degree of competition – and partisanship – in broadcasting.

In addition, there were a number of other important departures from the traditional model. Firstly, the new model of broadcasting appeared to depart from the principle that broadcasting should be independent of the state (the principle of 'Staatsferne'). In particular, the Land government, not the AKK, was to be actually responsible for choosing the new programme-operators, despite the technicality that the AKK granted the licences. Thus, the AKK participated formally in the process of allocation and possible withdrawal of franchises, but it was the CDU Rhineland-Palatinate government that ultimately made the real decisions. Moreover, the new regulatory agency was particularly vulnerable to 'agency capture': it soon became clear that the Assembly gave considerable representation to groups that were simultaneously associated with applications for broadcasting franchises. Furthermore, the Assembly's composition appeared to be politically rather unbalanced: one trade union representative faced no less than ten representatives of the employers' organisations.[31]

Similarly, the hand of the CDU Land government could clearly be seen at work in the appointment of the chief executive of the pilot-project. In fact, the choice of first chief executive of the AKK reflected very clearly the 'patronage politics' of the political parties (the extensive influence of the 'Parteienstaat') and the 'Verflechtung' (interpenetration) of party and business interests. Appointed in October 1982, Claus Detjen was a former journalist whose major distinction, apart from his obvious conservative political allégiance, was the fact that he had been first the new media spokesman and later managing director of the BDZV and as such a vocal protagonist of the private broadcasting lobby. In addition, he had played a leading role in the BDZV's first brief flirtation with satellite broadcasting, a liaison

---

31. M. Helmes, 'Erste Erfahrungen aus dem Kabelpilotprojekt Ludwigshafen aus der Sicht des DGBs', *Media Perspektiven*, 7/1984, pp. 570–1.

with RTL in Luxemburg which turned out to be unconsummated (the aim had been to establish a satellite television channel). However, in 1982 Detjen was appointed co-director of the Programming Company for Cable and Satellite Broadcasting (Programmgesellschaft für Kabel und Satellitenrundfunk – PKS), chosen as one of the first new operators for the Ludwigshafen cable television network. Within a short period of time, the PKS was to become a key participant in SAT 1, West Germany's first private commercial satellite television consortium which encompassed most of the country's large publishers including the Springer group, Bauer, Burda and Holtzbrinck. The degree of this 'Verflechtung' reached blatant proportions when the AKK selected SAT 1 to operate a channel on a European Communications Satellite (ECS 1) in order to feed the Ludwigshafen cable pilot-project.[32]

There were a number of other lesser, but still very significant, innovations, most notably relating to advertising and provision for an 'open channel'. Apart from the general prohibition of advertising on Sundays and national holidays, there was at first no limit to the amount of advertising that the cable services could run. Only later, in 1983, did the standing rules of the AKK decide to set an upper limit to advertising – and this was a very liberal 20% of daily transmission time![33] At least partially to sweeten the pill for the opponents of cable broadcasting and to legitimise the new media in the eyes of the larger public, the 1980 law also provided for a non-commercial 'open channel' to provide cost-free access to the general public.

Despite the early lead established by the state government of the Rhineland-Palatinate in preparing this pathbreaking new legislation, the pilot-project at Ludwigshafen did not open until 1 January 1984. By this time, over fifty applications for franchises had been made and by the end of 1983 twenty-two had received licences to broadcast. Among the channels offered were those of existing German and foreign public-service broadcasters: eight channels of the public-service broadcasters (SWF 1 and 3, HR 1 and 3, SW 3, BR 3, SDR 1, and ZDF); three French

32. K. Dyson, 'Regulating the New Media', in Dyson and Humphreys, *Broadcasting and New Media Politics in Western Europe*, London: Routledge and Kegan Paul, 1988, pp. 251–304, p. 284.
33. See the 'Satzung' of the AKK of 27.4.1983, Ludwigshafen: AKK, 1983.

The Controversy Over the Introduction of the New Media

channels (TF 1, Antenne 2 and FR 3); a new music channel run by ZDF; and an educational channel mounted by SWF. In addition, there was the 'Citizen Channel' ('Bürger Kanal') produced by a number of local public and community organisations and edited by the AKK itself. The network also ran all the major public-service radio channels as well as a number of new private channels. For the first time in the history of FRG's broadcasting system, there were also three private broadcasters: the English-language Sky Channel of Rupert Murdoch; a channel operated by the EPF ('Erste Private Fernsehgesellschaft') controlled by the major regional publishing group in the Rhineland-Palatinate, namely the *Rheinpfalz* Group; and also a channel operated by the PKS, financed by the Deutsche Genossenschaftsbank and the conservative daily, the *Frankfurter Allgemeine Zeitung* (*FAZ*) (subsequently, the PKS channel was given over to the SAT 1 satellite television channel mounted by most of the country's leading publishers, PKS retaining an important share).

However, the take-up rate remained disappointingly low. By 1984 only 5,000 of the projected 30,000 homes originally foreseen by the 1980 law were connected. By mid-1985, half-way through the three-year 'experiment', there were still only 17,000 of the 30,000 subscribers foreseen by the legislation. As will be seen, the AKK was actually abolished by a later Rhineland-Palatinate media law of 1986. This development reflected the view of the CDU policy-makers in the Rhineland-Palatinate that the experiment had duly run its course – passing with 'flying colours' – and that a more permanent regulatory structure was required to establish a framework for the future of all broadcasting and new media development in the entire region of the Rhineland-Palatinate. In its place a new law established the State Centre for Private Broadcasters (Landeszentrale für private Rundfunkveranstalter), but by then the AKK and the 'pilot-project' had primarily fulfilled their role, at least in the minds of the CDU policy makers in the Rhineland-Palatinate, of ushering in a new media era.

The Munich Pilot-Project

Unlike the CDU government of the Rhineland-Palatinate, the

CSU government of Bavaria appeared at first to be somewhat constrained, by the Bavarian constitution, about the degree of blatant deregulation that it could introduce. Following the people's referendum of 1972 the public-service nature of broadcasting had been powerfully reaffirmed in Bavaria, most notably by Article 111a of the state's constitution. Accordingly, the opponents of the cable project – namely the trade unions, the SPD, the Greens and a hastily established and very vocal citizens' initiative 'protest' group called the Munich Citizens' Initiative Against Cable Commercialism (Münchener Bürgerinitiative gegen Kabelkommerz, not to be confused with the earlier one of the 1972 controversy) – were able to draw attention to clearly established constitutional principles in their struggle to limit the CSU government's freedom of manoeuvre. However, this did not, in the event, prevent the CSU state government from gradually taking over the pilot-project in much the same fashion as the CDU had done in the Rhineland-Palatinate. Nevertheless, initially at least, it substantially delayed the privatising endeavours of the CSU policy makers with the result that the pilot-project was actually established under the terms of existing, not new, legislation.

Since the Bavarian constitution seemed to suggest that the ultimate responsibility for programming regulation resided with the existing public-service broadcaster, the Bavarian Broadcasting Service (BR), at first no new 'public-service' corporation was established along the lines of the AKK in the Rhineland-Palatinate. Instead, the project was to be run by a simple limited company called the Munich Pilot Company for Cable Communication (Münchener Pilotgesellschaft für Kabelkommunikation – MPK). However, like the AKK in the Rhineland-Palatinate, the MPK was to be responsible for the coordination and control of the pilot-project, the management of the cable head-end and the studio complex and for the all-important process of allocation of new channels. Significantly, a former chief editor of BR, Rudolf Mühlfenzl, was appointed director of the pilot-project. Between them, Mühlfenzl and the supervisory board ('Aufsichtsrat') of the MPK were to be ultimately responsible for the pilot-project. However, like Detjen in Ludwigshafen, Mühlfenzl was no neutral voice in the debate about the new media. He had travelled widely in the USA and was a firm protagonist of commercial

The Controversy Over the Introduction of the New Media

cable television. He was also associated with the ruling CSU Party in Bavaria. In September 1983 the MPK formally decided to launch the pilot-project on 1 April 1984 and to set the duration of the experiment at between three and five years.

The MPK's shareholders included the two public-service corporations, BR and ZDF, with 10% each, the Bavarian Chamber of Commerce and Trade, also with 10%, and the audiovisual production companies of Bavaria with a further 20%. Significantly, however, the Bavarian publishers were to gain at least a significant foothold in broadcasting through the new experiment. A stake of no less than 20% in the MPK was granted to the Bavarian Newspaper Publishers' Association ('Verband Bayerischer Zeitungsverleger') and the allied Bavarian Magazine Publishers' Association ('Verband Bayerischer Zeitschriftenverleger'). The state of Bavaria (CSU) also held 20% of the shares. Thus, between them the political forces pressing for commercial broadcasting held no less than 40% of the shares in the MPK. Finally, the City of Munich (SPD) was given a share of 10% in the company. However, the latter was to withdraw its support in May 1984, less than one month after the opening of the project. This move reflected the opposition of the ruling SPD city government to what now amounted to a very blatant attempt by the CSU state government of Bavaria to hijack the pilot-project entirely and imbue it with a degree of irreversibility.[34]

Less than two weeks after the opening of the pilot-project on 1 April 1984, the CSU Bavarian state government introduced new legislation embracing the whole range of electronic media – the 'Law for the Testing and Development of new Broadcasting Output and other Media Services' (the 'Gesetz für die Erprobung und Entwicklung neuer Rundfunkangebote und anderer Mediendienste' – MEG).[35] This legislation had been prepared in January 1984 by the Staatskanzlei (state government office) and it bore the unmistakeable stamp of the CSU's ambitions irrevo-

---

34. 'Stadt München: Ausstieg aus dem Kabelprojekt', *Media Perspektiven*, 6/1984, pp. 499–50.
35. 'Entwurf eines Gesetzes über die Erprobung und Entwicklung neuer Rundfunkangebote und anderer Mediendienste in Bayern (Medienerprobungs- und Entwicklungsgesetz – MEG)', *Media Perspektiven*, 4a/1984, pp. 305–14; and 'Gesetz über die . . . von November 1984', *Media Perspektiven Dokumentation*, 1/1985, pp. 1–10.

cably to open up Bavarian broadcasting to commercial enterprise while at the same time retaining a powerful degree of control over the process and the outcome. The MEG established a new body to take responsibility for the new media, and, significantly, now for all the programming side of operations of the cable pilot-project. This foresaw the removal of all the MPK's regulatory responsibilities no later than six months after the MEG came into effect on 1 November 1984 (i.e. by May 1985). The new regulatory body was to be a public law institution ('Anstalt des öffentlichen Rechts') like the existing broadcasting corporations and the AKK. It was to be called the Bavarian State Centre for New Media (Bayerische Landeszentrale für neue Medien). Like the Rhineland-Palatinate's law governing the Ludwigshafen cable pilot-project, the MEG had the function of legitimating fundamental changes in broadcasting regulation engineered by a party determined to introduce a commercial broadcasting sector while at the same time seeking to extend its grip on the medium. The establishment of a second public law broadcasting institution in Bavaria, alongside BR, was plainly an attempt to clear the way for the breaking of the public-service monopoly of broadcasting and allow for the introduction of a deregulated new private commercial broadcasting sector – now to be distinctly kept apart from the highly regulated existing public-service sector. At the same time, the policy-makers could appear to be visibly keeping faith with Article 111a of the Bavarian constitution.

Also like the Rhineland-Palatinate's law, there was a superficial similarity between the Landeszentrale and the traditional structure of the public-service broadcasting corporations. The Landeszentrale was constituted by two organs that appeared closely to resemble those of the public-service broadcasting corporations. It had an Assembly which gave representation to the 'socially significant groups', namely the state government, the state parliament (one representative for every twenty MPs), the state senate, the churches, the trade unions, the City of Munich, youth, sports and other associations, journalists, the education sector, etc. It had an Administrative Council ('Verwaltungsrat') which was composed of three members apiece from the Assembly, from the cable operating companies and from the television programme providers and one member apiece from the radio programme providers and from the providers of other new cable services. However, the reality of the matter was that, through party patronage, the CSU was now able to pack the membership of the Assembly of the Landeszentrale in its favour. It was as if the controversy of 1972 had never occurred. Moreover, the MEG had even gone so far as to give the very interests involved in new services a position of influence and representation on the Landeszentrale's Administrative Council. Furthermore, Articles 10 and 22 of the MEG made clear that the Landeszentrale was henceforth to work towards the organisation of cable companies throughout Bavaria thus paving the way for the eventual cabling of the whole of the state. This single provision was highly controversial in itself since it clearly negated the whole 'test' character of the pilot-project. In protest, the SPD city government of Munich withdrew its support for the pilot-project. At the same time, the unions too withdrew their 'cooperation' altogether and declared their total opposition.

When the pilot-project opened on 1 April 1984 only 500 homes were actually connected. The pilot-project offered sixteen television channels and twenty-four radio channels. For this the subscribers paid a monthly fee of DM 10.25. The sixteen television channels included the established West German public-service channels ZDF, ARD, BR 3 and SW 3, the two Austrian public-service channels ORF FS1 and ORF FS2, the Swiss public-service channel SRF 1, and the new French public-service TV 5 cultural channel. It also carried the new music channel mounted by ZDF. In addition, as with the Ludwigshafen pilot-project, it opened the door to a number of private commercial channels, notably Sky Channel, music box, a new educational programme called TV Kultur Klub, provided by cooperation between BR and private programme providers, a new private channel called Jugend-Sport-Spiel or simply 'Channel 8', and, of course, PKS, much of the programming of which drew on the film archives of the Munich-based Beta Taurus company of the Bavarian film entrepreneur Leo Kirch. Kirch stood very close to the CSU and was actively engaged in building up a multimedia empire based in Bavaria. As with the Ludwigshafen pilot-project, the PKS channel was subsequently given over to the SAT channel which replaced it. The Munich cable pilot-project also featured a teletext channel called 'Mbt', standing for Media Company of Bavarian Daily Newspapers for Cable Communication (Mediengesellschaft der Bayerischen Tageszeitungen für Kabelkommunikation) which was backed entirely by forty-eight local Bavarian newspaper publishing houses. Thus the Munich cable pilot-project was characterised by exactly the same kind of patronage politics and interpenetration of political and business interests as the Ludwigshafen project. Hardly surprisingly, the opening of the pilot-project was enthusiastically hailed as the dawning of 'a new era for the media' by the Bavarian press. Altogether less publicity was given to the critical voices condemning the CSU state government for declaring the project a success before it had even got underway.

Berlin

The pilot-project in West Berlin was the last of the three CDU pilot-projects to be established. It opened on 28 August 1985. By then it had gained an importance all of its own arising from the fact that, with 220,000 homes already connected and no less than 710,000 homes passed, West Berlin was by far the largest cable network in the country (indeed, in the world). It also became highly controversial, not least because its huge size belied its 'test' character from the start.

On 28 June 1984 the West Berlin Land parliament passed the 'Law on the Conduct of the Berlin Cable Project' ('Gesetz über die Durchführung des Kabelprojektes Berlin – Kabelpilotprojekt-Gesetz – KPPG) which supplied the legal basis for the five-year 'experiment'.[36] This law duly entered into force on 1 August 1984. The law established a Cable Corporation (Anstalt für Kabelkommunikation – AK) as an independent public law regulatory body composed of a Director and a 'Cable Council' ('Kabelrat') which was in turn composed of five independent public figures. Notionally, these public figures were selected according to the British practice of choosing from among the ranks of the 'great and the good'. For example, the chairman of the Cable Council was a former President of the Federal Consti-

---

36. 'Gesetz über die Durchführung des Kabelprojektes Berlin (Kabelpilotprojekt – KPPG)', *Media Perspektiven*, 8/1984, pp. 650–60.

The Controversy Over the Introduction of the New Media

tutional Court. This principle of independence was important, since the Cable Council was responsible for all the usual regulatory matters: allocation of franchises, safeguarding of diversity of opinion in programming, and general programmes supervision. A programme committee, giving representation to the programmers, was also established to help the Cable Council in its work.

The actual technical and organisational aspects of the pilot-project, on the other hand, were the responsibility of a private commercial body, the Cable Project Company Ltd (Projektgesellschaft für Kabelkommunikation mbH – PK Berlin). The PK Berlin was not itself a programme provider, rather it was intended to be a 'neutral' provider of the transmission facilities (studios, cable head-end, etc.). The PK Berlin was internally composed of a 'Supervisory Board' ('Aufsichtsrat'), a chief executive ('Geschäftsführer') and a 'Cable Centre' ('Kabelzentrale'). The third major element of the structure was the establishment of a 'Project Commission' ('Projektkommission') which was responsible for the research and evaluation work of the 'test'.

Controversy immediately centred, however, on the question of the 'independence' of the pilot-project from the state ('Staatsferne'), and therefore from the ruling CDU government in Berlin. Firstly, the Land of Berlin was the sole shareholder of the PK Berlin. Secondly, the members of the PK Berlin's Supervisory Board were all members of the CDU state government. This appeared to give the CDU government very considerable scope to influence the internal direction of the project, through the financial control exerted by the Supervisory Board. Thirdly, the independence of the public regulatory body, the AK, also seemed to be in doubt since the law contained a provision for it to fall under 'state supervision of the member of the Berlin Senate responsible for media affairs' (who was also CDU). Fourthly, the Cable Council was not composed of members of the 'socially significant groups'. Even the AKK Ludwigshafen and the Landeszentrale in Munich had provided for some public accountability of this kind. In the case of the Berlin pilot-project, however, the element of democratic representativeness was completely absent from the regulatory body. Worse still, the law provided for the members of the Cable Council to be elected by the Berlin Land parliament by two-thirds majority. However, in the event of a failure to produce such a majority, the law

225

allowed the highly sensitive question of the composition of this key regulatory body to follow the well-established 'Proporz' principle (i.e. CDU 3: SPD 2). This too gave the CDU state government the opportunity thoroughly to 'politicise' the project. As the Cable Council was to sit in closed sessions, there would be every opportunity for all kinds of shadowy manipulation. Finally, reflecting the policy of the ruling CDU Party in West Berlin, the law opted unequivocally for the 'external pluralism' model of programme regulation, going even further in the details of this matter than the Rhineland-Palatinate's law of December 1980.[37]

When the pilot-project opened on 28 August 1985 it ran the following television channels: the public-service programmes BR 3, WDR 3, 3SAT (a new satellite television channel mounted by ZDF in cooperation with Austrian and Swiss public-service broadcasters), ZDF's Musikkanal, and ARD's Eins Plus (another new public-service satellite television channel); in addition, the private commercial channel Teleclub (a subscription television channel), three new German private commercial satellite channels RTL Plus, SAT 1 and KMP musicbox, and two British-based private satellite television channels Music Box and Sky Channel. The pilot-project also ran a wide range of public-service and private commercial radio channels. One of the selling features of the Berlin project was supposed to be the weight it gave to innovative new local channels. Indeed, it did start with some: Berliner Kabelvision (a local news and information channel), the Mix-Kanal (an open channel), and Havelwelle (a cooperative venture of eighteen different local operators). However, Berliner Kabelvision proved to be an instant disaster, collapsing after only two weeks. Havelwelle lasted slightly longer, surviving as long as 100 days and costing its backers around DM 2 million in return for a paltry advertising return of DM 35,000. By 1987, the solitary successful local programming venture was a Turkish-language programme designed for West Berlin's huge immigrant and'guest-worker' ('Gastarbeiter') population.[38]

Of the three CDU/CSU pilot-projects, it was in the Ludwig-

---

37. For a more thorough critique see K. Betz, 'Das Berliner Kabelpilotprojekt', *Media Perspektiven*, 6/84, pp. 441–50.
38. V. O'Connor, 'Wall to Wall Cable', *Cable and Satellite Europe*, 10/87, p. 46.

The Controversy Over the Introduction of the New Media

shafen and Munich projects that the future pattern of press involvement emerged earliest and that the high degree of interpenetration of interests and 'policy networking' between CDU/CSU and the publishers was most clearly evident. In Berlin, by contrast, despite the entirely favourable political framework of the project, the local newspaper publishers decided not to become immediately involved, preferring instead to await satellite developments which by that time were moving very fast.[39]

Dortmund

The Dortmund cable pilot-project remained unique among the four experiments in that it was the only one bearing the imprint of SPD policy-making. In comparison to the CDU/CSU pilot-projects, SPD policy-making was quintessentially incrementalist rather than radical. The SPD bill in North-Rhine Westphalia, the 'Law Concerning the Conduct of a Pilot-Project for Broadband Cable'('Entwurf eines Gesetzes über die Durchführung eines Modellversuchs mit Breitbandkabel'), was prepared by the office of Ministerpräsident Johannes Rau, presented to the Land parliament on 22 June 1982 and passed into law on 20 December 1983.[40] It reflected the SPD's then total commitment to the defence of the traditional public-service broadcasting monopoly and the party's opposition to the introduction of any private commercial broadcasting whatsoever. The legislation excluded advertising (ironically, 'in particular to protect the press'), and instead opted for a fee-based financial structure for the pilot-project. Also in line with the party's media policy guidelines, private operators too, including the press, were entirely excluded from the project. In fact, it was intended that the pilot-project be entirely programmed by the existing public-service broadcasters, and that the cable services be operated jointly and exclusively by the regional public-service corporation, the WDR, and also by the ZDF. Accordingly, no new regulatory structures

---

39. M.-L. Kiefer, 'Kabelprojekt Berlin ohne Berliner Zeitungsverleger', *Media Perspektiven*, 4/1984, pp. 259–63.

40. 'Entwurf eines Gesetzes über die Durchführung eines Modellversuches mit Breitbandkabel in Nordrhein Westfalen', *Media Perspektiven*, 6/1982, pp. 409–17; 'Gesetz über die . . . (Kabelversuchsgesetz NRW – KabVersG NRW)', *Media Perspektiven*, 12/1983, pp. 886–91.

were deemed necessary, apart from a 21-member advisory board ('Projektbeirat') which was to be composed of representatives of the usual 'socially significant groups'. The legislation was very vague about the latter's functions, apart from the stipulation that it existed to guarantee the public interest. It was quite apparent that it did not in any sense fulfil the same function as the new regulatory bodies being established by the CDU/CSU policy-makers in Ludwigshafen, Munich and West Berlin.

In justification of their highly restrictive and incrementalist approach, the SPD policy-makers in North-Rhine Westphalia claimed to be adhering to the spirit and letter of the 1978 agreement of the Ministerpräsidentenkonferenz, which they suggested had been utterly betrayed by the CDU/CSU pilot-projects. They pointed out that this agreement had specified that the unified basic structure of broadcasting in the Federal Republic would not be altered during the trials. Clearly, the CDU/CSU pilot-projects were designed to do precisely that. Instead, the SPD policy-makers were insistent about the 'test' nature of the whole exercise. This incrementalist approach was reflected in the law's provision for a maximum of 10,000 cable connections, rather than the 30,000 foreseen by the CDU state government of the Rhineland-Palatinate or the 50,000 which was the ambitious goal of the CSU Bavarian state government. The Dortmund pilot-project eventually began operations in June 1985. However, by then there had been some important changes, most notably concerning the projected anti-commercial nature of the project's terms of reference. As will be seen, these changes reflected the powerful pressures to compromise over the question of commercial broadcasting which had been in the meantime exerted on the SPD in the period 1983–5. These pressures arose from a constellation of new factors that now came into play to suddenly bring about the conditions for a much more thoroughgoing transformation of the West German broadcasting system.

Thus, while CDU/CSU policy-makers continued to pay lip-service to the need to await the recommendations of the special Media Commission charged with the evaluation of the cable pilot-projects, in reality the whole character and conduct of the CDU/CSU pilot-projects testified to their impatience to use the

The Controversy Over the Introduction of the New Media

pilot-projects as a means to break the public-service broadcasting monopoly and introduce a commercial broadcasting sector. They had displayed a blatant disregard of the established broadcasting 'policy community' and instead established new 'policy networks', characterised by a marked degree of 'Verflechtung' of interest (and indeed of personnel) between party and business. They had already endowed the 'pilot-projects' with a model character for the future of broadcasting and established *faits accomplis*. Moreover, during the course of this 'experimental' phase, the special Media Commission, established by the Länder to evaluate the pilot-projects, quickly fell victim to internal bickering. By 1984 it had disbanded not least in recognition of the fact that the so-called pilot-projects had taken on a quasi-permanent character.

The 'Expert Commissions'

Alongside the pilot-projects, the establishment of expert commissions was a significant feature of this early stage of policy-making for the new media. The debate about the new media had been initiated by an expert commission, namely the KtK. During the period under discussion, two further expert commissions were established, namely the Expert Commission for New Media (Experten-Kommission Neue Medien – EKM) in Baden-Württemberg and a parliamentary commission of inquiry, the Commission of Inquiry into Information and Communications Technologies (Enquête-Kommission – Informations- und Kommunikationstechnologien – EK–IUK).

The EKM

The EKM was established in CDU-governed Baden-Württemberg in 1980. Very clearly, this commission reflected the particular interest which the Land government and its progressive and innovative CDU Ministerpräsident Lothar Späth had in the new media. Baden-Württemberg was already the heartland of the West German electronics industry and its Land government now saw the opportunity to improve the state's economic position still further by preparing for a rapid development of the

229

new information and communications technologies.[41] The composition of the commission was again 'pluralistic': a broad 'policy community' of political parties and all important associations and socially significant groups was apparently involved, although experts predominated. However, the resultant report suggested that the commission was in fact dominated by an insider 'policy network' of representatives of local industrial and commercial interests, technocrats and the ruling CDU government. The commission inquired into the whole field of information and communications technologies, but concentrated on the effects of the new media on the broadcasting system. However, although the commission's report contained some reference to possible negative effects of the introduction of private broadcasting, particularly cross-ownership of the press and broadcasting, its overall recommendation was much as to be expected. It expressed a generally positive attitude to the new media and gave positive approval to the measures that had already been taken by the Bundespost. In sum, the commission found in favour of the speedy introduction of broadband technology and private broadcasting, this time without even advocating the necessity of preliminary pilot-projects.[42]

The EK–IUK

The early 1980s saw increasingly bitter conflict about media policy between the CDU/CSU and the SPD, among other interests. The SPD parliamentary party in the Bundestag chose this moment to initiate a parliamentary commission of inquiry into the new media. This met with the immediate disapproval of the CDU and large sections of industry, which feared that a new commission would cause delays in the introduction and utilisation of the new technologies. Indeed, the establishment of the commission can be seen as a clear ploy by the SPD to delay the introduction of private broadcasting. In order to win time in the

---

41. See Späth (ed.), *Das Kabel*.
42. Expertenkommission Neue Medien – EKM – Baden-Württemberg, *Abschlußbericht*, 3 vols, Stuttgart: Kohlhammer Verlag, 1981. For a criticism, see: W. Hoffmann-Riem, 'Ein Anlauf zu privatem Rundfunk. Analyse der Vorschläge der baden-württembergischen "Expertenkommission Neue Medien",' *Zeitschrift für Rechtspolitik*, vol. 14, 1981, pp. 177–85.

field of broadcasting policy, the SPD now began to argue the case for the development of an integrated services broadband communications network using fibre-optic cable. The latter was technologically speaking far more promising than existing cable technology, but for the SPD it had the additional merit of not being likely to be widely available for a considerable time hence. It was unsurprising that when the CDU/CSU later came to power in 1982/3 they immediately discontinued this latter commission's work.[43]

Satellite Broadcasting

Ironically, however, in view of the direction taken by SPD media policy during the 1970s, it was a narrow 'policy network' of SPD policy-makers beyond the established media 'policy community' who were actually responsible for undertaking a 'technocratic' initiative which was henceforth to have a catalytic, and arguably the most dramatic, impact on the debate about the introduction of commercial broadcasting, namely the construction of a direct broadcasting satellite (DBS).

The SPD's Industrial Policy for DBS

The explanation for this development is in fact both simple and highly illustrative of the internal contradictions of SPD policies for the new media. While the party had been developing its defensive status quo orientation in media policy, a 'policy network' of SPD technocrats and economic policy makers had at the same time been developing an 'anticipatory' style of technology policy specifically designed to respond to the imperatives of industrial change and economic restructuring in the post oil-shock era. In 1975 leading SPD technocrats Horst Ehmke,

---

43. See the *Zwischenbericht der Enquête-Kommission 'Neue Informations- und Kommunikationstechniken'*, Bonn: Bundestag-Drucksache 9/2442, 28.3.83. For a critical analysis of the role of the various expert commissions and pilot projects in 'legitimising' the introduction of the new media and commercial broadcasting see W. Hoffmann-Riem, 'New Media Policy in West Germany: The Politics of Legitimation', in K. Dyson and P. Humphreys (eds.), *The Political Economy of Communications Policies*, London: Routledge and Kegan Paul, (forthcoming).

Volker Hauff and Fritz Scharpf had produced guidelines for a highly interventionist industrial policy programme, the so-called 'structural modernisation programme' ('Programm zur Modernisierung der Volkswirtschaft durch Technologie-Strukturpolitik'). This programme had considered satellite development to be a highly interesting field of activity because of its alleged future export potential for the Federal Republic.[44] Satellite developments were then given an additional spur when the World Administration Radio Conference of 1977 (WARC 77), convened by the International Telecommunications Union (ITU), on the subject of satellite broadcasting allocated a DBS orbit position to each European country.[45] The SPD-led Bonn government reacted promptly. Specific satellite technology studies were hastily conducted by the West German Experimental Research Institute for Aerospace ('Deutsche Forschungs-Versuchsanstalt für Luft- und Raumfahrt': DFVLR) for the Federal Ministry of Research and Technology ('Bundesministerium für Forschung und Technologie': BMFT). On the basis of the DFVLR's positive recommendations, and fearing an imminent round of European competition to enter the promising new field opened up by the WARC allocation, the BMFT had immediately expressed strong support for DBS development. Similarly strong support was unsurprisingly forthcoming from leading West German manufacturing firms with interests in aerospace, electronics and telecommunications – notably, Messerschmidt Bölkow Blohm (MBB), AEG-Telefunken, Dornier and SEL. At the same time, the Bundespost appeared characteristically keen to keep abreast of any development that concerned its telecommunications monopoly, and therefore also expressed a positive interest in becoming centrally involved in any such project.

During the early 1970s the West Germans had already been involved in a novel joint venture with the French to produce two communications satellites, namely the 'Symphonie' series launched in 1974 and 1975. Following this precedent, the two governments had conducted urgent discussions during 1979 as

44. V. Hauff and F. Scharpf, *Modernisierung der Volkswirtschaft: Technologiepolitik als Strukturpolitik*, Frankfurt/Main: Europäische Verlagsgesellschaft, 1975.
45. E. Blöhmer, 'Satelliten-Direktempfang. Ergebnisse der weltweiten Funkverwaltungskonferenz 1977 für den Satellitenrundfunk', in ZDF (ed.), *ZDF Jahrbuch 1977*, Mainz: ZDF, 1977, pp. 134–8.

a result of which a formal treaty on technical and industrial cooperation in the field of DBS was signed in April 1980.[46] Accordingly, it was agreed that two identical DBS satellites – TDF I (French) and TV SAT (West German) – would be constructed and placed in geostationary orbit by the French *Ariane* rocket. Thereafter, the West German satellite would be managed by the Bundespost. Later, back-up satellites might be constructed to render the new DBS systems fully (rather than pre-) operational. Decisions on these back-up satellites were to be made independently by the respective national authorities. In July 1982 satellite construction was formally contracted to a Franco-German consortium, Eurosatellite Ltd, with its headquarters in Munich. The estimated cost of the satellites was initially set at DM 225 million for TV SAT, and FFr 555 million for TDF 1 – with an additional cost of DM 115 million for each launch by *Ariane*. This huge investment – the lion's share borne by the state in each country – was to be offset by capturing a large share of a world market the volume of which was estimated variously to be between DM 25 billion and DM 50 billion.[47]

The Internal Contradiction of the SPD's DBS Policy

Thus, the West German DBS initiative started life purely as a result of decisions taken by a narrow 'policy network' of SPD technocrats, scientific experts and industrialists concerned to promote an 'anticipatory' technology and industrial policy and reap the advantages of early entry into what was at the time perceived to be a promising international market for communications hardware. At the same time, all too little consideration was apparently given to the consequences for broadcasting policy. However, serious reservations were expressed by certain SPD media-policy-makers ('Medienpolitiker') in the Federal Chancellor's Office (Bundeskanzleramt), notably by fierce opponent of commercial television Albrecht Müller.[48] Nevertheless,

---

46. 'Abkommen über die technisch-industrielle Zusammenarbeit auf dem Gebiet von Rundfunksatelliten', *Media Perspektiven*, 5/1980, p. 342.
47. G.-M. Luyken, *Direktempfangbare Rundfunksatelliten: Erklärung, Kritik und Alternativen zu einem 'neuen Medium'*, Frankfurt/Main: Campus Verlag, 1985, pp. 198–200.
48. Müller, 'Wieviel Medien braucht der Mensch?', pp. 49–56.

Chancellor Helmut Schmidt himself clearly did not judge the risks of DBS to be comparable to those surrounding cable television. Schmidt was doubtless much more impressed by the 'technocratic' logic of engineering an exciting new collaborative response to new international competitive pressures.

To be sure, the SPD's responsibility for producing the West German DBS initiative did not mean that the satellite was ever intended to open up the way for commercial broadcasting. The government seemed to reject the possibility of using it for commercial broadcasting by stating publicly that the DBS initiative was 'not to prejudice the development of [the government's] media policy'. In view of the SPD's determinedly anti-commercial stance on media policy, this naturally led to a general expectation that the three new TV SAT channels (in the operational stage this might be extended to five) would be allocated to the existing public-service broadcasters, one each to the ARD and the ZDF and the third devoted to radio programmes. Undoubtedly, the main value of the project was to be its 'demonstration' effect on future overseas customers for the hardware. It was therefore widely regarded as being of only of an 'experimental' nature. Nevertheless, by the early 1980s SPD media-policy-makers were beginning to wake up to the distinct possibility of an imminent explosion of satellite broadcasting. At this time, the cable pilot-projects were already running programmes transmitted by ECS satellite, most notably the British-based Sky Channel and the SAT 1 channel. Moreover, a phalanx of new foreign satellite channels was being prepared in neighbouring countries. In 1981 the West German publishers' federation (the BDZV) demonstrated a keen interest in taking a share in the so-called LUX–SAT satellite television venture planned by the neighbouring state of Luxemburg. Although the plans for LUX–SAT quickly collapsed, the worst fears of these SPD policy-makers were confirmed when in late 1982 the huge West German multimedia conglomerate Bertelsmann announced that it was to take a share of 40% with the Luxemburg broadcasting company Compagnie Luxembourgeoise de Télédiffusion (CLT) in a planned new commercial German-language satellite television channel, to be called RTL-Plus and broadcast 'off-air' in the first instance into West Germany from Luxemburg, where it would be immune from West German regulatory policies.

Therefore, despite the fact that they retained 'control' over DBS development within West Germany (although their loss of control was imminent, since as will be seen they very soon lost power in Bonn at the and of 1982), the spectre of satellite broadcasting began to play a key role in reshaping the attitudes of leading SPD politicians at the beginning of the 1980s. They began to realise that if the new commercial entrepreneurs were denied suitably attractive conditions in the FRG the latter would nevertheless seek and gain access to the West German television audience, if necessary by cooperating with foreign broadcasters and using foreign satellites. This would entail a loss of investment, without in any way protecting either West German culture or West German advertising markets. In fact, the 'technocratic' sprint to gain advantages in a 'hardware' market had diverted the attention of all but a handful of the most perspicacious SPD policy-makers from West Germany's vulnerability in the international broadcasting-related markets (programming and advertising). Thus, satellite broadcasting exposed the inherent weaknesses and contradictions of SPD policy as it had evolved during the 1970s.[49]

The FRAG Judgement

The establishment of the cable pilot-projects and the fateful 'technocratic' decision to construct a West German DBS satellite constituted a giant step towards the introduction of the new media. Naturally, all this gave very considerable encouragement to the coalition of forces pushing for the introduction of a private commercial broadcasting sector. Even greater encouragement was now suddenly furnished by another monumental ruling

49. On the origins and development of West German DBS policy see K. Dyson and P. Humphreys, 'Satellite Broadcasting Policies and the Question of Sovereignty in Western Europe', *Journal of Public Policy*, 6, 1, 1986, pp. 73–96; see also Humphreys, 'Satellite Broadcasting Policy in West Germany', pp. 107–12; M. Schmidbauer, *Satellitenfernsehen für die Bundesrepublik Deutschland*, Wissenschaftsverlag West Berlin: Wissenschaftsverlag Volker Spiess, 1983; Luyken, *Direktempfangbare Rundfunksatelliten*; for an interesting and informative neomarxist account see H. Holzer, 'Satellitenfernsehen mit TV SAT', in H. Holzer and K. Betz, *Totale Bildschirm-Herrschaft? Staat, Kapital und Neue Medien*, Cologne: Pahl-Rugenstein Verlag, 1984, pp. 85–123.

Media and Media Policy in West Germany

about the structures of broadcasting by the Federal Constitutional Court, the so-called FRAG Judgement of June 1981 (see Appendix 2(c)).

Chapters 3 and 4 have already made clear the centrality of the role of 'law in politics' in West German broadcasting policy. Most notably, the Federal Constitutional Court had made important rulings which had appeared to confirm the public-service broadcasting monopoly and to place important constraints on politicians seeking to introduce radical change. It cannot therefore be surprising that the Federal Constitutional Court has played a major role in the new media debate of the 1980s. This time, however, the Court has eased the legal brakes on fundamental change by actually opening the way for private commercial broadcasting. In fact, as will be seen, the Court has intervened twice, once in 1981 and more recently in 1986, to contribute to the current radical transformation of West German broadcasting policy. The first break-through came in 1981 in the shape of the FRAG Judgement ('FRAG Urteil'). This major ruling established effectively new guidelines for broadcasting policy which allowed for the expansion of broadcasting resulting from the introduction of new technologies such as cable and satellite.

In the TV Judgement of 1961 the Court had made a celebrated distinction between the press and broadcasting. It had ruled that pluralism of the press was automatically guaranteed by the large number of newspapers and magazines in circulation. However, it had also ruled that, by contrast, in the case of broadcasting, pluralism had to be actively ensured by a public-service monopoly because of the limited number of channels on offer resulting from the scarcity of broadcasting frequencies. At the time, this had appeared to rule out the possibility of allowing private commercial broadcasting.

However, matters were given an unexpected new twist when, after a period of fourteen long years, the controversy originally sparked off by the 1967 amendment to the Saarland's broadcasting law mentioned in Chapter 4, finally culminated in a Ruling by the Federal Constitutional Court in June 1981. The FRAG Judgement now ruled definitively that the specific conditions for the introduction of private commercial broadcasting foreseen by this amendment did not provide for sufficient public-service

The Controversy Over the Introduction of the New Media

safeguards. Much more importantly, however, it more generally, recognised that the 'scarcity of frequencies' line of reasoning was being rendered obsolete by the new technologies of cable and satellite. In fact, the monumental significance of the FRAG Judgement resided in its apparent acknowledgement that, in view of the future abundance of channels promised by cable and satellite, henceforth individual Land legislation might now open the way for private broadcasting. At the same time the Court sought to prevent any uncontrolled development whereby broadcasting fell victim to a 'free-for-all' ('freies Spiel der Kräfte'). In fact, the Court's ruling contained a number of strict qualifications on the scope of private enterprise. The Court explicitly rejected the extension of monopoly power, of the press or any other kind, into the realm of broadcasting. The Court also maintained that any private broadcasting system would still have to be in a position to guarantee balance, impartiality and mutual respect ('Ausgewogenheit, Sachlichkeit und gegenseitige Achtung') as well as diversity of opinion ('Meinungsvielfalt').

Moreover, the Court actually suggested how this new abundance might be combined with a concern for pluralism by means of an alternative regulatory model to the established pattern of 'internal pluralism' and 'internal control'. Accordingly, a new so-called 'external pluralistic' model could be envisaged wherein balance and diversity might be produced by virtue of provision of a greatly increased number of channels and programme schedules. These could be permitted to be individually biased so long as, in totality, they reflected an overall balance. The supervision of these channels might therefore be feasibly conducted by an 'external control' body placed above the broadcasters, rather than 'internal control' by an internal regulatory instance within the broadcasting corporation. As seen, the CDU pilot-projects had employed exactly this kind of 'external pluralism' regulatory model. Once again in the history of West German broadcasting policy, the Federal Constitutional Court thus demonstrated that it alone ultimately established the parameters and determined the boundaries of policy, thus assuring 'continuity in change' in terms of the enduring values of the 'Rechtsstaat'. At the same time, the Court actively anticipated dramatic structural changes in broadcasting as a result of new technologies and accordingly adopted a dynamic 'anticipatory' policy-making stance. Unsurprisingly, the protagonists of commercial broadcasting were greatly heartened by this new ruling. At the same time, the hollowness of the welcome given by the SPD to the in-built public-service safeguards of the Court's rulings could hardly conceal the party's discomfort, for this latest key ruling of the Court had at last eased the legal brakes on change. The way was now open for the CDU/CSU to move beyond the stage of pilot-projects in their campaign to radically restructure West German broadcasting.[50]

50. 'FRAG–Urteil des Bundesverfassungsgerichtes vom 16. Juni 1981 (1 BvL 89/78)', *Media Perspectiven*, 6/1981, pp. 421–43.

6
The 'Dual Broadcasting System' and Multimedia Diversification

The establishment of a few isolated cable pilot-projects and the arrival of SAT 1 to feed them were not, however, enough in themselves radically to transform the nature of broadcasting policy for the whole of the Federal Republic. The FRAG ruling of the Constitutional Court may now have theoretically allowed the Länder to proceed with new media legislation, but a change of power in Bonn was also necessary before the media revolution could actually occur.

The Constitution assigned responsibility for telecommunications policy to the federal authorities in Bonn. Therefore, while the Bundespost remained under its control, the SPD was still able to employ its federal competence for telecommunications to block widespread cabling of the country. At the same time, the SPD was able to restrict the use of communications satellites purely to data and telephone links. Without the federal governments's decision in favour of a nationwide installation of a technical infrastructure for new broadcasting services, namely cable and satellite, any new deregulatory media legislation by the CDU/CSU Länder, beyond that governing the pilot-projects, would be rendered pointless. In support of its cable 'blockade', the SPD could point to the KtK's lack of enthusiasm for any general cabling of the country. After all the KtK had considered West Germany's requirements for broadcasting services to be more or less fully satisfied already and in merely recommending the establishment of the four pilot-projects had not been at all enthusiastic about broadband systems.

Apart from these pilot-projects, it was true that the country could boast of a patchwork of 'low-tech' cable islands which had resulted from an incremental cabling effort by the Bundespost over the years designed to cover areas of poor 'off-air' broadcasting reception. This state of affairs might allow the 'go-it-alone' CDU state government of Baden-Württemberg to envis-

239

age the establishment of its own pilot-projects for new media services in competition with the other CDU/CSU cable pilot-projects. Yet this hardly opened the way for a thoroughgoing transformation of the existing framework by the forces pushing for commercial broadcasting. Moreover, the cable 'blockade' of 1979 had effectively set limits to this incremental kind of cabling by the Bundespost.

The 'Machtwende' (Change of Power) in Bonn

At this critical juncture, however, dramatic change came just as abruptly as the FRAG Judgement, this time as a direct result of the sudden although not entirely unexpected collapse of the longstanding SDP/FDP government and the subsequent confirmation in federal power, by the general elections of March 1983, of a new 'conservative liberal' CDU/CSU/FDP government. The new CDU Minister for Posts and Telecommunications (Bundespostminister), Christian Schwarz-Schilling, had long been a leading campaigner for commercial broadcasting. The occupation of this particular ministerial office in Bonn by a CDU media-policy specialist ('Medienpolitiker') suggested that telecommunications policy might now be enlisted in the cause of CDU/CSU media policy.

Almost immediately after the March 1983 elections, Schwarz-Schilling abruptly broke the SPD's former blockade of cable by massively raising the annual investment allocation for the Bundespost's cable plans to no less than DM 1 billion per annum. These new funds were to be employed to make improvements and rapidly extend the existing cable islands and also to link them into a national cable network. Moreover, Schwarz-Schilling now began to proclaim quite openly that his prime aim was to 'revolutionise broadcasting'. He emphasised that cable investment by the Bundespost would henceforth be channelled to those Länder which enacted new media laws permitting commercial exploitation of this 'revolution'. He even threatened repeatedly to suspend cabling in SPD-governed Länder that resisted introducing new legislation to allow private commercial television. Moreover, in order to further prepare the way for this broadcasting revolution, Schwarz-Schilling announced, at the close of 1983, that the Bundespost would make available abundant extra capacity for satellite broadcasting. The plethora of additional channels would, it was hoped, stimulate the speediest possible development of a West German commercial broadcasting industry to programme the country's cable networks now set for a massive expansion. The main aim was to attract new commercial programme providers. This policy initiative would involve two new channels on the ECS-1 communications satellite and no less than six new channels rented on an Intelsat-V satellite (these latter would later be replaced or complemented by seven channels on a new West German communications satellite system called DFS Kopernikus). In addition, four further television channels and one new radio channel would be provided by the West German direct broadcasting satellite (DBS) TV SAT.[1]

CDU/CSU Land Legislation

With the 'Machtwende' in Bonn, and the launch in 1983 of a radical new programme by the Bundespost to cable the whole country mainly using already widely available copper-coaxial cable, it suddenly became more apparent than ever that the economic and political forces pushing for commercial broadcasting did not intend to await the results of the pilot-projects.

The CDU/CSU States Join the Bandwagon: The 'Standortpolitik' Game

As a result of the new circumstances created by the 'Machtwende', other CDU Länder not involved in the limited pilot-projects now joined the new media bandwagon. There soon began to develop a fierce competition between the individual Länder to be the first to offer the most favourable local regulatory conditions for the geographical implantation of new broadcasting operations in their areas of jurisdiction. From now on,

[1]. P. Humphreys, 'New Media Policy Dilemmas in West Germany', Chapter Five in K. Dyson and P. Humphreys, *Broadcasting and New Media Policies in Western Europe: A Comparative Study of Technological Change and Public Policy*, London: Routledge and Kegan Paul, 1988, pp. 200–1.

the confrontation between the SPD and the CDU over media policy was to be gradually overlain and complicated by the efforts of individual Länder, regardless of their political orientation, to seek competitive advantage in a race to attract inward investment in the field of media and electronics. As will shortly be seen, progressively the economic pressures of this competition came to eclipse the guidelines of official SPD national media policy as even SPD Länder began to give precedence to regional and local policies designed to favour location of the expanding media industries ('Standortpolitik'). Typically, 'Standortpolitik' took the form of a pattern of competitive deregulation by the Länder as, following the example of the Rhineland-Palatinate's law of 1980, they engaged in a race to produce a wave of new deregulatory media legislation.

The first Land actually to produce a new state law governing broadcasting was the CDU state of Lower Saxony, which produced a law on 15 May 1984 explicitly permitting the establishment of a new commercial broadcasting sector.[2] The most controversial feature of this new legislation was that it gave major discretion to the state government, and more specifically to the CDU Ministerpräsident, Ernst Albrecht, in decisions concerning the allocation of new broadcasting franchises. In this respect, the role of the new regulatory body created by the law appeared to be restricted to a preparatory and advisory function. However, this power over franchising given to the state authorities appeared to infringe the well-established principle of the West German broadcasting 'constitution' that the state should be kept at a safe distance from broadcasting regulation (the principle of 'Staatsferne'). In fact, this feature of the new law merely followed the precedents already established by the Rhineland-Palatinate's law of 1981 governing the Ludwigshafen pilot-project and, even more blatantly, also by the structures of the Berlin pilot-project. Nevertheless, this time the legislation was no longer designed to cater for a limited 'experiment'. Therefore, the Lower Saxony law of 1984 quickly assumed a huge symbolic importance for the future shape of broadcasting regulation in the country at large, in that it became a 'test-case'

2. 'Niedersächsisches Landesrundfunkgesetz', reproduced in *Media Perspektiven* 6/1984, pp. 486–96.

for all deregulatory legislation currently being prepared by other CDU/CSU Länder. Accordingly, this time the SPD was quick to respond.

The SPD Complaint to the Federal Constitutional Court

More than one-third of the members of the Bundestag, all members of the SPD, now exercised their legal right to lodge a complaint with the Federal Constitutional Court in Karlsruhe.[3] In the words of one eminent analyst of West German politics, bearing out our repeated experience so far in this study, the 'well-known track to Karlsruhe' has been 'well trodden by the parties over the years'.[4] The SPD action alleged that the Lower Saxony law infringed the basic principle of 'broadcasting freedom'. In addition to the already mentioned excessive role of the state government in the franchising process, the SPD action pointed to the insufficient guarantee of a diversity of private commercial programming, the lack of appropriate powers granted to the new regulatory authorities, and the absence of any legal provisions against concentration of media power resulting from the cross-ownership of press and broadcasting concerns.

Although the Lower Saxony law related quite specifically to the arrangements for broadcasting in a single Land, all the interested parties were quite aware of the implications that yet another major ruling by the Court would bring for all future developments nationally as well as regionally. The Constitutional Court, too, was well imbued with the enormity and politically controversial nature of its task. According to the deeply ingrained West German 'policy style' of according primacy to consensus-seeking, the Court therefore invited submissions from all the interested parties. Subsequently, the verdict of the Court was awaited with impatience by all concerned, not least because the arrival of satellite broadcasting urgently necessitated some clear statement about the future direction to be

---

3. W. Hoffmann-Riem (Bevollmächtigter), 'Antrag gemäß Artikel 93. Absatz 1. Nummer 2 Grundgesetz des Bundestagsabgeordneten Dr. Hans-Jochen Vogel und weiterer 158 Mitglieder des Deutschen Bundestags. . . ' of 6.11.1984, copy in author's possession.
4. G. Smith, *Democracy in West Germany*, London: Heinemann, 1979, p. 190.

taken by the broadcasting system nationally. Satellite broadcasting would effectively have a national, rather than a regional, impact. Therefore, despite the principle of Land sovereignty for broadcasting, some new generally applicable ground rules would be required as well. The Constitutional Court's ruling would be bound to produce such guidance and therefore it would inevitably have a national significance beyond its immediate impact on Lower Saxony.[5]

The Trend Towards 'External Pluralism' and the Promotion of a New Commercial Broadcasting Sector

In the meantime, however, the other CDU/CSU Länder prepared their own draft legislation enabling commercial television. Mindful of the constitutional constraints upon them and ever conscious now of the deliberations set in motion in Karlsruhe, the CDU/CSU policy-makers trod with some care. Unlike the 'external pluralistic' model adopted by the 1981 Rhineland-Palatinate law for the Ludwigshafen cable pilot-project, strong features of which were also adopted by the Lower Saxony law, the draft-laws produced by the CDU states of Saarland, Schleswig-Holstein and Baden-Württemberg provided for an element of 'internal pluralistic' regulation during the introductory period of the new private, commercial services. These latter draft laws sought clearly to define conditions of minimum competition for the guarantee of 'diversity of opinion' ('Meinungsvielfalt') and the permission of 'external pluralism'. In the case of Baden-Württemberg, the conditions were even fairly restrictive, in that they specified as an absolute minimum reception of the programmes of the public-service stations, two further German-language local and regional channels and at least three German-language supra-regional channels.[6] Overall, however, the general drift was inexorably away from the 'inter-

---

5. See B. Hendriks, 'Verfassungsrechtliche Probleme des Niedersächsischen Landesrundfunkgesetzes', *Media Perspektiven*, 6/1984, pp. 433–40.
6. Rather than footnote individually each reference to the numerous versions of the draft laws and laws mentioned in the following, the author advises the reader to refer to *Media Perspektiven. Reihe Dokumentation*, from 1985 onwards. Moreover, there is a very useful synopsis of the content of all laws and draft laws up to 1986 in *Media Perspektiven. Dokumentation*, III/1986, pp. 125–211.

nal pluralism' model of regulation towards 'external pluralism': 'external pluralism' would in every case follow upon the attainment of a certain numerical threshold of new services. Exploiting the window-of-opportunity which had been opened to them by the 1981 FRAG ruling of the Constitutional Court, the CDU/CSU policy-makers at the Land level thus sought to create a suitably deregulated environment for new entrepreneurial, multimedia activity in their Länder.

The spate of CDU/CSU legislation also varied in the delicate matter of defining responsibility for the process of allocation of new franchises. Bavaria and Baden-Württemberg were very much more circumspect about laying themselves open to the charge levelled against the Lower Saxony law that the principle of 'Staatsferne' was being infringed. Thus, both the Bavarian and Baden-Württemberg laws delegated this responsibility to the new regulatory bodies they created (although, as seen, this had not been the case in the early days of the Munich pilot-project). Later, this was also to be the case when the second Rhineland-Palatinate law of June 1986, designating the move beyond the 'test' phase of the Ludwigshafen project, also adopted this principle (doubtless influenced by the Constitutional Court's ruling against the Lower Saxony law).

Nevertheless, in the case of Baden-Württemberg, the five-member Board of Directors of the resultant State Authority for Communication (Landesanstalt für Kommunikation) was to be elected by the state parliament. Moreover, the Landesanstalt remained subject to the legal supervision ('Rechtsaufsicht') of the state government. In the case of Schleswig-Holstein and the Saarland, similar State Authorities for Broadcasting (Landesanstalten für das Rundfunkwesen) were established, but they too remained ultimately subject to state supervision, by the state government in the former case and by the Ministerpräsident in the latter case. In this respect, it could be argued that 'Rechtsaufsicht' meant only a residual kind of supervision of the kind also provided for by the early post-war broadcasting legislation of the Länder. However, the inclusion of this kind of stipulation was further grist to the mill of the SPD, given the sensitivity of the issue as a result of the court case over the much more transparent and direct influence of the state in the case of the Lower Saxony law.

This frenetic drafting of new deregulatory legislation by CDU/CSU policy-makers in the Länder also produced a degree of variance in the role accorded to public-service broadcasters in this developing era of new media. The fundamental position shared by all CDU/CSU policy-makers alike was that the existing public-service broadcasters already benefited from an enormous built-in advantage of experience, skill and resources in broadcasting. However, the new legislation revealed a considerable variance of response to this advantage. The temptation was to restrict the role of the public-service broadcasters in order to leave the field as clear as possible for the new entrepreneurs. Indeed, this was the course of action preferred by most CDU policy makers. However, another strategy altogether was adopted by the CSU policy-makers in Bavaria. As a result of patronage politics, the CSU had managed to gain a particularly strong grip on the regional broadcasting corporation in Bavaria, the BR, and this despite the controversies of the early 1970s. Accordingly, the CSU harboured scarcely disguised ambitions of its own to promote the BR and to use the opportunities opened up by satellite (and notably the Bundespost's policy of making more satellite channels available) in order to find a national role for its regional public-service corporation. Generally, however, the CDU/CSU policy-makers all shared one major concern, namely to restrict the place of the ARD in future operations. The explanation was both simple and highly illustrative of the ulterior determinants of broadcasting policy in the Federal Republic. The ARD gave national coverage to the channels of NDR and WDR which were the most suspect (i.e. 'SPD') in the eyes of the CDU/CSU.

Despite this not inconsiderable divergence in details, the broad aims of the CDU/CSU policy-makers in the Länder reflected the parties' national policy, namely to promote the speediest possible development of a new commercial broadcasting sector which was confidently expected to be more favourable to their political philosophy. The creation of a similar situation for broadcasting to that already pertaining to the press would, it was felt, rebalance broadcasting politics to the disadvantage of the SPD. At the same time, this overriding aim did not preclude the outbreak of a very considerable degree of competition between the CDU/CSU Länder themselves in their

SPD Land Legislation

SPD policy-makers in the Länder now found themselves in a dilemma: they could persist in 'fundamentalist' opposition to commercial broadcasting; or, they could adopt a more 'cooperative' mode of opposition. There were some strong arguments in favour of the latter course. It was by now very evident that CDU/CSU policy was explicitly designed to attract new broadcasting entrepreneurs to establish their centres of activity and invest in CDU/CSU Länder. The SPD Länder therefore faced the danger that private media investment would be diverted to new CDU/CSU commercial 'media havens', such as Munich, Berlin, Mainz, and Hanover. Moreover, the Bundespostminister Schwarz-Schilling had repeatedly made it very clear that SPD Länder which refused to legislate for commercial broadcasting would forfeit valuable federal telecommunications investment. The arrival and imminent explosion of satellite broadcasting also played a key role in reshaping the attitudes of leading SPD politicians.

Hamburg Embarks on the Path to Compromise

In Hamburg, in particular, there were compelling pressures on the ruling SPD politicians to abandon 'fundamentalist' opposition. Hamburg was West Germany's preeminent media-centre, already host to the largest concentration of newspaper and magazine publishers in the country. The media industry was central to the city-state's local economy. As the result, the city's SPD policy-makers found themselves faced with a classic instance of the 'veto power' which powerful media concerns exercised over the city-state's political economy.

Ironically, the Springer group was particularly important both to the city's local economy and to its status as West Germany's

---

7. On the legal issues raised by the CDU/CSU legislation see R. Gross, 'Verfassungsrechtlich bedeutsame Schwerpunkte der Mediengesetzgebung', *Media Perspektiven*, 9/1984, pp. 681–95.

Media and Media Policy in West Germany

'press capital'. The city hosted such leading 'Springer' publications as *Die Welt* and *Bild*, including their Sunday editions, and also the *Hamburger Abendpost*, *Hör Zu* and *Funk-Uhr*. Next to the Springer concern, the Bauer group was also a very powerful lobby in the city. Bauer's *Neue Post*, *Neues Blatt*, *Neue Revue* and *TV Hören und Sehen* were all sited in Hamburg. Both of these groups were important backers of the SAT 1 commercial satellite channel and key players in the campaign to introduce a nationwide commercial broadcasting sector (in addition, such well-known newspapers as the *Hamburger Morgenpost* and *Die Zeit* and leading magazines as *Der Spiegel* and *Stern* were also based in Hamburg).

Moreover, the city was now faced by a powerful and ambitious domestic rival in the shape of Munich, the capital of CSU-governed Bavaria. According to a well-publicised report by the Munich and Upper Bavarian Chamber of Commerce (Industrie- und Handelskammer für München und Oberbayern), in 1985 the media industry of Munich accounted for nearly 90,000 employees in over 5,000 firms with a total annual turnover of DM 16 billion. Munich's media industry was registering very impressive annual growth (of between 5% and 6%) and significantly most of the new firms were in the field of the audiovisual media. Most alarmingly for the Hamburg SPD, the report suggested that Munich was now in an excellent position to challenge Hamburg's preeminence as a 'media centre'.[8] Moreover, Munich was not the only city in a position to challenge Hamburg. Mainz, the capital of the CDU-governed Rhineland-Palatinate, was already host to ZDF and now it was to become the base for SAT 1 as well. Also, CDU West Berlin presented a very special financial inducement to media firms anxious to relocate, on account of a long-established federal policy of encouraging business to the beleaguered city. In addition, as seen, West Berlin was fast developing the country's most extensive cable system.

The first inclination of the Hamburg SPD parliamentary group was to follow SPD national media policy and oppose an overhasty introduction of the new media and completely rule out the

8. See 'München mausert sich zum Medienzentrum', *Süddeutsche Zeitung* no. 246, 24 October 1985, p. 26.

possibility of commercial broadcasting. Bundespostminister Schwarz-Schilling's cable programme especially was vigorously attacked for using arguably 'obsolete' copper-coaxial technology. Moreover, the Hamburg SPD declared its intention to introduce a more modern fibre-optic system when this option became available at an as yet unspecified future date. However, the twin pressures of 'Standortpolitik' and the power of the city's resident media giants soon became overwhelming. In particular, the SPD policy makers in Hamburg began to fear that an investment flight would follow from their continued adherence to such a restrictive local policy for the new media.

Very considerable cross-party pressure soon built up within the city's parliament in favour of introducing an energetic cable initiative for the city under the Bundespost's new programme. This cross-party pressure also demanded the prompt passage of new legislation that would ensure the city's future attractiveness for media investors by opening the way forward for private, commercial broadcasters. The SPD mayor of Hamburg, also the city state's Ministerpräsident, Klaus von Dohnanyi, a very powerful voice within the SPD, both locally and nationally, argued fiercely for a new realism in media policy. However, he was opposed by a vocal minority of 'grass-roots' left-wingers, notably the Hamburg SPD's strong contingent of Young Socialists (Jungsozialisten). For two years the Hamburg SPD was therefore riven by very fierce intra-party debate. It quickly became apparent that the higher echelons of the Hamburg party and particularly those party officials actually responsible for governmental policy-making were impatient to act over the heads of the party 'grass-roots'. On October 1984, the Hamburg state government duly adopted a 'Law for the Provisional Retransmission of Broadcast Programmes in Cable Networks' ('Vorschaltsgesetz über die vorläufige Weiterverbreitung von Rundfunkprogrammen in Kabelanlagen'), which allowed commercial broadcasting. The following year, in December 1985, the SPD Hamburg state government then enacted a deregulatory Land media law to confirm this latter development.[9] This law came into effect on 1 January 1986. It followed the example of

9. See *Media Perspektiven*, 10/1984, pp. 833–9 as well as *Media Perspektiven. Dokumentation*, IV/1985, pp. 186–201.

the CDU/CSU media laws in accepting the new regulatory formula of 'external pluralism' and 'external control' by the creation of a Hamburg Authority for the New Media (Anstalt für Neue Medien HAM). However, like several more 'moderate' CDU laws, it attempted to combine this regulatory principle with certain 'internal pluralistic' ('binnenpluralistisch') elements.

The extent to which the law amounted to a very significant concession to local publishing interests was amply illustrated by its ingenious but largely symbolic attempt to conciliate party animosity towards the Springer press. Article 19 clause 2 of the law specified that 'any' applicant for a regional franchise, who already had a dominant position in the city's daily newspaper market (i.e. Springer), should not himself personally be eligible for a private broadcasting licence; moreover, his share in any company receiving a licence should not exceed 25%. At the same time, most revealingly, this threshold was established well above the level of the direct (though not indirect) shareholding of the Springer press in the new private, commercial satellite channel, SAT 1 (see Appendix 3).[10]

North-Rhine Westphalia Changes the Terms of Reference of the Dortmund Cable Pilot-Project and Develops an 'Alternative' Regulatory Model for Commercial Broadcasting

In the SPD-governed Land of North-Rhine Westphalia similar concern was displayed by the regional government to develop a new regulatory model which paid due attention to the requirements of regional 'Standortpolitik'. At the same time, however, much more serious effort was devoted to combining 'Standortpolitik' with a coherent political strategy towards developing a realistic and pragmatic alternative to simple deregulation. After a long period of soul-searching, which involved making a number of significant concessions to economic pressures, a very interesting and controversial alternative regulatory model was finally produced, which sought to employ regulatory instru-

10. See Humphreys, 'New Media Policy Dilemmas in West Germany', pp. 205–7; and P. Humphreys, 'Satellite Broadcasting Policy in West Germany', in R. Negrine (ed.), *Satellite Broadcasting. The Politics and Implications of the New Media*, London: Routledge and Kegan Paul, 1988, pp. 122–3.

'Dual Broadcasting System' and Multimedia Diversification

ments as a countervailing power to media-concentration. The pressures of 'Standortpolitik' were more obviously compelling than in Hamburg. Despite the collapse of the latter city's ship-building industry, the relative decline of its port, and unemployment figures above the national average, Hamburg could still boast the highest gross domestic product per capita in the Federal Republic (in 1986). The city, one of the most opulent in Western Europe, presented an image of spacious splendour, rivalled in West Germany only by Munich. It had always had far more going for it than its traditional industries. In a country deprived by post-war division of its natural capital, Hamburg could fairly lay claim to being West Germany's northern pole, and it was, after all, still the country's leading media centre. By contrast, North-Rhine Westphalia had the highest concentration of traditional and crisis-prone industries in the country and contained one of the Federal Republic's problem regions, namely the coal- and steel-producing 'Ruhrgebiet' (Ruhr area). Although relatively pleasant cities (in international comparison), the Ruhr's leading industrial cities of Essen, Duisburg, Bochum and Dortmund, with their surrounding dense networks of working-class satellite towns, presented a very different picture to the comfortable affluence of Hamburg. During the 1970s and 1980s they had begun to exhibit the unmistakable signs of seedy decline, as the region suffered recurrent waves of pit closures and rationalisation of steel production, involving massive reductions in the labour force. For example, between the 1960s and the early 1980s, the West German steel industry, once made world famous by names such as Krupp and Thyssen, had cut its workforce by over a half, from over half a million to under a quarter of a million employees. With some success, the SPD Land government of North-Rhine Westphalia had initiated ambitious plans to restructure the region, but it was still desperate for any new inward investment. On the other hand, as the most populous Land in the Federal Republic, with nearly 17 million inhabitants, accounting for a third of the West German population and more than that of neighbouring Holland, the Land was obviously highly attractive to new media entrepreneurs. While the state authorities were inclined to court inward investment, the new media entrepreneurs were equally keen to gain access to this dense concentration of viewers and listeners.

Therefore, the SPD Land government had a strong card to play in the process of reshaping media regulations. To put it simply, it could afford to adopt a more autonomous stance *vis-à-vis* the power of capital and, in particular, the publishers.

However, the first attempt by the SPD Land government to turn this state of affairs to its advantage ended in failure. It involved no less than a highly ambitious, ingenious and fairly blatant attempt to construct a new media force in North-Rhine Westphalia, which would be private and commercial in nature, but which would also be politically sympathetic to the SPD. In essence, the SPD Land government attempted to act as a 'marriage broker' between two powerful media forces already resident in the Land, namely the WDR, which was the Federal Republic's wealthiest and largest public-service broadcasting corporation, and the WAZ publishing group, which was one of the country's most powerful newspaper concerns. The WAZ group had a virtual monopolistic status in the Ruhr and also had the merit, in the eyes of the state government, of being 'social-liberal' in political orientation. Had this plan been successful, North-Rhine Westphalia would have been able to produce a new private commercial media force in West Germany with a truly commanding presence in the country's media system. It would have presented very grave economic competition, and simultaneously offered very serious editorial and political competition, to other new commercial operators such as the SAT 1 consortium, which as seen had been established by conservative media interests and which had been similarly 'sponsored' by the conservative Land government of the Rhineland-Palatinate.

Had the SPD Land government initiated this plan somewhat later, for example during the late 1980s, it would probably have succeeded. However, the time was not yet right for such a bold manoeuvre, the main reason being that, as in Hamburg and elsewhere, the SPD was still very deeply riven by a fierce internal party debate over whether to accept at all the principle of private commercial broadcasting. At this time, grass-roots party activists in North-Rhine Westphalia refused to countenance the prospect of any private commercial television whatsoever being introduced by an SPD government. It was also characteristic of the legalistic contours which the whole media-policy debate was beginning to assume that the CDU/CSU

'Dual Broadcasting System' and Multimedia Diversification

Ministerpräsidenten raised the subtle threat of litigation, by pointing to the complex constitutional 'problems' that the venture posed. As a result the climate for investment was at best rather uncertain. Before the matter could develop much further, the WAZ group itself decided the issue by withdrawing its initial support for the scheme in favour of backing a much more secure option, namely a 10% stake in Luxemburg-based RTL Plus alongside the other 'liberal' West German publishing group, the giant Bertelsmann concern. Thus the first serious attempt by SPD pragmatists at least to steer developments increasingly perceived as inevitable in a favourable direction was quickly disappointed. However, the significance of this desertion by the regional WAZ group to what was at that time a foreign-based enterprise was not lost on SPD policy-makers. Indeed, it had a catalytic effect on SPD attitudes more widely. It confirmed the fears of those actually responsible for regional economic policy-making that SPD media policy raised the danger of a flight of investment. This message now began to diffuse down to the party ranks and as a result the more pragmatic orientation of the SPD government slowly gained a wider acceptance.

Faced by the powerful twin pressures of 'Standortpolitik' and the obvious economic 'blackmail' power of the regional press, the SPD Land government was now forced to make a significant concession. In March 1985, a law was prepared which effectively opened the way forward for the reception and retransmission of private commercial television in the whole of North-Rhine Westphalia.[11] The extent of the retreat from earlier SPD national media-policy aims was dramatically illustrated by this law's alteration of the arrangements surrounding the Dortmund pilot cable television project. As seen in the preceding chapter, this pilot-project had been a powerful symbol of SPD 'principled' opposition to private commercial television. Alone among the country's four experimental cable projects, it had debarred all private commercial satellite channels and had chosen instead to rely entirely upon public-service programming. However, the

---

11. 'Nordrhein-Westfalen: Gesetz über die vorläufige Weiterverbreitung von Rundfunkprogrammen in Kabelanlagen (VorlWeiterverbreitungsG NW) vom 19 März 1985', *Media Perspektiven. Dokumentation* II/1985, pp. 105–12.

new legislation now provided for an abrupt reversal of this 'fundamentalist' opposition to commercial television. The desertion by the WAZ group to RTL Plus had exposed the complete bankruptcy of this policy stance in the age of trans-border broadcasting and free capital flows. Although grass-roots perceptions were now changing, the *volte-face* by the policy-makers did still provoke some very bitter condemnation from the party's more militant activists. It also met with considerable recrimination from the WDR and also from those involved in Kabelfunk Dortmund, who were now forced to review the station's programming schedule shortly before its opening. However, the pragmatic SPD officials who were actually responsible for governmental policy-making overruled these objections, repeating the pattern now established in SPD Hamburg.

Yet it very soon became evident that the SPD policy-makers in North-Rhine Westphalia did not intend to submit entirely to economic pressures and to downgrade cultural and broadcasting policy concerns. In the first place, the Land government financed the most comprehensive and detailed research project that has so far been conducted into the new media by any state authority in Western Europe. This involved commissioning in-depth studies conducted by academics, scientists and media experts into fields as diverse as: the effects of the new media on the family and children; local media and the political culture of Dortmund; behavioural studies of journalistic activity in local broadcasting; regulatory policy; and a host of other areas. These studies were notable in that they were conducted by independent and often critical experts, rather than by those who were obviously chosen because they were generally sympathetic to commercialisation and deregulation, or even highly enthusiastic about the 'brave new media world', as was the case in many other cases (e.g. the pilot-projects and commissions of the CDU/CSU Länder). Even more significantly, however, the SPD Land government set about elaborating a novel regulatory model for the new media which pointed towards a wholly different approach to the all-important business of combining economic and cultural concerns. This model was destined to provide a stark contrast to those chosen anywhere else in the Federal Republic. Although at the time of writing it remains too early to judge the success of implementation of this model, the

'Dual Broadcasting System' and Multimedia Diversification

new regulatory model clearly testified to the less submissive stance adopted by the SPD policy-makers in North-Rhine Westphalia than by their counterparts in Hamburg and demonstrated their determination to employ legislation as a countervailing power. When the legislation was finally enacted and came into effect, in January 1987, it contained a clever attempt to conciliate party sensitivities by responding to the pressures of 'Standortpolitik' whilst not conceding to the powerful interests of the publishers.[12]

The law provided for an ingenious 'twin-pillar' ('Zwei-Säulen') model for local broadcasting which was cleverly designed so as to detach regulations for editorial policy from those governing the financing of local commercial broadcasting. More precisely, the legislators foresaw the establishment of two special bodies, with distinct functions. On the one hand, an 'operational company' ('Veranstaltergemeinschaft') – composed pluralistically and involving the 'socially significant groups' – would be responsible for representing the public interest and solely responsible for all programming decisions. On the other hand, alongside this body, the law also established a 'management company' ('Betriebsgesellschaft') with the role of financing and drawing profits from regional broadcasting. In the latter body the publishers would be allowed to gain as much as 75% of the shares, but the remaining 25% would be allocated to the local authorities. In this bold and imaginative manner, the North-Rhine Westphalian SPD policy-makers determined explicitly to prevent the publishers from being in a position to exercise undue influence over the editorial policy of the new commercial programmes. At the same time, however, this 'twin-pillar' model was clearly intended not to deter, even to positively mobilise, the much needed new investment in the sector, since the allure of making profits from regional broadcasting in this highly populous Land was not in any way interfered with or restricted. It was also highly significant that the legislation stipulated the adoption of the 'internal pluralistic' model of programming regulation (see Appendix 3).[13]

12. 'Rundfunkgesetz für das Land Nordrhein-Westfalen (LRG NW) vom 19. Januar 1987', *Media Perspektiven. Dokumentation*, II/1987, pp. 120–37.
13. Humphreys, 'New Media Policy Dilemmas in West Germany', pp. 207–8, and p. 213.

255

The Hardline SPD States: Hessen and Bremen

Nevertheless, the initiatives of the Hamburg and North-Rhine Westphalian SPD governments alike were widely perceived as media-policy 'revisionism'. They engendered predictable accusations of 'betrayal' from the party 'grass-roots' and were not so easily adopted by policy-makers in two SPD-controlled Länder, namely Hessen and the small city-state of Bremen. Notwithstanding the pressures of 'Standortpolitik', for a long time these Länder refused to enact any legislation to allow commercial broadcasting. In both cases, the 'input' from the party activists and the grass-roots in the policy process was a very much more significant constraint on the official policy-makers' scope of action. Moreover, in Hessen, the situation was further complicated for SPD pragmatists by the fact that during the early 1980s the SPD had entered into a regional coalition (first informal, but later formal) with the Green Party.

In fact, the 'red/green' government of Hessen adopted the very confrontational policy of introducing advertising into its regional public-service broadcasting service in a naked attempt to disadvantage the new commercial operators (advertising was normally not carried by the so-called 'Third Programme'). This measure infuriated the CDU/CSU and became a serious obstacle to the negotiations which had meanwhile been entered into by the Ministerpräsidenten in order to reach some kind of compromise solution for a coherent national regulatory framework for the new media. In fact, by now the urgent need for a new nationwide consensus about the future shape of the broadcasting system had become a very major preoccupation.

Satellite Broadcasting and the Need for a New 'Staatsvertrag'

Following the 1981 FRAG ruling of the Constitutional Court and the 1982/3 change of power in Bonn, satellite broadcasting had suddenly become a major catalyst for the radical transformation of West German broadcasting policy, especially as far as the attitudes and sensibilities of leading SPD policy-makers in certain Länder were concerned. In fact, it had rapidly become an even more important factor in the wave of change than the cable pilot-projects, which had originally been the object of far more intense and bitter political debate. Stimulated by the chaotic particularism ('Kleinstaaterei') that had now become characteristic of the policies pursued by the individual Länder and given urgency by the uncertain issue of the law-suit against the CDU law of Lower Saxony, the main subject of national policy debate during the period 1983–6 quickly came to focus on the need for a comprehensive rethink by the Ministerpräsidentenkonferenz about the whole structure of broadcasting regulation in the Federal Republic – and in particular on the need for a 'Staatsvertrag' on broadcasting and new media.

The Ministerpräsidenten Confronted with the 'National' Scope of Satellite Broadcasting

By its very nature satellite television, especially DBS, amounted to 'national' broadcasting in that it could be received by the whole country. Franchising and regulatory decisions made in individual Länder – such as the Rhineland-Palatinate's decision to franchise and up-link the SAT 1 private commercial satellite channel – would have a national impact. Therefore, the Ministerpräsidenten, including those of the SPD, were faced with the increasingly urgent necessity of making some collective decisions about the national broadcasting system. To be more precise, they had to decide about the allocation of at least twelve potential satellite television channels, this being the sum of the channels to be made available by Bundespostminister Schwarz-Schilling plus the DBS channels to be provided by the eventual launch of TV SAT. As importantly, the Ministerpräsidentenkonferenz had also to agree common regulatory principles for the 'feeding' of cable systems. In future, satellite programmes would feed cable systems in individual Länder originating from beyond the latter's borders. The regulatory framework of the originating Land would often diverge from that of the Land whose cable systems would be on the receiving end. The list of matters of mutual concern to all the Länder did not stop here. New common principles for advertising on the satellite channels would also be required – since advertising revenue would be the 'life-blood' of the new broadcasters. Accordingly, the regulations for advertising too had repercussions beyond any particular purely regional jurisdiction. This latter matter was naturally of paramount concern to CDU/CSU Ministerpräsidenten concerned to establish the most favourable financial scenario for future commercial broadcasting.

In order to arrive at an arrangement for such matters that commonly affected all Länder alike, the traditional practice of West German broadcasting policy-making suggested that negotiation of a new 'Staatsvertrag' would be necessary. Such a process, however, implied a degree of consensus among the Ministerpräsidenten. At first, in view of the polarised debate between the parties and interest groups the basis for such a consensus did not appear to exist. The alternative, however, was the possible imminent disintegration of the Federal Republic's broadcasting landscape. As one West German broadcaster put it, the country could easily face a situation resembling a 'mosaic of individual media territories, a truly paradoxical situation in the day and age of satellites'.[14]

The Reorientation of National SPD Policy

The SPD, and especially its policy makers at Land level, were becoming increasingly aware of the negative effects of the national policy commitment made during the 1970s to the status quo in broadcasting. This policy was already being undermined by a combination of legal, economic, technological and political factors. The FRAG Judgement of 1981 *de jure* rendered void the SPD's single-minded commitment to maintenance of the public-service monopoly. Economically, the SPD Länder were in danger of missing out on important new media investment, even of falling prey to an investment flight, as the CDU/CSU states furnished legislation to make their Länder more attractive sites for the media. Technologically, satellite broadcasting was already making a *de facto* nonsense of federal state 'sovereignty'. Politically, it would be near impossible, and certainly very

---

14. W. Konrad in *Satellitenrundfunk – Medium der Zukunft?* Documentation of the Third International Media Conference of 18–20 November 1984 in Luxemburg, published by the Hans Seidel Stiftung, Munich, 1984. Also see Humphreys, 'Satellite Broadcasting Policy in West Germany', p. 121.

'Dual Broadcasting System' and Multimedia Diversification

damaging, to attempt technically to block satellite signals from beyond state borders. Not only would this lay any SPD public authority thinking of pursuing such an option open to the charge of a major infringement of the constitutional right of 'broadcasting freedom', and run counter to the basic liberal-democratic tenet of freedom of communications, there would be a certain obvious political cost involved in any such attempt to impede programming originating in a neighbouring Land (especially when many West German citizens already received 'off-air' broadcasts from the nearby German Democratic Republic). Finally, to persist in 'fundamentalist' opposition to commercial broadcasting, which quite unlike the situation during the 1970s was now a distinct reality, would mean that the SPD was abdicating any responsibility for actually trying to shape the direction of future developments by relinquishing a useful role for itself in the policy-making process. In sum, over the period 1982–4 there was increasing recognition within the SPD policy-making organs that existing national SPD policy had been overtaken by events.

Accordingly, in May 1984 at its national party conference at Essen the SPD adopted a new Media Action Programme ('Medienpolitisches Aktionsprogramm'), albeit after a vigorous and polarised debate by the delegates and a very close vote.[15] This new programme was much more pragmatic in its approach, accepting the introduction of private commercial broadcasting alongside the existing public-service system. It amounted to little less than a major *volte-face*. At the same time, the SPD Land governments of Hamburg and North-Rhine Westphalia, if not those of Hessen and Bremen, were busily drawing up deregulatory legislation to facilitate the introduction of commercial broadcasting at the regional level.

The Deadlock Within the Ministerpräsidentenkonferenz

Thus freed of all previous policy constraints, the SPD

---

15. SPD, *Medienpolitik: Eingeschränkte Öffnung für private Veranstalter: Beschlüsse des Essener Parteitages der SPD zur Medienpolitik*, Bonn: SPD, 1984; a shortened version of this 'Medienpolitisches Aktionsprogramm' is reproduced in *Media Perspektiven*, 2/1984, pp. 149–51.

259

Ministerpräsidenten immediately opened negotiations with their CDU/CSU counterparts about a new 'Staatsvertrag' for cable and satellite broadcasting. During the course of the subsequent long-drawn-out negotiations between 1984–7 the CDU/CSU sought to bully the SPD Ministerpräsidenten into making major concessions, especially over the future distribution of advertising resources between the public-service broadcasters (which the CDU/CSU wanted to limit) and the new commercial operators (which the CDU/CSU wanted to maximise). Another serious source of conflict between the Ministerpräsidenten was the balance of apportionment of future DBS channels between the public-service and the commercial broadcasters. Finally, certain SPD Länder exhibited a definite intransigence about the whole matter of commercial broadcasting.

In order to 'blackmail' the SPD Ministerpräsidenten, those of the CDU/CSU now raised the spectre of a breakaway of the CDU/CSU states from the ARD and the possibility that they might compose their own 'rump' 'Staatsvertrag' for broadcasting and new media. Such a threat to the unity of the West German broadcasting landscape and the cooperation between the public-service broadcasters was made in the knowledge that it would have a disastrous impact on certain 'SPD' broadcasting corporations. For example in Bremen, the broadcasting organisation of that small 'city-state' was totally dependent on cooperation within the ARD. Bremen's broadcasting corporation was too small to contemplate continuing to operate without the ARD financial equalisation structure and contributions of programming from other members of the ARD network. The SPD state of Hamburg also felt the sharp edge of this threat, in this case because its broadcasting organisation, the NDR, was based on a 'Staatsvertrag' with the neighbouring CDU Länder of Lower Saxony and Schleswig-Holstein. Chapter 4 has described how both these CDU Länder had already threatened to break up the NDR, because of its alleged SPD bias: the NDR was distinctly vulnerable to pressure of this kind. In addition, another threat was employed to even greater effect by the CDU/CSU Ministerpräsidenten hinting darkly that SPD 'intransigence' would meet with their refusal to support the raising of the television licence-fee, upon which the public-service broadcasters depended, when it next came up for renegotiation.

Over the period 1984–7, agreement was repeatedly blocked by the obdurate refusal of one party or another to compromise. For example, a general and comprehensive agreement was very nearly achieved by the Ministerpräsidenten at their first annual summit to reorganise broadcasting and produce a 'State Treaty for the Restructuring of Broadcasting' ('Staatsvertrag zur Neuordnung des Rundfunkwesens') – held at Bremerhaven in October 1984.[16] However, hopes were soon dashed by the refusal to accept the draft Bremerhaven 'Staatsvertrag' by two SPD Länder, North-Rhine Westphalia and Hessen. Both of these states objected to CDU/CSU-inspired measures to peg advertising by the pubic-service broadcasters at present levels. Such a measure, it was argued, would amount to a very serious long-term handicap for the public-service broadcasters and give the new commercial sector an unfair advantage. Other attempts to produce an agreement were blocked by the stubborn resistance of the hard-line SPD states of Bremen and Hessen. In fact, the negotiations were doomed to remain laboriously deadlocked for a further two and a half years, a fact which contributed to the impression of increasing gloom both at home and abroad among potential investors in the new industry.

Nevertheless, the negotiations did result in one early compromise decision of considerable importance. In 1984, the Ministerpräsidenten managed to agree on the allocation of two channels rented by the Bundespost on the ECS communications satellite. As the result, the 'east beam' was allocated to a new public-service satellite channel called 'Drei SAT' (3SAT). This channel demonstrated the new confidence of the public-service broadcasters about their ability to confront the new commercial operators in the arena of the new media. 3SAT was mounted by ZDF in collaboration with the public-service broadcasters of Austria and Switzerland. It was ostensibly designed to be a German-language cultural channel, but this hardly concealed the ambition of the public-service broadcasters to deploy their vastly superior resources to 'occupy the market', compete with, and if possible strangle at birth, the new commercial operators.

16. The draft 'Bremerhafener Staatsvertrag' is reproduced in *Funk Korrespondenz* 43/26 (October 1984); also see 'Vorläufiges Ergebnisprotokoll der Ministerpräsidentenkonferenz vom 17.–19. Oktober 1984 in Bremerhafen', *Media Perspektiven*, 10/1984, pp. 791–3.

The other channel, the 'west beam', was allocated to the SAT 1 consortium, which duly began operations in January 1985, initially feeding the country's growing cable infrastructure. Moreover, after August 1985 3SAT was compelled to share its 'east beam' with the commercial rival of SAT 1, namely RTL Plus which had been broadcasting 'off-air' from Luxemburg into the Saarland and adjacent parts of the Federal Republic since January 1984. These new commercial satellite channels were accepted by all SPD Länder with the notable exceptions of Hessen and Bremen. However, this noteworthy compromise aside, no further major progress was made over a future common nationwide regulatory framework for the West German broadcasting system until events began moving again in the period 1986/7.

In the meantime, the broadcasting system of the Federal Republic seemed to be becoming increasingly threatened by dangerous fragmentary pressures. Firstly, the competition between public-service broadcasters and the new commercial operators was given a new twist when the ARD stations decided to launch a second public-service satellite television channel called Eins Plus in 1986, using a transponder rented by the Bundespost on the Intelsat-V communications satellite. Secondly, the particularistic competition ('Kleinstaaterei') between the Länder escalated when Bavaria's CSU policy-makers decided to use another of the rented channels on the Intelsat-V satellite in order to broadcast Bavaria's 'third programme' – Bavaria Three ('Bayern Drei' or BR3) – nationally across West Germany as the 'voice of CSU Bavaria'. This provoked apprehension among CDU politicians about the CSU's national political ambitions and the CDU Ministerpräsident of Schleswig-Holstein, Uwe Barschel, even refused to grant it access to his Land. Moreover, it soon prompted a response in kind from the SPD policy-makers of North-Rhine Westphalia, who immediately applied to the Bundespost for another rented transponder in order that the WDR's 'third programme' might also 'go national' as the 'voice of SPD North-Rhine Westphalia'. Thirdly, the SPD and CDU/CSU Ministerpräsidenten seemed to be unable to reach a compromise over the future organisation of the broadcasting system. CSU Bavaria and CDU Baden-Württemberg refused to accept the legality of Eins Plus and denied it access to their cable systems. Moreover, during 1986 the CDU/CSU Länder escalated the

'Dual Broadcasting System' and Multimedia Diversification

pressure by actually drafting two 'rump' 'Staatsverträge', one for the south and one for the north of Germany, thereby preparing the way for the threatened break-up of the ARD system. The pressures of 'Standortpolitik' even led SPD Hamburg to accede to the latter 'rump' 'Staatsvertrag'.[17]

In sum, in several ways the economic and political particularism of the Länder seemed to have replaced 'cooperative federalism' – the basis of the ARD network – with a dangerous fragmentation of the West German broadcasting system. The crisis had gravely escalated beyond the already precarious situation caused by the polarisation between the SPD and the CDU/CSU over media policy. Moreover, as the result of this media policy impasse, Bundespostminister Schwarz-Schilling appeared to be becoming increasingly reticent about signing his name to the DM 400 million contract for TV SAT 2, the back-up satellite which would eventually complete the proposed national DBS system. In fact, Schwarz-Schilling had become increasingly concerned at the disappointingly slow pace of his 'broadcasting revolution'.

Dramatic Action by the Bundespost to Rescue National Media Policy: New Measures to Promote Commercial Broadcasting

Therefore, during the period 1983–6, despite the coincidence of important factors highly favourable to a broadcasting revolution in the Federal Republic – namely, the FRAG Judgement, the 'Machtwende' and the advent of satellite broadcasting – the prospect of a speedy achievement of the radical reform of the broadcasting system sought by the CDU/CSU had begun to fade seriously at the edges. The CDU/CSU policy-makers' radical plans appeared to be blocked by the hard-bargaining and even downright obduracy of certain SPD members of the Ministerpräsidentenkonferenz. Moreover, the constitutional complaint signed by 201 SPD Bundestag members against the Lower Saxony media law had been a further serious, if not

---

17. Both of these are reproduced in *Media Perspektiven. Dokumentation*, I/1986, pp. 43–56.

entirely surprising, setback. The Court was bound to deliberate long and hard over its verdict, which was not expected much before the end of 1986, and the outcome was by no means certain to be favourable to the CDU/CSU. The SPD plaintiffs had demanded no less than the declaration of the contested CDU law completely null and void. Such an outcome would inevitably be a declaration against the whole gamut of deregulatory legislation being hurriedly prepared by the CDU/CSU state governments. To make matters much worse, the radical infrastructural programme for cable and satellite, launched in 1983 by Bundespostminister Schwarz-Schilling, had resulted in much early disappointment.

Disappointments of the Bundespost's Plans for the New Media

During the period 1984–6, massive investment by the Bundespost, to the tune of DM 1 billion per annum, had been poured into the cable programme. However, by the end of 1985 barely 1.5 million German homes had been connected to cable and were receiving the new satellite television channels. One year later the figure was still only 2.3 million cabled homes. A government-commissioned report of 1984 into the 'amortization capacity of broadband systems' had considered 4.4 million homes connected to be the necessary threshold for financial viability of the new commercial broadcasting sector. Moreover, the actual figures represented a thoroughly disappointing penetration rate of only one-third of homes passed. The scenario was made even gloomier by the fact that the Bundespost had not yet completed its network of earth stations to facilitate reception of the new satellite channels. Therefore, some cable systems were even unable to receive them (amounting to about 300,000 homes in 1985).[18]

Matters were made worse by growing public and official criticism of the Bundespostminister's ambitious project. In June 1984 a highly critical report of the Federal Auditor's Office (Bundesrechnungshof) into the 'economic viability of public

18. E. Witte, *Neue Fernsehnetze im Medienmarkt; die Amortisationsfähigkeit von Breitbandverteilsystemen*, Heidelberg: R. v. Decker's Verlag, G. Schenck, 1984; cable figures from *Cable and Satellite Europe*, 4/1987, p. 22.

broadband networks' had publicly questioned the financial viability of the national ('flächendeckende') dimensions of the programme. This report had stimulated criticism of the Bundespostminister, even within his own party (the CDU), and had furnished the SPD opposition with valuable political ammunition. The Bundespost had been accused of 'milking' post users, letter-writers and telephone customers in order to promote an enterprise which was an economically shaky as it was dubiously ambitious in terms of media policy. The effect of this damaging report was to compel Schwarz-Schilling to revise downward the projected extent of the cable programme. Thenceforth, the word 'flächendeckend' was dropped from discussions about the cable programme while the Bundespostminister himself seemed to disavow that this had ever been his goal. Now it appeared that only about half the country was to be cabled. The other half would remain dependent on 'off-air' reception. Thinly-populated areas would eventually reap the benefits of the new media by means of DBS.[19]

At the same time, the Bundespost was incurring huge extra expense from the fact that much of the channel capacity that Schwarz-Schilling had acquired in order to promote the CDU/CSU dream of a broadcasting 'revolution' remained unsubscribed. Evidently, the Bundespost had wildly overestimated the commercial demand for new satellite channels: only SAT 1, RTL Plus and a third new private commercial channel based in Munich called KMP musicbox had been prepared to take the plunge of making a huge loss-leading investment in order to enter the new commercial satellite broadcasting business. To some extent, these disappointments resulted from the political problems described above. The business confidence of potential investors in the new media was being seriously undermined or deterred by the failure of the Länder to agree a unified approach and give stability to the country's broadcasting future.

The Bundespost and the CDU/CSU policy-makers were not the only disappointed parties in the affair: the equipment suppliers and the backers of commercial television were becoming

---

19. See Dietrich Jorn Weder, 'Finanzielle Grenzen der Verkabelung – Bundesrechnungshofbericht zur Wirtschaftlichkeit öffentlicher Breitbandverteilnetze', *Media Perspektiven*, 6/1984, pp. 451–6.

Media and Media Policy in West Germany

increasingly impatient. The latter, in particular, were anxious about the lack of 'reach' for their new services, given the disappointing rate of cable connections. The Bundespost itself might be concerned about the need for action designed to recoup its massive expenditure, but the situation was beginning to appear even more desperate for the new commercial broadcasters themselves. Moreover, the 'broadcasting revolution' at the heart of CDU/CSU media policy depended above all upon the business confidence of the new commercial actors. Having encouraged the West German publishers to take the plunge and make huge loss-leading investment in satellite channels, the CDU/CSU policy-makers had a special interest, as well as a political obligation, to act so as to maximise their audiences. At this stage, therefore, CDU/CSU policy-making appeared to be in serious danger of running out of steam. Despite the radical 'heroism' with which it had been launched in 1983, the policy process seemed to be degenerating into the very kind of incrementalism that would allow the SPD the best prospects of sabotaging the whole enterprise. However, the CDU/CSU possessed one very major trump card; namely, their incumbency in Bonn and accordingly the CDU's control of the Bundespost.

The Bundespost Liberalises SMATV Regulation

As in 1983, with its launch of an ambitious national cable programme, the Bundespost now intervened once again to exploit the constitutional loophole that allowed its sole jurisdiction over 'telecommunications' to impinge on the jurisdiction of the Länder in broadcasting affairs. Accordingly, in July 1985 the Bundespost relinquished its monopoly of satellite reception (SMATV) in order to allow all MATV systems ('master antenna television' systems, i.e. cabled housing blocks receiving the signal from one 'master' antenna) in the country to install their own satellite reception dishes. By this simple expedient almost eight million West German households would potentially be opened up to the new commercial satellite broadcasters (much housing in the Federal Republic is of the 'housing block' kind). Moreover, this new radical policy measure was accompanied by a directive from Bundespostminister Schwarz-Schilling to West

German dish manufacturers explicitly granting an element of relaxed technical standards and encouraging them to start production. This liberalisation of SMATV brought a further major benefit to CDU/CSU media policy. It had a dramatic impact on the hitherto deadlocked political debate within the Ministerpräsidentenkonferenz over regulatory policy for satellite television. In particular, it made it highly problematical now for recalcitrant SPD politicians to persist in holding out against the reception of private commercial satellite television. The SPD policy-makers in Hessen and Bremen had argued that their regulatory jurisdiction extended to blocking undesirable programmes from being admitted to their Länder. However, they were now faced with the sheer impossibility of regulating against the direct reception of satellite signals by a multitude of MATV systems as well as a steadily growing number of local cable systems. Moreover, to attempt to do so would cast them in a very unattractive political light indeed. Article 5 of the Constitution (the 'Basic Law') gave West German citizens the 'basic right' to inform themselves from any available source of information. By liberalising SMATV regulations, Bundespostminister Schwarz-Schilling thus unleashed strong political pressure in support of the CDU/CSU members currently embroiled in frustrating negotiations with their SPD counterparts within the Ministerpräsidentenkonferenz. The result was that in 1985 and 1986 even the hardline SPD state governments of Bremen and Hessen felt compelled to introduce state laws respectively permitting the 'provisional retransmission of broadcast programmes in cable networks' ('Gesetz über die vorläufige Weiterverbreitung von Rundfunkprogrammen in Kabelanlagen') and the 'retransmission of satellite channels' ('Gesetz über die Weiterverbreitung von Satelliten-programmen') (see Appendix 3).[20]

The Bundespost Relaunches Its Cable Programme with the Private Sector

Nor was this latter measure an end to the interventionism of the

---

20. See Humphreys, 'Satellite Broadcasting Policy in West Germany', pp. 107–43. Texts of these laws are reproduced in *DLM Jahrbuch 88*, produced by the Direktorenkonferenz der Landesmedienanstalten (DLM), Munich: Verlag Neue Mediengesellschaft Ulm, 1988, pp. 599–601 and 605–8.

Bundespost during the period 1985-6. On 25 June 1986 it launched a new federal programme aiming 'to improve the general conditions surrounding the private broadcasting market' ('Programm zur Verbesserung der Rahmenbedingungen des privaten Rundfunkmarktes'). This aimed to increase the cable channel capacity to no less than thirty-five channels and to improve the marketing of cable systems. The Bundespost had learned one major lesson from the experience of the cable pilot-projects, namely that the promotion of cable needed a commercial strategy and in particular an efficient and modern marketing approach. The handful of private marketing companies upon whose services the Bundespost had already called in its 'national' cabling drive had shown the way forward. Generally, they had achieved far better results than the Bundespost itself by adopting a hard-nosed and aggressive ('American-style') marketing strategy, including door-to-door campaigns and heavy advertising. Accordingly, the new programme increased the Bundespost's marketing budget for its own cable programme from DM 8.5 million in 1985 to DM 15 million in 1986, rising to no less than DM 20 million in 1987. This now took the form of regular advertising through press and broadcasting outlets, and even postmarks on letters! The Bundespost had by now also recognised the importance of providing a more efficient service. Accordingly, the new programme determined to equip the majority of cable networks as quickly as possible with the latest satellite reception equipment and to take urgent measures to remove outstanding technical obstacles to satellite reception. The Bundespost's cable programme had so far been dogged by the so-called 'Sonderkanal' problem, namely the problem presented by old cable systems in need of up-grading before they could receive new satellite programmes by cable. In order to overcome these problems, in 1986 the Bundespost increased its annual investment rate to the colossal figure of DM 1.5 billion.

Moreover, the Bundespost now took the unprecedented step of opening up its jealousy-guarded monopoly of cable installation. In June 1986 it founded a subsidiary company called 'Telepost Kabel-Servicegesellschaft' (TKS) with DM 1 million of capital. The Bundespost retained a 95% stake in this new company, but the latter was intended in turn to establish about 55

Regional Cable Service Companies (Regionale Kabel-Service-gesellschaften – RKS) which would combine private and public finance and initiative. These regional companies would act as consultancies and financiers for regional and local cable drives. In effect, the new RKS companies would subsidise the connection of new cable subscribers to the tune of around DM 450 per customer. Furthermore, once this programme was under way, the Bundespost intended to reduce progressively its 95% stake to a 51% controlling stake, by attracting investment from banks, additional private commercial marketing companies and cable programmers. By these means, the Bundespost hoped to attract new private capital for its cable programme, raise the rate of connections and overcome delays in the actual business of connecting customers who had registered an interest. By the end of 1987, 3.2 million households were connected to cable, representing a take-up rate of 34.4% of homes passed (8.86 million households).[21] By 1990 7 million are expected.

The Bundespost Releases Massive New 'Off-Air' Broadcasting Capacity

However, none of these major interventions in the media-policy process by the Bundespost – namely, the deregulation of SMATV, the launch of a new marketing drive and the partial liberalisation of cable installation – had nearly as much impact as the next dramatic step taken by Bundespostminister Schwarz-Schilling. One way of suddenly increasing the availability of the new channels was to provide new outlets in addition to cable and satellite. Accordingly, in the late summer of 1986, Schwarz-Schilling announced that the Bundespost would give a new priority to allocating spare 'low power' frequencies to 'local' private commercial television in all West German cities with populations over 100,000. All in all sixty-five West German towns and cities, with a total population of 16 million viewers,

---

21. V. O'Connor, 'Vorsprung durch Marketing', *Cable and Satellite Europe*, 4/1987, pp. 22–4. The figures on cabling are given by a second Bundesrechnungshof report of 1988, a copy of which is in the author's possession: Bundesrechnungshof 'Bericht über die Entwicklung der Wirtschaftlichkeit des Breitbandverteildienstes der Deutschen Bundespost', Bonn: January 1988 (Aktenzeichnis III 6–70–550–G/87m), Anlage 4, p. 2.

were to be given their own 'local' television frequencies (a further thirty-five frequencies were subsequently found). By this method, the Bundespost would be in a position to retransmit the programmes of the new commercial broadcasters into local 'off-air' networks all over the country thereby helping to furnish the commercial broadcasters with the audiences that they desperately needed in order to become viable. The two new CDU/CSU, northern and southern 'rump Staatsverträge' (incorporating SPD Hamburg) made explicit in their opening articles that DBS programmers (to be franchised according to arrangements also laid out in the treaties) should have access to the new 'low power' terrestrial frequencies.

Nobody supposed seriously that this last measure of Bundespostminister Schwarz-Schilling, for all his emphasis on 'local' broadcasting, was designed for any other purpose than mainly to benefit SAT 1 and RTL Plus. The latter now keenly anticipated reaching a potential audience of no less than 16 million citizens in the Federal Republic. Once again, *faits accomplis* had been established by Bundespostminister Schwarz-Schilling in the process of ushering in the CDU/CSU broadcasting revolution. An end seemed at last in sight to the endless procrastinations and delaying tactics of the SPD members and the resultant frustrations of the CDU/CSU members within the seemingly hopelessly deadlocked Ministerpräsidentenkonferenz. The SPD policy-makers were being relentlessly compelled by factors beyond their control to see the writing on the wall. In this respect, it was the Constitutional Court that was the next, and final, actor to intervene in the policy process and bring the reform of broadcasting in the Federal Republic to within a breath of its final consummation.

A Dual Broadcasting System

After more than two years of deadlock, an imminent solution was suddenly made more likely when on 4 November 1986 the Federal Constitutional Court at Karlsruhe finally made its long and anxiously awaited ruling on the Lower Saxony media law. The CDU and CSU were greatly encouraged by the Court's judgement of the law to be 'essentially' in conformity with the federal Constitution. However, the SPD was also gratified by the Court's finding that nine of the law's detailed provisions were regarded as incompatible with the constitutional principle of 'broadcasting freedom'. In particular, the SPD's main objection to the law was vindicated. The Court found that the law's provision for franchising by the state chancellory, in other words, the Ministerpräsident, offended against the principle of broadcasting's independence from the state ('Staatsferne') (see Appendix 2(d)).[22]

The Court Recommends a 'Dual Broadcasting System'

However, by far the most significant outcome of the case was the Constitutional Court's suggestion of the legal possibility that a 'dual' broadcasting system might be established consisting of a private commercial sector alongside the public-service sector. In such a 'dual' system, it was now suggested, the public-service broadcasters would remain responsible for providing the basic broadcasting services to the whole of the population and fulfilling their classical public-service duties. Indeed, the Court saw the role of the public-service broadcasters as being more vital than ever in the age of an expanded broadcasting system. Moreover, the Court specified that the public-service broadcasters should continue to be assured all the means – of a technical, structural and financial kind – that were necessary for the complete fulfilment of their public-service mission. The Court therefore gave the public-service broadcasters the kind of guarantee of their future that they, and the SPD, were seeking in the face of the threatened dramatic changes. This latest ruling seemed to banish any future attempt by CDU/CSU politicians to constrain the public-service sector, for instance by means of refusal or procrastination during the business of negotiation over the periodic appropriate adjustments to the licence-fee. The Court also appeared to reject the argument, advanced by the commercial lobby, that the range of programming offered by the public-service broadcasters should in future be pared of much of the entertainment category and that these 'rich pick-

---

22. 'Urteil des Bundesverfassungsgerichts vom 4. November 1986–IBvF 1/1984', *Media Perspektiven. Dokumentation*, IV/1986, pp. 213–47.

ings' be more or less reserved to the private sector. In its monumental 'Fourth TV Judgement' ('Viertes Fernsehurteil') of 1986 the Court thus saw the future of public-service broadcasting in the fullest possible terms, and not simply as a cultural ghetto.

In addition, the Court's ruling deemed the existing pluralistic structure of the public-service corporations, organised according to the 'internal control' regulatory model, to be – whatever its weaknesses – better suited to guaranteeing a balanced diversity of opinions, therefore 'broadcasting freedom', than the 'external control' model foreseen by the spate of new CDU/CSU legislation. However, to the SPD's great chagrin, the Court also now suggested that the same high requirements about diversity and balance of programming expected of the public-service broadcasters were not to be expected of or imposed upon the new private broadcasters. This was the bombshell: in the supremely authoritative view of the Federal Constitutional Court the private commercial sector should be allowed to benefit from very considerable deregulation.

For this latter ruling, the Court gave several important justifications. In the first place, it believed that the private commercial broadcasters were going to be confined to the new media. At the time of the ruling there was no public inkling that the Bundespost Minister was about to grant the new private sector widespread access to terrestrial frequencies. Therefore, the Court had assumed that the new private sector would need far more freedom than the public-service sector to maximise ratings in order to attract enough advertising income on the basis of a much more limited audience size, at least for many years to come. Moreover, unlike the public-service broadcasters, the new operators would be wholly dependent on advertising revenues. The Court seemed to accept that a certain amount of commercialisation would inevitably follow from this simple fact. The Court acknowledged too that, in order to cover their enormous start-up costs, the new operators would have to schedule predominantly the more 'popular' kind of programming and could not be expected to produce the more esoteric kind of public-service broadcasting straightaway.

Finally, the Court had grasped the fundamental significance of satellite broadcasting, namely that single Länder could no

'Dual Broadcasting System' and Multimedia Diversification

longer act as if they remained fully sovereign in broadcasting regulation. It followed that no individual Land could be expected to organise by itself a complete balance of programming, much of which would henceforth originate from beyond state and even national borders. Given these very real difficulties, the Court had chosen a pragmatic solution designed to facilitate the birth of a commercial sector while ensuring the survival of the strongest possible elements of public-service broadcasting. The element of disequilibrium caused by the new private commercial sector would not be entirely compensated, but would at least be counterbalanced, as much as was feasible under the new circumstances, by the generous guarantees given to the public-service broadcasters. Hence, in a 'dual' system the health of the public-service broadcasting sector was seen as the very precondition for an opening to a new private commercial sector.

The Legal Basis for a Deregulated Private Commercial Sector

More precisely, the Court suggested that, while basic standards of balance and diversity of opinion were to remain the fundamental norms of the private sector, there would be no expectation of a strict mathematical balance between diverse tendencies. There would be no requirement for regulatory intervention in the case of slight or unavoidable imbalances. In an attempt to provide for the greatest possible diversity and balance in the new private commercial sector, the Court made explicit the requirement that an important role in the new private sector be given to minority (non-powerful) tendencies. Moreover, the Court also prescribed the need for Land regulation to counter the 'danger of concentration' with the development of 'multi-media power over opinion' (i.e. a combination of influence through both broadcasting and the press). The existence of the Federal Cartel Office was therefore not deemed sufficient to counter concentration in the field of broadcasting and new media. Furthermore, the Court's ruling clearly precluded any manifest or clandestine legislative provision that sought to give any advantage to the press in the new private commercial sector. The press had long argued for the need for some 'compensatory preference' in view of the alleged impact of broadcasting on its advertising revenues (this had been the

273

rationale for establishing the Michel Commission in the 1960s – see Chapter 2). Such 'compensatory preference' was now definitively ruled unconstitutional.

Lastly, the Court reiterated the constitutional division of powers between the federation in Bonn and the Länder which would remain entirely unchanged in the case of the establishment of a 'dual' broadcasting system. The Länder would remain solely responsible for broadcasting regulation, a field of cultural policy, while the federation would have jurisdiction over telecommunications. At the same time, the Court alluded to the very real complication of this principle brought by satellite broadcasting – with its national and transnational scope. Accordingly, the Court suggested the need for an inter-state regulation of all matters thereby affected, most notably the allocation of future satellite broadcasting channels. The Court therefore encouraged the Länder to speedily find a mutually acceptable formula for a new 'Staatsvertrag'. In addition, it stressed the requirement of 'bundesfreundliches Verhalten' (behaviour that was conscious of federal responsibilities). This was clearly both an admonishment of the chaotic 'Kleinstaaterei' of the Länder described above and a demand for the urgent resurrection of the principle of 'cooperative federalism'.[23]

Although the 'Fourth TV Judgement' appeared to guarantee 'continuity in change', and in particular the important future role of public-service broadcasting, it did provoke some criticism. According to Martin Stock, for example, the ruling marked a major shift in the fundamental premises which had hitherto underpinned West German broadcasting, away from the public-service concept. Moreover, Stock (among others) questioned the effectiveness of the new safeguards and guarantees suggested by the Court.[24]

Above all, the timing of the judgement reflected the dangerously chaotic character taken by developments in broadcasting

23. See K. Berg, 'Weichenstellung. Das Niedersachsen-Urteil als Leitlinie der Künftigen Rundfunkordnung', *Media Perspektiven*, 11/1986, pp. 689–91. For an evaluation of this law in English see K. Berg, 'The Fourth TV Judgement of the Federal Constitutional Court', *EBU Review*, vol. XXXVIII no. 3, May 1987, pp. 37–43.
24. M. Stock, 'Ein fragwürdiges Konzept dualer Rundfunksysteme', *Rundfunk und Fernsehen*, 35 Jg. 1987/1, pp. 5–24.

policy in the Federal Republic during the early 1980s. The content of the judgement, for its part, reflected an attempt by the ultimate arbiter of all policy-making in the Federal Republic, namely the Federal Constitutional Court, to find a characteristically German consensual outcome. In fact, such an outcome was finally achieved by the successful conclusion of a 'Staatsvertrag' in April 1987, for which the monumental 'Fourth TV Judgement' of November 1986 had thus patently prepared the way.

The 'Staatsvertrag for the Reform of the Broadcasting System of the Federal Republic'

At last, at the beginning of April 1987, the Ministerpräsidenten signed a 'Staatsvertrag for the Reform of the Broadcasting System in the Federal Republic' ('Staatsvertrag zur Neuordnung des Rundfunkwesens'). Over the following six month period, the parliaments of the individual Länder duly ratified the treaty and published its contents in their respective gazettes of laws and ordinances. The treaty became law on 1 December 1987. The comprehensive sixteen-article 'Staatsvertrag' sought to guarantee the basis of a 'dual broadcasting system' for several decades ahead well into the era of the new media. It amounted to a characteristically German compromise snatched out of the jaws of a most untypical and seemingly intractable dissension. Although it was immediately apparent that the SPD Ministerpräsidenten had made rather more concessions than their CDU/CSU negotiating partners, the SPD policy-makers had still managed to gain some important safeguards for the public-service broadcasters.[25]

The Establishment of a 'Dual Broadcasting System'

In this latter respect, the 'Staatsvertrag' had clearly been heavily influenced by the 'Fourth TV Judgement' of the Federal Constitutional Court. Most notably, it envisaged a future broadcasting

---

25. 'Staatsvertrag zur Neuordnung des Rundfunkwesens (Rundfunkstaatsvertrag) vom 12. März 1987' (signed on 1–3 April 1987), *Media Perspektiven. Dokumentation*, II/1987, pp. 81–8; see also the 'Begründung' for the above in the same, pp. 89–102.

'duopoly' with a private commercial sector coexisting alongside the public-service sector. At the same time, the 'status and further development' of the public-service broadcasting sector was 'to be guaranteed'. Moreover, this guarantee was now extended to a share for the public-service broadcasters in all new technical possibilities offered by the new media. It also included an explicit commitment to the future maintenance of the ARD system with its concomitant financial equalisation system. The reference to the financial equalisation system safeguarded the future financial viability of the smaller public-service broadcasting corporations (like 'SPD' Radio Bremen). Certain aspects of the 'Staatsvertrag' went even further than the 'Fourth TV Judgement' in detailing guarantees for the public-service broadcasters and as such they predominantly reflected the influence of the SPD Ministerpräsidenten.

At the same time, the 'Staatsvertrag' opened the way for the development, based on sufficient transmission capacity and adequate sources of revenue, for the private commercial sector. An important concession gained by the CDU/CSU Ministerpräsidenten was represented by the provision for private commercial broadcasting on terrestrial frequencies as well as by means of the new media (as seen, in the late summer of 1986 Bundespostminister Schwarz-Schilling announced his intention to liberate a large number of 'low power' frequencies and make them available to 'local' private commercial television). This aspect of the 'Staatsvertrag' also went way beyond anything considered by the 'Fourth TV Judgement' and in this instance it was clearly designed to benefit the two main private commercial channels that had established a significant foothold in the Federal Republic's broadcasting system by feeding the country's cable systems from communications satellite, namely SAT 1 and RTL Plus. Reflecting a major victory of the CDU/CSU Ministerpräsidenten over the SPD 'hardliners', the 'Staatsvertrag' opened the way for this major new development of the private commercial sector by giving it the official legal blessing of the totality of the Länder.

The Allocation of DBS Channels

The SPD Ministerpräsidenten had also conceded a greater

amount of the transmission capacity of the TV SAT DBS satellite series to the new private commercial operators. When the first satellite started to transmit, it had been agreed that it would house two public-service television channels and two private commercial channels. As seen, both ZDF and ARD had each been running new satellite broadcasting services, namely the former's 3SAT started in 1984 and the latter's Eins Plus started in 1986. Like SAT 1 and RTL Plus they had used communications satellites to feed the country's cable systems and it was now duly expected that they would transfer to DBS when launched. However, when the second satellite planned for launch in 1990 eventually became available, a third private commercial channel would start on TV SAT 1 and ZDF's 3SAT would then have to transfer to TV SAT 2. Partly to compensate for this imbalance in television channels in favour of the private commercial sector, the 'Staatsvertrag' contained a special provision for digital radio services to be mounted by the ARD. However, it seemed unlikely anyway that any new private commercial operators would become seriously interested in digital radio in view of the very high costs involved and its much lower audience appeal than satellite television. The new private channels were all to have local 'windows' ('Fensterprogramme'), to provide specialised local and regional services.

The Financial Basis of the New Broadcasting Duopoly

The provisions of the 'Staatsvertrag' relating to advertising also reflected significant concessions by the SPD Ministerpräsidenten. The 'Staatsvertrag' determined that the ban on Sunday and public holiday advertising should be lifted and it also allowed the new private commercial broadcasters to run advertising after 20.00 hours. These measures at last empowered private commercial television to enter the SPD states of Bremen and Hessen despite those states' banning of Sunday advertising.

The SPD Ministerpräsidenten were, however, to gain appropriate compensation for these major concessions. Firstly, the 'Staatsvertrag' explicitly stated that the licence-fee was to continue to be the 'prime source of funding' for ARD and ZDF. Furthermore, in order to safeguard this source of income to the

Media and Media Policy in West Germany

public-service broadcasters, the 'Staatsvertrag' explicitly linked payment of the licence-fee to the possession of broadcasting reception equipment. In other words, even if the public were in future to develop a much greater inclination to watch private commercial television than public-service broadcasting, there could be no refusal to pay the licence-fee which exclusively funded the latter. Moreover, the 'Staatsvertrag' provided for the regular upward revision of the licence-fee every two years. This reflected the extraction by the SPD Ministerpräsidenten of a very significant additional safeguard for the public-service broadcasters. In future, it should be impossible for the CDU/CSU Ministerpräsidenten to delay increases in the licence-fee in order to gain political advantage, to apply political pressure or to benefit the private commercial sector.

However, the advertising regulations which the 'Staatsvertrag' contained were considerably more favourable to the private commercial sector than to the public-service broadcasters. The former was granted the possibility of running as much as 20% advertising in its daily programming. At the same time, advertising by the public-service broadcasters was to be kept restricted to its present level: namely 20 minutes of weekday television advertising between 18.00 and 20.00 hours on ARD and ZDF with no advertising at all on 'third programmes'. The HR, which as seen had broken with this convention and started to run advertising on its 'third programme' Hessen Drei (HR3), was to stop the practice. The public-service broadcasters were to be granted the same right as the new private commercial operators to run advertising on Sundays and public holidays but significantly only if it did not lead to increased total advertising revenue for the ARD and the ZDF.

Thus, the 'Staatsvertrag' reflected clearly the aim of the CDU/CSU Ministerpräsidenten to furnish the most favourable financial conditions for the private commercial sector and to delimit the commercial operations of the public-service sector. However, there were limits to the degree of commercialism that would be acceptable given the conservative sensibilities of many in the CDU/CSU as well as the SPD regarding this matter. The 'Staatsvertrag' therefore adhered to the established principle of block advertising for both public and private sectors and stipulated that advertising continue to be kept strictly apart from the rest of the schedule and that it should not influence programme content.

Programming Regulation

However, as regards programme regulation, the 'Staatsvertrag' interpreted the spirit of the recommendations of the 'Fourth TV Judgement' of 1986 very liberally indeed. So long as a fully functioning public-service broadcasting system existed, the 'Staatsvertrag' saw little need to impose more than a distinctly 'light touch' regulation on the private commercial sector. The fairly minimal nature of the regulatory requirements was made clear by Article 8 of the treaty. The threshold for 'external pluralism' was held to be the availability of no more than three complete private programme schedules provided by different companies. Achievement of this threshold would be deemed to provide the requisite diversity of opinion in the private sector. In the event of fewer than three complete channels being provided, then each must 'essentially express the diversity of opinion'.

The individual private operator would have to allow for the establishment of a programme advisory committee to ensure that no individual groups had a distorting influence on opinion formation and to ensure that a range of social, political and ideological groups, including minorities, gained an appropriate measure of expression. However, no such precautions would be required in the event of the new channel being operated by a consortium of programme providers in which no one individual or group had more than a 50% stake. Given that the SAT 1 channel was owned by just such a diversely constituted consortium, but nevertheless largely composed of similarly politically conservative publishers of the press, the CDU/CSU Ministerpräsidenten had clearly won a famous victory. There hardly seemed to be any necessity for the additional stipulation that private commercial broadcasters be limited to ownership of a single whole television channel with the possibility of an additional specialised service in both radio and television (i.e. a programme or segment of a channel).

There was no reflection in the 'Staatsvertrag' of the demands made by the SPD for firm quotas for certain programme categories. The treaty merely called for a 'proper amount' of news and information, culture, and education, together with a 'substantial proportion' of in-house programmes and of programmes commissioned from the German-speaking area and from Europe. All in all, the 'Staatsvertrag' was therefore very generous to the commercial broadcasting lobby in the regulatory terms which it had dictated for their sector. Moreover, the way was now opened up for the nationwide distribution of private commercial programming. This latter provision was contained in Article 11 of the treaty. Similarly, the way was also opened up now for the nationwide distribution of the services provided by individual ARD corporations. The satellite operations conducted by the BR and the WDR were thus made definitively legitimate. Finally, the 'Staatsvertrag' opened up the way for the wholesale legitimate 'import' of foreign programmes – which formally included RTL Plus (which in any case transferred its headquarters to Germany in 1988 so as to become eligible for a franchise for a channel on the West German DBS satellite TV SAT) – so long as these programmes fulfilled the above requirements of the treaty.

The treaty entered into force on 1 December 1987 for an unlimited period. It could not be terminated for at least ten years, and thereafter only with difficulty. Once again, this latter stipulation reflected the success of the CDU/CSU Ministerpräsidenten in achieving their aim of securing the best possible conditions and a favourable legal basis for the implantation of a durable and viable private commercial broadcasting sector in the Federal Republic.[26]

Patterns of Multimedia Diversification and Cross-ownership of the Press and Broadcasting in the Dual Broadcasting System

As a result of the developments described in this chapter and the preceding one, the traditional West German broadcasting system has undergone a very radical structural transformation.

---

26. For a very useful discussion of the treaty's main provisions in English see K. Berg, 'The Inter-Land Treaty on the Reform of the Broadcasting System in the FRG, and the Fifth Decision of the Constitutional Court', *EBU Review*, vol. XXXIX no. 2, March 1988, pp. 40–9.

'Dual Broadcasting System' and Multimedia Diversification

The introduction of the dual broadcasting system marks a very major break with the previous exclusively public-service model. To the British observer at least, the establishment of a dual public/private broadcasting system in itself might hardly be considered to be a cause for a major concern. What, however, is much more controversial in its long-term implications is the pattern of multimedia diversification and, in particular, cross-ownership of the press and broadcasting that has accompanied the arrival of a commercial broadcasting sector. Indeed, arguably this latter development stands in contradiction to the established West German principle of the independence of broadcasting from powerful sectional interests in society.

The New Private Commercial Broadcasting Sector

As a result of the series of deregulatory legislative measures by the Länder culminating in the 1987 'Staatsvertrag', a host of new private local actors interested in broadcasting suddenly sprang up all over the Federal Republic. During 1987 the number of new private radio operators grew steadily, a pattern that seemed set to endure. In 1987 the first licences for local radio were allocated in Baden-Württemberg. Further frequencies were in the process of being allocated in those states, such as Berlin and Bavaria, which already had private radio stations. Similarly, in SPD-controlled Länder, two frequencies were allocated to private operators in Hamburg, while in North-Rhine Westphalia the licensing process had started. Finally, frequencies were almost certain to be allocated shortly to private operators in Bremen, Hessen and Saarland, all SPD states (the Saarland had been traditionally CDU but it had swung to the SPD in 1986; on the other hand, in 1987 Hessen fell to the CDU/FDP).[27] Significantly, nearly all of the new local radio operating companies were in the majority ownership of, or completely owned by, publishers. Often the latter already enjoyed a dominant position in the local daily press market. Moreover, both Springer and the Bertelsmann subsidiary 'Ufa' were often involved. Nevertheless, in the field of radio at least, a considerable plurality of

---

27. H. Röper, 'Formation deutscher Medienmultis 1987', *Media Perspektiven*, 8/1987, pp. 481–95.

operators still existed.[28]

However, in the field of commercial television the picture was quite different. Many would-be commercial television operators quickly developed cold feet and withdrew from the field which was soon dominated by a few financially strong companies, mainly the largest publishers in the FRG. The already well established process of media-concentration was clearly taking a new turn. In fact, the pattern was already clear in 1986: the future private commercial television market in the Federal Republic was to be contested by two leading companies, RTL Plus and SAT 1. Each had obtained a communications satellite (ECS) channel and was clearly destined to transfer to DBS when available. The franchise for the third private commercial DBS channel appeared almost certainly to be allocated to the KMP musicbox channel. This left very little room for any other would-be private broadcasters to operate at the national level.[29]

At the local level, hopes had been raised that the new terrestrial frequencies, released by the Bundespost since late 1986 in order to promote the 'broadcasting revolution', would permit smaller local interests to flourish. However, the measure unleashed an intense wave of competition among the new private-sector actors, both between the larger corporate interests and between the latter and a host of smaller local interests. In the event, it soon transpired that the large new private commercial broadcasters, especially SAT 1, were also the main beneficiaries of the allocation of these terrestrial channels.

The Patterns of Corporate Ownership of the New Commercial Channels

Since the late 1970s, the publishers had combined within their collective lobbying organisations, namely the BDZV and the Federal Association for Cable and Satellite (Bundesverband Kabel und Satellit – BVKS), in order to push for the introduction of a commercial broadcasting sector. The term 'policy network' would be a very appropriate description of the kind of interac-

28. S. Hiegemann, *Kabel- und Satellitenfernsehen; die Entwicklung in der Bundesrepublik Deutschland unter politischen und inhaltlichen Aspekten*, Bonn: Bundeszentrale für politische Bildung, 1988, pp. 119–20.
29. See Röper, 'Formation deutscher Medienmultis 1987', pp. 481–95.

tion that had come to characterise their relations both between themselves and with their various political sponsors over the twin issues of new media and commercial broadcasting. There were, however, considerable competitive tensions between them. Therefore, they might be said to constitute a rather loose 'policy network' (indeed, as will be seen, a number of more regionalised and localised 'policy networks'). Moreover, the patterns of corporate ownership of the new channels were also quite fluid.

The first group of private-sector actors to constitute itself was the SAT 1 consortium, initially 'sponsored' by the state government of the Rhineland-Palatinate. Originally the SAT 1 consortium involved: a 40% share by the PKS company originally established by the Deutsche Genossenschaftsbank (DG Bank) and the *Frankfurter Allgemeine Zeitung* (*FAZ*) to programme the Ludwigshafen cable pilot-project; a 20% share by a company called Aktuelle Presse Fernsehen (APF) based in Hamburg which supplied the SAT 1 news service (this was itself a company of over 160 daily newspapers among which the right-wing Springer press held a 30% share); a 9.9% share by the Springer group in its own right; an 8.2% share by Burda; a 6.1% share by Bauer; a 5.4% share by Holtzbrinck; and several other minor shareholders, including the *FAZ* in its own right. However, this complex pattern of corporate ownership soon produced considerable structural problems of intra-organisational coordination. SAT 1 was very quickly plagued by competition and duplication of effort by its various constituent members. Business efficiency was undoubtedly impaired by the decentralised nature of the organisation with each component member independently being responsible for its own budget, programme production and programme buying. This was, in turn, reflected in higher costs than anticipated at a time when the early hopes of commercial success were rapidly being disappointed.

As a result, by October 1986 the major publishers Burda, Bauer, *FAZ* and the Kabel-Media Programmgesellschaft (KMP) had all pulled out and the Aktuelle Presse Fernsehen company had reduced its holding to 15%, leaving the distribution of capital shares in SAT 1 highly favourable to the PKS and the Springer group. Thus, the shake-out reflected a disturbing trend towards rapid concentration within the new industry. Moreover, although strictly speaking a subsidiary company of the Deutsche Genossenschaftsbank in Frankfurt, the PKS was very much under the influence of the leading West German film dealer Leo Kirch. Kirch soon engaged in a campaign to increase his influence within the Springer group in the wake of Axel Springer's death in 1985. Together, the Springer group and the PKS had come to control a majority of SAT 1 shares (55%). Furthermore, the Springer group was also the major shareholder in the APF, which in turn owned a further 15% of the SAT 1 shares. If this is taken into consideration, then by 1987 no less than 70% (i.e. over a two-thirds majority) of SAT 1 had rapidly fallen under the web of influence of the Springer/PKS/Kirch combination, which was clearly a potential multimedia enterprise in the making (see Table 6.1).[30]

This pattern of concentration is confirmed when attention is turned to the SAT 1 channel's private commercial rival, RTL Plus. Through its offshoot company 'Ufa', the huge West German multimedia multinational Bertelsmann had held a 40% stake in RTL Plus since the beginning. Later the West German *WAZ* newspaper group took a 10% share in the channel. In mid-September 1986, RTL Plus transferred its headquarters from Luxemburg to the Federal Republic in order to make itself eligible for the DBS franchise on TV SAT and also for the allocation of the new terrestrial frequencies. The resultant RTL Plus Deutschland Fernsehen GmbH & Co KG was ceremoniously established at Gütersloh, the West German home of Bertelsmann. By the late summer of 1987, Compagnie Luxembourgeoise de Télédiffusion (CLT) held 46.5% of the shares, the Bertelsmann subsidiary 'Ufa' held 38.5%, the *WAZ* group continued to hold 10%, the *FAZ* held 1% and the Deutsche Bank had become trustee of 4% of the shares, 2% of which were snapped up by Burda for around DM 2.5 million.[31]

Thus, the new private commercial television sector had quickly developed very strong features of oligopolistic competition between giant publishers, most notably the Springer/Kirch group versus the Bertelsmann/*WAZ* group. The only mitigating

30. Ibid., p. 483.
31. See Hiegemann, *Kabel- und Satellitenfernsehen*, p. 118.

'Dual Broadcasting System' and Multimedia Diversification

Table 6.1 Shareholders in SAT 1

Name of the shareholder	% shares in SAT 1		
	launch	July–86	Oct–86
Programmgesellschaft für Kabel- und Satellitenrundfunk (PKS)	40	35	40
Aktuell Presse Fernsehen (APF)	20	13	15
Springer	9.9	12	15
Burda	8.2	12	–
Bauer	6.1	12	–
Holtzbrinck	5.4	12	15
Neue Mediengesellschaft Ulm	1.4	1	1
Frankfurter Allgemeine Zeitung (FAZ)	1.4	1	–
Otto-Maier Verlag	1	1	1
Kabel-Media Programm- gesellschaft (KMP)	6.6	1	–
'Special Funds' (on which Springer and the APF each have an option of 5%)	–	–	13

Sources: *Medien Bulletin*, July 1986, p. 22; *Media Perspektiven*, 6/86, pp. 417–18; *Media Perspektiven*, 10/86, p. 686.

factor that could be considered significant was that at least a limited political 'balance' of sorts seemed to be promised between the social-liberal-oriented Bertelsmann/*WAZ* group and the highly conservative Springer/Kirch combination. In fact, both Bertelsmann and Springer were also 'partners' each with a significant stake in a Pay-TV company called Teleclub, which commenced operations in the Hanover cable system in 1986. This particular example of the 'Verflechtung' (capital interconnection) that characterised the new commercial sector was highly symbolic of the degree to which virtually unrestricted cross-ownership of the press and broadcasting in the new sector had entailed a further massive step towards media-concentration in the Federal Republic.

The third major group in the picture was the Kabel-Media

Programmgesellschaft (KMP) in Munich, which had established the German 'musicbox' channel during 1985 using one of the Intelsat-V transponders made available by the Bundespost. At first, this channel consisted almost completely of music videoclips. Significantly, the KMP musicbox was owned by the Munich publisher Wolfgang Fischer, who had close links with the CSU. However, it soon encountered serious financial difficulties and became vulnerable to predators. In 1987, the conservative publishers Bauer and Burda stepped in, though still leaving Fischer with a majority stake. Bauer and Burda brought new programming resources to the 'musicbox' channel from their earlier satellite broadcasting venture. As the result, it appeared that KMP musicbox was destined to become a more conventional channel, adding news and information programmes and more varied programming generally to its musical fare.[32]

The Battle over the Springer Inheritance

This pattern of concentration was clear enough. Less clear had been the future of the Springer press empire after the death of its creator in 1985. In fact, the corporate manoeuvres surrounding the Springer inheritance threatened to produce even more concentration and multimedia cross-ownership. In particular, the death of Axel Springer opened the way forward for a new would-be multimedia magnate, Leo Kirch.

Axel Springer had long presided over a veritable press empire, which over the years had been the object of several inquiries by the Federal Cartel Office. However, only rarely had the Federal Cartel Office refused to countenance its significant extension (for instance, in November 1981 when it had intervened to prevent an effective merger with the Burda group). In 1986, the annual turnover of the Springer group was in the order of DM 2.5 billion and it controlled about 28% of the market for daily newspapers (the 'Tagespresse') as well as enjoying a virtual monopoly of Sunday papers and the popular national tabloid market (through the notorious *Bild-Zeitung*). Towards the end of his life, and particularly after the death of his sole male heir, Axel Springer appeared progressively to lose

32. 'SAT 1 Defectors for musicbox', *Cable and Satellite Europe*, 1/1987, p. 6.

interest in directing his press empire. In July 1985 he actually relinquished 49% of the capital and sold the shares on the stock market to private shareholders. However, he retained a blocking minority and continued to exercise the post of honorary president of the board of directors until his death in September 1985, at the age of seventy-three. At this time, 24.9% of the shares were in the hands of the three Burda brothers, Franz, Frieder and Hubert. In addition, Axel Springer's own heirs now inherited a further 26.1% of the shares.

There immediately ensued a very bitter three-cornered struggle for control of the Springer empire between the Springer heirs, the Burda brothers and another formidable predator, Leo Kirch, the Munich-based film entrepreneur. In the event, the Federal Cartel Office refused to allow the Burda brothers to increase their stake, in view of their already extensive publishing activities. Kirch, on the other hand, was initially more successful and snapped up 10% of the public shares, later increasing this share still further to near 20% (and as high as 26% through shadowy intermediaries). However, in his bid to gain control of the Springer group, Kirch was frustrated by the determined opposition of the Springer heirs, who managed in the end to consolidate their control by buying out the Burda brothers. For a while it appeared that Leo Kirch's ambitions were to remain completely disappointed and the prospects of his establishing a multimedia empire by this quick route entirely dashed. However, Kirch was not so easily thwarted. Blocked entrance into the SAT 1 consortium by one route, he immediately contrived to find another. In 1988, he bought a controlling stake in PKS, the single largest shareholder of SAT 1. The resultant Kirch/Springer axis within SAT 1 amounted to a very significant development in media concentration, spanning the press, broadcasting and film sectors. This picture of 'Verflechtung' is completed by the fact that Kirch was the third major shareholder, alongside Bertelsmann and Springer, in the new West German Pay-TV company, Teleclub. Such a degree of media concentration was entirely unprecedented in the postwar history of the West German media.[33]

33. R. Woldt, 'Real Life Soap Opera', *Media Bulletin*, vol. 5, no. 2, June 1988, pp. 9–10, Manchester: European Institute of the Media.

Leo Kirch: The 'New Hugenberg'?

Leo Kirch was a powerful but shadowy figure who was on close terms with both CDU Chancellor Helmut Kohl and Franz Josef Strauss, the CSU leader in his home state of Bavaria. Kirch was also a committed supporter of the CSU. He enjoyed very important contacts in the financial world, most notably with his 'housebanker' ('Hausbankier') Helmut Guthardt. The latter was very influential within the board of the Deutsche Genossenschaftsbank, a fact that had doubtless helped Kirch to muscle in on the PKS consortium (the DG Bank was one of the originators of the PKS).[34]

Notwithstanding the fact that he had to 'share' SAT 1 with the 'headless' Springer group, in the late 1980s Leo Kirch appeared to be strategically extremely well-placed to fulfil his ambition of becoming the mightiest multimedia magnate in the Federal Republic's new dual broadcasting system. His Munich-based Beta/Taurus company provided him with an excellent base for his multimedia diversification operations, command over a scarce resource which even the Springer group could not match – namely, programmes. His Munich warehouse was reported to store no less than a million cans of film, amounting to a potential of over 50,000 hours of television, including 15,000 feature films and numerous series, valued at around DM 1 billion. Indeed, according to *Der Spiegel*, Kirch was in a position to supply his own television company with enough material for eight years of programming, and he already supplied both the ARD and the new private commercial sector. It was, therefore, hardly surprising that the heady expansion of Kirch's media empire invited comparisons from certain quarters with the Weimar Hugenberg empire. In this connection, the programme director of RTL Plus, Helmut Thoma, is alleged to have stated 'that the CDU/CSU media policies [had] led to a politicisation of the new media to an extent that was never the case with the public-service broadcasters'.[35]

---

34. *Der Spiegel* no. 42/1987, p. 84.
35. Ibid., pp. 84–5.

The Private Commercial Sector and 'Standortpolitik'

However, in the first instance at least, the new commercial broadcasting sector was confronted by serious problems of consolidation. As seen, the new terrestrial frequencies then being distributed among private commercial television companies had been intended to help the new private commercial broadcasters to achieve financial viability. Bundespostminister Schwarz-Schilling had released these unused frequencies in order to give the CDU/CSU 'broadcasting revolution' a badly needed second wind. Prior to this action, the new private commercial television operations had been confined to an audience of around 2.5 million cable viewers. This had meant that they remained generally uninteresting to the advertising industry. As a result, the new operators had been obliged to sell their advertising slots cheap and therefore their income remained very disappointingly low. In 1987 RTL Plus and SAT 1 were expected to make losses of between DM 70 million and DM 100 million.[36]

The new terrestrial frequencies were supposed to lead the commercial broadcasters out of the 'cable ghetto' (in the words of SAT 1 manager Jurgen Doetz). However, according to West German regulatory law, although the Bundespost made the frequencies available in the first place, it remained the responsibility of the Länder to decide their allocation. The Länder themselves were engaged in a fierce competition to become media centres. The complexity of the power-relations within the new commercial broadcasting sector became strikingly evident as the public policy-makers in the Länder now sought to turn their media-policy-making competence to advantage *vis-à-vis* the new commercial broadcasters. The new commercial broadcasting groups suddenly found themselves implicated in the difficult business of establishing a diffuse web of localised 'policy networks' with policy-makers at the regional and local level. Within these 'policy networks' the bargaining position of the new commercial operators *vis-à-vis* the official policy-makers in the Länder was severely weakened by the internecine rivalries of the former. On the other hand, the local officials of certain

36. *Wirtschaftswoche* no. 42/1987, pp. 17–20.

regions and cities were now in a classic position to turn the tables on the power of the publishers.

In particular, city-states such as Berlin, Hamburg, and Bremen, and large populous states such as Bavaria and North-Rhine Westphalia offered potentially very large audiences. In return for the local terrestrial franchises the public authorities of these populous Länder and cities were now able to extract promises of very generous inward investment (e.g. studios, channels, business offices, etc.) from the new television operators. These resulted a kind of auction (or 'Standortpoker' as it was described by the economic journal *Wirtschaftswoche*) between the new commercial operators in the race to obtain franchises. In order to win the competition for the highly desirable 'big city' frequencies, the major private commercial operators soon discovered the need to make considerable commitments to invest and locate production centres in these rival metropolitan centres. For example, in its bid to obtain the West Berlin frequency from the Berlin Anstalt für Kabelkommunikation, SAT 1 had to promise to take a 51% share in a Berlin-based production company producing programmes worth DM 20 million per year. According to one report, SAT 1 was supposed to have promised to invest no less than a total of DM 32.4 million in the city.[37] Although unsuccessful, RTL Plus had promised to cooperate with local programmers to open up an office in West Berlin and to produce DM 10 million worth of programmes in 1987 rising to DM 20 million in 1988.[38]

Similarly, SAT 1 promised to establish a headquarters in Hanover and to cooperate in the establishment of regional 'window programmes' ('Fensterprogramme') with local partners in Schleswig-Holstein, Bavaria and Hamburg. Not to be outdone, RTL Plus promised to move its operational headquarters to Cologne (to gain entrance to the populous and viewer-rich state of North-Rhine Westphalia) and offered to establish 'window programmes' in other regions and localities.[39] The position of the major new private commercial channels was further complicated by the requirement that they coordinate

37. Ibid., pp. 17–20.
38. V. O'Connor, 'A Private Affair', *Cable and Satellite Europe*, 5/1987, pp. 16–23, p. 20.
39. *Wirtschaftswoche*, no. 42/1987, pp. 17–20.

with local programmers in each location. For example, although SAT 1 became the main beneficiary of the Munich frequency, two hours per day were to be given over to twelve local programmers. In 1987 SAT 1 made 'local window' agreements with programmers all over the country.

Future Financial Prospects of the Commercial Broadcasters

Therefore during 1988, the new private commercial broadcasting sector faced the distinct danger that the new broadcasting operations could become highly splintered and overstretched. The requirement to provide the promised regional 'window programmes' for local broadcasters threatened to place a very serious financial constraint on the new multimedia giants and postpone the day when they could hope to break even and make a profit. The local operators were highly unlikely to be able to cover the costs by themselves and the generous commitments made by the giant operators in order to obtain the terrestrial frequencies suggested that they would be left to foot the bill of local broadcasting. Past experiments in local broadcasting augured badly: for instance, the experimental local channels in Munich and Ludwigshafen had for years run up a deficit of millions of marks.[40] Moreover, it also appeared that the Bundespost had been over-sanguine about the extent of the new audiences that the release of the new terrestrial frequencies would provide. It seemed probable that many households would require additional reception equipment (switches and boosters) in order to ensure that the new frequencies provided a good picture.[41]

Worse still, in December 1987 the launch of TV SAT 1, the first of the series of two West German DBS satellites, was rewarded by its complete failure to function. This latter disaster cost the Bundespost around DM 400 million in lost investment. However, this did not amount to such a huge setback for the new commercial broadcasters as might at first be imagined. In order to salvage the situation, the Bundespost immediately entered into negotiations with Télédiffusion de France (TDF) about the

40. *Wirtschaftswoche*, no. 34/1987, pp. 64–5.
41. *Wirtschaftswoche*, no. 42/1987, pp. 17–20.

Media and Media Policy in West Germany

possibility of running the channels that were to have operated on TV SAT 1 on the French DBS satellites instead (as well as on TV SAT 2 when launched). This seemed to be a mutually promising solution, since until this point the French had appeared to be having their own difficulties in finding takers for their DBS satellite channels. Moreover, by this time, the new West German commercial operators were at least as keen to operate 'off-air' by means of the new terrestrial frequencies released by the Bundespost as they were interested in transferring to DBS satellite. Moreover, they still had their communications satellite channels and, from 1989, also Kopernikus.

In the final analysis, the dramatic transformation of the broadcasting system was irreversible; the commercial broadcasters would certainly survive these early problems and disappointments. The new multimedia giants undoubtedly had the resources, and also the motivation, to weather the long haul ahead. In order to stake their claims in the commercial broadcasting sector, they were prepared to accept very considerable losses in the short term. Moreover, their investment in the sector was a mere fraction of their annual income. In 1987, the Springer group's annual turnover was of the order of DM 2.7 billion. The Bertelsmann group was the world's second mightiest multimedia company with an annual turnover of DM 9.2 billion (in 1987). As seen, Leo Kirch possessed arguably the most important asset of all, namely a seemingly inexhaustible flow of programmes. Moreover, viewed in another light, the extremely high costs involved in establishing their market position merely confirmed the unlikelihood of any major rivals appearing to contest the new giant entrepreneurs' mastery of the commercial broadcasting sector. Although the Bundespost too had encountered a number of disappointments in the process of introducing the new media, it had undoubtedly achieved its CDU Minister's primary political objective, in line with his party's media policy, namely the successful introduction of a 'broadcasting revolution' in the Federal Republic.

Conclusion

The following conclusion will attempt briefly to summarise the main results of this investigation. Particular attention will be paid to the main specificities and peculiarities of the German media system, in the course of which some general points of comparison with other media systems will be raised. Finally, there will be some comment upon the West German response to major challenges to the established system arising from international market forces and new technologies. In this latter respect, the theme is one of the likely continuing distinctive character of important aspects of the West German media system: a system especially bound to respect the principle of pluralism enshrined in the country's liberal-democratic written Constitution. At the same time, some important reservations are expressed about the recent departure from certain of the 'first principles' which have hitherto ensured the 'balanced' nature of the West German media system.

The Historical Legacy

The West German media system has a fairly ignominious history. During the Imperial period, the press had been subject to the authoritarian state ('Obrigkeitsstaat'). While this did not impede the rapid commercial development of a mass press, it certainly did severely inhibit the development of a genuinely free press confident about its ability to give expression to political opinions beyond the narrowly circumscribed conservative orthodoxy. As a result, the mass press remained generally apolitical and objectively conservative. During the Weimar Republic, the press became more pluralistic but also 'hyperpolitical'. This, however, meant that it was generally unable to contribute to the consensus-building that was so sorely needed to give Germany's first experience of democracy a chance of survival. A significant section of the mass press was excessively partisan, often little more than an instrument for the representation of the interests of political groups and entrenched social interests. Moreover, the press system soon fell victim to a high degree of concentration of media power in the shape of the Hugenberg 'multimedia' empire spanning news supply, newspapers and film. The Hugenberg empire supported the antidemocratic right and later the National Socialists, and it contributed greatly to the poisoning of the political culture and the subsequent collapse of Weimar democracy.

The Weimar broadcasting system, too, proved itself to be hardly more conducive to the consolidation of liberal democracy. In this case, the state exercised a controlling influence over the new medium right from the start. There were no constitutional safeguards to ensure the freedom, democratic representativeness or public accountability of broadcasting, which instead was treated as an important function of public administration and governed by largely undemocratically inclined state officials. This lack of any serious commitment to liberal-democratic values paved the way for the National Socialist takeover, after which broadcasting was misused as a powerful instrument of totalitarian rule.

Post-War West German Media Policy

By contrast, the media system of post-war West Germany exhibits a number of very pronounced core features:

(1) The deep-rooted, historically-determined and highly self-conscious concern to legally safeguard the free expression of opinion, information and culture against control or interference either by the state or by any dominant social or economic interest.

(2) Following on from this, the very special role of law in media policy, which reflects the developed role of law, and constitutional principles more broadly, in regulating West German politics and society and in resolving political conflict. Whilst the legal system often appears to have enshrined the power of the publishers in the field of the

press, and has patently failed to act against many abuses (e.g. of Springer's *Bild-Zeitung*), it has conversely acted as an important guarantee of the enduring principle of public-service regulation in the field of broadcasting, ensuring the emergence and maintenance of a carefully 'balanced' media system.

(3) The fact that, while the press, as elsewhere in the Western world, has been generally free from direct regulation, the West German broadcasting system has been typically subject to an exceedingly strict and painstakingly defined degree of public regulation. The highly regulated broadcasting system, with its constitutional duty to 'manufacture' pluralism, has acted as a crucial counterbalance to the lack of regulation and, in practice, only limited pluralism of the press sector. This has been the central feature of the 'balanced' media system.

(4) In this latter respect, the West German broadcasting system can be said to have had a somewhat unique 'model' character in the lengths to which it has gone in ensuring democratic accountability to the 'socially significant groups' in a pluralistic liberal-democratic society. The West German broadcasting system has been, by international standards at least, very 'open' and 'representative'.

The West German Press System

After the Second World War, the Allied occupation period has been shown to have been crucial for giving the post-war West German press system its current shape and character. 'Stunde Null' marked a profound hiatus in the history of the German press. Few of the great newspapers of the Weimar period reappeared after the war. Instead, the licensed press benefited from the initially highly restrictive policies of the Allies and a host of new publishers soon established themselves as the main providers of the major post-war newspapers. At first the Allied occupation powers imposed major constraints on the 'pure' capitalistic nature of the press (witness the early provisions against shareholding, and of course licensing), in order to prevent the reemergence of the great press empires of the past. In

Conclusion

practice, however, their measures quickly led to the consolidation of a quintessentially capitalistic press system. Nevertheless, this system was 'free' from state control and the West German Constitution explicitly protected the press from censorship. Moreover, it seemed to be characterised by a fairly high degree of pluralism.

The reality, however, was somewhat more prosaic. Once released from the early Allied controls, the press system very quickly fell under the influence of powerful economic forces, which led it into a state of marked concentration of ownership, characterised by the reappearance of giant oligopolies and monopolies. The right-wing Springer concern, in particular, was able to establish a large degree of market dominance. Partly as a result of Allied policies, partly as a reflection of the balance of political forces in the early Federal Republic, radical alternatives were certainly marginalised and the proprietorial right of publishers to more or less exclusively establish the social, political and philosophical orientation of their publications was enshrined in the controversial 'Tendenzschutz', against the generally weak opposition of the journalists' organisations and the trade unions. Writers such as Rudiger Liedtke are undoubtedly correct to draw attention to the primacy of economic factors in explaining these developments (although Liedtke's tendency to blame the Allied occupation powers exclusively is inaccurate). Indeed, there can be little doubt that 'press freedom' has been too narrowly interpreted as freedom from the state: there has not been similar emphasis on independence from big business or the advertising industry. The pluralistic ideal which places a high value on the prevention of monopolies and concentrations of media power has been seriously abridged. In particular, the excessive power wielded by the stridently right-wing Springer press has been a constant reminder of the how far the system has fallen short of its noble ideal.[1]

Nevertheless, the West German press sector certainly does exhibit what might be described as a reasonable degree of 'limited pluralism'. The dominance of the right-wing Springer press is, to some extent, counterbalanced by the existence of

1. Rüdiger Liedtke, *Die verschenkte Presse – die Geschichte der Lizenzierung von Zeitungen nach 1945*, Berlin: Verlag für Ausbildung und Studium in der Elefanten Presse, 1982.

such worthy and influential newspapers as the left-inclined *Frankfurter Rundschau* and *Süddeutsche Zeitung*, the intellectual/liberal *Die Zeit* and the widely read and left-of-centre magazines *Stern* and *Der Spiegel*, and even the politically conservative but otherwise often fairly liberal *Frankfurter Allgemeine Zeitung*. Together, these magazines and newspapers have been monuments to the post-war achievements of liberal and 'critical' journalism, setting a high standard for the rest of the West German press to follow. Unlike the rest of the West German press, they can all boast a fairly wide national ('überregionale') readership. Moreover, much of the overwhelmingly regional press is composed of very stolid and respectable daily newspapers, which may be rather conservative in style as well as politics but which are also very information-oriented, and on the whole both 'responsible' and 'serious'.

Moreover, apart from the *Bild-Zeitung*, which admittedly has a very wide national readership indeed, there is, in fact, very much less of the sensationalist kind of 'gutter press' so richly in evidence in Britain. Furthermore, press-concentration in West Germany may have proceeded to a wholly unwelcome extent, but there is still a greater degree of pluralism than, for instance, in the case of Britain, where between 1958 and 1976 seven multinational companies bought no fewer than 552 British papers and magazines with total circulations of 49 million.[2] The Springer empire may be exceedingly large and powerful, with around a quarter of the West German market for dailies and a clear dominance of the market for Sunday papers, but in Britain Rupert Murdoch's News International owns no less than five leading national newspapers, Robert Maxwell owns three and the three 'Lords' – Rothermere, Hartwell and Stevens – between them own another seven, leaving only the *Guardian*, the *Independent* and the *Financial Times* (combined circulation of around a mere million) in truly independent hands.[3]

The West German Public-Service Broadcasting System

In the case of the West German broadcasting system, the influ-

---

2. F. Allaun, *Spreading the News*, Nottingham: the Spokesman Press, for the Campaign for Press and Broadcasting Freedom, 1988, p. 18.
3. See ibid., p. 27.

Conclusion

ence of the Allied occupation powers was shown to have been no less crucial for the development of the West German broadcasting system. Above all concerned that this powerful medium should never again be abused by overweening state power, the Allied powers rejected the reconstitution of a centralised broadcasting system and took many key precautions to ensure that the broadcasting stations were taken out of the hands of the state and made the responsibility of autonomous and publicly accountable public-service organisations. In this singly important respect, the highly respected British model was far more influential than either the commercial American model or the *étatiste* French one.

Without a doubt, the West German broadcasting system can justifiably claim much distinction: it has widely been praised as one of the best television systems in the world. In the words of John Ardagh, 'if the BBC, ITV and Channel Four constitute . . . the least worst television in the world, then the West German networks might be regarded as the second least worst in Europe'.[4] Unlike the French broadcasting system, it has avoided the worst excesses of the unashamed kind of blatant politicisation that inevitably arises from a state-controlled system, even if it has clearly not avoided a certain degree of politicisation (and even the British system has not always been able to keep the politicians at bay). Moreover, the decentralised nature of the West German broadcasting system has ensured that political bias has been evened out by regional counterbalances. At the same time, as a self-consciously public-service system, the West German broadcasting system has, at least until now, offered a very meritworthy alternative to the kind of brash and rampant commercialism which has long characterised the American system. Furthermore, the West German system's complex regulatory structure, with its emphasis on the role of the diverse 'socially significant groups', is undoubtedly far more democratic, open and accountable than the rather elitist British system, with its predominance of the 'great and the good' within the IBA and the BBC.

Undoubtedly, the secrets of the past successes of the West German public-service broadcasting system are to be found in

4. J. Ardagh, *Germany and the Germans*, Harmondsworth: Penguin, 1988, p. 308.

Conclusion

the peculiarities of its policy-making and regulatory system. First of all, in view of the historical legacy, great care has been taken to ensure that the state is kept at a healthy distance from the broadcasting system (the principle of 'Staatsferne'). In addition, the complex structure of the public-service broadcasting corporations, with 'internal control' assured by the pluralistically composed 'broadcasting councils', has been a rather exceptional feature of the system which has undoubtedly contributed to the generally pluralistic and representative nature of broadcasting. The decentralised structure of the system too has ensured that there is a strong regional input into West German broadcasting. The interaction between the regional corporations within the ARD 'network' and between the Länder representatives within ZDF have greatly contributed to the socially 'integrative' function of broadcasting in West Germany. Together these two features – control by the 'socially significant groups' and the interactive national/regional quality of broadcasting – have led West German media analysts proudly to refer to the system as 'integrational broadcasting' ('Integrationsrundfunk'). Moreover, the central commitment to pluralism has been powerfully bolstered by the centrality of the Constitution and constitutional law which is a very special characteristic of the wider West German political system. A series of landmark rulings by the Federal Constitutional Court quickly established the objective parameters of broadcasting policy-making and continuously guided the cautious and highly incremental evolution of the broadcasting system in a manner that was very conducive to the maintenance of this commitment to pluralism.

However, certain weaknesses are also very apparent: the shortfalls are equally to be explained by the peculiarities of this system. Most seriously, the system has clearly not avoided a certain degree of politicisation despite the interventions of the Constitutional Court. The pervasive influence of the West German political parties has been a generally positive feature of the West German state, given the profoundly undemocratic historical legacy. During the authoritarian past the democratic parties had been objects of an unhealthy contempt rather than the respected agents of liberal democracy. However, a negative feature of West Germany's post-war democracy is the 'party book' state, where appointments to the bureaucracy are all too often decided by political allegiance. The 'party book' qualification has meant that very quickly the parties' influence extended into the broadcasting corporations. As a result, there soon appeared to exist a very evident tension between, on the one hand, a 'broadcasting constitutionalism' that stressed the principles of 'Staatsferne' and pluralism and, on the other, an emerging reality of significant politicisation.

Nevertheless, an important measure of political pluralism has been guaranteed by the traditionally German 'Proporz' principle which has assured both major political parties a measure of influence within *each* broadcasting corporation. Coupled with the regional counterbalances, determined by simple electoral geography, this has meant that *no single political party* has ever enjoyed undue influence over the entire public-service broadcasting system. In fact, a very approximate political balance has generally prevailed between the majority of northern German corporations, with their various degrees of overall SPD bias, and the southern German corporations, which have been generally sympathetic to the CDU/CSU. Moreover, the most politicised of the corporations have balanced each other out: the 'red' Hamburg-based NDR and the 'black' BR in CSU Bavaria. (Obviously, this pattern is not fixed: during the 1980s, for example, the NDR has lost its SPD orientation and become a veritable battleground of conflicting tendencies.) On the debit side, the 'Proporz' system has produced negative effects. On the one hand, it has led to a rather restrained style of broadcasting where too often the concern for 'balance' within programmes and programme schedules has acted as a kind of 'straitjacket' on reporting, with the effect that much of the latter can seem 'dull and timid'. On the other hand, the broadcasting system has tended to be 'cramped by politics in ways that were never intended, and this has had a harmful effect on the news and current affairs output'.[5]

Another feature of the broadcasting system has both positive and negative qualities. On the one hand, concern for the 'rules of the game' and a profound respect for the status quo has prevented several determined attempts by various exclusive 'policy networks' to drastically alter the model of broadcasting

5. Ibid., pp. 308–9.

established by the Allies and by the paternalistic and earnestly 'democratic' post-war West German elites. The in-built checks and balances and countervailing powers (e.g. the Constitutional Court, the principle of 'cooperative federalism', the role of the 'socially significant groups', 'Proporz', etc.) has ensured that the public-service broadcasting system in West Germany has remained the restricted preserve of a stable, fairly representative and pluralistic 'policy community'.

On the other hand, as John Sandford has suggested, 'throughout the sixties and seventies, the West German broadcasting system remained, from an organisational point of view, one of the most conservative in Europe . . . at a time when [elsewhere] fundamental changes were taking place, in particular in the form of the introduction of commercial broadcasting'.[6] As a result, the devoutly public-service style of German broadcasting (which as seen has long carried commercials) has led much broadcasting fare to appear rather serious-minded in a fashion somewhat reminiscent of the BBC before the stimulus which followed the introduction of ITV. Entertainment has been kept strictly separate and this has often been at the expense of lively programming. Yet, this same rather peculiar 'conservatism' has had its merits: in particular, it has ensured that the recent 'broadcasting revolution', documented in the last two chapters of this volume, has seen the establishment of a 'dual broadcasting system' which safeguards 'continuity in change' and, above all, an enduring commitment to high-quality public-service broadcasting.

The Performance of Key Media Functions

All in all, the above-mentioned weaknesses notwithstanding, the balance so far must be acknowledged to be fairly positive: the West German media can be said to have performed reasonably well in respect of a number of key functions. With a considerable degree of success, the West German media have fulfilled the following functions:

6. John Sandford, 'Wollt ihr das totale Fernsehen? – the New Media Debate in West Germany', *Journal of Area Studies*, no. 12, Autumn 1985, p. 24.

Conclusion

(1) *An important democratisation function*. Both the press and the public-service broadcasters have contributed vigorously to the liberal-democratic process of public and individual opinion-forming ('Meinungsbildung'). At least in large part through the media, the early post-war West German citizen (Bundesbürger) was relatively quickly 'reeducated' and socialised into acceptance of the social mores and political norms of liberal democracy. Since the inception of the media system, the West German citizen has undoubtedly been presented with a reasonably wide range of different political, philosophical and cultural viewpoints.

(2) *A crucial stabilisation and legitimation function*. The West German media made a very important contribution to the process by which the infant Federal Republic was very quickly stabilised and legitimated as a viable economic, social and political order, albeit in its early years a fiercely anti-communist one. Some newspapers, most notably those of the Springer empire, undoubtedly gave too much priority to the internal and external consolidation of the new state, mobilising public opinion against presumed internal and external threats which were all too often hardly justified. Yet this was as much a function of the Cold War and also of the idiosyncratic bias of Axel Springer himself as of the structures and values of the overall West German media system.

(3) *A valuable integration function*. The public-service broadcasting system, in particular, has conscientiously given expression to the diverse range of interests in West German society. Over the years, and particularly in the wake of 1968, the media system has been flexible enough to incorporate new social concerns and movements at least to a certain extent.

(4) *A critical 'check' function*. Both the press and the public-service broadcasters have acted as an important 'check' on the political system, frequently drawing attention to blatant abuses of political power when these have occurred. Very early on, the *'Spiegel* Affair' of 1962 testified to the way the press had already developed a distinct consciousness of its critical control function and its mission to act as

Conclusion

an important constraint on the exercise of political power. On this occasion virtually the entire press, with the notable exception of the Springer papers, rallied to the defence of the *Spiegel*. Since this crucial moment, this important function has been admirably performed by the *Spiegel*, along with other worthy titles such as the somewhat less intellectual *Stern* magazine, in addition to other highly distinguished quality 'critical' liberal newspapers (see above).

However, attention might be drawn to a less positive function of the media:

(5) *A social control function.* According to radical critics of the West German media system, the West German media have served decisively to limit the political, economic and cultural agenda. They are held to have manufactured 'acceptance' and 'support' for the dominant groups in society, thereby creating a deeply 'bourgeois' ('bürgerlich') public sphere ('Öffentlichkeit'). This is to some extent undeniable, yet West Germany is quintessentially a quietly 'bürgerlich' country. Measured against its unstable, violent and profoundly illiberal history, many would argue that 'bourgeois' liberalism is the country's major achievement. Apart from which, the word 'bürgerlich' (which only very inadequately translates into 'bourgeois' anyway) simply denotes a rather class-less kind of society, in comparison at least with its still class-ridden neighbours, Britain and France, a state of affairs to which the tenor and content of much of the print media in Britain at least has undoubtedly greatly contributed. In West Germany, only one or two exceptions, most notably, Springer's *Bild-Zeitung*, have seriously tarnished this image, by pandering to vulgar and populist (rather than bourgeois) prejudices. Nevertheless, while the press remains the dominant preserve of Sethe's 'two hundred rich men' (see quote introducing this volume), there is certainly more than an ounce of truth in this critique.

Consideration of the last-named function inevitably leads to

Conclusion

mention of one final important function, which has been performed increasingly spectacularly in West Germany (with far more energy and imagination than in Britain or in France):

(6) *A mobilisation of alternatives function.* The West German media system has undoubtedly expanded, during the 1970s and 1980s, in response to the above critique. Arguably, the themes, issues and style of the 'new social movements' of the post-'68 period have had a more enduring a deeper impact on politics and society in West Germany than in any other Western society (witness the success of the Greens). This major social and political transformation has had an undoubted resonance within the 'established' West German media, striking exciting new currents and contributing to a greater pluralism and diversity than had existed previously. Within the broadcasting corporations, the 'statutes movement' actually achieved much to elevate and safeguard the position of the investigative and socially-aware journalist (also to an extent a product of the '1968 wave'). At the same time, the 'alternative' press, symbolised by the spectacularly successful *Tagezeitung*, gave expression and impetus to the broader emergence of new values and pointed the way forward to a new style and substance of communication, centred on community and social issues, and throwing down the gauntlet to the giant conservative concerns, and especially to the Springer press.

Whither the Media? The Deregulation Debate

However, during the late 1970s and 1980s, media policy, like many other areas of social and economic activity, has been characterised by powerful forces pushing for a movement towards 'deregulation'. This, it is legitimately feared, will inevitably entail a debasement of standards and an increase in crass commercialism in the media. To some extent, this new development can be seen as an American (or Anglo-Saxon) ideological import, which has certainly very little in common with the heavily legalistic and highly regulated German tradition. This is very

Conclusion

clearly reflected in the especially agonised public debate which, as much of this book has described, the issue of broadcasting deregulation has provoked in the Federal Republic. Indeed, the characteristic combination of thoroughness ('Gründlichkeit') and emotiveness of this debate in West Germany presents a striking contrast with the paucity and belatedness of debate in Britain.

On the other hand, to a large extent this development can also be seen, as generally elsewhere in the Western world, as the more or less direct result of powerful technological changes and international market developments which have presented far-reaching and unavoidable, even fundamental, challenges to existing policies. Technological change, in the shape of cable and especially satellite, and the onrush of 'cross-frontier' media operations, have everywhere confronted traditional patterns of regulatory policy with the prospect of decreased autonomy for media systems, not only at the regional level, as in West German broadcasting, but also on a national basis. In addition, industrial and international market considerations have increasingly played as important a role as the traditional cultural policy concerns of the established 'policy community'. The collapse of the precarious boundary between the broadcasting and the telecommunications sector coupled with the concern of governments to promote the information technology industries have inevitably led to pressures to establish a new, much looser and more flexible regulatory framework for broadcasting services.[7]

Under the impact of technological change and of new corporate and political pressures, the broadcasting system of the Federal Republic has been shown to have recently undergone an important transformation. Most dangerously of all, the hitherto established 'first principle' of the 'balanced' West German media system, namely that of a strict separation of the press and broadcasting sectors, especially in matters of ownership, has now been dispensed with and a deregulated sector has been introduced within the previously highly regulated broadcasting system. The combined pressures of 'Standortpolitik' (the competition for investment) and the power of the publishers have

---

7. K. Dyson and P. Humphreys, *Broadcasting and New Media Policies in Western Europe. A Comparative Study of Technological Change and Public Policy*, London: Routledge and Kegan Paul, 1988.

Conclusion

compelled the SPD, as the political party dedicated to the maintenance of this 'balance' of media power, progressively to move from a position of 'fundamentalist' opposition to commercial broadcasting to a final position of acceptance of a new commercial broadcasting sector.

An indicator of the new prime allegiance to industrial and technological imperatives has been the new role of the central state, in the shape of the Bundespost, in the media-policy community. The Bundespost has been an important factor in maintaining the momentum of this 'broadcasting revolution', and indeed in constraining the local and regional SPD policy-makers to accept centrally determined *faits accomplis*. The Bundespost's enormous powers of investment and control over technological resources (satellite channels, cable systems, terrestrial frequencies) has allowed the CDU/CSU federal government to become a central actor in the broadcasting policy community (at last fulfilling Konrad Adenauer's dream, although in a way that would have surprised him in the 1960s). Although the Bundespost has clearly encountered a number of disappointments in the process of introducing the new media, it has undoubtedly achieved its CDU Minister's primary political objective, in line with his party's media policy, namely the successful introduction of a commercial and considerably deregulated broadcasting sector. This recent activism of the central state in media-policy-making represents another significant departure from a 'first principle' of the established media system, namely the principle of avoiding state manipulation of broadcasting policy ('Staatsferne').

At the same time, however, the SPD's resort to the characteristic avenue of 'legalistic opposition' and the resultant intervention of the all-powerful judicial system (the 'Rechtsstaat'), as the ultimate guardian of constitutional 'first principles', has been shown to be a crucially important factor in the creation of an acceptable and workable new consensus about the future of broadcasting in the age of satellite broadcasting. As in the past, the Federal Constitutional Court at Karlsruhe has established the detailed principles to guide the policy-makers in their deliberations. The result has been the emergence of a 'dual broadcasting system' which safeguards an important measure of 'continuity in change'. Thus, the future of the public-service

Conclusion

broadcasting system has been guaranteed, while at the same time a considerable measure of deregulation has been allowed for the new commercial broadcasting sector.

Nevertheless, it is clear that the introduction of a new commercial broadcasting sector marks an historic landmark in the annals of media-concentration in the Federal Republic. Unsurprisingly, the new sector has very quickly become dominated by a few giant combines of leading publishers which have already long enjoyed a very dominant position in the press sector. Moreover, the introduction of the new media and a commercial broadcasting sector dominated by the publishers of the press has been shown to be, in an important respect, a goal deliberately pursued by political parties (i.e. the CDU/CSU) seeking to 'reorientate' the political balance of the broadcasting system. Both of these developments also mark important departures from hitherto established 'first principles' of the 'balanced' media system. Of course, in reality, politics has been shown to have always played a key role in media-policy-making. Until recently, however, such blatant attempts to 're-balance' the entire broadcasting system had failed. Equally, perhaps even more, disturbing is the current onward march of the press barons. The final achievement by the Springer press of its long-cherished goal of entering into mass broadcasting operations and the sudden rise of Leo Kirch undoubtedly present a formidable challenge to the guardians of media pluralism.

There is however cause for some optimism, or at the very least for tempering undue pessimism. This work has described how both the West German media system and the country's political system contain important countervailing powers to the hungry power of the publishing barons. Firstly, the Federal Constitutional Court: the 'guardians of the Constitution' have demonstrated consistently their commitment to upholding the principles of pluralism and balance in the country's media system. The Court has ensured that, at least formally, a manifestly incremental and cautious deregulatory approach has been taken to the introduction of a new private commercial broadcasting sector. Distinct, if fairly liberal, limits have been set to the degree of private media-concentration which will be tolerated and, just as importantly, important guarantees have been established for the future health of the public-service broadcasting sector. Secondly, the regime characteristics of a federal system and a legalistic political culture have reinforced this propensity towards incrementalism and ensured an important degree of 'continuity in change'. Federalism may have complicated the process of policy formulation and adaptation to new market and technological pressures, yet at the same time it has meant that significant boundaries have been set to CDU/CSU-inspired deregulation. The SPD policy-makers have been able to achieve a very significant measure of success in establishing important guarantees for the future of the public-service broadcasting sector (in large part by recourse to the Federal Constitutional Court). It is noteworthy that the SPD itself has undergone a learning process in the course of events: by adopting a 'cooperative' and 'legalistic' style of opposition, it has been able to steer developments in a manner which would not have been possible had it maintained a stance of 'principled' opposition. Such behaviour is entirely characteristic of the well-established pattern of West German politics and will come as no surprise to political scientists specialising in the government system of the Federal Republic. The 'twin-pillar' regulatory model of North-Rhine Westphalia symbolises what may be achieved in the way of combining economic and cultural policy concerns, while placing constraints on media-concentration and reasserting the principles of editorial independence and public-service regulation. Thirdly, it should be pointed out to an Anglo-Saxon readership that, as Christian Democratic parties, the CDU/CSU are not instinctively neo-liberal parties. They contain strong elements – in particular, the Christian 'Wertkonservativen' (moral conservatives) – which continue to adhere to a certain respect for regulation. They too have undoubtedly undergone a learning process and have realised the dangers of breaking too much from the country's established public-service traditions. Moreover, the CDU/CSU have discovered, to their certain disappointment, that the new media entrepreneurs are less amenable to political control than the semi-politicised public-service broadcasting corporations. Moreover, the former seem so far to have been far more interested in providing anodyne and inexpensive entertainment programmes than the kind of programme which could conceivably be said to carry an overt political message. The continuing commitment of the Christian Democrats to the

Conclusion

public-service sector is perhaps nowhere more clear than in CSU Bavaria, where the public-service broadcasters have even been given pride of place in new media developments. This is, of course, because BR remains very much a CSU-influenced corporation. However, whether this latter observation should be taken as a cause for optimism about the future is, as this volume has described, a moot point.

Nevertheless, for all their obvious shortcomings, the public-service broadcasters themselves are an important counterweight to the power of the publishers. They have manifestly responded with increasing confidence to the new commercial challenge, not least in the shape of their own initiatives in the field of the new media. Although this volume has shown how their role can be cast in a critical, as well as a generally positive, light, they are at least responsible to the 'socially significant groups' of West German society in a very direct manner. Moreover, as already explained, the mere existence of so many different public-service corporations, with their varying degrees of political bias, in itself guarantees an important degree of pluralism and confrontation of viewpoints and philosophies. Moreover, it would be mistaken to view the press interests themselves as homogeneous and uniform in their political and philosophical stances. Finally, with respect to the danger of a drift down-market towards 'lowest-common-denominator' commercial broadcasting, it might be suggested that the West German public itself has become accustomed to enjoying a very high quality service: it is doubtful whether they would react positively to an overdose of 'Dallas'-type programmes and game shows and a marked deterioration in quality programming.

All in all, the situation in West Germany stands in stark contrast to that pertaining in certain neighbouring countries. For instance, in Britain during the 1980s, radical deregulatory political currents have held sway, promising a very considerable deregulation of broadcasting and the possible marginalisation ('ghettoisation') of the very public-service broadcasting corporation, the BBC, which ironically did so much to inform and influence the infant West German system. By contrast, in West Germany, public-service broadcasting would seem to have an assured future, as an enduring counterweight to unhealthy concentrations of private commercial media power.

Afterword

In 1989, there are no less than four private commercial television operations offering a full programme schedule ('Vollprogramm'). SAT 1 and RTL Plus continue to be the main new channels with the largest audiences. However, they are being challenged by two other channels, one of them with very strong foreign backing. Wolfgang Fischer's KMP musicbox had for several years offered a primarily thematic, and distinctly limited, schedule ('Spartenprogramm') of music and videoclip programmes delivered nationwide to cable systems by means of Intelsat communications satellite. However, it has undergone a transformation into a major new channel, now called TELE 5, with a much fuller programme schedule. Fischer's Munich-based company KMP now owns only 10% of the shares. As many as 45% of the channel's shares have been taken by Tele München under another Munich entrepreneur, Herbert Kloiber. Kloiber is the German representative of the American network CBS and he has brought the valuable resource of CBS news and entertainment services to TELE 5. In addition, the remaining 45% of the shares have been taken by the Italian media magnate, Silvio Berlusconi, who already had a 25% stake in the French channel, La Cinq, as well as shares in operations in Belgium, the Netherlands, Portugal and Spain. Very clearly, TELE 5 has Europe-wide ambitions.[1]

The fourth channel is a company called PRO 7. This channel had started operations in 1987, again using Intelsat, under the name 'Eureka'. Until recently, the channel has had a very limited audience, since it was mainly a news and information service – heavily reliant on American (World-Net) supplies – transmitting to doctor's waiting rooms and suchlike. However, it too has experienced a radical transformation as the result of Leo Kirch's son, Thomas Kirch, taking a 49% stake in the

1. K. Wenger, *Kommunikation und Medien in der Bundesrepublik Deutschland*, Munich: Iudicium Verlag, 1988, pp. 69–70.

channel – now renamed PRO 7. Significantly, this development has brought the channel within the orbit of the Kirch multimedia empire. Moreover, it now has access to the latter's massive entertainment programme resources of films and series, making it too a serious addition to West Germany's new private commercial sector.[2]

According to one source, by the late summer of 1989 PRO 7 reached an audience of about 3.3 million cabled households, TELE 5 reached 5.7 million, SAT reached 5.2 million and RTL Plus reached 5.3 million. Reportedly, SAT 1 reached a further 5.2 million homes via off-air transmission by means of the new 'local' terrestrial frequencies and RTL Plus accessed 7.1 million homes by this means.[3] The latter channel has gained as many as 5 million viewers in North-Rhine Westphalia alone by gaining frequencies in the SPD ruled state.[4] Similarly, SAT 1 had gained access to nearly 2 million 'affair' viewers in Berlin. Both channels could reach around 2 million viewers in Hamburg, a similar number in Munich, and nearly 1 million in Hanover. TELE 5 had also gained a frequency in Munich, giving it the ability to reach a further 2 million (approx.) viewers.[5] In view of the still limited density of cabled households, and despite the additional 'reach' of the private commercial broadcasters provided by new terrestrial frequencies, the public-service broadcasters are still well ahead in viewing figures for the country at large. In 1988, ARD could boast an audience share of 40.5% of the viewing audience, the ZDF was close behind with 38.2%, and the 'third programme took 10.7 % (the remainder being accounted for by a mixture of the new public-service and private commercial channels, plus cross-border overflows in frontier regions). However, the public-service broadcasters cannot afford to be complacent: the two major West German private commercial channels, SAT 1 and RTL Plus, have achieved considerable success in terms of audience shares in cabled households. According to figures

2. Ibid., pp. 70–1.
3. European Institute of the Media, *Fiche no. 10 – Diffusion of programmes*, Manchester: European Institute of the Media, 1989, pp. 4–5.
4. Wenger, *Kommunikation und Medien*, p. 62.
5. More detailed figures, giving a more comprehensive coverage of the FRG, are supplied by the *DLM Jahrbuch 88*, produced by the Direktorenkonferenz der Landermedienanstalter (DLM), Munich: Verlag Neue Mediengesellschaft Ulm, 1988, pp. 288–96.

Afterword

produced by ZDF, by 1988 SAT 1 had achieved an audience share of 21.5% and RTL Plus 9.2% among adults (among children the figure was even higher). Significantly, SAT 1 and RTL Plus were broadcasting respectively 70% and 66% entertainment programming compared to the ARD's 44% and ZDF's 37%.[6]

In view of this increased competition for the public-service broadcasters, the question of an adequate licence-fee has assumed an even more crucial importance. However, despite the political compromise seemingly achieved by the 1987 'Staatsvertrag for the Reform of the Broadcasting System in the Federal Republic', the television licence-fee has disappointingly continued to be a source of politicking. The CDU Ministerpräsidenten have continued to dispute the need to award the size of increase requested by the public-service broadcasters. Only after a bitter political battle have the Ministerpräsidenten finally agreed to raise the licence-fee to DM 19.00 per month operative from 1 January 1990.

Finally, a development has occurred in the field of industrial relations which may well be important in the future. By 1989 West German media workers' interests were being represented, alongside the journalists' unions and the RFFU, by a new union, namely IG-M (shortened version of 'Industriegewerkschaft Medien – Druck und Papier, Publizistik und Kunst'). This union is an amalgamation of IG-Druck und Papier and the artistic and cultural workers' union, the Gewerkschaft Kunst. In no small measure, this latter development can be seen as a result of the increasingly convergent nature of the print, film and electronic media described by this volume (exemplified by the multimedia activities of groups such as the Springer concern, Kirch and Bertelsmann).

---

6. Wenger, *Kommunikation und Medien*, p. 103 and p. 107.

Appendix 1(a)

Economic concentration in the daily press ('Tagespresse'): market-shares of the ten largest publishers in daily newspapers in 1987

Publisher	Circulation & market-share
1. **Axel Springer Verlag AG**, Hamburg, Berlin. (*Bild, Hamburger Abendblatt, Die Welt, Berliner Morgenpost, B.Z. Berlin* and five other dailies.) Plus a near monopoly of Sunday papers	5.8 million 28.6%
2. **WAZ Group**, Essen. (*Westdeutsche Allgemeine Zeitung, Westfälische Rundschau, Neue Ruhr-Zeitung, Westfalenpost* and several other large publishing houses in the Ruhr area.)	1.2 million 6%
3. **Verlagsgruppe Süddeutscher Verlag**, Munich. (*Süddeutsche Zeitung, Abendzeitung, Donau-Kurier, Frankenpost, Neue Presse.*)	709 560 3.5%
4. **Verlagsgruppe M. DuMont Schauberg**, Cologne. (*Kölner Stadt-Anzeiger, Express, Düsseldorf Express.*)	647 298 3.2%
5. **Verlagsgruppe Stuttgarter Zeitung**, Stuttgart. (*Stuttgarter Nachrichten, Stuttgarter Zeitung, Die Rheinpfalz, Südwestpresse,* and a large number of other daily newspapers mainly in South Western Germany.)	626 083 3.1%
6. **Verlagsgruppe Münchener Zeitungsverlag**, Munich. (*Münchner Merkur* and many others.)	542 332 2.7%
7. **Rheinische-Bergische Verlagsgesellschaft**, Düsseldorf. (*Rheinische Post.*)	416 893 2.0%

Appendices

Appendix 1(a) *continued*

Publisher	Circulation & market-share
8. **Verlagsgruppe Madsack/Gerstenberg**, Hanover. (*Hannoversche Allgemeine Zeitung, Neue Presse* (Hanover), *and others* in the Hanover area.)	365 325 1.8%
9. **Frankfurter Societätsdruckerei**, Frankfurt. (*Frankfurter Neue Presse, Frankfurter Allgemeine Zeitung.*)	337 249 1.7%
10. **Ruhr-Nachrichten Verlagsgesellschaft**, Dortmund. (*Ruhr-Nachrichten, Recklinghäuser Zeitung, Münstersche Zeitung.*)	296 721 1.5%

Note: The ten largest publishers of daily newspapers together account for a total market-share of 54% (decimals rounded up to nearest tenth).
Source: Media Perspektiven. *Daten zur Mediensituation in der Bundesrepublik. Basisdaten 1987* (ISSN 1070–1762). The figures originally appeared in H. Röper: 'Daten zur Konzentration der Tagespresse in der Bundesrepublik Deutschland im 1. Quartal, 1987', *Media Perspektiven*, 9/1987 pp. 563–73.

Appendix 1(b)

Market-shares of the five largest newspaper publishing groups (at given moments in time)

Source	Year	Market-share
Diederichs[1]	1963	36.1
Günther-Kommission[2]	1968	50.2
Noelle-Neumann/Schulz[3]	1971	38.5
Diederichs[1]	1971	37.7
Diederichs[1]	1972	36.1
Aufermann/Lange/Zerdick[4]	1972	49.0
Diederichs[5]	1974	42.9
Diederichs[6]	1975	45.0
Holzer[7]	1978	48.4
Diederichs[8]	1982	47.0
Röper[9]	1987	44.4

Notes: Figures relate to the daily newspaper market only ('Tagespresse')
[1] H.H. Diederichs, *Konzentration in den Massenmedien. Systematischer Überblick zur Situation in der BRD*, Munich: Carl Hanser Verlag, 1973, p. 57.
[2] Günther-Bericht, *Schlußbericht*. . . ., Bonn: Bundestags-Drucksache V/3122 von 3 Juli 1968, pp. 154 ff.
[3] E. Noelle-Neumann and W. Schulz (eds.), *Publizistik* (Das Fischer Lexikon), Frankfurt/Main: Fischer, 1971, p. 227.
[4] J. Aufermann, B.-P. Lange and A. Zerdick, 'Pressekonzentration in der BRD: Untersuchungsprobleme, Ursachen und Erscheinungsformen', in J. Aufermann, H. Bohrmann and R. Sulzer (eds.), *Gesellschaftliche Kommunikation und Information*, Vol. I, Frankfurt/Main: Athenäum, 1973, pp. 278 ff.
[5] H.H. Diederichs, *Media Perspektiven*, 4/1975, pp. 148 ff.
[6] H.H. Diederichs, *Media Perspektiven*, 5/1976, pp. 209 ff.
[7] H. Holzer, *Medien in der BRD. Entwicklungen 1970–1980*, Cologne: Pahl Rugenstein Verlag, 1980, pp. 27–8.
[8] H.H. Diederichs, *Media Perspektiven*, 7/1983, pp. 482 ff.
[9] H. Röper, *Media Perspektiven*, 9/1987, pp. 563 ff.
Source: This table is adapted from M. Knoche *Einführung in die Pressekonzentrationsforschung* Berlin: Wissenschaftsverlag Volker Spiess, 1978, p. 471.

Appendix 1(c)

Economic concentration in the market for popular illustrated magazines ('Publikumszeitschriften'): market-shares of the four main publishers of popular illustrated magazines in 1986

Publisher	Market-Share
Axel Springer Verlag AG, (*Hör zu, Funk-Uhr, Journal für die Frau*, among others.)	10.20% (17.57%)
Verlagsgruppe Bertelsmann/Gruner & Jahr. (Among others, *Stern, Brigitte, Capital, Eltern, Schöner Wohnen*, with a 49% stake in *Frau im Spiegel*, and a 24.9% stake in the *Spiegel* Verlag Rudolf Augstein.)	7.74% (7.00%)
Bauer (Among others, *Fernsehwoche, TV Hören und Sehen, Wochenende, Neue Post, Neue Revue, Quick, Das Neue Blatt, Bravo.*)	19.20 (31.52)
Burda (Among others, *Freizeit-Revue, Freundin, Das Haus, Bild und Funk, Bunte, Meine Familie + ich, Burda-Moden.*)	10.72 (9.98)
Total	47.86 (66.07)

Note: The figures in brackets give a truer picture. They are the market-shares based on a weighting of the circulation figures to take into account the frequency of appearance of the magazines.

Source: H.H. Diederichs, 'Daten zur Konzentration der Publikumszeitschriften in der Bundesrepublik Deutschland im IV. Quartal 1986', *Media Perspektiven*, 8/1987, pp. 496–506, p. 503.

Appendix 1(d)

Economic concentration in the market for popular illustrated magazines ('Publikumszeitschriften'); development of the market-shares of the four main publishers since the early 1970s (figures for the fourth quarter of each year)

Publisher	Market-shares in % Unweighted							
	1972	'74	'76	'78	'80	'82	'84	'86
1) Bauer	19.9	20.6	21.3	20.9	20.5	19.9	20.1	19.2
2) Burda	19.9	21.4	18.5	13.6	12.2	12.2	11.4	10.7
3) Springer	9.1	8.9	8.5	8.8	8.4	8.2	10.5	10.2
4) Gruner & Jahr[1]	10.1	8.4	7.6	6.2	6.7	6.5	5.8	7.7
Total	59.0	59.3	55.9	49.5	47.8	46.8	47.8	47.8

	Market-shares in % Weighted							
1) Bauer	28.6	30.5	32.9	31.7	32.1	32.0	31.9	31.5
2) Springer	14.1	13.7	13.3	13.4	13.0	13.0	17.0	17.6
3) Burda	12.7	13.3	12.1	12.4	11.0	11.2	10.4	10.0
4) Gruner & Jahr[1]	10.0	8.8	8.2	5.8	6.1	5.9	5.0	7.0
Total	65.4	66.3	66.5	63.3	62.2	62.1	64.3	66.1

Note: [1] Verlagsgruppe Bertelsmann/Gruner & Jahr.
The weighted figures give a truer reading. They are the market-shares based on a weighting of the circulation figures to take into account the frequency of appearance of the magazines.
Source: H.H. Diederichs, 'Daten zur Konzentration der Publikumzeitschriften in der Bundesrepublik Deutschland im IV. Quartal 1986', *Media Perspektiven*, 8/1987, pp. 496–506, p. 503. The original figures have been rounded up to the nearest decimal point.

Appendix 1(e)

Market-shares of the leading papers sold on the street ('Boulevardzeitungen') in the third quarter of 1979

Title	Market-share
Bild[1]	72.4%
BZ[1]	8.9%
Express	6.1%
Abendzeitung	3.7%
Hamburger Morgenpost	3.3%
tz (Munich, not to be confused with the *taz*)[1]	2.3%
Abendpost	1.9%
Der Abend	1.4%

Note: With *Bild*, *BZ* and a 24.99% share shareholding in the *tz* the Springer Press had thus achieved a market share of no less than 82% of the 'Boulevardpresse' by the end of the 1970s

Source: P. Brummond and P. Schwindt, *Der Pressemarkt in der Bundesrepublik Deutschland*, Cologne: Pahl-Rugenstein Verlag, Hochschulschriften 110, 1982, p. 66

Appendix 2

The Key Broadcasting Judgements of the Federal Constitutional Court: a *Résumé* of the Main Points with Selected Extracts

(a) *The 'First TV Judgement' of 28 February 1961*

This judgement ruled against CDU Chancellor Konrad Adenauer's plans to introduce a second television channel, called 'Deutschland Fernsehen GmbH'. Adenauer had intended that this channel be both national (i.e. controlled by Bonn) and commercial. In response to an appeal by the Länder, the Federal Constitutional Court found constitutional grounds to reject both of these features. In the first place, the Court ruled that culture, and therefore broadcasting, fell within the jurisdiction of the Länder: accordingly, Bonn could not organise a broadcasting service. In the second place, the Court *appeared to rule against private commercial broadcasting* by arguing for the retention of existing public-service arrangements. In particular, the Court pointed out that technological and financial hurdles prevented the provision of 'pluralism' through the free establishment of numerous radio and television stations in a manner analogous to the press sector:

> The difference between the press and broadcasting resides in the fact that the German press is characterised by a relatively large number of publications which are independent and mutually competitive according to their aims ('Tendenz'), political leaning or philosophical stance; while in the field of broadcasting the number of operators must necessarily remain relatively small, both for technical reasons and because of the extraordinarily high financial costs involved.[1]

Pluralism, therefore, would continue to be the result of public-service structures. Although the Court did not rule out the possibility of private commercial broadcasting, this ruling was in fact widely interpreted as a confirmation of the public-service broadcasting monopoly.

(b) *The 'Second TV Judgement' or the 'Valued Added Tax Ruling' of 27 July 1971*

In the first instance, this ruling resulted from the appeal to the Federal Constitutional Court by the Länder of another piece of controversial

319

federal legislation. In this case, the Court ruled that the payment of the broadcasting licence-fee should not be made subject to a value added tax. However, the Court's deliberations ranged widely beyond this immediate legal problem. In particular, the Court appeared to confirm the exclusively public-service nature of broadcasting. On this occasion, the Court seemed to rule positively against the possibility of broadcasting as a commercial activity.

> The activity of the broadcasting organisations takes place in the public domain. The broadcasting organisations are publicly accountable; they perform tasks of public administration; they fulfil an integrating function for the whole of the state. Their activity is not of a commercial kind.[2]

(c) *The 'Third TV Judgement' or 'FRAG Judgement' of 16 June 1981*

The major significance of this ruling is that it at last removed the legal brakes on the radical reform of the West German broadcasting system and prepared the way for the introduction of new commercial channels. As with the 'VAT Judgement', the Court used a very concrete and narrow specific issue in order to make a far-reaching pronouncement on the fundamental constitutional principles of the West German broadcasting system. In this case, after a very long-standing legal and political controversy, the Court had been called upon to rule on the legality of an amendment, dating back to 1967, which had been made to the original Saarland broadcasting law of 1957 with the specific aim of providing for the introduction of commercial television in that Land. With respect to this single case, the Court found the specific conditions of the Saarland law wanting and unsuitable for the introduction of commercial television. However, more generally, and far more importantly, the Court now seemed positively to accept the possibility of private commercial broadcasting, so long as it remained subject to legal regulation in the cause of 'broadcasting freedom'. It recognised that the shortage of frequencies underpinning the public-service monopoly was being replaced by potential abundance as a result of the new media.

> Article 5, Paragraph 2 of the Basic Law ['Grundgesetz'] requires for the provision of private broadcasting a legal regulation, which provides for measures designed to guarantee broadcasting freedom. This remains a requirement, even if the exceptional constraints placed on broadcasting by the scarcity of frequencies and the high financial investment involved should be removed by modern developments.[3]

(d) *The 'Fourth TV Judgement' of 4 November 1986: the ruling on the Lower Saxony broadcasting law*

This ruling arose as the result of a complaint raised by the SPD against a

Appendices

specimen piece of CDU deregulatory legislation, namely the Lower Saxony media law of 23 May 1984. In the event, the Constitutional Court judged the Lower Saxony law to be 'essentially' in conformity with the federal constitution.

> The Lower Saxony state broadcasting law of the 23 May 1984 is in its essentials in conformity with the Basic Law ['Grundgesetz'].[4]

However, the real significance of the ruling was its suggestion of the legal possibility that a 'dual' broadcasting system might be established consisting of a private commercial sector alongside the public-service sector. In such a 'dual' system, it was now suggested, the public-service broadcasters would remain responsible for providing the basic broadcasting services to the whole of the population and fulfilling their classical public-service duties. However, the Court also suggested that the same high regulatory requirements placed on the public-service broadcasters should not be imposed upon the new private broadcasters: the private commercial sector should be allowed to benefit from considerable deregulation. At the same time, in the 'dual' system the health of the public-service broadcasting sector was seen as the very precondition for an opening to a new private commercial sector.

> So long and in so far as the observation of the specified requirements by the public-service broadcasters is effectively assured, it appears justified not to place upon private broadcasters similarly high requirements for a wide range and balanced diversity of programming.[5]

This ruling provided the stimulus and basis for the successful conclusion, in April 1987, of a 'Staatsvertrag' between the Länder for the 'reorganisation of the broadcasting system' into just such a 'dual broadcasting system'.

Notes

1. 'Der Unterschied zwischen Presse und Rundfunk besteht aber darin, daß innerhalb des deutschen Pressewesens eine relative große Zahl von selbständigen und nach ihrer Tendenz, politischen Färbung oder weltanschaulichen Grundhaltung miteinander konkurrierenden Presseerzeugnissen existiert, während im Bereich des Rundfunks sowohl aus technischen Gründen als auch mit Rücksicht auf den aussergewöhnlich großen finanziellen Aufwand für die Veranstaltung von Rundfunkdarbietungen die Zahl der Träger solcher Veranstaltungen verhältnismäßig Klein bleiben muß'. *Das Rundfunkurteil ('Erstes Fernsehurteil') vom 28. Februar 1961*, BVerfGE, 12/205. The relevant section of this law is reproduced in H. Kleinsteuber, *Rundfunk-*

Appendices

politik in der Bundesrepublik, Opladen: Leske Verlag, 1982, pp. 127–31, p. 129.
2. 'Die Tätigkeit der Rundfunkanstalten vollzieht sich im öffentlichen Bereich. Die Rundfunkanstalten stehen in öffentlicher Verantwortung, nehmen Aufgaben der öffentlichen Verwaltung wahr und erfüllen eine integrierende Funktion für das Staatsganze. Ihre Tätigkeit ist nicht gewerblicher oder beruflicher Art'. *Mehrwertsteuer Urteil vom 27. Juli 1971*, BVerfGE, 57/295. The relevant section of this law is reproduced in H. Kleinsteuber, *Rundfunkpolitik in der Bundesrepublik*, Opladen: Leske Verlag, 1982, pp. 131–5, p. 131.
3. 'Artikel 5 Absatz 2 GG ['Grundgesetz'] fordert für die Veranstaltung privater Rundfunksendungen eine gesetzliche Regelung, in der Vorkehrungen zur Gewährleistung der Freiheit des Rundfunks zu treffen sind. Diese Notwendigkeit besteht auch dann, wenn die durch Knappheit der Sendefrequenzen und den hohen finanziellen Aufwand für die Veranstaltung von Rundfunksendungen bedingte Sondersituation des Rundfunks im Zuge der modernen Entwicklung entfällt'. *FRAG Urteil des Bundesverfassungsgerichts vom 16. Juni 1981*, 1 BvL 89/78. The relevant section of this law is reproduced in H. Kleinsteuber, *Rundfunkpolitik in der Bundesrepublik*, Opladen: Leske Verlag, 1982, p. 135.
4. 'Das Niedersächsische Landesrundfunkgesetz vom 23 Mai 1984 ist in seinen Grundlinien mit dem Grundgesetz vereinbar'.
5. 'Solange und soweit die Wahrnehmung der genannten Aufgaben durch den öffentlichen-rechtlichen Rundfunk wirksam gesichert ist, erscheint es gerechtfertigt, an die Breite des Programmangebots und die Sicherung gleichgewichtiger Vielfalt im privaten Rundfunk nicht gleich hohe Anforderungen zu stellen wie im öffentlich-rechtlichen Rundfunk'. *Urteil des Bundesverfassungsgerichts vom 4 November 1986*, 1 BvF 1/84. This law is reproduced in *Media Perspektiven Dokumentation*, 4/1986, pp. 213–47. For an evaluation of this law in English see K. Berg, 'The Fourth TV Judgement of the Federal Constitutional Court, *EBU Review* vol. XXXVIII, no. 3, May 1987, pp. 37–43.

Appendix 3

New regulations for broadcasting adopted by the Länder

Land	Laws	Model adopted
Rhineland-Palatinate	Dec. 1980: Cable Law	External pluralism
	June 1986: Broadcasting Law	External pluralism
Bavaria	November 1984: Media Experimentation Law	External pluralism
Berlin	July 1984: Cable Law	External pluralism
North-Rhine Westphalia	Dec. 1983: Cable Law	Internal pluralism
	January 1987: Media Law	Mixed 'twin pillar' model
Lower Saxony	May 1984: Broadcasting Law (subsequently revised Oct. 1987)	Mixed model with bias towards external pluralism
Schleswig-Holstein	Nov. 1984: Broadcasting Law	Mixed transition model – leading to external pluralism
Baden-Württemberg	Dec. 1984/Dec. 1985: Media Law	External pluralism upon attainment of threshold of three private channels
Saarland	Nov. 1984/August 1987: Broadcasting Law	External pluralism with certain safeguards
Hamburg	Dec. 1985/Nov. 1987: Media Law/Broadcasting Law	Mixed model with elements of external pluralism
Bremen	June/July 1985: Law for retransmission of outside broadcasts	Mixed model
Hessen	Jan. 1987: Law for retransmission of outside broadcasts	Mixed model

Appendices

Source: The texts of these laws are published in *Media Perspektiven. Dokumentation*, I–IV/1987 and 1/1988.

Glossary

Abonnement	subscription
AKK	Anstalt für Kabelkommunikation or 'Authority for Cable Communication' (Ludwigshafen)
Altverleger	old (established pre-war) publishers
APF	Aktuelle Presse Fernsehen – a company of over 160 publishers (dominated by the Springer concern), with a stake in the SAT 1 commercial satellite television channel
ARD	Arbeitsgemeinschaft der öffentlich-rechtlichen Rundfunkanstalten in der Bundesrepublik Deutschland or 'Association of Public Service Broadcasters in West Germany' (the public-service 'network')
Ausgabe	edition
Außenkontrolle	external control (regulatory body external to broadcasting organisations)
Außenpluralismus	external pluralism (overall pluralism resulting from multiplicity of channels)
Basic Law	the name given to the West German Constitution of 1949
BDZV	Bundesverband Deutscher Zeitungsverleger or 'Federal Association of German Newspaper Publishers' (the interest group of the West German newspaper publishers)
Bezirksausgabe(n)	local edition(s) (see 'Nebenausgabe')
Binnenkontrolle	internal control (regulatory body within the public-service corporation)
Binnenpluralismus	internal pluralism (pluralism within channels and programmes)
Boulevardblatt	'boulevard' paper, a popular newspaper sold on the street
BR	Bayerischer Rundfunk or the 'Bavarian Broadcasting Service', public-service broadcasting corporation
Bund	the West German federation, or central state authority

Glossary

Bundespost	Federal Post Office (the Post, Telegraph and Telecommunications authority or PTT – with its own Minister, the Bundespostminister)
Bundesrat	upper house of the West German parliament (consisting of representatives of the Länder)
Bundestag	lower house of the West German parliament
Bundesverfassungsgericht	Federal Constitutional Court (the highest court in the Federal Republic and the pinnacle of the country's highly developed system of judicial review)
CDU	Christlich-Demokratische Union or 'Christian Democrat Union' (i.e. the German Conservative Party)
CSU	Christlich-Soziale Union or 'Christian Social Union' (the CDU's Bavarian sister party)
DBS	direct broadcasting (by) satellite
DDP	Deutscher Depeschendienst or 'German Dispatches Service' (West German news agency)
Deutscher Presserat	German Press Council
DFS	Deutsches Fernsehen or 'German Television' (the so-called 'first channel' otherwise known as 'ARD')
DGB	Deutscher Gewerkschaftsbund or 'German Trade Union Federation'
DG Bank	Deutsche Genossenschaftsbank
DJU	Deutsche Journalisten Union or 'German Journalists' Union'
DJV	Deutscher Journalisten-Verband or 'German Journalists' Association'
DLF	Deutschlandfunk or 'Radio Germany' (one of the two national radio stations)
DNVP	Deutschnationale Volkspartei or 'German National Peoples Party' – Weimar extreme conservatives
DPA	Deutsche Presse-Agentur or 'German Press Agency'
Drei SAT (3SAT)	public-service satellite television channel mounted by the ZDF with Austrian and Swiss public broadcasting corporations
DW	Deutsche Welle (literally the 'German Airwave', one of the two national radio stations)
ECS 1	European communications satellite (used for satellite broadcasting)
Eins Plus	public-service satellite television service mounted by the ARD
EK–IUK	Enquête-Kommission – Informations- und Kommunikationstechnologien or 'Commission of Inquiry

Glossary

	into Information and Communication Technologies
EKM	Experten-Kommission Neue Medien or 'Expert Commission for New Media' (Baden-Württemberg)
FAZ	*Frankfurter Allgemeine Zeitung*
FDP	Freie Demokratische Partei or 'Free Democratic Party' (West German Liberal Party)
Fernsehrat	television council (i.e. the 'broadcasting council' of the ZDF)
Feuilleton	Cultural, artistic and intellectual section of newspaper
Finanzausgleich	financial equalisation scheme (between different sized broadcasting corporations)
GDZV	Gesamtverband Deutscher Zeitungsverleger or 'General Association of German Newspaper Publishers' (the interest group of the 'licenced press')
Generalanzeiger	provincial commercial mass-circulation newspaper
Genossenschaft	cooperative
GEZ	Gebühreneinzugszentrale or 'Licence-Fee Office'
Gleichschaltung	'coordination' within the Nazi order
Grundgesetz	the Basic Law (see above)
Hauptausgabe(n)	main edition(s)
Heeresgruppenzeitungen	'army-group newspapers' produced by the Allies
Heimatpresse	small town press
Heimatzeitung	local newspaper
HR	Hessischer Rundfunk or the 'Hessian Broadcasting Service', public-service broadcasting corporation for the mid-German Land of Hessen
IG Druck und Papier	German print workers' union
Impressum	obligatory section of newspaper carrying details of the printer, publisher, editors and journalists
Initiativezeitung (blatt)	publication by single-issue organisations
Intelsat-V	communications satellite upon which the Bundespost rented a number of channels
Intendant(en)	director-generals of the public-service broadcasting corporations
Kampfblatt	agitprop paper
'Kleinstaaterei'	provincial particularism and rivalry (between the Länder)
KMP	Kabel-Media Programmgesellschaft or 'Cable-Media Programming Company' (see next entry)

Glossary

KMP musicbox	private commercial satellite television channel (jointly owned by the Munich publisher Wolfgang Fisher, Bauer and Burda)
Kopfblatt	main edition (Hauptausgabe); parent paper'
KPD	Kommunistische Partei Deutschlands or 'Communist Party of Germany'
KtK	Kommission für den Ausbau des technischen Kommunikationssystems or 'Commission for the Development of the Technical Communications System'
Land (pl. Länder)	West German federal state (i.e. a region or province)
'Machtwende'	the change of power in Bonn of 1982 (from SPD/FDP to CDU/CSU/FDP)
MATV	Master antenna television, the term used to describe a cable network limited to a single aerial serving a single building or housing estate; in West Germany, typically serving an apartment block.
Ministerpräsidenten	prime minister(s) (i.e. heads of government) of the Länder
Mitbestimmung	'co-determination', management participation by employees
MPK	Münchener Pilotgesellschaft für Kabelkommunikation or 'Munich Pilot Company for Cable Communication'
NDR	Norddeutscher Rundfunk or the 'North of Germany Broadcasting Service', public-service broadcasting corporation for the Länder of Schleswig-Holstein, Hamburg and Lower Saxony
Nebenausgabe(n)	supplementary local edition (multiple editions)
NSDAP	Nationalsozialistische Deutsche Arbeiterpartei or 'National Socialist German Workers Party' – the 'Nazi' Party
NWDR	Nordwestdeutscher Rundfunk or the 'North West German Broadcasting Service', early post-war broadcasting corporation for the North of Germany subsequently split up into NDR, WDR and SFB
Öffentlich-rechtlich	public-service
PKS	Programmgesellschaft für Kabel und Satellitenrundfunk or 'Programming Company for Cable and Satellite Broadcasting' (in 1988 Leo Kirch bought a controlling stake of this company, which has an important stake in the SAT 1 channel)

Glossary

Programmbeirat	programme advisory council (in the NDR and WDR)
Proporz	the principle of proportionality or 'proportional representation' (e.g. in political appointments)
Publikumszeitschrift	popular illustrated magazine
publizistische Einheiten	independent editorial units
RB	Radio Bremen, the radio and television broadcasting corporation serving the north German city-state of Bremen
Redaktion	editorial office (or team)
RFFU	'Rundfunk-Fernseh-Film-Union' or 'Radio, Television and Film Workers' Union'
RIAS, Berlin	'Rundfunk im Amerikanischen Sektor', or 'Radio in the American Sector (Berlin)'. A radio station established by the Americans
RTL Plus	private commercial satellite television channel (in which the Bertelsmann concern has an important share)
Rundfunkrat	broadcasting council (socially representative regulatory body)
SAT 1	private commercial satellite television channel (in which the Springer group has an important share)
'Scene'-blatt	publication of the 'alternative scene'
SDR	Süddeutscher Rundfunk or the 'South German Broadcasting Service', public-service broadcasting corporation for the Land of Baden-Württemberg
SFB	Sender Freies Berlin or the 'Free Berlin Broadcasting Service', public-service broadcasting corporation for the city-state of West Berlin
SMATV	satellite master antenna television, a form of MATV (see above), where the television signals are received by a satellite 'dish' antenna rather than by an aerial from a terrestrial transmitter
SPD	Sozialdemokratische Partei Deutschlands or 'Social Democratic Party of Germany' (i.e. German Labour Party)
SR	Saarländischer Rundfunk or the 'Saarland Broadcasting Service', public-service broadcasting corporation for the Land of Saarland
Staatsferne	the principle of independence from the state (i.e. of the broadcasters)

Glossary

Staatsvertrag	inter-state (i.e. Inter-Land) treaty (this kind of law has special relevance to broadcasting regulation). Plural form: Staatsverträge
Stadtmagazine	metropolitan 'alternative' magazine
Stadtzeitung	metropolitan 'alternative' newspaper
Standortpolitik	policies to attract inward investment and, in this context, local and regional measures to favour location of expanding media industries
SWF	Südwestfunk or 'South West Broadcasters', a public-service broadcasting corporation covering parts of the Rhineland-Palatinate and Baden-Württemberg
Tagesschau	daily ARD television news programme
Tagespresse	daily press
Tageszeitung	daily newspaper
Tendenz	the general editorial orientation of a newspaper
Tendenzschutz	the privileged right of newspaper proprietors to determine the editorial (including political) orientation of their publications
TV SAT	West German DBS satellite
Überregionale Zeitung	newspaper with a supra-regional readership
VDZV	Verein Deutscher Zeitungsverleger or 'Association of German Newspaper Publishers' (the interest group of the 'old publishers')
'Verflechtung'	interlocking web of interests (e.g. capital integration, interpenetration of ownership, business/political links, etc.)
Verwaltungsrat	administrative council of the public-service broadcasting corporations
Vielfalt	the principle of pluralistic 'diversity'
WAZ group	*Westdeutsche Allgemeine Zeitung* group (of newspaper publishers)
WDR	Westdeutscher Rundfunk or the 'West of Germany Broadcasting Service', public-service broadcasting corporation for the Land of North-Rhine Westphalia
ZAW	Zentralausschuß der Werbewirtschaft or 'Central Committee of the Advertising Industry'
ZDF	Zweites Deutsches Fernsehen or 'Second German Television', public-service broadcasting corporation producing the second national public-service channel
Zeitung(en)	newspaper(s)

Chronology

Note: For the sake of simplicity, the following chronology leaves out the dates of the many individual Land laws and 'Staatsverträge' on the press and broadcasting, unless they are held to mark a crucial turning-point in media development (see Appendix 3).

The Press Sector

12 May 1945	Law no. 191 and 'Information (lit: news) control' regulation ('Nachrichtenkontroll-Vorschrift') no. 1 of the Military Government of Germany deny to the defeated Germans the right to use any form of public communication without a licence.
June 1945	The Soviets issue the first newspaper licences.
July 1945	The Americans issue their first newspaper licences.
August 1945	The French issue their first newspaper licences.
January 1946	The British issue their first newspaper licences.
18 June 1948	The currency reform unleashes a wave of fierce competition among the licenced publishers.
23 May 1949	Basic Law promulgated.
August 1949	First federal elections. Adenauer elected Chancellor.
18 August 1949	Decision of the zonal news agencies to merge and found the Deutsche Presse-Agentur.
1 September 1949	The Arbeitsgemeinschaft für Pressefragen e. V. of the 'Altverleger' adopts the name of the Weimar publishers' association, namely Verein Deutscher Zeitungsverleger (VDZV). On the very same day, the various organisations of the licenced publishers establish Der Gesamtverband der Deutschen Zeitungsverleger e. V. (GDVZ).
21 September 1949	Law no. 5 of the Allied High Commission 'concerning the press and broadcasting' lifts compulsory licencing. The 'Altverleger' can return to business.
10 December 1949	Foundation of the Deutscher Journalisten-Verband (DJV).
1 April 1951	Foundation of the Berufsgruppe der Journalisten und Schriftsteller in der IG Druck und Papier (fore-

331

Chronology

	runner of the Deutsche Journalisten Union – DJU).
19 July 1952	Enactment of the first Betriebsverfassungsgesetz (a subsequent one was enacted on 15 January 1972) containing the 'Tendenzschutz' for the publishers of the press.
May–December 1952	Intermittent strikes in the press sector in protest against the 'Tendenzschutz'.
15 July 1954	The VDZV of the 'Altverleger' and the GDZV of the licensed publishers merge to form Der Bundesverband Deutscher Zeitungsverleger (BDZV).
20 November 1956	Foundation of the Deutsche Presserat.
October 1962	The *Spiegel* Affair' breaks out. Augstein and Ahlers arrested, the *Spiegel* offices searched.
May 1965	The Federal Constitutional Court rules that there had been no treasonable offence committed by *Spiegel* publisher Augstein or journalist Ahlers.
25 September 1967	The Michel Report is produced. It rejects the publishers claims that broadcast advertising is detrimental to the press.
14 June 1968	The Günther Report is produced. It recommends a catalogue of measures against press-concentration.
25 July 1974	Draft 'press framework law' is produced. This draft foresees a considerable expansion of journalists' rights. However, this draft is subsequently dropped, because of the opposition from the publishers.
28 June 1976	Amendment of competition law to control more strictly mergers and takeovers in the press sector.
February–March 1978	Serious strike action by the print workers over the introduction of new technologies.

The Broadcasting Sector

4 May 1945	The last Nazi broadcasting station in Hamburg falls into the hands of the British. It continues operations as 'Radio Hamburg', around which the NWDR is later formed.
12 May 1945	'Radio Munich' (later the BR) begins operations in the American zone. These two stations are soon followed by others all over Germany.
1 January 1948	By Verordnung 118 of the British military government the NWDR is the first broadcasting station to be returned to full German control. During 1948, all

Chronology

	the others pass into German control.
5 August 1950	Foundation of the ARD.
1953–6	Break up of the NWDR into the NDR, the SFB and the WDR.
20 February 1953	First draft federal law produced by Adenauer government seeking to establish a federal broadcasting station. This draft is subsequently dropped in face of very considerable opposition.
27 March 1953	The ARD members agree to operate a joint network to produce the first national television channel, DFS or 'ARD'.
19–20 June 1958	ARD members announce their intention to establish a second national television channel.
8 December 1958	Establishment of the Freies Fernsehen GmbH, by publishers and industrial interests with plans to launch a private commercial television channel.
19–20 June 1959	Ministerpräsidentenkonferenz at Kiel produces a proposal of its own for a second public-service television channel.
30 September 1959	Adenauer government counters this move by producing yet another draft law to establish a second national television channel. The latter promises to be 'Adenauer TV'.
29 June 1960	The above law is enacted by the Bundestag.
19 August 1960	SPD Hamburg is the first Land to appeal this law to the Federal Constitutional Court. Others soon follow suit.
28 February 1961	The 'First TV Ruling' of the Federal Constitutional Court rules against this second more serious attempt by Adenauer to introduce a Bonn-directed television channel and confirms the sole jurisdiction of the Länder for broadcasting.
6 June 1961	The Ministerpräsidenten sign a 'Staatsvertrag' in Stuttgart to establish the ZDF.
22 September 1964	The BR is the first public-service broadcasting organisation to open a 'Third Channel'. It is followed by the HR in October. Others soon follow suit.
27 July 1971	The 'VAT Ruling' of the Federal Constitutional Court confirms the public-service structure of broadcasting in West Germany. It rejects the federal government's attempt to subject payment of the licence-fee to VAT.

333

Chronology

21 January 1972	The CSU produce an amendment to the Bavarian broadcasting law in a naked attempt to gain greater control of the BR.
1 March 1972	The above amendment is passed by Bavarian state parliament against SPD opposition. However, a wave of popular protest follows, leading to demands for a plebiscite. As a result the CSU is forced to reconsider its goal and eventually back down.
8 May 1973	An amendment to the Bavarian state constitution is enacted which explicitly enshrines the principle of public-service broadcasting in Bavaria.
3–4 July 1979	Lower Saxony withdraws from the NDR 'Staatsvertrag'. This follows the CDU election victory of 1978 in that state.
12 July 1979	CDU Ministerpräsident of Lower Saxony, Ernst Albrecht, announces plans to break the SPD's control of broadcasting in northern Germany by founding another 'NDR' for his state and neighbouring CDU Schleswig-Holstein.
28 May 1980	The Bundesverwaltungsgericht rules against Albrecht's withdrawal from NDR 'Staatsvertrag'. As the result, a compromise 'Staatsvertrag' is drafted between Hamburg, Schleswig-Holstein and Lower Saxony during the summer and autumn of 1980.
1 January 1981	The compromise NDR 'Staatsvertrag' becomes law. The 'NDR crisis' is finally over (for the time being at least).

The New Media

27 February 1974	The KtK is established in Bonn to explore the question of the future development of the West German telecommunications system.
27 January 1976	The KtK produces its 'telecommunications report', recommending the establishment of a limited number of cable pilot-projects.
1–2 February 1978	The Ministerpräsidenten agree on the sites for four cable pilot-projects.
12 April 1980	The French and German governments sign an agreement jointly to construct a DBS series. The two German DBS satellites, called 'TV SAT', will eventually provide five new television channels and a new radio channel.
12–14 November	The Ministerpräsidenten agree on the financial-

Chronology

1980	arrangements and mode of evaluation of the cable pilot-projects.
27 November 1980	The Rhineland-Palatinate passes a deregulatory media law for the Ludwigshafen pilot-project. This sets the pattern for a series of deregulatory CDU/CSU media laws across the country (see Appendix 3).
16 June 1981	The FRAG Judgement by the Federal Constitutional Court eases the legal brakes on the introduction of commercial broadcasting. It recognises that, in the cable and satellite age, there will no longer exist a 'scarcity of frequencies'.
March 1983	Bundespostminister Schwarz-Schilling (CDU) launches a massive programme to cable the country.
August 1983	The CDU/CSU/FDP coalition cabinet adopts a plan to develop a German communications satellite system called 'Kopernikus'. This will provide seven further television channels.
1 January 1984	The (CDU) Ludwigshafen pilot-project opens.
2 January 1984	The German-language private commercial television channel 'RTL Plus' starts broadcasting 'off-air' from Luxemburg, where it escapes West German regulation, into southern Germany. In August it transfers to ECS 1 (also, see following entry).
23 February 1984	The Ministerpräsidenten allocate the two television channels rented by the Bundespost on ECS 1: one goes to the public-service 'Drei SAT' channel mounted by ZDF; the other goes to the private commercial 'publishers' channel SAT 1, franchised in and up-linked from the Rhineland-Palatinate (CDU).
1 April 1984	The (CSU) Munich pilot-project opens.
15 May 1984	Lower Saxony (CDU) passes the first deregulatory Land law which allows private commercial broadcasters to operate generally (in other words, on more than an 'experimental' basis).
May 1984	Essen party conference of the SPD adopts a more pragmatic approach, recognising the futility of continued 'fundamentalist' opposition to commercial broadcasting. The SPD resolves to fight instead for strict guarantees for the public-service model.
23 October 1984	The SPD parliamentary party decides to take the Lower Saxony law to the Federal Constitutional

335

Chronology

	Court. This action effectively becomes a test of all CDU/CSU deregulatory media legislation.
1 June 1985	The (SPD) Dortmund pilot-project opens.
10 July 1985	The Bundespost liberalises SMATV regulations.
28 August 1985	The (CDU) Berlin pilot-project opens.
29 March 1986	The second public-service satellite television channel Eins Plus, mounted by the ARD, goes on air broadcasting from Intelsat-V.
25 June 1986	The Bundespost launches a new federal programme 'to improve the general conditions surrounding the private broadcasting market'. The cable programme's budget is dramatically increased. Cable installation is liberalised. This is followed up with the release of numerous terrestrial 'low power' frequencies by the Bundespost.
4 November 1986	Federal Constitutional Court finally rules on the Lower Saxony law (see above). It recommends the adoption of the principle of a 'dual broadcasting system'. This breaks the political deadlock over regulatory reform.
1–3 April 1987	As a result, the Ministerpräsidenten sign a 'Staatsvertrag' for the reform of the broadcasting system, adopting the 'dual broadcasting' model.
1 December 1987	The 'Staatsvertrag' becomes law. The 'dual broadcasting system' is legally established.

Bibliography

General

Haler, M., *Basic Law Guarantees Freedom of Opinion – Mass Media in the FRG*, Bonn: Inter Nationes, 1982
Kepplinger, H.-M., *Massenkommunikation*, Stuttgart: Teubner Studienskripte, 1982
La Roche, W. and Maassen, L., *Massenmedien. Fakten – Formen – Funktionen in der Bundesrepublik Deutschland*, Heidelberg: C.F. Müller Juristischer Verlag, 1983
Lehr, W. and Berg, K., *Rundfunk und Presse in Deutschland – Rechtsgrundlagen der Massenmedien – Texte*, Mainz: von Hase und Koehler Verlag, 1971
Mahle, W. and Richter, R., *Communication Policy in the Federal Republic of Germany*, Paris: Unesco Press, 1974
Meyn, H., *Massenmedien in der Bundesrepublik Deutschland*, Berlin: Colloquium Verlag, 1979
Sandford, J., *The Mass Media of the German-Speaking Countries*, London: Oswald Wolff, 1976

Press

Abel, K., *Presselenkung im NS-Staat. Eine Studie zur Geschichte der Publizistik in der nationalsozialistischen Zeit*, Berlin: Colloquium Verlag/ Wissenschaftsverlag Volker Spiess 1987 (2nd edn)
Arbeitsgruppe Alternativpresse, *Riesengroßes Verzeichnis aller alternativen Zeitungen*, Bonn: Arbeitsgruppe Alternativpresse, 1981 (also, see the 'Extra-Ausgabe' of 1982)
Arens, K., *Manipulation: Kommunikationspsychologische Untersuchung mit Beispielen aus Zeitungen des Springer-Konzerns*, Berlin: Wissenschaftsverlag Volker Spiess
Brokmeier, P. (ed.), *Kapitalismus und Pressefreiheit. Am Beispiel Springer*, Frankfurt/Main: Europäische Verlagsanstalt, 1969
Bruseke, F. and Grosse-Ötringhaus, H.-M., *Blätter von unten; Alternativzeitungen in der Bundesrepublik Deutschland*, Offenbach: Verlag 2000 GmbH., 1981
Bundeszentrale für politische Bildung, *Die Presse in der deutschen Medienlandschaft*, Themenheft 6, Bonn: Bundeszentrale für politische

Bibliography

Bildung, 1985

Fischer, H.-D., *Parteien und Presse in Deutschland seit 1945*, Bremen: Schünemann Universitätsverlag, 1971

——, *Reeducations- und Pressepolitik unter britischem Besatzungstatus. Die Zonenzeitung 'Die Welt' 1946–1950*, Düsseldorf: Droste Verlag, 1978

Funke, K.-D., *Innere Pressefreiheit. Zu Problemen der Organisation von Journalisten* (Unter Mitarbeit von W. Brede; von der IG Druck und Papier zur Mediengewerkschaft), Pullach/Munich: Verlag Dokumentation, 1972

Giebel, K., *Mediendschungel. Eine kritische Bestandsaufnahme*, Stuttgart: Bleicher Verlag, 1983

Greuner, R., *Lizenzpresse – Auftrag und Ende. Der Einfluß der angloamerikanischen Besatzungspolitik auf die Wiedererrichtung eines imperialistischen Pressewesens in Westdeutschland*, Berlin (East): Rütten und Loening, 1962

Gross, H.-W., *Die Deutsche Presse-Agentur* Frankfurt/Main: Haag & Herchen, 1982

Gross, R., *Presserecht. Einführung in Grundzüge und Schwerpunkte des deutschen Presserechts*, Wiesbaden: Deutscher-Fachschriften Verlag, 1987 (new edn)

Guratzch, D., *Macht durch Organisation. Die Grundlegung des Hugenbergschen Presseimperiums*, Wiesbaden: Westdeutscher Verlag, 1974

Hagemann, W., *Publizistik im Dritten Reich. Ein Beitrag zur Methodik der Massenführung*, Hamburg: Hansischer Gildenverlag – Joachim Heitmann & Co., 1948

Hale, O., *The Captive Press in the Third Reich*, Princeton: Princeton University Press, 1974 (original German edn: *Presse in der Zwangsjacke 1933–45*, Düsseldorf: Droste Verlag, 1965)

Hermann, E., *Zur Theorie und Praxis der Presse in der sowjetischen Besatzungszone Deutschlands*, Berlin: Colloquium Verlag, 1963

Hoffmann-Riem, W., *Innere Pressefreiheit als politische Aufgabe*, Neuwied and Darmstadt: Luchterhand, 1979

Holtz-Bacha, C., *Mitspracherechte für Journalisten – Redaktionsstatuten in Presse und Rundfunk*, Cologne: Studienverlag Hayit, 1986 (Serie Kommunikation)

Hurwitz, H., *Die Stunde Null der deutschen Presse*, Cologne: Verlag Wissenschaft und Politik, Berend von Nottbeck, 1972

Inter Nationes, *Press Laws. Documents on Politics and Society in the Federal Republic of Germany*, Bonn: Inter Nationes, 1980

Jansen, B. and Klönne, A. (eds.), *Imperium Springer: Macht und Manipulation*, Cologne: Pahl-Rugenstein Verlag, 1968

Klemm, P., *Machtkampf einer Minderheit; der Tarifkonflikt in der Druckindustrie*, Cologne: Informedia Verlags Gmbh, 1984

Bibliography

Koszyk, K., *Pressepolitik für Deutsche 1945–1949*, Part IV of *Geschichte der deutschen Presse*, ed. B. Sösemann, Berlin: Colloquium Verlag, 1986

Leithauser, J., *Journalisten zwischen zwei Welten. Die Nachkriegsjahre der Berliner Presse*, Berlin: Colloquium Verlag, 1960

Liedtke, R., *Die verschenkte Presse – die Geschichte der Lizenzierung von Zeitungen nach 1945*, Berlin: Verlag für Ausbildung und Studium in der Elefanten Presse, 1982

Löffler, M., *Presserecht*, Vol. 1: *Die Landespressegesetze der Bundesrepublik Deutschland mit Textanhang*; Vol. 2: *Geschichte und Theorie des Presserechts*, Munich: Beck'sche C.H. Verlag, 1983 (new edn)

Matz, E., *Die Zeitungen der US-Armee für die deutsche Bevölkerung (1944–46)*, Studien zur Publizistik, Bremer Reihe, Band 12. Münster: Verlag C.J. Fahle, 1969

Müller, H.-D., *Press Power: A Study of Axel Springer*, trans. J. Cole, London: MacDonald, 1969 (original German edn: *Der Springer-Konzern: Eine kritische Studie*, Munich: R. Piper & Co. Verlag, 1968)

Ossario-Capella, C., *Der Zeitungsmarkt in der Bundesrepublik Deutschland* Frankfurt/Main: Athenäum, 1972

Otzen, K., *Lizenzpresse, Altverleger und Politik. Kontroverse um die 'Kieler Nachrichten' in den Jahren 1945–1952* (Duisburger Studien), St Augustin: Hans Richarz Publikation Service, 1980

Pätzold, U. and Schmidt, H. (eds.), *Solidarität gegen Abhängigkeit. Mediengewerkschaft.*, Darmstadt and Neuwied: Hermann Luchterhand Verlag, 1973

Pross, H. (ed.), *Deutsche Presse seit 1945*, Berne/Munich/Vienna: Scherz Verlag, 1965

Richter, R., *Kommunikationsfreiheit = Verlegerfreiheit. Zur kommunikationspolitik der Zeitungsverleger in der Bundesrepublik Deutschland 1945–69* (Dortmunder Beiträge zur Zeitungsforschung), Pullach/Munich: Verlag Dokumentation, 1973

Ring, W., *Deutsches Presse- und Rundfunkrecht. Textsammlung mit Anmerkungen, Verweisungen und Sachregister*, Munich: F. Rehm Verlag, 1986

Schenk, U., *Nachrichtenagenturen*, Berlin: Vistas Verlag, 1985

Schoelzel, S., *Die Pressepolitik in der französischen Besatzungszone 1945–1949* (Veröffentlichung der Kommission des Landtags für die Geschichte des Landes Rheinland-Pfalz), Mainz: Hase Koehler Verlag, 1986

Schoenbaum, D., *The Spiegel Affair*, Garden City, New York: Doubleday, 1968

Schöps, J., *Die Spiegel Affäre des Franz Josef Strauss* (Spiegel-Buch no. 40), Reinbek: Rowohlt Taschenbuch Verlag, 1983

Schulze, V., *Der Bundesverband Deutscher Zeitungsverleger*, Düsseldorf: Droste Verlag, 1985

Bibliography

Wallraff, G., *Der Aufmacher. Der Mann, der bei Bild Hans Esser war*, Cologne: Verlag Kiepenhauer und Witsch, 1977
——, *Zeugen der Anklage: Die 'Bild'-Beschreibung wird fortgesetzt*, Cologne: Verlag Kiepenhauer und Witsch, 1979
——, *Bild-Störung. Ein Handbuch*, Cologne: Verlag Kiepenhauer und Witsch, 1985
Weichler, K., *Gegendruck. Lust und Frust der alternativen Presse*, Reinbek/Hamburg: Rowohlt Verlag, 1983
Wulf, J. (ed.), *Presse und Funk im Dritten Reich. Eine Dokumentation*, Gütersloh: S. Mohn Verlag, 1964

Media Concentration

Arndt, R., *Die Konzentration in der Presse und die Problematik des Verleger-Fernsehens*, Berlin: Alfred Metzner Verlag, 1967
Aufermann, J., Lange, B.-P. and Zerdick, A., 'Pressekonzentration in der BRD: Untersuchungsprobleme, Ursachen und Erscheinungsformen', in J. Aufermann, H. Bohrmann and R. Sülzer (eds.), *Gesellschaftliche Kommunikation und Information, Forschungsrichtungen und Problemenstellungen. Ein Arbeitsbuch zur Massenkommunikation*, Vol. 1, Frankfurt/Main: Athenäum, 1973
Bericht der Bundesregierung über die Lage von Presse und Rundfunk in der Bundesrepublik Deutschland. 1974, Bonn: Bundestags-Drucksache VII/2104, 1974
Bericht der Bundesregierung über die Lage von Presse und Rundfunk in der Bundesrepublik Deutschland.'Medienbericht' (1978), Bonn: Bundestags-Drucksache VIII/2264, 1978
Diederichs, H.H., *Konzentration in den Massenmedien. Systemischer Überblick zur Situation in der BRD*, Munich: Carl Hanser Verlag, 1973
——, 'Daten zur Konzentration der Publikumszeitschriften in der Bundesrepublik Deutschland im IV. Quartal 1986', *Media Perspektiven*, 8/1987, pp. 496–506
Farin, K., and Zwingmann, H.-J., *Pressekonzentration. Daten. Fakten. Trends*, Ettlingen: Doku-Verlag, 1981
Günther-Bericht, *Schlußbericht der Kommission zur Untersuchung der Gefährdung der wirtschaftlichen Existenz von Presseunternehmen und der Folgen der Konzentration für die Meinungsfreiheiten in der Bundesrepublik – Pressekommission*, Bonn: Bundestags-Drucksache V/3122 vom 3. Juli 1968
IG Druck und Papier, Landesbezirk NRW, *Pressekonzentration in Nordrhein-Westfalen*, Düsseldorf: IG Druck und Papier, 1977
——, *Tendenzschutz und Pressekonzentration*, Stuttgart: IG Druck und Papier, 1971

Bibliography

Kisker K., Knoche, M. and Zerdick, A., *Wirtschaftskonjunktur und Pressekonzentration in der Bundesrepublik Deutschland* (Dortmunder Beiträge zur Zeitungsforschung), Munich: K.G. Sauer Verlag, 1979

Knoche, M., *Einführung in die Pressekonzentrationsforschung. Theoretische und empirische Grundlagen – Kommunikationspolitische Voraussetzungen*, Berlin: Wissenschaftsverlag Volker Spiess, 1978

——, 'Ansätze und Methoden der Konzentrationsforschung im Pressebereich', *Media Perspektiven*, 5/1979, pp. 288–300

——, 'Der Konzentrationsprozeß der Tages-Presse 1954–1978. Typenorientierte Einzellfallanalysen zum Wegfall Publizistischer Einheiten', *Media Perspektiven*, 10/1978, pp. 731–47

Kunert, W., *Pressekonzentration und Verfassungsrecht*, Berlin: Duncker und Humblot, 1971

Lerche, P., *Verfassungsrechtliche Fragen zur Pressekonzentration*, Berliner Abhandlungen zum Presserecht, Heft 14, Berlin: Duncker und Humblot, 1971

Moeschel, W., *Pressekonzentration und Wettbewerbsgesetz. Marktbeherrschung, unlauterer Wettbewerb und Sanierungsfusionen im Pressebereich*, Tübingen: Mohr Verlag, 1978

Röper, H., 'Daten zur Konzentration der Tagespresse in der BRD im I. Quartal 1987', *Media Perspektiven* 9/1987, pp. 563–3

Schütz, W., 'Deutsche Tagespresse', *Media Perspektiven*, 9/1987, pp. 585–97

In addition, numerous articles over the years in *Media Perspektiven* by H.H. Diederichs and W. Schütz.

The Broadcasting Sector

Arnold, W. (ed.), *Die elektronischen Medien*, Heidelberg: R. v. Decker & Co., F. Müller, 1984

Bausch, H., *Rundfunkpolitik nach 1945. Erster Teil 1945–62*, Vol. III of the series *Rundfunk in Deutschland*, ed. H. Bausch, Munich: Deutscher Taschenbuch Verlag (dtv.), 1980

——, *Rundfunkpolitik nach 1945. Zweiter Teil 1963–80*, Vol. IV of the series *Rundfunk in Deutschland*, ed. H. Bausch, Munich: Deutscher Taschenbuch Verlag (dtv.), 1980

Brack, H., Herrmann, G. and Hillig, H.-P., *Organisation des Rundfunks in der Bundesrepublik Deutschland 1948–62*, Hamburg: Verlag Hans-Bredow-Institut, 1962

Diller, A., *Rundfunkpolitik im Dritten Reich*, Vol. II of the series *Rundfunk in Deutschland*, ed. H. Bausch, Munich: Deutscher Taschenbuch Verlag (dtv.), 1980

Engler, J., 'Das Rundfunksystem der Bundesrepublik Deutschland', in

Bibliography

Hans-Bredow-Institut/Hamburg (ed.), *Internationales Handbuch für Rundfunk und Fernsehen 1988/89*, Baden-Baden: Nomos Verlagsgesellschaft, 1988, pp. B70–87

von Gottberg, H., *Initiativen zur Errichtung kommerziellen Rundfunks*, Berlin: Wissenschaftsverlag Volker Spiess, 1979

Hans-Bredow-Institut/Hamburg (ed.), *Internationales Handbuch für Rundfunk und Fernsehen 1988/89*, Baden-Baden: Nomos Verlagsgesellschaft, 1988

Hessischer Rundfunk, *Radio und Fernsehen in der Bundesrepublik Deutschland*, Frankfurt/Main: Hessischer Rundfunk, June 1980

Hoffmann-Riem, W., *Redaktionsstatute im Rundfunk*, Baden-Baden: Nomos Verlagsgesellschaft, 1972

Inter Nationes, *Broadcasting Laws. Series: Documents on Politics and Society in the Federal Republic of Germany*, Bonn: Inter Nationes, 1984 (2nd edn)

Jank, K., *Die Rundfunkanstalten der Länder und des Bundes. Eine systematische Darstellung ihrer organisatorischen Grundlagen*, Berlin: Duncker und Humblot, 1967

Kleinsteuber, H., *Rundfunkpolitik in der Bundesrepublik*, Opladen: Leske Verlag & Budrich GmbH, 1982

Lerg, W., *Rundfunkpolitik in der Weimarer Republik*, Vol. I of the series *Rundfunk in Deutschland* ed. H. Bausch, Munich: Deutscher Taschenbuch Verlag (dtv.), 1980

——, and Steininger, R. (eds.), *Rundfunk und Politik 1923–73*, Berlin: Wissenschaftsverlag Volker Spiess, 1975

Maassen, L., *Der Kampf um den Rundfunk in Bayern. Rundfunkpolitik in Bayern 1945 bis 1973*, Berlin: Wissenschaftsverlag Volker Spiess, 1979

Mettler, B., *Demokratisierung und Kalter Krieg. Zur amerikanischen Informations- und Rundfunkpolitik in Westdeutschland 1945–49*, Berlin: Wissenschaftsverlag Volker Spiess, 1975

Noelle-Neumann, E., *Die Schweigespirale. Öffentliche Meinung – Unsere soziale Haut*, Munich: R. Piper & Co. Verlag, 1980

Pohle, H., *Der Rundfunk als Instrument der Politik. Zur Geschichte des deutschen Rundfunk von 1923–28*, Hamburg: Verlag Hans-Bredow-Institut, 1955

Riese, H.-P., *Der Griff nach der vierten Gewalt*, Cologne: Bund-Verlag, 1984

Ring, W.-D. (ed.), *Deutsches Presse- und Rundfunkrecht. Textsammlung mit Anmerkungen, Verweisungen und Sachregister*, Munich: Franz Rehm Verlag für Verwaltungspraxis, 1986

Ross, D., 'Der Rundfunk in Deutschland', in Hans-Bredow-Institut/Hamburg (ed.), *Internationales Handbuch für Rundfunk und Fernsehen*, Baden-Baden: Nomos Verlagsgesellschaft, 1986, p. B58

Bibliography

Seifert, J., 'Probleme der Parteien und Verbandskontrolle von Rundfunk- und Fernsehanstalten', in D. Prokop (ed.), *Massenkommunikationsforschung: 1 Produktion*, Frankfurt/Main: Fischer Taschenbuch Verlag, 1972
Sontheimer, K., 'Zum Problem der gesellschaftlichen Kontrolle des Rundfunks und seiner Organisation', in Gemeinschaftswerk der Evangelischen Publizistik, *Herrschaft und Kritik. Probleme der Rundfunkfreiheit*, Frankfurt/Main: Verlag Haus der Evangelischen Publizistik, 1974, pp. 48–77
Williams, A., *Broadcasting and Democracy in West Germany*, London: Bradford University Press/Crosby Lockwood Staples, 1976
Wulf, J. (ed.), *Presse und Funk im Dritten Reich. Eine Dokumentation*, Gütersloh: S. Mohn Verlag, 1964

The New Media

Bleuel, H.-P., *Die verkabelte Gesellschaft. Der Bürger im Netz neuer Technologien*, Munich: Kindler Verlag, 1984
Dyson, K. and Humphreys, P., *Broadcasting and New Media Policy in Western Europe: A Comparative Study of Technological Change and Public Policy*, London: Routledge and Kegan Paul, 1988
—— (eds.), *The Politics of the Communications Revolution in Western Europe*, London: Frank Cass, 1986
Ebinger, H., *Neue Medien. Strategien von Staat und Kapital*, Frankfurt/Main: Nachrichten-Verlags GmbH, 1983
Expertenkommission Neue Medien – EKM Baden-Württemberg, *Abschlußbericht*, 3 vols., Stuttgart: Kohlhammer, 1981
Hiegemann, S., *Kabel- und Satellitenfernsehen; die Entwicklung in der Bundesrepublik Deutschland unter politischen und inhaltlichen Aspekten*, Bonn: Bundeszentrale für politische Bildung, 1988
Holzer, H. and Betz, K., *Totale Bildschirm-Herrschaft? Staat, Kapital und Neue Medien*, Cologne: Pahl-Rugenstein Verlag, 1984
Humphreys, P., 'Satellite Broadcasting in West Germany' in Negrine, R. (ed.), *Satellite Broadcasting. The Politics and Implications of the New Media*, London: Routledge and Kegan Paul, 1988, pp. 107–43
Kleinsteuber, H. et al. (eds.), *Medien: Thema Kabelfernsehen*, Berlin: Wissenschaftsverlag Volker Spiess, 1980
Kubicek, H., *Kabel im Haus – Satellit überm Dach*, Reinbek/Hamburg: Rowohlt Taschenbuch Verlag, 1984
——, *Neue Informations- und Kommunikationstechniken. Die medienpolitische Diskussion über Kabelfernsehen und Breitbandverteilnetze – ein 'Nebenkriegsschauplatz' aus Arbeitnehmersicht?*, Stuttgart: Hauptvorstand der Gewerkschaft Öffentliche Dienste, Transport und Verkehr, 1984

Bibliography

Kühn, F. and Schmitt, W. (eds.), *Einsam, überwacht und arbeitlos: Technokraten verdaten unser Leben*, Stuttgart: Die Grünen, 1984

Landesregierung Rheinland-Pfalz, *Versuch mit Breitbandkabel. Zwischenbericht*, Mainz: 1985

Lang, U. (ed.), *Der verkabelte Bürger. Brauchen wir die neuen Medien?*, Freiburg/Breisgau: Dreisam Verlag, 1981

Luyken, G.-M., *Direktempfangbare Rundfunksatelliten: Erklärung, Kritik und Alternativen zu einem 'neuem Medium'*, Frankfurt/Main: Campus Verlag, 1985

Meyn, H., *Die neuen Medien. Neue Chancen und Risiken*, Berlin: Colloquium Verlag, 1984

Rau, J. and von Rüden, P. (eds.), *Die neuen Medien – Eine Gefahr für die Demokratie?*, Frankfurt/Main: Büchergilde Gütenberg, 1984

Schmidbauer, M., *Kabelfernsehen in der Bundesrepublik Deutschland*, Munich: K.G. Sauer Verlag, 1982

——, *Satellitenfernsehen für die Bundesrepublik Deutschland*, West Berlin: Wissenschaftsverlag Volker Spiess, 1983

Späth, L. (ed.), *Das Kabel. Anschluß an die Zukunft*, Bonn: Bonn Aktuell, 1981

Wenger, K., *Kommunikation und Medien in der Bundesrepublik Deutschland*, Munich: Ludiciun Verlag GmbH, 1988.

Witte, E., *Neue Fernsehnetze im Medienmarkt; die Amortisationsfähigkeit von Breitbandverteilsystemen*, Heidelberg: R.v. Decker's Verlag, G. Schenck, 1984

Index

Abendzeitung, 83–4, 111, 313, 318
Abonnement, 15, 69, 74, 78
Ackermann, Josef, 48
Adenauer, Konrad, 8, 38, 45, 63, 67, 96, 138, 155, 157–61, 162, 181, 184, 191, 306, 319
'Adenauer TV', 157–61, 162, 184, 191, 319
administrative council (broadcasters), *see* 'Verwaltungsrat'
advertisers (-ing), 15, 35, 36, 47, 69–71, 79–81, 88, 103, 157, 170, 173–5, 199, 200–1, 203, 204, 209, 218, 227, 235, 257–8, 260, 268, 273, 277–9, 289, 296
advisory council (ARD), *see* 'Fernsehbeirat'
Agence France Presse (AFP), 60, 62
Ahlers, Konrad, 72–3
Albrecht, Ernst, 182–4, 203, 242
Allied Press Service (APS), 33
Allies, 2, 3, 4, 24–42, 43, 44, 49, 52, 55, 60, 62, 65–6, 68, 76, 128–31, 132, 134–6, 139, 148, 153, 154, 155, 295–6, 298
  occupation, 2, 3, 5, 24–42, 62–4, 65–7, 79, 128–31, 137, 149, 155, 295–6, 298
anti-fascism, 25, 26, 29, 31, 131
anti-semitism, 19, 20, 21, 22, 23, 127
APF (Aktuelle Presse Fernsehen), 283–5
alternative press, 89, 117–23, 304
Alternativen, 89, 92, 117–23, 147, 178, 210–11
Altoner Nachrichten, 92–3
Altverleger, 24, 31, 34, 37, 39, 40–3, 45–6, 47, 51
Angriff, Der, 21
anti-communism, 29–30, 96–7, 302
Arbeitsgemeinschaft für Pressenfragen e.v., 45–6
ARD, 134, 140, 144, 148–52, 153, 155, 157, 159, 162, 164, 165, 166, 168, 169, 172–3, 175, 176, 181, 182, 190, 191, 223, 226, 234, 246, 260, 262–3, 276–8, 280, 288, 299, 311
army-group newspapers, *see* 'Heeresgruppenzeitungen'
Article 5 (Basic Law), 39, 53, 72, 104, 116, 132, 267, 320
Associated Press (AP), 60, 61
AtK-Presse, 199
Augstein, Rudolf, 73, 96, 316
Auskunftspflicht, 56, 133
Außenkontrolle, 216–17, 237–8, 250, 272
Außenpluralismus, 216–17, 226, 237–8, 244–6, 250, 272, 279, 323
authoritarian (-ism), 13, 15, 61, 65, 154, 159, 293–4

Bad Harzburg, 18
Baden-Württemberg, 55, 67, 129, 137, 203, 213, 214, 229–30, 262, 281
  new media legislation permitting commercial broadcasting, 244–5, 323
balance (editorial), 142, 154, 165, 205, 216–17, 237, 273
  see also 'duty of impartiality' *and* 'politicisation'
Basic Law (Grundgesetz), 1, 38, 39, 45, 53–4, 71, 72, 104, 107, 108, 116, 132–6, 141, 157, 161, 188, 190, 195, 239, 267, 293, 296, 299, 320–1
Bauer Group, 84, 85, 86, 248, 283–5, 316–17
Bavaria, 55, 67, 129, 138, 202, 203, 209, 248, 262, 281, 288, 290, 300, 309
Bavarian Broadcasting Service, *see* Bayerischer Rundfunk
Bavarian Constitutional Court, 178–9
Bavarian controversy (broadcasting), 177–80, 184, 191
Bavarian Higher Regional Court, 69
Bavarian plebiscite/referendum,

345

Index

179–80, 219
new media legislation permitting commercial broadcasting, 219–24, 244–6, 323
  see also 'cable, pilot-project, Munich'
Bayerischer Rundfunk (BR), 69, 129, 138, 140, 152, 169, 173, 175, 177, 178, 179, 180, 209, 218, 220, 221, 222, 223, 226, 246, 280, 300
Bayern-Kurier, 91
BBC (British), 129, 154, 169, 298, 301, 309
BDZV (Bundesverband Deutscher Zeitungsverleger), 43, 47–8, 54, 64, 69, 87, 100, 107, 108, 112, 116, 198–9, 217, 234, 282
Berlin, 30, 35, 36, 44, 53, 55, 67, 74, 78, 85, 92, 93, 96, 97, 117, 118, 119, 129, 137, 138, 153, 155, 183, 191, 214, 247–8, 281, 290
  crisis/blockade, 30, 35, 96
  new media legislation permitting commercial broadcasting, 224–7, 242, 323
  see also 'cable, pilot-project, Berlin'
  pilot-project (cable), 224–7
  Wall, 93
Berliner Morgenpost, 83, 85, 93, 313
Berliner Tageblatt, 16
Berliner Zeitung (BZ), 85, 93, 318
Berlusconi, Silvio, 310
Bertelsmann AG, 84, 85, 86, 90, 200, 234, 253, 281, 284–5, 287, 292, 312, 316–17
Beta Taurus, 223, 288
Betriebsverfassungsgesetz, 51, 65, 105
Bild am Sonntag, 85, 248, 313
Bild und Funk, 84, 316
Bild-Zeitung, 74, 83, 85, 87, 90, 93, 94, 95, 96, 97, 98, 200, 248, 286, 295, 297, 303, 313, 318
Binnenpluralismus, 141, 142, 237, 244–5, 250, 255, 272, 299, 323
  Binnenkontrolle, 141, 161, 168, 237, 272, 299
Bismarck, Count Otto von, 14, 15
Böll, Heinrich, 97
boulevard press, *see* 'Boulevardzeitung'
Boulevardzeitung, 15, 69, 79, 85, 317

Brandt, Willi, 101–2, 108, 110
Bravo, 84, 86, 316
Bredow, Hans, 125, 126, 148–9
Bremen, 39, 55, 67, 136, 153, 161, 183, 256, 259, 260, 262, 267, 277, 281, 290
  new media legislation permitting commercial broadcasting, 267, 323
Bremerhafen, 136
Bremerhafen 'compromise', 261
Brigitte, 84, 121, 316
broadcasting
  advertising regulations, 173–5
  commercial, 10, 11, 69–71, 84–5, 98–9, 135–6, 153, 157, 159, 161, 163, 172, 174, 178–80, 189, 190–2, 193, 195, 199, 201, 202, 193–292 *passim.*, 301, 306, 309, 319–21
  dual system, 172, 239–92 *passim*, 301, 306–7, 321
  electoral importance, 182, 202
  federal legislation, 138, 149, 150, 155–61
  finance, 170–6, 277–9
  franchising, 158, 159, 192, 217–19, 225, 242, 250, 290
  freedom (concept of), 11, 53, 132, 259, 320
    internal broadcasting freedom, 187
    see also 'broadcasting, independence of', 'internal democracy'
  independence of, 128, 132, 139, 140, 141, 150, 151, 153, 156, 176, 187, 188, 192, 217–18, 225–6, 242, 281, 299
    see also 'Staatsferne'
  jurisdiction of the Länder, 134, 148, 157, 161, 164, 197, 214, 274, 319
  Land legislation, 134, 135, 136–47, 148, 153, 178, 190, 215–29 *passim.*, 241–56, 267, 272, 323
  law (general), 124, 131, 132–47, 154
  licence-fee, 159, 163, 170–3, 175, 176, 206, 209
  network, 150–3, 165, 169
    see also 'ARD'
  party political influence, *see* 'broadcasting, politicisation'
  politicisation, 8, 138, 146–7, 155,

Index

156, 157, 162, 164, 166, 167–8, 169, 176–87, 188, 189, 288, 298–301, 308
public-service monopoly, 190–1, 193, 199, 202, 203, 206, 208, 210, 227, 236–8, 258, 281, 319, 320
regulation,
corporate principle/model, 130, 145, 147, 166, 177–80, 184–6
parliamentary principle/model, 130, 145, 146, 147, 176, 180, 184–5
see also 'Außenpluralismus', 'Außenkontrolle', 'Binnenpluralismus', 'Binnenkontrolle'
standards, 204–5, 206, 210, 211
transmission, 133–5, 157, 193
see also 'frequencies'
broadcasting council *see* 'Rundfunkrat'
Bundesgerichtshof, 116–17, 235–8
Bundesministerium für Forschung und Technologie (BMFT), 194, 232
Bundespost, 133, 134, 135, 157, 158, 164, 172, 194, 195–7, 198, 212–14, 230, 232–3, 239–41, 246, 249, 261–70, 282, 289, 291–2, 306
Bundespost Minister, 164, 194
see also 'Schwarz-Schilling'
Bundesrat, 72, 156
Bundesrechnungshof, 264–5
Bundestag, 57, 70, 72, 99, 100, 103, 156, 157, 159, 230
Bundesverband der Deutschen Industrie (BDI), 198
Bundesverband Kabel und Satellit (BVKS), 282
Bundesverfassungsgericht, 73, 135, 140, 141, 161–4, 183, 190–2, 193, 206, 235–8, 239, 243–6, 263–4, 270–5, 299, 301, 306–8, 319–22
Bundesverwaltungsgericht, 183–4, 191
Bunte Illustrierte, 84, 86, 316
Burda Group, 84, 85, 86, 103, 200, 218, 283–5, 286–7, 316–17
brothers, 287
Burda-Scope, 200
Bürgerinitiative(n), *see* 'citizens' initiative groups'

cable (television, systems, etc.), 193–292 *passim*, 305–6, 311
copper-coaxial, 198, 241, 249
fibre-optic, 198, 231, 249
pilot-projects, 195, 206–29 *passim*, 230, 238, 239, 241, 257
Berlin, 224–7, 242
Dortmund, 227–9, 250–5
Ludwigshafen 215–19, 226–7, 242, 244–5, 283
Munich, 219–24, 226, 245
cartel law, 102–3
Catholic Centre Party, *see* 'Zentrum'
Catholic church, 145, 209–10
Catholic press (Weimar), 16, 19
CBS, 310
censorship, 10, 13, 14, 23, 32, 53, 132, 296
see also 'Nachzensur', 'Vorzensur'
Central Association of the Electronics Industry, *see* 'Zentralverband der Elektronischen Industrie'
Central Committee of the Advertising Industry *see* 'Zentralausschuß der Werbewirtschaft'
centrality of law in German politics, 52–3, 183, 236, 299, 306–8
see also 'law', 'courts', 'Rechtsstaat'
Channel Four (British), 169, 298
churches, 57, 61, 130, 145, 154, 166, 167, 185, 194, 204, 209–10, 216, 222
citizens' initiative groups, 6, 117, 178–9, 211, 219
CLT, 234, 284
codetermination, *see* 'Mitbestimmung'
Cold War, 29, 35, 66, 71, 96, 302
collective bargaining, 49, 50, 52, 105, 107, 108, 114–16, 187
Cologne, 138, 153, 172, 290, 313
Commission of Inquiry into Information and Communication Technologies, *see* 'Enquête-Kommission'
commissions of inquiry, 70, 87, 99–101, 214, 229–31
see also 'Michel commission', 'Günther commission', 'Medienkommission', 'Expertenkommission Neue Medien', 'Enquête-Kommission'
Communism (-ist), 26, 30, 128

347

Index

communist press (Weimar), 16, 19, 22
community, *see* 'policy community'
concentration (of the press, media, etc.) 4, 7, 8, 11, 15, 16, 27, 38, 39–40, 41, 42, 43, 48, 64–5, 66, 74–88, 99–104, 106, 110, 112, 121, 123, 204, 205, 206, 209, 251, 273, 282–8, 294, 296–7, 308–9, 313–18
confiscation (of newspapers, documents, etc.), 57–8, 120–1
conservative press (Weimar), 16, 17
Constitution *see* 'Basic Law'
constitutionalism, 132–6, 140
 see also 'Basic Law', 'centrality of law', 'Rechtsstaat'
control (state, political), 10, 13, 22, 23, 24, 27, 30, 32, 38, 59, 65, 68, 71–3, 125, 128, 134, 139, 152–3, 155, 159, 294, 298
cooperative federalism, 136, 153–4, 162, 164, 176, 212, 263, 274, 301
cooperatives, 7, 37, 51, 52, 64–5, 76, 87–8, 226
corporatism, 10, 122, 154, 178
costs of production, 82, 103, 200, 206
counter-culture, *see* 'Alternativen'
courts (general), 52, 69, 73, 116–17, 135, 140, 141, 161–4, 178–9, 183, 190–2, 206, 235–8, 239, 243–4, 245, 256, 263–4, 270–5, 299, 301, 306–8, 319–22
 see also 'Bundesgerichtshof', 'Bundesverfassungsgericht' 'Bundesverwaltungsgericht', 'law'
Cron, Helmut, 48
cross-subsidisation, 150
 see also 'financial equalisation'
cultural jurisdiction of the Länder, *see* 'Kulturhoheit der Länder'
currency reform (of 1948), 34–5, 63

denazification, 25–31, 37, 49, 128–31
Detjen, Claus, 217–18
Deutsche Bank, 284
Deutsche Genossenschaftsbank, 219, 283–4, 288
Deutsche National-Zeitung, 92
Deutsche Postgewerkschaft, 208–9
Deutsche Presse-Agentur (DPA), 48, 52, 60, 63–5, 199
Deutsche Presserat, 59

Deutsche Welle (DW), 138, 139, 140, 150, 159, 170, 176
Deutscher Depeschendienst (DDP), 60
Deutscher Nachrichten-Agentur (DENA), 62–3
Deutscher Presse Dienst (DPD), 62–3
Deutscher Rundfunk, 149
Deutsches Fernsehen, 159
Deutsches Nachtrichtenbüro (news agency), 23, 62
Deutschland Fernsehen GmbH., 149–61, 319
Deutschland Funk (DLF), 138, 139, 140, 150, 159, 170, 176
DFS (Deutsches Fernsehen), 151–2, 165, 181
 see also 'ARD'
DFS Kopernikus, 241
DFVLR, 232
DGB (Deutscher Gewerkschaftsbund), 50, 51, 207–9
Director General *see* 'Intendant'
diversity of opinion (Vielfalt), 7, 87, 141, 142, 154, 165, 205, 237, 244, 272–3, 279
DJU (Deutsche Journalisten-Union), 50, 51, 105–6
DJV (Deutscher Journalisten-Verband), 49, 50, 51, 60, 105–6, 114
DNVP (Deutschnationale Volkspartei), 17, 18, 19
Dohnanyi, Klaus von, 249
Donau-Kurier, 84, 313
Dortmund, 78, 214, 227–9, 250–5
Drei SAT (3 SAT), 226, 261–2, 277
DuMont-Schauberg Group, 83–4, 313
Dutschke, Rudi, 94, 97
duty of impartiality, 58–9, 133, 141, 165, 205, 237
duty to inform *see* 'Auskunftspflicht'

East Germany, *see* 'German Democratic Republic'
Eastern Europe, 11, 96
ecologists, 119–20
economic miracle, 52, 82, 95
ECS 1, 218, 234, 241, 261–2, 282
editorial policy, 8, 22, 23, 49–50, 51, 52, 59, 65, 67, 68, 98, 104–11, 142, 166, 187, 255
 see also 'Mitbestimmung',

Index

'Tendenzschutz'
editorial statutes, 110–11
 see also 'statutes movement'
Eher Verlag, 22, 23
Ehmke, Horst, 194, 231
Eins Plus, 226, 262, 277
Eisenhower, General Dwight, 27
electronics industry, 157, 196, 197–8, 203, 229
Emergency Laws, see 'Notstandgesetze'
employee management participation, see 'Mitbestimmung'
employers' organisations, 57, 130, 145, 166, 167, 185, 216, 217
Enquête-Kommission (EK-IUK), 230–1
environmentalists, 119–20, 147
Enzensberger, Hans Magnus, 119
EPF (Erste Private Fernsehgesellschaft), 219
Erhard, Ludwig, 35
Eureka TV, 310
European Broadcasting Union (EBU), 149
Evangelischer Pressedienst (EPD), 60
Expertenkommission Neue Medien (EKM), 214, 229–30
external pluralism, see 'Außenpluralismus'
external control, see 'Außenkontrolle'
extra-parliamentary opposition, 101, 118, 188
 see also 'students'
extreme right, 91–2

fascism, see 'National Socialism'
Federal Administrative Court, see 'Bundesverwaltungsgericht'
Federal Association for Cable and Satellite, see 'Bundesverband Kabel und Satellit'
Federal Association of German Industry, see 'Bundesverband der Deutschen Industrie'
Federal Auditor's Office, see 'Bundesrechnungshof'
Federal Cartel Office, 102–3, 104, 273, 286–7
Federal Constitutional Court, see 'Bundesverfassungsgericht'
Federal Court of Justice see 'Bundesgerichtschof'
Federal Ministry for Research and Technology, see 'Bundesministerium für Forschung und Technologie'
Federal Statistics Office, 103
feminism, 119–20, 121
Ferlemann, Erwin, 112
Fernsehbeirat, 151
Fernsehrat, 165–8
Fernsehwoche, 84, 86, 316
feudalism, 11
feuilleton, 28, 94
film (industry), 18, 25, 86, 158, 214, 287
 see also 'Beta Taurus', 'Kirch, Leo'
financial equalisation (Finanzausgleich), 175–6, 181, 276
First Television Judgement, 141, 161–2, 164, 184, 236, 319
First World War, 17, 18
Fischer, Wolfgang, 286, 310
Fourth TV Judgement, 270–5, 276, 279, 320–1
FRAG Judgement, 191–2, 235–8, 239, 245, 256, 258, 263, 320
Frankfurt, 74, 78, 118, 145, 159, 314
Frankfurter Allgemeine Zeitung, 1, 74, 90, 219, 283–5, 297, 314
Frankfurter Neue Presse, 30, 314
Frankfurter Rundschau, 29, 36, 74, 90, 297
Free Berlin Broadcasting Service, see 'Sender Freies Berlin'
Free Broadcasting Company Ltd., see 'Freie Rundfunk AG'
freedom of information, 100, 116–17, 132
freedom of opinion, 128, 132
free-sheets (free papers), 81
Free Television Company Ltd., see 'Freies Fernsehen GmbH.'
Freie Rundfunk AG (FRAG), 192
Freies Fernsehen GmbH. (FFG), 158–9
French Revolution, 13
frequencies, 157, 191, 236–8
 allocation, 157
 see also 'broadcasting, transmission', 'broadcasting, franchising',
'off-air' local television, 269–70, 272, 276, 282, 284, 289–92, 306,

349

Index

311
  scarcity of, 191, 193, 236–8, 320
Freundekreise, 167, 186
Führer, see 'Hitler'
Funk Uhr, 84, 248, 316

GDZV (Gesamtverband Deutscher Zeitungsverleger), 43, 46, 47
Gebühreneinzugszentrale (GEZ), 172
Generalanzeigerpresse, 14, 16, 37, 94
German Broadcasting Service, see 'Deutscher Rundfunk'
German Democratic Republic (GDR), 25–6, 96, 128, 156, 259
German Post Workers' Union, see 'Deutsche Postgewerkschaft'
German Press Agency, see 'Deutsche Presse-Agentur'
German Press Council, see 'Deutsche Presserat'
German Television, see 'Deutsches Fernsehen'
Germany Television Company Ltd., see 'Deutschland Fernsehen GmbH.'
Gleichschaltung, 23, 126–7
Goebbels, Josef, 21, 23, 127
Grand Coalition (CDU/CSU/SPD), 70, 72, 99, 100, 162
Grass, Günter, 97
Great War, see 'First World War'
Greens, 6, 119, 122, 147, 178, 210–11, 219, 256, 304
Groth, Otto, 48
Gruner und Jahr, 84, 85, 86, 90, 121, 316–17
Günther commission, 99–101, 315
Günther report, 99–101
Gutenberg, Johannes, 13

Habe, Hans, 28
Habermas, Jürgen, 119
Hamburg, 55, 60, 67, 73, 74, 85, 92–3, 97, 117, 129, 137, 146, 153, 161, 180–5, 251–2, 254, 259–60, 281, 283, 290, 300, 311
  accedes to CDU/CSU 'rump' Staatsvertrag, 263, 270
  new media legislation permitting commercial broadcasting, 247–50, 323
Hamburger Abendblatt, 30, 83, 85, 93, 94, 248, 313

Hamburger Morgenpost, 89, 248, 318
Hamburger Rundschau, 117
Hammerschmidt, Helmut, 189
Handelsblatt, 74, 86
Hanover, 184, 247, 285, 290, 311, 314
Harzburger Front, 18
Hase, von Karl Günther, 186
Hauff, Volker, 232
Heeresgruppenzeitung (-en), 25, 62
Heimatzeitung (-en), 16, 18, 37, 40
Hensche, Detlev, 108, 113
Hess, Werner, 186
Hessen, 39, 55, 67, 103, 129, 145, 161, 163, 186, 256, 259–60, 262, 267, 277, 281
  new media legislation permitting commercial broadcasting, 267, 323
Hessen Broadcasting Service, see 'Hessischer Rundfunk'
Hessischer Rundfunk (HR), 129, 140, 143, 145, 148, 152, 169, 177, 186, 218, 278
Heuss, Theodor, 29
Hindenburg, Field Marshal von, 18
Hitler, Adolf, 19, 21, 127, 128
Holtzbrinck Group, 86, 218, 283–5
Hör zu, 30, 84, 93, 248, 316
Hören und Sehen, 84, 86, 248, 316
Hugenberg, Alfred, 4, 16, 17, 18, 19, 21, 61, 66, 74, 288, 294

IG Druck und Papier, 50, 52, 106, 108, 110, 112, 113, 114, 312
IG-Medien, 312
impartiality, see 'duty of impartiality'
Imperial Broadcasting Company, see 'Reichsrundfunkgesellschaft'
Imperial Interior Ministry, see 'Reichsinnenministerium'
Imperial Post Ministry, see 'Reichspost'
Imperial Press Law, see 'Reichspressegesetz'
Impressum, 58
industrialisation, 13, 14, 61
Initiativenzeitung (-en), see 'alternative press'
integrational broadcasting, see 'Integrationsfunk'
Integrationsfunk, 205, 299, 320
intellectuals, 72, 94, 119
Intelsat-V, 241, 262, 310

Index

Intendant (-en), 99, 130, 131, 142, 143, 144, 149, 150, 151, 162, 165, 166, 186, 187, 188, 189, 190
internal control, *see* 'Binnenkontrolle'
internal democracy, 187, 189
internal pluralism, *see* 'Binnenpluralismus'
inter-state treaty, *see* 'Staatsvertrag'
ITV (British), 157, 298, 301

joint programming, *see* 'broadcasting, network'
journalists' organisations, 48–52, 54, 59, 65, 67, 82, 104–11, 113–14, 166 *see also* 'DJU', 'DJV'
Jungsozialisten, 101, 178, 249

Katholische Nachrichten-Agentur (KNA), 61
Kiel, 159, 184
Kirch, Leo, 223, 284–8, 292, 307, 310, 312
Kirch, Thomas, 310
Klabunde, Erich, 48
Kleinstaaterei, 257, 262, 274
Kloiber, Herbert, 310
Kluge, Alexander, 119
KMP (Kabel Media Programmgesellschaft), 283–6, 310
KMP musicbox, 226, 265, 282, 286, 310
see also 'Fischer, Wolfgang'
Kohl, Helmut, 288
Kreuzberg (Berlin), 119
Kristall, 93
KtK, 194–5, 199, 202, 207, 208, 209, 212
Kulturhoheit der Länder, 53, 134, 148 *see also* 'broadcasting, jurisdiction of the Länder'
Kulturkampf, 14
Krupp concern, 17, 251

Labour government (British), 63
law, 70, 104, 106–7, 108–10, 116–17, 124, 131, 132–47, 178, 183, 184, 294–5
see also 'centrality of law', 'courts', 'Rechtsstaat'
leasehold contracts (for printing presses), 31, 34, 40, 42, 43, 45, 47
liberal press (Weimar), 15, 17, 22
licence-fee, 159, 163, 170–3, 175, 176, 206, 209, 214, 260, 271, 277–8, 311, 320
Licence Fee Office, *see* 'Gebühreneinzugszentrale'
lockouts, 114, 117
Lower Saxony, 55, 67, 129, 137, 146, 161, 180–5, 203, 260
new media law permitting commercial broadcasting, 242–245, 270, 320–1, 323
legal action against this law by the SPD, 243–4, 257, 263, 320–1
Ludwigshafen, 78, 213, 215–19, 242, 244, 283, 291
see also 'cable, pilot-projects'
Luxembourg, 234, 253, 262, 284, 253, 262, 284

Madsack Group, 314
Mainz, 78, 153, 165, 215, 247–8
Mann, Thomas, 28
marginal (minority/fringe) groups, 10, 57, 95, 97, 117–23, 147
Marx, Karl, 15
MATV, 266–7
Maxwell, Robert, 85, 297
Media Commission, *see* 'Medienkommission'
media freedom *see* 'broadcasting, freedom', 'press, freedom'
media reports, 100–1
Medienkommission (der Länder), 214, 228–9
Meinungsbildung, 56, 122–3, 127, 132, 133, 142, 302
merger control, 102–3, 104, 110
Michel commission, 70, 199, 274
Michel report, 70
Mitbestimmung, 47, 49, 51, 65, 104–11, 187–90
Monitor, 187
monopolies, 8, 11, 23, 32, 33, 65, 77–9, 80, 85, 135, 189, 190–1, 196, 202, 209, 237, 296
see also 'concentration'
Mosse, Rudolf, 15
Mühlfenzl, Rudolf, 220–1
Müller, Albrecht, 213, 233
multimedia activities, 70, 86, 90, 98–9, 223, 239–92 *passim.*, 305, 307–9, 310
multiple editions, 36, 66, 74–8, 80–1,

351

Index

103–4
Münchener Zeitungsverlag Group, 103, 313
Münchner Merkur, 103
Munich, 20, 27, 69, 78, 117, 150, 151, 153, 209, 213, 214, 219–24, 247, 248, 251, 288, 291, 310, 311, 313
see also 'cable, pilot-projects'
Murdoch, Rupert, 85, 219, 297

Nachzensur, 14, 32
Napoleonic Wars, 13
National Front, 26
National Socialism, 4, 7, 11, 15–23 *passim*, 24, 28, 31, 32, 39, 49, 50, 53, 62, 65, 71, 91–2, 93, 126–8, 132, 149, 153, 294
'Nazi', see National Socialism
press 16, 19, 20, 21, 22
network, policy, see 'policy network'
Neue Rheinische Zeitung, 15
Neue Zeitung, 25, 27–8
Neues Deutschland, 26
new media, 11, 193–292 *passim.*, 293, 305, 306, 309, 320
new politics, 119
new right, see 'extreme right'
new social movements, 119, 122, 178, 185, 304
see also 'ecologists', 'environmentalists', 'feminism', 'peace movement'
new technologies, 8, 10, 11, 14, 61, 82, 88, 111–16, 189, 293, 305
see also 'new media'
news agencies, 17, 23, 33, 45, 60–5
news blackouts, 57
Norddeutscher Rundfunk (NDR), 137, 138, 140, 144, 145, 146, 147, 152, 167, 168, 169, 170, 173, 175, 176, 177, 180–5, 186, 187, 188, 189, 246, 260, 300
controversy, 180–5
Nordwestdeutsche Hefte, 93, 94
Nordwestdeutscher Rundfunk (NWDR), 129, 130, 131, 136, 137, 138, 145, 155, 180–1
North German Broadcasting Service, see 'Norddeutscher Rundfunk'
North-Rhine Westphalia, 56, 67, 86, 90, 129, 137, 138, 181, 214, 227–9, 311, 323
new media legislation permitting commercial broadcasting, 250–5, 259
'twin-pillar' regulatory model, 255, 308
see also 'cable, pilot-projects, Dortmund'
North West German Broadcasting Service, see 'Nordwestdeutscher Rundfunk'
Notstandgesetze, 71–2
Nouvelles de France, 25
NSDAP (Nationalsozialistische Deutsche Arbeiterpartei), see 'National Socialism'

obligation of accuracy, 57
Obrigkeitsstaat, see 'authoritarianism'
oligopolies, see 'monopolies'
Olympiad (1936), 127
Ostpolitik, 96

Panorama, 187
Papen, von, 126
Parliamentary Council, 45
Parteienstaat, 178, 186, 189, 192, 217, 299–300
'party-book state', see 'Parteienstaat'
peace movement, 119–120, 147
people's party (see 'Volkspartei')
people's ratio (see 'Volksempfänger')
Pfalzischer Merkur, 78
pilot-projects, see 'cable'
PKS, 218–19, 223, 283–5, 287–8
police raids 72–3, 120–1
policy community, 9, 10, 11, 52, 54, 135, 147, 158, 159, 164, 230, 231, 300, 305–6
policy network, 9, 10, 11, 148–9, 158–9, 230–3, 282–3, 289–90, 300
political strikes, 52, 117
post-publication censorship, see 'Nachzensur'
Pravda, 26
pre-publication censorship, see 'Vorzensur'
press
committees 54, 60
federal legislation, 47, 51, 54–5, 102, 107, 108–11
freedom, 1, 11, 21, 38, 53, 55, 56, 68, 71–3, 100, 104–11, 116–17, 132, 296
internal press freedom, 104–11,

352

Index

118
legislation, 14, 52–59
legislation of the Länder, 55–9
licensed press, 40–3, 44, 45, 46, 47, 51, 62, 93, 295
licensing (of publications), 14, 24–38, 39, 40, 44, 45, 56, 66, 76, 93
removal of licences, 28–9, 30, 44
multiple editions, 36, 66, 74–8, 80–1, 103–4
nationalisation, 104
new technologies, 111–17
political orientation, 89–98
political press, 14, 15, 16, 19, 20, 21, 29, 42, 89, 91–5
right of reply, 58
Statistics Law, 103–4
street sales, *see* 'Boulevardzeitung'
subscription, *see* 'Abonnement'
Sunday papers 79, 286, 313
 see also 'Bild am Sonntag', 'Welt am Sonntag'
supplements 81
 see also 'concentration'
printworkers, 8, 106, 112–16, 207
PRO 7, 310–11
propaganda, 21–3, 127
Proporz, 59, 145, 146, 154, 166, 167, 176, 180–1, 184, 189, 213, 226, 300–1
Protestant church, 145, 209–10
provincialism, 136, 153
 see also 'Kleinstaaterei',
Prussia, 17
publishers' associations, 43, 46–8, 59, 107–8, 157
 see also 'BDZV', 'GDZV', 'VDZ', 'VDZV'

racism, 91–2
 see also 'anti-semitism'
Radio Bremen (RB), 129, 136, 138, 140, 152, 155, 169, 175, 176, 177, 260, 276
Radio Frankfurt, 129
Radio Munich, 129
Radio Stuttgart, 129
rationalisation (of jobs), 111–16, 207, 208, 211
rationing (of paper, print etc.), 28, 45
Rau, Johannes, 227
Rechtsstaat, 6, 53, 55, 178, 183, 184,
237, 306
 see also 'centrality of law', 'courts', 'law'
Red Army Fraction, 57
re-education, 25–8, 128
refusal of testimony, 57–8
Reichsinnenministerium, 125–6
Reichspost, 124, 125, 126, 134
Reichspressegesetz, 14, 53
Reichsrundfunkgesellschaft (RRG), 125–6
Reichssender, 127
Republican Party (Die Republikaner), 92
Republikaner, Der, 91–2
restoration theory, 3, 4, 7, 66, 79
Reuter, 60, 61
Revolution of 1848, 15
RFFU, 187, 312
Rhein Neckar Zeitung, 29
Rheinpfalz, 78, 83, 219, 313
Rhineland-Palatinate, 55, 56, 67, 78, 137, 203, 213, 248
 new media legislation permitting commercial broadcasting, 215–19, 220, 242, 244, 245, 323
 'sponsors' SAT 1, 218, 252, 257, 283
 see also 'cable, pilot-projects, Ludwigshafen'
RIAS, 138, 139, 140, 150, 170, 176
rotary printing, *see* 'Rotationsdruck'
Rotationsdruck, 14
RTL, 218
RTL Plus, 226, 234, 253–4, 262, 265, 270, 276–7, 280, 282, 284, 289, 290, 310–11
Ruhr, 17, 86, 90, 103, 251–2, 313
Rundfunkrat, 130, 142, 143, 144, 145–7, 149, 154, 165–8, 178, 181, 184, 185, 188, 299

Saarbrücken, 153
Saarbrücker Zeitung, 78, 86, 111
Saarland, 55, 56, 67, 78, 130, 137, 183, 191–2, 262, 281
 the 'FRAG' affair, 235–8, 320
 see also 'FRAG Judgement'
 new media legislation permitting commercial broadcasting, 244–5, 323
Saarland Broadcasting Service, *see* 'Saarländischer Rundfunk'

353

Index

Saarländischer Rundfunk (SR), 137, 138, 140, 152, 175, 176, 177
Sänger, Fritz, 48, 63–4
SAT 1, 218–19, 223, 226, 234, 239, 248, 250, 252, 257, 262, 265, 270, 276–7, 279, 282–3, 287–9, 290–1, 310–11
satellite (television), 84, 152, 169, 193–292 *passim.*, 305, 306
  direct broadcasting (DBS), 231–5, 257, 260, 263, 265, 270, 276–7, 282, 284, 291–2
  see also 'TV SAT'
Scherl, August, 15, 16
Schleswig-Holstein, 56, 67, 137, 146, 180–5, 260, 290
  new media legislation permitting commercial broadcasting, 244–5, 323
Schleyer, Hanns-Martin, 57
Schmid, Professor Carlo, 45
Schmidt, Helmut, 102, 110, 114, 204, 213, 234
Schriftleitergesetz, 22
Schwarz-Schilling, Christian, 240–1, 247–8, 257, 263–70 *passim.*, 276, 289
Second Television Judgement, 162–4, 319–20
Second World War, 2, 3, 127
SED (Sozialistische Einheitspartei Deutschlands), 26
Sender Freies Berlin (SFB), 137, 138, 140, 144, 152, 169, 175, 176, 177, 191
Sethe, Paul, 1, 303
Setzmachine, 14
Sky Channel, 219, 223, 226, 234
SMATV, 266–7, 269
socialist press (Weimar), 14, 15, 16, 19, 22
social-liberal coalition (SPD/FDP), 89–90, 101–4, 108, 111, 177, 203
socially significant groups, 6, 57, 130, 144–7, 154, 159, 161, 166, 167, 177, 178–9, 184–5, 216, 222, 225, 228, 255, 295, 298–301 *passim.*, 309
South German Broadcasting Service, *see* 'Süddeutscher Rundfunk'
Sourth West Broadcasters, *see* 'Südwestfunk'
Soviets, 25, 26, 35, 96
Sozialistengesetz, 14
Späth, Lothar, 203, 213
Spiegel, 72–3, 86, 90, 248, 297, 302–3, 316
Spiegel Affair, 72–3, 96, 302–3
Springer, Axel, 1, 30, 34, 37, 61, 74, 79, 83–5, 92–9, 200, 205, 284, 286–7, 295, 302, 303
Springer Auslandsdienst (SAD), 61
Springer Group, 61, 74, 79, 83–5, 90, 92–9, 100, 101, 103, 117, 123, 200, 205, 218, 247–8, 250, 281, 283–92, 295–6, 302–4, 307, 312, 313, 316–18
Staatsferne, 140, 153, 156, 217, 225, 242, 245, 271, 299, 300, 306
Staatsvertrag, 137, 139, 142, 144, 146, 159, 162, 164, 165, 166, 172, 180–5, 256–63, 270, 274–80, 281, 311, 321
Stadtmagazine, *see* 'alternative press'
Stadtteilzeitungen, *see* 'alternative press'
Stadtzeitungen, *see* 'alternative press'
Standortpolitik, 241–2, 247, 249, 250–6, 263, 289–91, 305
state security, 71–3
statute movement, 110–11, 187–90, 304
Steinbeck, John, 28
Stern, 84, 86, 90, 111, 248, 297, 316
Stoltenberg, Gerhard, 183
Strauss, Franz Josef, 38, 73, 162–3, 203, 288
strikes, 52, 113–17
  see also 'political strikes'
students, 72, 94, 97, 99, 119
  see also 'extra-parliamentary opposition'
'Stunde Null', 2, 3, 11, 65–7, 131, 152–4, 295
Stürmer, Der, 21
Stuttgart, 153, 313
Stuttgarter Zeitung Group, 83, 313
subversion, 71, 119, 121
Süddeutsche Zeitung, 74, 84, 89, 111, 297, 313
Süddeutscher Rundfunk (SDR), 129, 137, 140, 152, 177, 218
Süddeutscher Verlag Group, 84, 313
Südena (Südwestdeutsche Nachrichten-Agentur), 62–3
Südwestfunk (SWF), 130, 137, 138, 140, 155, 173, 177, 189, 218–19

Tagesschau, 181
tageszeitung (*taz*), 74, 117, 120, 121–2, 304

Index

Tägliche Rundschau, 25
technocratic policy-making, 9, 196, 230, 231–5
TELE 5, 310–11
Tele München, 310
Teleclub, 226, 285, 287
telecommunications, general, 196–7, 208
  industry, 194, 196
  investment power (as political instrument), 196–7, 240, 247, 258, 306
  jurisdiction of the Bundespost (federation), 133, 134, 157, 161, 164, 195–6, 214, 239–41, 274
  monopoly of the Bundespost, 196, 208, 209, 232, 239–41
Telegraphen-Union (news agency), 17, 61
television council (ZDF), *see* 'Fernsehrat'
Tendenzschutz, 51, 52, 59, 65, 67, 89, 105–6, 296
terrorism (-ists), 57, 97, 121
Third Channel ('third programmes'), 134, 168–9, 173, 278, 311
Third Reich, 4, 21–3, 24, 28, 92–3, 126–8, 131, 134
Third Television Judgement, *see* 'FRAG Judgement'
Tip, 118, 120
trade unions, 47, 48–52, 57, 59, 65, 67, 72, 88, 105–6, 108, 111–16, 118–19, 130, 145, 147, 166, 167, 185, 207–9, 211, 216, 217, 222, 223
TV SAT, 233–4, 241, 257, 263, 276–7, 280, 284, 291–2
typesetting machine, *see* 'Setzmachine'

Ufa-TV (Bertelsmann), 200, 281, 284
Ullstein, Leopold, 15
Ullstein AV (Springer), 200
Ullstein publishing concern, 93
unification (national), 13, 14, 53
United Press International (UPI), 60, 61

VAT Affair, 162–4, 319–20
VAT Ruling, *see* 'Second Television Judgement'
VDZ (Verband Deutscher Zeitschriftenverleger), 198

VDZV (Verein Deutscher Zeitungsverleger), 43, 46, 48
Verflechtung, 64, 83, 186, 217–18, 224, 285, 287
Verlag DuMont Schauberg, 83
Verwaltungsrat, 130, 142, 143, 144, 145–7, 148, 149, 165–6, 167, 181, 184, 222–3
Vogel, Bernhard, 203, 215
Völkischer Beobachter, 20, 27
Volksempfänger, 127
Volkspartei, 91
Vorwärts, 15, 16, 91, 111
Vorzensur, 14, 32

Wallenberg, Hans, 28
Wallraff, Günter, 98
WARC 77, 232
WAZ Group, 83, 86, 87, 90, 103, 252–4, 284, 313
Weimar Republic, 3, 4, 15–21, 27, 38, 61, 62, 65, 66, 71, 74, 91, 121, 124–6, 127, 131, 134, 148, 149, 152, 288, 293–4
Welt, Die, 1, 25, 74, 83, 85, 90, 93, 95, 97, 248, 313
Welt am Sonntag, 85, 248, 313
West of Germany Broadcasting Service, *see* 'Westdeutscher Rundfunk'
Westdeutsche Allgemeine Zeitung, 83, 86, 87, 103, 313
  see also 'WAZ Group'
Westdeutscher Rundfunk (WDR), 137, 138, 140, 144, 145, 146, 147, 152, 168, 169, 175, 176, 177, 180, 181, 185, 187, 188, 226–7, 246, 252–4, 262, 280
Wirtschaftswoche, 86
Witte, Professor Eberhard, 194
Wochenzeitung, 91
Wolff, Theodor, 16
Wolffsches Telegraphen-Büro (WEB), 61
women, 145–6, 166
women's organisations, 146, 166
Works Constitution Law, *see* 'Betriebsverfassungsgesetz'
Württemberg-Baden, 39, 129

Young Socialists, *see* 'Jungsozialisten'

ZDF, 134, 140, 151, 152, 162, 164–8,

355

P
95.82
.G3
H86
1990

Humphreys, Peter.
Media and media policy in West Germany

DATE DUE